AGAINST PROGRESS

AGAINST PROGRESS

Intellectual Property and Fundamental Values in the Internet Age

Jessica Silbey

Stanford University Press
Stanford, California

STANFORD UNIVERSITY PRESS
Stanford, California

Printed in the United States of America on acid-free, archival-quality paper

Library of Congress Cataloging-in-Publication Data is available upon request.

ISBN 9781503608306 (cloth)
ISBN 9781503631915 (paper)
ISBN 9781503631922 (electronic)

Cover design: Black Eye Design
Typeset by Newgen in Minion Pro 10.2/14.4

To Charlotte Silbey Dresser and Harper Silbey Dresser

Table of Contents

Acknowledgments

I wrote this book because I was not finished with my first one. I now understand that the feeling of being unfinished is a gift, not a burden, even if it haunts me. And so, I am grateful to friends, colleagues, and family, who keep me company and encourage me to continue in what seems like a project without end.

The intellectual property law community has been my academic home for fifteen years. In a book about intellectual property and fundamental values, I would be remiss not to acknowledge the exemplary moral leadership from some of the community's senior scholars who model thoroughness, inclusivity, and broad-mindedness. To Maggie Chon, Rochelle Dreyfuss, Rebecca Eisenberg, Wendy Gordon, Jessica Litman, and Pamela Samuelson, thank you. So many of us humbly follow in your footsteps with profound gratitude and admiration.

Generous and insightful colleagues in both the IP and constitutional law communities helped me refine and rethink some of the book's arguments. I am especially grateful to Olufunmilayo Arewa, Margo Bagley, Barton Beebe, Dan Burk, Colleen Chien, Margaret Chon, Danielle Citron, Julie Cohen, Frank Cooper, Carys Craig, Rebeca Curtin, Peter DiCola, Stacey Dogan, Abraham Drassinower, Rochelle Dreyfus, Christine Haight Farley, Brett Frischmann, Jeanne Fromer, Bill Gallagher, John Golden, Eric Goldman, Wendy Gordon, K. J. Greene, Leah Chan Grinvald, Woodrow Hartzog, Laura Heymann, Steve Jamar, Peter Jaszi, Ed Lee, Mark Lemley, Jessica

Litman, Orly Lobel, Michael Madison, Linda McClain, Bill McGeveran, Mark McKenna, Michael Meurer, Joseph Miller, Lateef Mtima, Kali Murray, Ruth Okediji, Matthew Sag, Zahr Said, Pamela Samuelson, Miguel Schor, Patrick Shin, Robert Spoo, Kathy Strandburg, Eva Subotnik, Kara Swanson, Rebecca Tushnet, and Ari Waldman.

Northeastern University and the Northeastern University School of Law provided me with substantial support for this book. Deans Jeremy Paul and James Hackney supported my research every year with time, money, and enthusiasm. Northeastern University law students stoked my passion to connect constitutional values with intellectual property law, helping me to launch the Center for Law, Innovation, and Creativity (CLIC). The impressive interdisciplinary research and collaborations at Northeastern University also fueled this project. Thanks to Northeastern University's Humanities Center and the 2017–2018 Humanities Center Fellows for the year of engaging conversations, especially Lori Lefkowitz and Marina Leslie, and to the lively company and community of scholars at the NULab for Texts, Maps, and Networks for promoting the progress of science through the digital humanities.

I was honored to receive a Guggenheim Fellowship in 2018 to write this book. The Fellowship was vital to finishing the project and sharing it with a wider audience. More humbling than the award was for me meeting the other Fellows, diverse artists and scholars who are deeply engaged in their fields. This book is in large part about the kind of work to which they devote their lives and the values that sustain them.

A special thank you to my research collaborators Peter DiCola, Eva Subotnik, and Mark McKenna. I believe the best aspect of empirical research is teamwork. I will be on your team any time. Other team members include research assistants Todd Thurheimer, Jeremy Sternberg, and Brittany Von Rueden, transcriber Nita Sembrowich, and Atlas.ti guru Ayn Cavicchi. Our joint empirical work was supported by several grants: the Innovation Grant from the Spangenberg Center for Law, Technology, and the Arts at Case Western Reserve University School of Law (the photographer study) and the FSRP Initiation Grant from the University of Notre Dame (the design study).

At critical stages of this project, I received invaluable help from Nausicaa Renner, Stephanie Sykes, and the team at Stanford University Press (Michelle Lipinski, Kate Wahl, and Marcela Maxfield). Thank you for seeing this project through from beginning to end. Thank you also to Stanford University Press for committing with me to contract terms that assure accessibility of this book on terms that support both writers and readers.

I shared this work as it evolved with colleagues and students around the United States and abroad. Thank you for inviting and engaging with me: the American Bar Foundation, Bournemouth University (International Society for the History and Theory of Intellectual Property (ISHTIP 2021)), Boston College Law School, Boston University School of Law, Cardozo School of Law (the Roundtable on Empirical Methods in Intellectual Property), Case Western Reserve University School of Law, Chicago-Kent College of Law, Columbia University Law School (Kernochan Center for Law, Media, and the Arts), DePaul College of Law (IPSC 2018), Golden Gate University School of Law, Harvard Law School (the Berkman Klein Center and especially Susannah Tobin's seminar), the Munich Summer Institute, Northwestern University, New York University School of Law (the Engelberg Center on Innovation Law and Policy), Stanford University (IPSC 2016), Toronto University School of Law (International Society for the History and Theory of Intellectual Property (ISHTIP 2017)), Texas A&M University School of Law, University of California Irvine School of Law, University of Connecticut School of Law, University of Georgia, University of Indiana McKinney School of Law, University of Miami School of Law, University of New Hampshire Franklin Pierce School of Law (MOSAIC 2019), University of North Carolina School of Law, University of Pennsylvania Law School (Copyright Scholarship Roundtable 2018), University of San Diego School of Law, University of Texas School of Law, University of Tulsa College of Law, University of Washington School of Law, Washington College of Law at American University, and Yale Law School (Information Society Project).

Portions of the book are adapted from previously published work. Parts of the introduction and Chapter 2 appeared in "Against Progress: Interventions about Equality in Supreme Court Cases about Copyright Law," *Chicago-Kent Journal of Intellectual Property Law* 19 (2020): 280–309 and in "Reading Intellectual Property Law Reform through the Lens of Constitutional Equality," *Tulsa Law Review* 50 (2015): 549–69. A short-form adaptation of Chapter 5 appeared as "Intellectual Property Harms: A Paradigm for the Twenty-First Century," *Boston University Law Review* 99 (2019): 2447–77. I published three other articles focusing on various aspects of the digital photographer case study. Those articles are Jessica Silbey, Eva Subotnik, and Peter DiCola, "Existential Copyright and Professional Photography," *Notre Dame Law Review* 95 (2019): 263–326; Jessica Silbey, "Justifying Copyright in the Age of Digital Reproduction: The Case of Photographers," *University of California Irvine Law Review* 9 (2019): 405–54; and Jessica Silbey, "Control over Contemporary Photography: A Tangle of Copyright, Right of Publicity, and the First Amendment," *Columbia Journal of Law and the Arts* 42 (2019): 351–64. And Eric Goldman and I wrote "Copyright's Memory Hole," *Brigham Young University Law Review* (2019): 929–96, which inspired portions of Chapter 3.

The tail end of this project was completed as I began my tenure at Boston University School of Law. I am excited for what lies ahead and full of appreciation for the new academic family I am joining at Boston University. Thank you especially to Dean Angela Onwuachi-Willig for providing summer research funds to complete this manuscript.

My home family – Keith, Charlotte, Harper, and our canine companions Louis and Oscar – have been patient with me and provided perspective when most needed. Susan Silbey and Ruth Walsh complete the village. They are two of the kindest, fiercest, and smartest women I know. Together with Keith's equal partnership, my mother and Ruthie have more than anyone enabled my professional aspirations, helping me become a better teacher and scholar. I am lucky to love my work, and they create healthy and sustaining foundations for both work and love in my life. I am so very grateful.

Finally, this book exists because busy people, creators and innovators of all kinds, agreed to talk with me about their work and aspirations. To the photographers, designers, artists, writers, scientists, engineers, lawyers, and entrepreneurs who generously shared details of their work, thank you.

AGAINST PROGRESS

FIGURE 1 Photograph used with the permission of David Slater, a wildlife photographer whose work can be found at DJSphotography.com. This photo can also be found on Wikipedia, https://en.wikipedia.org/wiki/Monkey_selfie_copyright_dispute. Wikipedia describes it as "Macaca nigra self-portrait" and claims that it is in the public domain, although Slater asserts authorship of the photograph. According to correspondence with the U.S. Copyright Office, Slater registered the photograph in 2012 as part of a large unpublished collection of photographs. I corresponded with Slater in the process of writing this book. He described frequently licensing the use of this photograph and others through his agency.

Introduction: Is Progress More?

THIS IS A PHOTOGRAPH of a crested macaque named Naruto. At the time of this photograph in 2011, Naruto was three years old and lived on a reserve on the island of Sulawesi, Indonesia. Naruto took this photo herself. It is a monkey selfie.[1]

Working weeks in the jungle, David Slater, a British wildlife photographer, had been thwarted in his attempts to take close-up photographs of the monkeys. Encouraged by the monkeys' playfulness and curiosity, however, Slater set up his camera to entice the troop of monkeys to engage with the equipment. He installed the camera on a tripod with a wide-angle lens and settings optimized for close-ups, and then he lured the curious animals to the machine.[2] In one interview about the photo shoot, Slater describes the monkeys as "looking at the reflection in the lens, which they found amusing."[3]

The idea paid off eventually, and the monkeys took dozens of selfies. Once the photographs were published in British newspapers, they understandably attracted significant attention.[4] Thereafter, an editor on Wikimedia Commons uploaded Naruto's selfie, asserting that the photograph was in the public domain, as "it has no human author in whom copyright is vested."[5] Slater contested this assertion. He claimed authorship and ownership of the photograph, emphasized the hard work and significant skill that went into producing it, and asked for the photograph to be taken off the site.[6] Wikimedia Commons refused.

While experts debated whether nonhuman animals could be copyright authors, Slater complained about lost revenues from his photograph's unlicensed use and his precarious financial circumstances.[7] In December 2014, Slater published the monkey selfies in a book, titled *Wildlife Personalities*, through Blurb, Inc., a San Francisco–based self-publishing website. In the book, Slater described the photo of Naruto as the monkey "star[ing] at herself with a new found appreciation, and mak[ing] funny faces . . . just as we do when looking in a mirror. She also . . . made relaxed eye contact with herself, even smiling. . . . Surely a sign of self-awareness?"[8] The book identifies Slater and Wildlife Personalities, Ltd. as copyright owners of the photographs, despite the U.S. Copyright Office having issued an opinion several months earlier, in August 2014, that "only works created by a human can be copyrighted under United States law."[9] The Copyright Office further stated that it would "refuse to register a claim if it determines that a human being did not create the work. The Office will not register works produced by nature, animals, or plants,"[10] giving as examples of excluded works "a photograph taken by a monkey" and "a mural painted by an elephant."[11]

The dispute between David Slater and Wikimedia Commons centers on control over and access to photographs on the internet. Wikimedia Commons is an internet platform for freely usable media files to which anyone can contribute with a mission of building a vast, accessible public domain of information and expression on the web.[12] Slater, a professional photographer, understandably cares about being paid for his work and is invested in maintaining rights in his photographs on the internet. These are weighty concerns and plausibly in conflict. A year later, another related dispute arose that raised even more fundamental questions.

In 2015, People for the Ethical Treatment of Animals (PETA) sued Slater, Blurb, Inc., and Wildlife Personalities, Ltd., for copyright infringement on behalf of Naruto. PETA argued that the monkey was the author and owner of the photograph, not the man. PETA, the largest animal rights organization in the world, describes itself as "establishing and protecting the rights of all animals" and operating "under the simple principle that animals are not ours to eat, wear, experiment on, or use for entertainment."[13] PETA sought recognition for Naruto under copyright law and, ostensibly, under law generally in order to elevate animals as worthy of respect and rights to be free from harm. Intellectual property law became the vehicle to make these arguments. At this point, David Slater had to defend not only his right to be paid by Wikimedia Commons for the use of Naruto's photograph but also his supremacy of authorship over a monkey.[14]

PETA's case was filed in federal court, which preliminarily had to decide whether PETA could sue on behalf of Naruto as the monkey's "next friend"—a term denoting legal status of a person or organization representing another who is otherwise unable to maintain suit on their own behalf. If PETA could not be Naruto's "next friend," the court had to decide whether Naruto could sue on her own. On its face, this might sound silly. But in 2004, a different federal court held that the cetacean community, composed of all the world's whales, porpoises, and dolphins, could sue President George W. Bush and Secretary of State Donald Rumsfeld under a specific provision of the 1973 Endangered Species Act to challenge injuries caused by the U.S. Navy's use of underwater sonar. If whales, porpoises, and dolphins could successfully allege injury against the U.S. Navy, why not crested macaques, whose creativity and likeness were purportedly taken and commercialized without permission?

PETA's federal lawsuit lasted four years, cost tens of thousands of dollars, and generated contested decisions at the trial and appellate courts. David Slater and his partners eventually prevailed, convincing the court that animals cannot be authors. But is that so obvious? Children can be copyright authors. Corporations can be copyright authors. Capacity and humanness are not essential features of copyright authorship. PETA was not asserting that animals are human but that they should have some of the same basic rights of humans—namely, to be free from exploitation and harm. PETA brought this suit to assert the dignity of animals in the manner that authorship provides: as an expression of will in the world. Using copyright as an expedient framework, PETA argued for equality, dignity, and an opportunity to thrive on a shared planet with rapidly diminishing resources. At its foundation, PETA's demand was empathy for all forms of life at a time when interspecies cooperation may become necessary for continued survival.

Naruto is now a famous monkey. But copyright law, the vehicle for her fame, is one of several branches of intellectual property (IP) law that remain obscure to most laypeople. And yet, as the twenty-first century progresses with its proliferating networked communication systems and innovative digital technologies, intellectual property law is more frequently the focus of public debate and personal disputes. Intellectual property is growing in relevance and renown. And as it becomes increasingly relevant to everyday life, it is becoming a vital terrain over which fundamental values are being contested in light of twenty-first-century technological progress. This book maps the contours of this terrain and the features of the debate.

*   *   *

The founders of the United States conceived intellectual property as the means to achieve progress of science and the useful arts. The first article of the United States Constitution explicitly says this much. It gives to Congress the power to "promote the progress of science and useful arts by securing for limited times to authors and inventors the exclusive right to their respective writings and discoveries."[15] And yet, more than two hundred years later, what "progress" means and whether intellectual property promotes it remain unclear.

Uncertainty over the meaning of "progress" is one source of destabilizing tension. Technological advances occur at a rapid pace, while wealth inequality and political divisiveness related to these technological resources appear to be at unprecedented levels without foreseeable amelioration.[16] *Against Progress* explores this tension by attending to intellectual property disputes in court and in everyday life in such a way that calls into question the shifting meaning of "progress of science and useful arts" in the age of digital reproduction and rapid technological change.[17] Rather than focusing on the nature of inventorship, authorship, and commercial incentives, which are typical intellectual property concerns, I focus on how disputes about intellectual property revolve around more basic fundamental values. In a world rich with technology but facing rising global political instability and looming ecological disaster, this book sets aside conventional accounts of intellectual property's justification and reimagines progress of science and the useful arts for the Anthropocene. Fundamental values like equality, privacy, and distributive justice are central to human flourishing and human dignity but have been largely absent from intellectual property law and policy. The book frames current intellectual property law and its role in everyday life as about these values and their contested contours as a bellwether of changing social justice needs in the Digital Age.

The old story is that copyright and patents promote the progress of science and the useful arts by granting to authors and inventors, for a limited time, a property right in the work made. This story explains that to encourage the work of intellectual labor, which is easily copied and resold (think a song or an invention), an author or inventor needs exclusive control over the work to recuperate the economic investment that produced it. Without property-like rights, the story goes, the progress of science and useful arts will slow if not stop altogether. This is the "grand incentive narrative" justifying intellectual property laws. This story requires revision in the Digital Age.[18]

Maturing conversations about the roles that creativity and innovation play in flourishing economies, in communities, and with everyday labor reveal that exclusive property rights may degrade rather than develop community sustainability. Technological progress and ubiquitous internet networks have not fostered or equitably spread general welfare or strengthened democratic governance, although they have enabled more copying and sharing and more iterative, derivative, and radical transformations of expressive and inventive work through those networks. These pioneering Digital Age behaviors are not rooted in exclusivity as much as in a newly imagined commons or a revised notion of the public sphere. In other words, private property rights are old news. Instead, values promoting social well-being and democratic politics such as equality and fairness structure relationships that foment creativity and innovation. The new story is that twenty-first-century creativity and innovation are developed through both human and digital networks bound together by evolving relations of mutual interdependence, all of which is reconfiguring twentieth-century society and politics for our internet age. Democratic and fundamental human values today—equality, privacy, distributive justice, and institutional accountability—orient disputes and practices concerning authorship, inventorship, and intellectual property generally, which is a departure from twentieth-century intellectual property justifications. Tracing intellectual property's contested place in the Digital Age, *Against Progress* uncovers new accounts of intellectual property and pivotal shifts in a legal regime that promises progress of science and the useful arts in a society more technologically advanced than ever but struggling with destabilizing wealth disparities, uncertain political institutions, and ideological division.[19] By studying everyday creative and innovative practices and contemporary intellectual property disputes, the book explores these new theories of "progress" for the internet age.

What does "progress" mean in the Constitution? The history of the constitutional clause is sparse, and thus policy preferences drive contemporary debates about its meaning.[20] Is "progress" simply more copyrighted works or patented inventions? Is it measured by welfare economics, job creation, or health outcomes? Is "progress" achieved if we know more today about breast cancer than we did ten years ago but diagnostic tests are widely inaccessible because of the high costs related to patent licensing practices? Contemporary music-making technology, such as the ability to self-record and self-publish on the internet, may not be "progress" for musicians and audiences if fewer reliable filters exist for promotion and quality and if substantial capital investment is needed to build and keep an audience. Perhaps "progress" in scientific fields occurs through iterative improvements to understanding the natural world, but what is "progress" in the aesthetic fields, such a visual arts, music, and writing?[21] Can we say that films are better today than in the 1950s? Is contemporary art an improvement over impressionism? The lightning-speed facility to copy, share, and transform almost anything with our cell phones combined with the ability to alter political stability and personal identity with digital clicks requires that we rethink the meaning of "progress" promoted by intellectual property incentives and measured by the quantity, not quality, of intellectual property.

The meaning of "progress" may be ambiguous, but we do know that when the United States was founded, "science" meant the systemized study of a branch of learning, as in the "science of commerce," "political science," or the "science of war," books about which were within the scope of copyright law.[22] It did not mean, as it does today, the specific practice of sciences such as biology, chemistry, or physics. "Useful arts" referred to practical skills and applied sciences, including manufacturing, agriculture, and civil engineering.[23] It did not mean fine arts, such as poetry or painting. Whether the fine arts, including photography, film, video, and music, were meant to encompass "sciences" protected by intellectual property law remains a subject of ongoing inquiry.[24] But since the Supreme Court's 1903 decision extending copyright protection to circus advertisements and lithography, copyright law has protected expanding forms of human expression and broader forms of art without discrimination as to their aesthetic merit or market value.[25] Today, it is common to accept that "science and useful arts" means technological innovation and artistic creations, which is quite different from the phrase's origins. As the constitutional clause evolves over time, so too may the nature of the progress that it addresses.

Intellectual property law is anti-copying regulation. But digital technology and the internet depend for their existence and functioning on the ability to copy, transform, and distribute. The rise of digital technology is thus an existential challenge to laws restricting copying, remaking, and distributing. As the Industrial Revolution gave way to both the Information Age and internet capitalism in the twentieth century, predictable tensions emerged between those claiming as proprietary the new technologies and ever-flowing creativity made possible by digital tools and those asserting as essential the freedom or openness of those very same mechanisms and behaviors in order to innovate or create in the first place. In newspapers, calls to prevent digital file-sharing and to strengthen rights management online appeared alongside claims that file-sharing and open research networks are essential to the advance of science and knowledge. Patents, allegedly necessary to produce groundbreaking medical treatments, also drive up health care costs. Are so-called patent and copyright "trolls" new finance mechanisms and investment vehicles of the twenty-first century, or are they an unintended negative consequence of intellectual property rights run amok?[26]

The result of these tensions is paradoxically an increase in the amount of intellectual property itself—more copyrighted works, more patents, and more trademarks covering an increasing substantive breadth.[27] The Digital Age's copy, iterate, share, and resell affordances contributed to the expansion of intellectual property's relevance and scope. The more copying was possible, the more necessary anticopying regulation was felt to be. Today, we have more intellectual property and more problems related to intellectual property. The specific legal basis for this "progress is more" story is straightforward.

Copyright protection for "original works of authorship" initially (in 1790) lasted only fourteen years and covered only "maps, charts, and books," which were reasonably understood to promote knowledge about our world.[28] But in a series of statutory amendments during the nineteenth and twentieth centuries, copyright scope grew to include art reproductions, translations, technical drawings, photographs, film, advertising, manufacturing labels, and sound recordings. The Supreme Court boosted this expansion in *Bleistein v. Donaldson Lithographing Co.* (1903), in which it extended copyright to a circus advertisement, stating that it would be a "dangerous undertaking for persons trained only to the law to constitute themselves the final judges of the worth of pictorial illustrations."[29] The case inaugurated what is called the "nondiscrimination principle" in copyright law, in which aesthetic judgment is left to the market. Almost one hundred and twenty years later, copyright subject matter covers everything from everyday Instagram photographs to shampoo labels. Copyright's term also grew from its original fourteen years to its current term: the life of the author plus another seventy years. Everyday emails, today undoubtedly copyrightable as original works of authorship, may be protected from unlawful copying for seventy years after the author's death.

Patents endure for twenty years, an increase of only a few years since the first Patent Act in 1790. But over the twentieth century, patentable subject matter expanded dramatically. Patents protect novel, nonobvious, and useful inventions; initially, these were signature innovations for the early U.S. economy—fertilizer, flour mills, punch types for printing, and early factory machinery.[30] The twentieth century brought new machines and businesses in the form of computers and biotechnology. Would patent law reach these innovations? In the 1980 *Diamond v. Chakrabarty* decision, the Supreme Court held, in what would become a famous turn of phrase, that "anything under the sun that is made by man" can be patented as long as the invention meets the statutory criteria of novelty, utility, and nonobviousness.[31] Since that decision, patentable subject matter has broadened to include algorithms, financial business methods, and living organisms such as genetically modified seeds, animals, and DNA.[32] The U.S. Patent and Trademark Office has issued over ten million patents, with an average of approximately three hundred thousand per year during the first decade of the twenty-first century.[33]

Trademark law's reach has also expanded over time.[34] Trademarks are authorized by Congress's power to regulate interstate commerce, not by the "progress" clause.[35] But trademarks are essential forms of intellectual property subject to similar dynamics as copyrights and patents. Trademarks are devices—typically words or symbols—that convey information to consumers about who makes the good or provides the service. The Nike swoosh tells consumers that Nike stands behind the product. The golden arches tell passersby that the restaurant is McDonalds and not Burger King. Trademark law's aim is to prevent confusing or misleading use of these kinds of source-signaling devices to promote fair competition and improve information in the marketplace. Copying someone's trademark and affixing it to your good or service to mislead or divert customers is trademark infringement and harms both the trademark owner and the consumer. Trademark's progressive function is to incentivize the flow of goods and services, to further investment in consumer goodwill, and to promote competition in the marketplace.

Like patents and copyrights, more trademarks might be better: more source identification, more branding and differentiation, more competition. And like patents and copyrights, trademarks have proliferated, and their scope has increased over the twentieth and early twenty-first centuries. Trademark protection now includes trade packaging and "trade dress," which means the look and feel of an object, such as the rounded corners of the iPhone or the tripod design of the classic Weber grill. Trademarks also now include single colors—like Tiffany's robin's-egg blue—and even smells.[36] The trademark statute was amended in the middle of the twentieth century to extend protection to any mark, without regard to its nature, that identifies the source of the good or service to which the mark is affixed.[37] Courts and commercial entities have taken that broad language to heart. At the end of the twentieth century, the Supreme Court upheld trade dress for a Mexican restaurant described as a "festive eating atmosphere."[38] There are very few limitations on trademark subject matter today.

What kind of story is this whose plot is growth and accumulation of intangible assets? It is a story that begins optimistically and focuses on economic investment and opportunity driven by an idealized free market. The moral of the story is clear: accumulate lots of intellectual property, and the market will distribute it fairly and efficiently. Penned at the political founding of a new nation—both the Copyright and Patent Acts were passed in 1790 by the first U.S. Congress, the first Trademark Act in 1905—the story accelerated at the turn of the twentieth century. Intellectual property law hit its growth spurt in the 1950s to the 1970s, when the United States inaugurated a new Trademark Act, Patent Act, and Copyright Act, which were then interpreted generously by courts.[39] In the backdrop is the mid-century boom of manufacturing and scientific discovery, advertising, and the entertainment industries in the United States. The twentieth-century expansion of intellectual property was part of an exuberant race to maximize the benefits of a consumerist society, which were described as abundance, choice, opportunity, and individuality.[40] When the personal computer revolution arrived in the 1980s, it is fair to say that intellectual property law appeared to be doing exactly what people expected it to: it was promoting progress as capital growth, employment opportunities, and wealth.[41]

The internet and the Digital Revolution disrupted that trajectory. The transformation of civil society in the Digital Age threatens to render obsolete intellectual property laws that control copying, making (or remaking), and distributing by anyone, even users at home. Intellectual property law's exclusive rights of control may justify constraints on copying to promote creativity and innovation, but the excessive generativity of the internet and twenty-first-century digital technologies challenge intellectual property's modus operandi. The accumulation and expansion of intellectual property may be a reaction to twentieth-century technological revolutions, but those very same trends bring about an enclosure of the public domain that twenty-first-century Digital Age affordances resist because the public domain and digital technology fuel contemporary creative and innovative practices.[42] The debate going on today centers around whether "progress" is in fact "more" IP and if other ways to evaluate progress deserve our attention.

The protagonists in the "progress is more" narrative within intellectual property law are not everyday creators and innovators but those who hold most of the revenue-generating intellectual property assets—companies like Disney, Unilever, and Bayer. In the political parlance of the era, intellectual property's winners are "the one percent." The twentieth-century focus on neoliberal economic rationales and incentive-based reasons for exclusive rights to work that intellectual labor produces increased the scope of federal intellectual property rights with wealth benefits for a relative few. The distributional consequences of the broadening and strengthening of intellectual property rights has in turn challenged the economic rationale that more intellectual property means progress for all.

Our Digital Revolution, with its focus on technologies that enable sharing and distribution and resist an enclosure of the public domain, counsels critiquing and reimagining progress for the twenty-first century. This book joins others in the conversation suggesting that it is time to rethink intellectual property's relation to progress, given that what intellectual labor is and how it is produced have so radically shifted off its 1790 foundations.[43] Perhaps surprisingly, intellectual property is not only a legal concept but a cultural, social, and political concept as well. Less surprisingly, intellectual property is transforming as it becomes more mainstream in everyday life.

Intellectual property is becoming mainstream in various ways. Since the mid-1990s and the Digital Revolution, the Supreme Court has decided intellectual property cases at a rate more than double that of previous decades.[44] The highest national court is a tone setter, selecting content and focusing the debate among legal elites in ways that reverberate to national media and the public. Intellectual property law was previously a domain of technicians, a legal specialty that was isolated in practice and in law schools. Now, intellectual property law is a central part of legal education, with law schools building intellectual property and technology law research and advocacy centers to highlight the field's importance in contemporary legal practice.[45] Intellectual property is such a prevalent legal field that it is taught not only in law schools but also in business schools, graduate science and humanities programs, undergraduate schools, and even high schools. The mainstreaming of intellectual property has led it from an obscure corner of the law to a common-knowledge baseline that even teenagers acquire, transfiguring copyrights, patents, and trademarks into subjects of everyday importance. Today, it is unexceptional to read about intellectual property law in news headlines or for intellectual property to be the subject of popular television shows.[46] Children return home from school with admonitions not to copy or download from the internet without permission; they put copyright (©) or trademark (™) symbols on their work, and they aspire to be "inventors" or "entrepreneurs."

This mainstreaming—or domestication—of intellectual property affects the popular conception of creativity and innovation and also thus the demands made on law that regulates both. New stories about progress and human welfare decouple classical or dominant theories about markets and money from creativity and innovation, instead linking fundamental human rights and democratic values to intellectual property's structure and purpose. This diversification of the property-as-incentive story and mainstreaming of intellectual property into everyday culture expose ongoing debates about the progress of science and useful arts that expose changing and challenging social justice concerns in the internet age.

Once historically and doctrinally focused on economics and consequentialist balancing of harms and benefits related to quantitative measure of innovation and creativity, intellectual property today debates other, more fundamental qualitative values and principles central to our constitutional system. In this book, I employ various methodological interventions—namely, close reading of court cases and empirical studies of everyday creative and innovative practices—to describe these debates about intellectual property as framed by values such as equality, privacy, and distributive justice that are central to human dignity and flourishing and are under assault in the advancing Digital Age.

When subject to public debate and popular cultural conversations, intellectual property is not simply an economic incentive in the form of a limited monopoly. It concerns rights of attribution and integrity, community relations, equal access, individual autonomy, and ecologically sustainable business practices. It is about reputation, privacy, nationalism, free speech, and labor justice. Dignity, equality, privacy, and community welfare are constitutional values in the United States whose scope and achievement have been debated since the nation's founding. This book shows how today, intellectual property debates also address these paramount sociopolitical issues.

*   *   *

Against Progress provides accounts of intellectual property from court cases as well as the lives of everyday creators and innovators working in intellectual property–rich fields. As described more below, the interpretation of court cases in chapters 2 and 3 is intended to surprise intellectual property lawyers and scholars who—if they are like me—read these cases in consonance with the traditional understanding of intellectual property law in the United States. The analyses of court decisions may be less surprising to readers working in other professional fields for whom court opinions may be strange as a matter of course. By contrast, the analysis of accounts from everyday creators and innovators in chapters 1, 4, and 5 will resonate with nonlawyers. The detailed personal stories in these chapters explain how intellectual property is enmeshed in but sometimes undermines progress desired through creative or innovative work. Wedding photographers, folk musicians, biologists, computer scientists, videographers, and designers have surprisingly fresh and important things to say about intellectual property's relevance to their working lives and communities. For the lawyers and legal scholars, I hope that these accounts are provocative if also discomfiting in the way that they defy or resist legal doctrine and established legal theories. In sum, these intellectual property stories—what intellectual property is, how it works, and whom it serves—demonstrate nuance and diversity as compared to the often single-sided view of what intellectual property is for and how it functions. The accounts, both empirical and legal, from interviews and court cases, evidence the changing demands on the regulation of art and science as everyday people assert multifaceted roles for intellectual property in our Digital Age.

Fundamental and constitutional values central to our nation's laws and social fabric necessarily assume fresh contours and expanded importance when debated within the new context of intellectual property. Excavating these debates within intellectual property law reveals embedded tensions about these fundamental values related to Digital Age affordances and how intellectual property laws affect us all. Like criminal law, contracts, property, torts, and constitutional law—all the bases of everyday legal practice and structure—intellectual property law bares its relevance for contemporary society. This is not to say that intellectual property law is central to social welfare; most legal regimes operate in the background and are invoked on the margins only at times of dispute, crisis, or assertion of control. Instead, but controversial still, intellectual property law, like other legal fields with which people are more familiar, is infused with primary societal and legal values. *Against Progress*'s five chapters attend to these values that animate creative and innovative work, illuminating various dimensions of "progress" that intellectual property should promote. Wealth or property accumulation features infrequently; instead, progress signifies the amplification of values central to U.S. common law and constitutional law, such as equality, self-determination, privacy, fairness, and resilient organizations that sustain community welfare. These values call for a broader understanding of intellectual property's contours to guide the reformation of law and policy in the twenty-first century.

The book focuses on these values as primary—equality, privacy, distributive justice, and institutional resiliency. Each chapter other than the first begins with a mini-history of the fundamental value and its place and evolution in U.S. law and philosophy. These are streamlined and modest accounts of complex and historically contingent ideas that have been pragmatically and imperfectly enacted through United States law over time. Nonetheless, each mini-history explains the material terms for the discussion of intellectual property that follows. Each chapter then proceeds to re-narrate contemporary accounts of intellectual property disputes and its regulation, or of creative and innovative practices, in terms of these values. Reframing traditional property-like claims of ownership, exclusivity, and investment incentives in terms of deontological values that ostensibly belong to and benefit all charts a new course for intellectual property's function and meaning in the twenty-first century. As the book title suggests, these values are positioned "against" the idea of progress as measured by private property rights and their accumulation. One might say that private property and the ability to possess, control, and benefit from it is also a fundamental value that forms a basis in the U.S. constitutional and common-law framework. That would be true. But the book's aim is to demonstrate how contemporary debates about intellectual property may be moving away from this old story of private property rights that incentivize creativity and innovation and are embracing new stories with other fundamental values at their center.[47]

The first chapter, "Everyone's a Photographer Now," introduces the book's themes through a case study of professional photographers. This creative and entrepreneurial community has experienced industry-wide cataclysmic change in the Digital Age. Based on interviews with a wide range of photographers as well as observations at their studios and professional gatherings, chapter 1 describes their adaptive aesthetic and business practices and the particular problems they confront in order to continue to make pictures, work together, and earn a living with digital technology and internet platforms. In an age of rapid digital reproduction, when anyone can be a photographer (including, apparently, a macaque monkey), the century-old medium of photography wrestles with inapt intellectual property laws, ubiquitous copying and sharing capacity, and consolidated, powerful media companies. Accounts from photographers illuminate how equality, privacy, distributive justice, and institutional precarity feature centrally in their adapting aesthetic practices and business methods and how copyright authorship—core to their power and identity as artists—is being reconfigured in light of the personal and professional concerns being made salient today. Our world is overflowing with amateur photographers and altered images (some would say "remade" images; others would say "faked")—which intellectual property rules inadequately address. Interviews with photographers illuminate ethics of professional picture-making built on both authenticity and fastidious craftsmanship, topics about which intellectual property rules are agnostic. The accounts reveal coherent and flexible business and aesthetic norms among photographers that the internet threatens, pitting the photographers' embrace of a massive internet audience and the unquestionable value of photographs in the Digital Age against fears of a ravaged professional practice of photography, one on which vital democratic industries such as journalism and education depend. How photographers adapt in the Digital Age—identifying the nature of their struggles and possible solutions—provides a contextual application of Digital Age concerns linking intellectual property with the fundamental values more fully explored in the four chapters to follow.

Chapter 2, "Equality," uncovers equality principles structuring milestone intellectual property cases at the U.S. Supreme Court. This chapter reorients analysis of these cases from a market-driven intellectual property framework to one debating the contours of equality in our constitutional system that adapts to evolving technological contexts. The chapter shows how these intellectual property cases focus the idea of equality around the principles of "non-discrimination" (or "sameness") and "anti-hierarchy," which also structure analogical legal reasoning and ground the experiment of democratic self-governance that is an ideological core of American constitutionalism.[48] As such, basic equality principles that ground American jurisprudence also suffuse the resolution of intellectual property disputes at the highest court. The chapter is anchored by several Supreme Court copyright and patent cases. One such case is *Eldred v. Ashcroft* (2003), the "Mickey Mouse" case upholding an extra twenty years of copyright term granted by the 1998 Digital Millennium Copyright Act, which was passed to protect Disney's Mickey Mouse copyright for two more decades.[49] Another case is *Golan v. Holder* (2012), the "Peter and the Wolf" case that restored copyright protection to millions of foreign works, including Sergei Prokofiev's symphony, making them less accessible and more expensive, stealing them from the public domain where they lay for most of the twentieth century, free for all to use and build upon.[50] Yet another case is *Bowman v. Monsanto Co.* (2013), a patent case upholding Monsanto's ability to restrict a farmer's use of genetically modified seeds to a single harvest despite centuries of seed-saving and replanting among the nation's farmers.[51] These are considered by some scholars to be troubling decisions from the perspective of innovation and technological progress. This chapter digs into the cases' details and narrative structures, interpreting them and many others like them as forming part of a larger family of equality jurisprudence.[52] Concerns to prevent discrimination and subordination initially raised by photographers in chapter 1 are doctrinally analyzed in this chapter. It canvases categorical variations of equality's meaning, considering important distributional questions such as "equality of what?" and "equality for whom?" Applying that analysis to milestone intellectual property cases reveals new and urgent stakes for everyday creators and innovators grounded in contemporary equality concerns. As such, it begins the refinement of "progress of science and useful arts" for the twenty-first century for those who aim to continue producing and distributing creative and innovative work.

Chapter 3, "Privacy," examines the large and growing set of disputes linking copyright and some patent and trademark law to privacy interests. These disagreements range from authors and heirs attempting to shield work from unwanted exposure (such as protecting diaries and unpublished manuscripts) to authors, owners, or subjects of copyrighted works and trademarks suppressing dissemination for reputational and emotional reasons. Authors like J. D. Salinger and his heirs may seek to suppress the critique or recontextualization of a published work (such as the critical sequel to *Catcher in the Rye* called *60 Years Later*) because it offends or devalues previous work or because the author wants the old story to stop being told.[53] Subjects of copyrighted works, such as a medical doctor whose patient reviews are online, may seek to suppress their dissemination because of unflattering content. Privacy claims are usually barred when brought on behalf of the deceased, but heirs and estates bring them with frequency under copyright law, which, as stated above, lasts for three generations beyond the author's death. Copyrights and trademarks endure, whereas privacy claims die with a person. Also, privacy rights are personal and cannot be assigned. But when they are dressed as intellectual property claims, the interest is transferrable, marketable, and for some a lucrative business model. The

First Amendment might be a barrier to many privacy claims, especially when the information and work has already been published or otherwise disseminated. And yet when authors, heirs, and owners or assignees bring these privacy disputes as IP cases, they are tenacious disputes that resist First Amendment constraints.

Chapter 3 describes how intellectual-property-as-privacy cases draw media attention and sympathy from the courts because of the heightened privacy concerns in the Digital Age. For example, *Garcia v. Google* (2015) is a case in which a defrauded actress sought to suppress dissemination of a film in which she unwittingly performed because its unexpected and offensive content, which was virally disseminated, caused her to be subject to death threats.[54] Google refused to take the film off the internet and sued to resolve its liability on the copyright and privacy claims that Ms. Garcia alleged. Google won eventually, but not until a federal court of appeals issued two opinions (and two dissents) declaring rights and remedies of the parties. Ms. Garcia sued to protect her bodily autonomy (a species of privacy), but her best chance of prevailing was to allege copyright infringement. Another example is *Hill v. Public Advocate* (2014),[55] which featured a photographer and her subjects, a gay couple whose engagement had been photographed. Together, they sued to prevent an anti–same sex marriage organization from using one of the engagement photographs scraped from the photographer's website to promote its political agenda. This case, like many others in chapter 3, used copyright to constrain critique under the guise of relational privacy rights. This should be a nonstarter for copyright law.[56] Instead, these copyright cases got farther than they would have in past decades—the photographer in *Hill* prevailed—in part because of the heightened harms and challenges of the internet's accessibility and virality.

Chapter 3 also discusses *Moore v. Regents of California* (1990), a patent case in which cells from John Moore's spleen were used without his consent to produce lucrative, patented medical research results. Dressing a patent case as an invasion of informational and bodily privacy complaint raises challenging questions for patent law, which is traditionally framed as promoting public disclosure (not seclusion) of novel and useful inventions. The chapter explores many such intellectual property disputes in terms of privacy's constitutional and common-law contours—bodily privacy, spatial privacy, relational privacy, and informational and intellectual privacy—illuminating the transformation of conflicts among artists, inventors, and audiences in our new age of rapid distribution when privacy (if not creativity) feels scarce.

Chapters 4 and 5 draw on interviews with creators and innovators to examine distributive justice principles and harms particular to contemporary creative and innovative Digital Age practices. Whereas the previous two chapters discuss legal disputes and court data, chapters 4 and 5 rely on accounts from nearly one hundred face-to-face interviews conducted over the past ten years, including the photographer interviews from chapter 1. Chapter 4, "Distributive Justice (or "Fairer Uses")," explores the broader tolerance that artists and scientists exhibit for borrowing, derivation, and adaptation than our intellectual property system currently allows, defying intellectual property's exclusivity in favor of more granular and community-based sharing norms. Chapter 5, "Precarity and Institutional Failures," describes emerging harms that take the form of personal and professional precarity in creative and innovative practices threatening institutional trust and resiliency in the internet age.

Chapter 4 examines how everyday creators and innovators consider a range of borrowing behaviors essential to their professional work and personal well-being. This range evidences a misalignment between formal intellectual property law, which would treat that borrowing as unlawful infringement, and grounded everyday practices that do not. This chapter troubles the strict liability model of intellectual property infringement in which legal principles of intentionality, negligence, or knowledge rarely matter. And it generates from personal accounts of creative and innovative work nuanced and refined categories of borrowing, sharing, and adaptation that are explained by other principles of moderation and reasonableness, mutual obligation and interdependence, fair apportionment, expansion of opportunities, and avoidance of undeserved windfalls. The variations described in this chapter provide a new lexicon for tolerated uses, or "fairer uses."[57] The common features of the accounts put pressure on intellectual property regimes and their rationales, displacing dominant market approaches and economic incentives with a focus on organizational and community sustainability and well-being, which requires attention to equitable resource allocation and a more inclusive conception of community and its stakeholders.

The chapter's detailed accounts from individual creators and innovators, as well as from companies and other institutions, are remarkable for their common focus on a narrower infringement scope. According to those interviewed, a reduction of restraints on copying is needed to promote good work. Accounts range from pharmaceutical researchers, corporate vice presidents, and novelists to freelance photographers, business consultants, and software engineers. Their stories of tolerating or engaging in copying can be understood as based on a capabilities framework of human dignity. And yet the language they use to explain their borrowing practices is neither philosophical nor economic. It is pragmatic and moral, aimed at elevating the quality of work, sustaining social relationships, and promoting fair labor practices. "Quality" and "fair" define the experiences as "progress" for them. Emphasizing distributive fairness rather than asserting needs to appropriate and accumulate releases the pressure of "property-talk" (e.g., ownership and exclusion) and shifts the debate to community welfare in order to meet diverse, interdependent needs. The focus on shared responsibility for sustainable creative and innovation practices is especially notable in the Anthropocene era, as we reckon with balancing more innovation and people with the need for reducing waste, employing nonrenewable resources, and equitably distributing security, comfort, and opportunity for humanity and the planet.

Chapter 5, "Precarity and Institutional Failures," is intended to be an inverse of chapter 4. It builds from the interviewees' diverse accounts and focuses on descriptions of harms and, as some say, "abuses" suffered within creative and innovative communities. Conspicuously left unmentioned in their accounts are the harms that intellectual property law is theoretically understood to prevent. Typically, intellectual property injuries are described in legal arguments in individual terms and as economic harm. An infringer is a thief. A corporation overclaiming intellectual property rights is engaged in greedy financial conquest. Intellectual property injuries are conceived in law and legal theory as uncompensated benefits, foregone licensing fees, or substitutional rivalry. The individualized and economic terms are unmistakable. But accounts from everyday creators and innovators instead describe harms to communities, systems, and institutions. They concern patterns of violence, institutionalized corruption, incumbency biases, and disproportionality. The underlying concern is that these harms, which intellectual property law in the digital ecosystem appears to promote, erode the interdependent connections and mutual obligations that secure individuals in groups (communities, organizations, and institutions) on which we rely to live and work. This leads to a sense of personal and professional precarity that further degrades essential structure and relations as well as institutional trust and resiliency, threatening an essential faith in our shared fate in these times of hyperconnectivity.

Interviewees describe a longing for affective relations with invigorated political, economic, and social power built around the new forms of Digital Age alliances that can resist the power of supercapitalized platforms and other corporate entities with nearly limitless reach and influence. The accounts from everyday creators and innovators conjure a pragmatic structure with moral narratives of collaboration, accountability, and quality standards. These are antidotes to the Digital Age's exacerbation of intellectual property's doubling down on private and individual ownership, exclusive rights, and "progress as more" narratives of accumulation or appropriation. When translated to more generalizable values, interviewees call for reciprocity, transparency, and proportionality as features of IP law, which are (whether or not interviewees know it) basic rule of law principles. In doing so, everyday creators and innovators revive the rule of law's fundamental purpose and what, in intellectual property law, is an ultimate goal: to promote the common good by fostering and protecting a healthy public sphere. After all, as a constitutional proposition, intellectual property is a means to an end, not an end in itself. The surprising conclusion is that accounts of intellectual property harms do not champion the protection of private property to maximize science and the useful arts but champion instead the sociopolitical systems that promote fundamental values and the public good, which are (or supposed to be) supported by law.

I explore the implications in the conclusion. That fundamental values, such as those studied in chapters 2 through 5, should guide the law and policy of intellectual property if we hope to preserve respect for the rule of law in our Digital Age seems self-evident, if not yet widely examined. Analysis of the interviews and cases demonstrates that the "progress" today promoted by intellectual property is not more money or things, but a "progress" the dimensions of which our constitutional democracy has already set and has been debating for a long time. The fundamental values of equality, privacy, distributive justice, and institutional accountability have deep roots in our legal system and yet remain subject to ongoing evolution and refinement from socioeconomic and political shifts in our contemporary era. *Against Progress* elucidates these legal and popular debates over progress within creative and innovative practices and intellectual property law in terms of their moral and personal narratives that shape our collective choices today.[58]

*   *   *

Considering the place of fundamental values within intellectual property law exposes a dystopian dimension of technological evolution. It also transforms intellectual property into unfamiliar terrain for lawyers. Instead of its usual subjects and goals—copyrights, patents, or trademarks and their facilitation of art, science, and fair competition—the intellectual property stories in this book concern political speech and identity politics, misinformation, unfair labor standards, unjust social hierarchies, restrictions on health care access, and the sustainability of agriculture. Intellectual property so transformed rejects "progress" as an anchor in the modernist project, featuring authors and inventors who if they work hard may benefit themselves and society with their output. Instead, contemporary intellectual property stories reveal cracks in that modernist armor, undermining the optimism of Information Age capitalism, and expose competing claims to intellectual property law's progress in terms of an expanding public purpose.[59]

Plotting intellectual property's mainstreaming in contemporary sociolegal culture reveals ways in which the economic status quo has languished for many since the Digital Age's commencement (and for many, worsened), despite writers and scholars describing our culture as optimistically postmodern and technologically advanced.[60] The prediction of a technologically advanced society was, in the words of Paul Starr, that "disparities in income and welfare would remain but would be smaller than in the past and would diminish in moral significance."[61] Digital connectivity was expected to close income gaps and allow both self-determination and democratic capitalism to flourish. To be sure, the benefits of our technological age include more communication with friends and loved ones, more efficient and targeted medicines, online learning, accessible entertainment, and beloved portable devices. And yet education costs skyrocket without proportionate quality or accessibility. Wages for most working people in the United States have stagnated over the past three decades despite a rising cost of living. U.S. mortality rates are up (including maternal mortality), and health care is more expensive than ever.[62] The global climate crisis that will displace and potentially starve entire communities of people may at this point be irreversible. Technological development has not fundamentally altered the socioeconomic or political structures characterized by hierarchy and need, nor has it made the world more habitable. With the increased connectivity tying our well-being to each other in ways both welcome and precarious, privacy wanes. Some say we are freer, others that we are more regulated. This book shows how the Constitution's intellectual property and progress clause, once a dusty corner of the revered founding document and now a mainstream attraction, plays a role in these debates and challenges.

In one of his last essays for the *New York Review of Books*, the historian and political commentator Tony Judt, writing about the new century's promises and perils, complained of "a prejudice" in modern thought that is the "the universal contemporary resort to 'economism,' the invocation of economics in all discussions of public affairs."[63] He wrote:

> Why is it that here in the United States we have such difficulty even *imagining* a different sort of society from the one whose dysfunctions and inequalities trouble us so? We appear to have lost the capacity to question the present, much less offer alternatives to it. Why is it so beyond us to conceive of a different set of arrangements to our common advantage? Our shortcoming—forgive the academic jargon—is *discursive*. We simply do not know how to talk about these things. . . . [T]he last thirty years, in much of the English-speaking world (though less so in continental Europe and elsewhere), when asking ourselves whether we support a proposal or initiative, we have not asked, is it good or bad? Instead we inquire: Is it efficient? Is it productive? Would it benefit gross domestic product? Will it contribute to growth? This propensity to avoid moral considerations, to restrict ourselves to issues of profit and loss—economic questions in the narrowest sense—is not an instinctive human condition. It is an acquired taste.[64]

To me, this sounds like the debate about "progress" around which intellectual property law and policy now revolves. Judt's answer was to search for a "moral narrative in which to situate our collective choices."[65] He implored us to fill the emptiness at the center of economic discourse. The following chapters exploring intellectual property in court cases and in the everyday lives of creators and innovators do just that.

I do not claim that investigating intellectual property's twenty-first-century contours will help see our way through to a political philosophy or practical reality that promises more social justice to those working to sustain their everyday. But it is nonetheless a critical move for intellectual property law and policy because of intellectual property's deeply rooted economic foundations since the 1960s. Long described as a balance between private rights and individual incentives with public access and the common good, the superficial and stark cost-benefit analysis of intellectual property has robbed it of the human values that structure law's purpose and function.

Throughout the book, I engage this discursive project in terms of intellectual property law and investigate how debates around creativity and innovation today are attempts to posit values and concepts in order to fill the center that Judt identified. As the linguist and philosopher George Lakoff wrote, "Language wars are policy wars."[66] To be sure, intellectual property debates are not explicitly about the language we use to define and structure creativity and innovation policies; words like *equality, privacy, subordination,* or *hierarchy* are seldom marshaled for intellectual property rights. And yet, close reading and deeper analysis of the disputes and practices, both in the courts and on the ground among creators, innovators, employers, and firms, reveal disagreements about precisely these concepts, sometimes using precisely these words. Disregarding this language and these concepts, which are common and so deeply rooted in other areas of law, in debates over intellectual property—or worse, excommunicating it—disserves the people for whom the laws exist.

Law is language that acts upon us. And the discursive analysis of law is central to its practice and its ability to peacefully and justly order societal relations. As the stories unfold in the following chapters, I hope to show how beneath the superficial economic analysis of intellectual property law are many other substantive layers of analysis exposing concerns and contests that the language of efficiency and transaction costs can neither substantiate nor justify. The language of efficiency and market transactions detaches both lay and legal communities from the regulation of everyday creative and innovative practices in which many participate to pursue fuller and freer lives. A richer understanding of what we are talking about when we talk about intellectual property can help us be more precise and more aware of what we are doing and who we are doing it to when we regulate creative and innovative practices through intellectual property law.[67]

Creativity and innovation are optimistic buzzwords of the twenty-first century, with all its promise of enhanced connectivity and inventive opportunity. The legal regulation of innovation and creativity as intellectual property often gets credit for the technological triumphs of this era. But intellectual property laws as framed through "free-market" or corporatist economic models are grossly inadequate to explain or facilitate the human flourishing that should anchor claims of progress in the Digital Age. Intellectual property laws do not explain coherence and cooperation among diverse communities that instantiate collective creative and innovative work. Intellectual property law currently cannot accommodate equality, privacy, or distributive justice claims, nor can it address institutional failures of creative and innovative industries. The new intellectual property stories told herein introduce these themes—along with characters, crises, and resolutions—that resonate with old values for our new times. They upend traditional intellectual property explanations and break new ground for evaluating progress as a matter of social justice and dignity in the internet age. Posing the question "Is life getting better or worse?," *The New Yorker*'s Joshua Rothman wrote in 2018 that "the spirit of progress is also the spirit of discontent."[68] These new intellectual property stories are evidence of dissatisfaction with legal frameworks unable to accommodate radically altered social relations in our digital era. Read together, they are moral narratives that situate our community debates, describe choices we face, and underscore the role in democratic society of fundamental human values as central to developing sustainable creativity and innovation in the internet age.

1 Everybody's a Photographer Now: The Case of Digital Photography

> Photography must realize its destiny as the "language" of the twentieth century.
> —Berenice Abbott, 1944[1]

> The practice of photography is no longer for recording reality. Instead it has become reality itself.
> —Ai Weiwei, 2006[2]

THE STORY OF PHOTOGRAPHY in the twentieth century is the story of humanity's struggles with technology. From photography's beginning, debates raged over photography's proper status as an art or a science.[3] Its mechanical reproduction of reality is both a fact and its flirtation. Photographs are not simply windows onto the world, they are communications about the world. "We think of photographs as works of art, as evidence of a particular truth, as likenesses, as news items. Every photograph is in fact a means of testing, confirming and constructing a total view of reality. Hence the crucial role of photography in ideological struggle," John Berger wrote in 1970.[4] But a century earlier, Oliver Wendell Holmes wrote this about the possibilities of the new photographic devices: "By this instrument that effect is so heightened as to produce an appearance of reality which cheats the senses with its seeming truth."[5] As art does, would this new visual medium clarify old phenomena and enable novel experiences, prompting humanistic and philosophical discussions about civilization and society? As technology, would photography also develop new businesses, help old ones, establish new professions, and bring human societies into closer contact?

There is no neutral position from which to evaluate the benefits and burdens of new technologies. Consider the mass-produced Ford Model T at the beginning of the twentieth century or self-driving cars in the twenty-first century. With cars, we weigh benefits of autonomous mobility and swift transport against human congestion and earth-devastating pollution. And so it is with photography. Since its inception, skeptics worried that widespread and uncontrolled photography would destabilize communities and governments by spreading lies and invading privacy. This anxiety arose in the early years of the Kodak camera, when its popularity combined with the spread of yellow journalism to produce invasive and misleading photographs. These concerns persist today with ubiquitous digital camera phones, deep-fake videos, and the viral internet.[6] Then and now, arguments about how cameras work and the power of photographic expression concern personal lives, international politics, and public justice.

Then again, photography might save us—as did technologies of the past, such as lifesaving medicine, sanitation, and electricity. Photography was considered the consummate democratic art *and* technology of the twentieth century. Cameras, at first huge, heavy, and slow, are now palm-sized, portable, and snappy. Photography might be the great unifier in a world whose human diversity and divisions can feel threatening, where anyone can make a memorable photograph and instantaneously share it globally, igniting empathy and connectedness. Gerry Badger, in his 2001 book *The Genius of Photography*, described photography this way:

> It is a time machine . . . projecting us into visual contact with . . . someone at the furthest end of the earth, or a human being who no longer exists. Photography has taken us to the moon and to the depths of the ocean. . . . The medium has been one of the primary forces in shaping the myths, manners and morals of our contemporary civilization.[7]

Photography as an art and a technology transcends geographical, political, cultural, and temporal boundaries. This is especially true when paired with cell phones, which have made us into instant messengers, and with the internet, which has made us into global witnesses. Photographic technology has made us all into photographers and photographic audiences, whether or not we comprehend the extent of our agency and acquiescence. Its widespread influence is thus worthy of reflection as we consider the omnipresence of digital technology, its mushrooming networks, and its roles in promoting or preventing justice in the twenty-first century.

This story begins not with photography, however, but with photographers. They are the protagonists in this tale about technology and social justice in the twenty-first century. The story's plot is photographers' fight for recognition, respect, and fair opportunities to thrive while adapting to rapid technological changes. The scene is the ubiquitous internet terrain. Mechanical reproduction and a public audience have always been the foundation of the photographer's art and technology; ironically, the internet's high-speed digital reproductive and disseminative capacities and global reach have become the photographer's nemesis.

As the story unfolds, the photographer's story becomes a shared one. The accounts below are of working photographers I interviewed during years of field research.[8] But the descriptions of their conflicts and struggles with technological "progress" to sustain twenty-first-century professional lives—and the values to which they are professionally devoted, such as truth, fairness, and respecting skilled work—resonate with ordinary working people who experience the joy and pain born of the Digital Age. This may seem a strange alignment since this book is about intellectual property. What do ordinary working people have to do with this story? Photographers wrestle with intellectual property in the Digital Age to sustain their professional lives, communities, and values. These challenges involve fundamental values that everyday people cherish: equal treatment and dignity, status and security, reasonable working conditions, and self-determination through speech, privacy, and community sustainability. The photographers' stories of thriving and struggling in the Digital Age pertain to these more basic and broadly experienced human rights and interests; at the same time, they also concern intellectual property adapted for the internet age.

Digital technology begets new equipment at rapid rates. It inaugurates new business models with opportunities related to scale and speed that produce faster trend cycles and cultivates more people with diverse tastes and entrepreneurial aspirations to harness these tools. As photographers transition from film to digital, darkrooms to photo-editing software, agents and art directors to web platforms and social media, they struggle to transform their labor and skills into sustainable income. This struggle is amplified by the global consolidation of media and advertising companies, which wield enormous economic and business leverage, and by the corresponding reduction in staff positions providing regular salaries or lucrative freelance contracts on which working photographers long relied. Whereas in the past, photographers may have freelanced for dozens if not hundreds of organizations and clients that copiously licensed their photographs for global distribution, now only a handful of entities purchase professional photographs at prices that sustain a photographer's business. Also, these entities frequently borrow from amateur photographers and citizen journalists, who give away their photographs. This is not to say that professional photographers do not welcome young or new photographers who are populating and diversifying the field. Established photographers describe the pleasure of teaching and mentoring. But the volume of amateur and aspiring professional photographers has exploded in the twenty-first century in conjunction with the cell phone, the digital camera industry, and the self-publishing potential of the World Wide Web. These amateur or aspiring photographers often work for lower wages or produce and distribute photographs for free. And many do not insist on established professional standards of aesthetics or business practices.

The photographer's struggle to earn a living in the twenty-first century is not only a story of low-end competition and changing Digital Age norms. It is also a story of outsized corporate power and reduced reward for the labor and skill of otherwise hardworking and passionate people. It is a story about how the wealth generated from their labor and skill accumulates disproportionately in the new internet companies (or companies that primarily do business over the internet) on the basis of donated or low-cost goods. These are the companies that primarily aggregate and distribute photographs, such as Getty, Adobe, Flickr, and Shutterstock, as well as those that rely on photographs as integral to their primary services of search, information, and communication, such as Google, Facebook, and Instagram (which is owned by Facebook). In other words, photographers tell the story that they contribute essential and valuable labor and capital to these thriving internet companies without reaping sufficient rewards.

For photographers, professional skills and hard work combined with copyright, which protects their photographs from being reused without payment or permission, are critical to achieving the status and leverage that would justify the rewards they seek. Yet the internet age and the companies that fuel it have disrupted the efficacy of photographers' copyright and undermined their skill set and labor for which they contract to produce, distribute, and sell photographs. Giant internet companies have rendered copyright and contracting—the essential tools of the photographer's business—inadequate, even impotent. By asserting the primacy of efficient internet traffic and easy access to information, the internet's commercial giants paint copyright and contract as nuisances. To be sure, the internet is a global copying machine and could not work as intended if copyright prevented expression by means of linking, cutting, pasting, forwarding, or editing. If Google search results entailed copyright infringement or were otherwise unlawful (or if every search result required contractual agreement or payment to the website owner), what would be left of the utility of its search feature for the trillions of searches its users conduct every day?[9]

Everyday business on the internet tends to be one-click shopping, with one-sided "take it or leave it" terms of service and use. This essentiality, which promotes the internet's speed and predictability, is one version of the internet's upside. The photographer's less rosy version is this: more photographs, more internet traffic, more uses for photographs, more photographers, less expensive equipment, and no meaningful way to be paid for these multiplying uses or to control the integrity or quality of their reproduced and repurposed photographs. To photographers, the Digital Age has gutted the photography profession. Those left able to earn a living are mostly elite photographers. Despite the primacy of photography on the internet, the everyday working photographer is becoming extinct.

Like typesetters of the early twentieth century or the human computers of the mid-twentieth century, we might wonder if professional photographers are worth saving. New advances in technology render prior skills and old forms of labor obsolete. This is one form of progress—redundancy and evolution. But photography is not obsolete, and photographers are not redundant. The profession and its output are unlike coal or other fossil fuels on which we seek to reduce our dependence. Skilled photography is vital to the internet's power and promise. Photographs circulate more widely and swiftly on the internet than other messages, perhaps because they transcend linguistic boundaries or because of their direct and primal effect on their audience.[10] Journalism and the free press, considered essential to democracy and democratic values, rely as much on accurate, relevant, and outstanding photographs as on written articles. And advertising, the fuel of the internet giants, itself depends on photography and film. Skilled photography remains necessary to human communication and institutional resiliency in the Digital Age.

Demand for photographic images has grown in the twenty years of digital photography's prominence. By the second decade of the twenty-first century, most photographers were working with digital (not film) cameras, speeding the making and processing time of professional photographs for clients and employers.[11] Also by the end of the 2010s, many working photographers still make photographs for traditional print outlets, but they also make photographs and moving images (videos and GIFs) for the multitude of social media venues that clients and employers require. And yet, despite persisting as a critical art and technology in the Digital Age, the sustained quality of photography and the diversity of its professional production suffers. There are more photographs than ever before. But, according to the photographers' stories recounted in this chapter, dependable and reputable photographic work producing a wide array of quality images is imperiled. Making sense of professional photographers' stories about their struggles to survive in the internet age and of their straitened circumstances and the effects on their livelihoods and communities exposes new considerations for the twenty-first-century story of human welfare, social stability, and technology.

Photographers' concerns about the future of photography pertain to the quality of our shared fate and interactions in the vital public space that is the internet: the distributed digital networks through which all essential human activity today travels. Photographers do not say this explicitly; this is my interpretation of their stories, which develop an overarching theme of the digital era's discrediting of public space and public goods. This story proceeds in three parts and is structured around three related plots: (1) the virtue and vexatiousness of the internet, with its flourishing economic models that make infringement easy but also easily contestable; (2) camera technology that turns everyone into a photographer, while few are able to critically appraise or skillfully make a photograph; and (3) disputed ownership and control of photographs relating copyright law to trust, fidelity, and fair remuneration as conditions of a sustainable internet age.

Photographers explain through the lens of their particular art and technology that our shared fate depends on the internet as a public space sustaining certain human decencies: the ability in the Digital Age to speak and be respected, to maintain relationships and communities that sustain us, and to rely on stable employment and institutions. Of course, public space and public goods take other forms—clean air and water, open space, quality public education, and safe roads, to name a few. Photographers emphasize the public space of the internet and the public goods of free expression and human dignity as essential to their art and its technology. They also explain that these public goods need shoring up, with more attention to equality, privacy, and respect for professional skill, all of which Digital Age affordances are degrading.

Speech, like other public goods, is neither unpaid for nor unsubsidized. But it is unrestricted by the government to the extent necessary to support a flourishing democracy and individual self-determination. Photographers rely on the robust promise of free speech to make pictures and comment on the world they see through the camera. Similarly, the internet is a public forum for speech and expression, although not everything on the internet is free, nor is it unregulated, equally accessible, or evenly beneficial. Photographers, like most of us, rely on the internet to work and live every day. It is the tolled road on which we all travel, experiencing varied risks and rewards, which we wish to be safe, open, and equitable. A question critical to the future of professional photography is how to maintain the road as a public good and include the internet's reproductive, distributive, and transformative capacities in view of intellectual property laws, which photographers describe as dysfunctional but worth saving.

In the photographers' stories of their evolving art and business practices, they implicitly reconfigure copyright's control over expression to promote free speech, human dignity, and a flourishing internet—which align with copyright's aim of "progress of science" and incorporate the goals of knowledge accumulation and dissemination. Copyright is supposed to be an engine of free speech, facilitating individual expression and a robust marketplace of ideas. By promoting diverse and democratic authorship, copyright may also support intellectual privacy, social fulfillment, equality of treatment, and self-government. That copyright may facilitate all these things in photographers' accounts is remarkable, if also fanciful.

Formal and doctrinal copyright law understand copyright as an economic asset, an investment vehicle that relies on legally created exclusivity to recuperate costs of production and dissemination to encourage more of it. It is a private investment tool that eventually, in a trickle-down kind of way, nourishes the common weal. Photographers' stories, by contrast, conceive of copyright primarily as a mechanism for improving the public good. Their stories propose a profound reconfiguration of copyright law anchored in fundamental values such as equality, privacy, and distributive justice, which are notably distinct from the formal intellectual property legal regime practiced by lawyers and courts. Whether or not copyright law specifically—or intellectual property law generally—can or will sustain these fundamental values, the photographers' dreams of an improved legal system signal the stakes in the internet age amid the disruption of twenty-first-century technology.

The photographers' three-part story follows below. Each part elaborates Digital Age tensions between intellectual property and fundamental values. Professional photographers struggle to embrace twenty-first-century technology and its promises of progress in their field by insisting on fundamental values as part of an updated IP system that they believe is central to human flourishing in contemporary society.

I. FAST AND LOOSE ON THE INTERNET
A. A Twentieth-Century Business under Siege

Internet and digital camera technologies threaten the photographer's primary business model of paid photographic services. Traditionally, professional photographers are paid for their skill and labor and for the photographs they make. Time and reputation are substantial components of freelance photographers' client fees. High-quality work explains client loyalty and why salaried photographers remain longtime employees. Typically, copyright law features in the background of these business practices, attaching the photographer to the photographic image as the attributed author in the case of employee/employer relationships. And in the case of freelance photography, contractual agreements for cost of services largely structure the original payment to the photographer, while copyright helps photographers retain the right to be paid again for future uses of the photograph, as long as they retain ownership through copyright. Both copyright and contract rely on professional norms respecting bargained-for benefits and restrained image sharing, which are undermined in the Digital Age. Everyday internet travelers frequently ignore copyright and act as though images available on the internet are free to use without restrictions. The proliferation of photographs on the internet has elevated demand while driving down prices. And click-to-contract e-commerce rules have eroded bilateral negotiations that uphold professional expectations of bargained-for prices based on discriminating skill and expertise.

Steve Giralt is a commercial photographer in New York City with high-end advertising clients. He explained the standard, sustainable commercial photography deal, which the internet age has disrupted:

> In the commercial space there might be a flat day rate, let's say five thousand dollars a day, and then depending, let's say they want rights for just billboards in Florida for one year, then they might pay five thousand dollars for that, and then if they come back later, then "Oh, we wanna use it on billboards nationwide," then that's a separate thing.

This standard contract includes time and materials, cost of assistants and editing, and an initial license fee for the photograph's use on billboards (a "usage fee"). If the client wants to use the image again later, in another venue, they relicense for another usage fee.

In the internet age, one might think that more venues for photographs means more opportunities for photographers to earn more fees. But as Steve explained, that is not how it works in the digital realm:

> I would consider myself a high-end image-maker. You know, I'm not the cheap guy that does the little jobs. . . . With high-end image making comes a high level of production value, and the amount of [assistants] we need, and the amount of equipment, and all that stuff. And then, as I explained, the brands buy usage rights, that . . . determines my fee, with global print advertising being the greatest fee. . . . And the fact that they now want to pay, "Oh, we just want to pay you the fee for, you know, Snapchat, which [they think] can't possibly be that much, 'cause the image is gonna be living in such a tiny little world for a second of time." Like, "We want eight-second rights, we just wanna show it to each person for eight seconds." But with that, the production fee, the cost of making that imagery is still the same to me. . . . And that's the fight that the industry's having. . . . So many companies feel that they need to make all this content, like "Oh, we need a new image to put

on Facebook every day." . . . What's happening even more and more is that same client [says] "Oh, this is just for social," [and] even though it's just for social, they're like, "Oh, but we want all rights to it." . . . And I'm saying it's just a downward spiral, and they don't wanna pay for production costs, they don't wanna pay properly for usage, and suddenly, what are they paying for? And then also suddenly, what do their images look like?

Steve's account combines the explosion of opportunities for photographic work on the internet and the resistance of photographic clients to pay for all of those new placements. Some clients justify smaller usage fees by the short duration of the internet image or by the reduced size. These are understandable metrics, but Steve explained that the images he makes are of the same high quality and cost the same to produce, whether they're displayed for eight seconds or a year, whether they're the size of a computer screen or a billboard. And as clients want more and more of these images, new ones every day, they resist paying for the costs and multiple usage fees that go along with every new photograph. They want more but do not want to pay for more. Furthermore, clients insist on "all rights" to a given photograph, meaning they seek an "unlimited license" or ownership of the image—a copyright transfer—so that they don't have to renegotiate and pay for later uses. Clients want an upfront price to own the copyright in the image and all future uses of it. But they want this bundle of rights for much less than would be the photographer's regular fee if the photographer retained copyright and future uses were relicensed, as was the practice in prior decades.

I repeatedly heard this account of the economic "downward spiral" of the price for photographs on the internet, which are increasing in number but decreasing in cost. Lou Jones, a photographer since the 1970s, has experienced the evolution of the business firsthand. He maintains a busy commercial practice with a staff of assistants, making photographs for companies' annual reports and advertisements. He also pursues editorial photography that is largely funded by his commercial work, such as his 1996 book *Final Exposure: Portraits from Death Row*.[12] Funding one genre of work with another is becoming commonplace among photographers who believe that photojournalism and documentary photography are important even as fewer paying opportunities exist for such work in the Digital Age. Lou's account of digital era changes to professional photography describes the paradox of underpayment or nonpayment for photographs accompanied by a widely held belief in a photograph's intrinsic value. Lou's story begins in the 1970s in the heyday of glossy magazines and broadcast television:

[Being a photographer in the 1970s] was such a scummy way to make a living, but then it changed, you know, the TV, there's photographers . . . for the *Sports Illustrated* swimsuit thing, there's photographers at *National Geographic*. . . . It evolved, it was a steady evolution, [and] the photographers started to get a little more of a cachet. [But] . . . the thing that nobody talks about . . . is that we are [now] in an era . . . [when] photography continues to have a stranglehold on the premier way of communicating in the world. It is the universal language. People do not have to be able to speak your language to be able to see a photograph and to be able to communicate, and we use it in every computer, . . . every newspaper, every magazine, every brochure, we are inundated with photographs. If somebody has a fire in their house, the thing that they're most wor[ried about is], "We've lost all the family photographs." [Photographs] are being produced at a rate higher than ever in history, and nobody wants to pay for them. So that is the bizarre thing that changes our industry. Whether it be stock or commercial, . . . it's purely a[n] economic sea change.

I sought to confirm with Lou that despite this "sea change," he continues to earn a sustainable living, because I saw his busy studio and met his numerous assistants. I wanted to understand if he was describing a phenomenon about disruptive technology to which he can adapt and survive, or if, despite his reputation and long career, he too struggles to maintain a professional photographic practice. I asked him, "But you still get paid, right? . . . You still can command a price? I mean, I'm looking at these pictures. These are extraordinary pictures." He responded:

[It's] rarer and rarer. [It's] harder and harder to get those clients. And the deals we make are . . . [for] less [money] and [are] less interesting. We're making [deals that say], "Yes, you can use this for this purpose and this purpose, and oh, you wanna use it on the internet? Oh, OK, for another hundred dollars I'll let you use it on the internet." [When] I said, "Well, you can use it for a year," [the client says], "No, we've got our website, it's gonna be up [for a long time]," you know. [And then I say], "OK, well you can use it [for] . . . two years. We'll give you three," you know. . . . It's like, ugh.

Lou described as uncontrollable the accretion of client usage combined with decreasing client fees. The frustration at the end of his explanation—his capitulation to extending duration for no more money punctuated by his "ugh"—was notable and authentic. He recounted the widespread appreciation for photographs and the perception that they are personally precious and commercially valuable. And yet he seemed to see no way out of the business paradox of reducing earnings but increasing work demands. His work is valued—but no longer enough for him to be paid as he once was. To him and others, this devolution of payment represents a degradation of professional status and personal control. One could see it as a leveling of the photographic industry—a leveling down—that generates access for many. But for photographers like Lou, the flattening demeans photographers and the professional photography field and is produced through unjust market domination by internet platforms and consolidated media industries.

That is how Stan Rowin talks about it. Stan has been a professional photographer for over four decades. His work spans the photographic genres of commercial photography, portraiture, and editorial. Stan is the author of a famous portrait of Claude Shannon—one of the pioneers of the internet—juggling in his backyard. (Shannon's research on information theory, digital circuitry, and natural language processing were essential precursors to the internet.) Stan told an origin story about one of the first standardized freelance contracts he was asked to sign that required photographers to produce and license more photographs for much less money, inaugurating the era of form contracts in professional photography that left photographers with very little leverage. The story (and the form contract) dates from the mid-2000s just after the Time Warner–AOL merger. It is not only a personal history of this soon to be widespread contract. It is also a general story about the costs of maintaining professional integrity in the face of outsized business leverage on the part of a global media company that employs thousands of photographers. Stan recalled:

That was the first time that Condé Nast came up with a contract that said, basically, "We can use [the photograph] for whatever we want in perpetuity on-

line or in print." That's the first generation of contract. I gave it to my attorney
. . . and he said, "Well, you can't sign that contract." I said, "I know I can't sign
this contract, but . . . what am I gonna do, call them back and say, "I can't do
this, I can't do this, I can't do this, I can't do this?" And he said, "Yeah. That's
what you're gonna do. That's what you paid me for, and that's what you're
gonna do." So I was dealing with the legal department now [at Condé Nast],
as opposed to the art department. . . . Then I faxed . . . back the crossed-out
things, and I got a phone call back, [saying], "I think we can work with you
on this." And I'm saying, "This is too . . . odd. There's somethin' wrong here."
So [Condé Nast] wrote me a new contract, without those terms in it. . . .
Right after I signed the contract, I never got work from them again.

Stan's account has multiple inflection points worth noting. First, he con-
sulted his lawyer, which should have strengthened his negotiating position.
Lawyers are expensive, and everyday authors rarely rely on them except in
unusual circumstances or emergencies. Stan's lawyer helped him with this
particular negotiation, but he could not prevent the eventual demise of
Stan's contractual leverage or future opportunities. Second, by repeating
"I can't do this" four times in his story, Stan appears to understand that the
contractual term demanding all rights in perpetuity to his photographic
work was a game-ending move for professional photographers. By insisting
on deleting the "all rights" contract term, he as the photographer could
continue to earn revenue for the image in the future because he remained its
owner. But Condé Nast never hired him again. If he instead had capitulated
to Condé Nast's "all rights" language, he would perhaps have continued to
work for Condé Nast, but for much less money. Stan insisted that the term
be deleted and kept his pride but not his client. Not many photographers
could afford to make that choice.

B. A Collective Action Problem

Stan recounted this tale as if it were David versus Goliath. One way to beat
Goliath without a lucky slingshot is to organize an army. At that time,
Stan was a rising leader in the American Society for Media Photographers
(ASMP), a photography organization that promotes professional standards
and educates clients about those standards, including contract terms,
license fees, day rates, and reasonable budget practices. Despite what

Stan described as tireless organizing around these issues, photographers nonetheless succumbed to deleterious contract terms, because, as Stan explained, they needed the work, and Condé Nast was a huge employer with desirable assignments. (Condé Nast's publications include *Vogue*, *The New Yorker*, *Architectural Digest*, *Vanity Fair*, *Bon Appetit*, and *GQ*, among many others; its publications claim an audience of over 150 million readers.) Stan recounted the following history of failed collective action in the context of negotiating with another magazine that soon thereafter adopted the same terms as the Condé Nast agreement:

> Steve, [a colleague,] called me up and said, "Did you receive the contract from [so-and-so]," I don't remember th[e] name [of the computer magazine]. And I said, "Yeah, I'm not gonna sign it." And he said, "Neither am I." . . . [But] Shelly signed it. I saw her at a meeting of the ASMP. I said, "How could you sign that contract?" She says, "I didn't even read it. I just signed it and sent it. I wanted to get it off my desk." . . . This was a contract for future jobs. So Steve and I stopped working for the magazine, and she kept working for a while, but now I don't even know if they're in business anymore. It was a magazine publishing company, the trade magazines for computers. And it was good money for us in Boston, 'cause we have a lot of computer-related stuff. So there are enough people to sign the contracts who need the work, so that you can yell all you want, and just say "No, don't sign the contract," and somebody's gonna sign the contract.

Stan initially thought that collective resistance would prevent wholesale adoption of the Condé Nast contract's onerous terms. But the combination of working photographers signing contracts without reading them and a glut of photographers in need of work fractured the resistance. Goliath won.

At the turn of the century, a confluence of political and economic events was a game changer for photographers. At the height of the dot-com bubble in the early 2000s, publishers covering the September 11, 2001, tragedy insisted that photographers produce more photographs in less time and allow their photographs to be used without restriction worldwide. This created another form of pressure on photographers: transition to using digital cameras or stop working for news and media companies. The combination of the events of 9/11, the rise of internet communication, media consolidation, and adaptation to digital technology had drastic consequences for working photographers. Publishing weekly magazines became a luxury; on-time content was the new standard. And with on-time content and digital cameras came more photographs and less time for postproduction editing—quantity gave way to quality, or so the photographers say. And with that shift came the rise of amateur and just-starting-out photographers who would work for less.

Before the dot-com crash and the transition to web-based publishing in the mid-2000s, business and technology magazines hired thousands of photographers to cover the technological revolution and its consumer and business opportunities in magazines like *Business Week, InfoWorld, and PC Today.* But on the edge of the crash, these weekly magazines started to fold. A few migrated online but still published a print version. (*WIRED* magazine, bought by Condé Nast in 1998, is often heralded as one of the success stories.) Craig Dale, a Hoboken-based photographer, worked for many of these magazines at this time. He trained as a medical photographer and often worked for hospitals, scientists, and medical companies, but he also freelanced for technology companies and magazines. Craig's description of the photographer's experience of the dot-com boom and bust adds specificity to Stan's account of the losing battle over professional contract and copyright standards:

> I was doing really well for probably about four or five years. [But then there was] [t]he *Business Week* contract. . . . I had a meeting with . . . the photo director of *Business Week* [to insist on proper contract terms]. Boy, he got his head handed to him, but he had a job to do, you know. . . . The bean counter said, "Nope." . . . And then I can remember going to places and hearing, "We'd love to hire you. And here's our contract," and they would always say "work for hire," you know, in perpetuity. All manners of reproduction existing and to be invented in the future. [laughs] But I'm not gonna sign that contract.

Craig's story resonates with Stan's, except that by now, the photography contract was "take it or leave it." The terms now included a complete transfer of copyright (the "work for hire" provision) and, if that term did not stick, permission was granted for all uses of the photograph now and in perpetuity. It was a one-size-fits-all contract for the publisher—a precursor to the "click to agree" contracts now ubiquitous online. With no negotiation possible, the value of and respect for professional photography as skilled and independent expression was dying.

Craig continued his story by introducing the photographers' organization Editorial Photographers (EP). EP is a professional group like the ASMP that at the time urged photographers to resist the contract grab that depleted their income and professional independence while demanding more services. Craig recalled:

> There was a time when . . . Editorial Photographers . . . was [telling us], "Just say no." [pause] "Just say no. We'll all just say no." Well, the trouble is that the photo schools are pumpin' out 150 new graduates every month, or every trimester, and there they are, and they'll shoot for free. They're like, "Yeah, I'll do it. That guy won't do it? I'll do it. For what? Sure." And, you know, I think . . . the whole industry was just toppling. . . . I can remember when the dotcom bubble burst because my phone started to ring, and it was Andrew from *Teledotcom*: "Hey, man, really bad news. We're closin' the magazine." And the next phone call was a guy from . . . *Internet Week*: "Hey, man, really bad news. The magazine is closing." Like everything stopped.

Craig's story adds to Stan's the detail of young photographers just out of school and eager to work. Unlike Stan's story, in which professional photographers agree to onerous contract terms from long-standing clients in order to retain them, Craig's story describes new or amateur photographers who become the low-end competition to the established photographers, who were trying to hold the line for better working terms. The young photographers, the new contract terms, and the demand for digital speed (in making and processing photography) combined to decrease the cost of doing business for publishers, who themselves were struggling to transition in a Digital Age when readership was moving online and demanding more real-time content but for less money or for free. Reducing photographers' fees was another way to save money in the evolving business of media publishing. Without a union or other powerful organization to represent the photographers as a group, the media companies would prevail in slashing their costs, reducing photographers' wages, and weakening photographers' control over contract terms concerning copyright retention and licensing fees. Faced with economic and professional precarity and with reduced standards for quality photographs, photographers continue to describe their futures as uncertain.

C. Risks and Rewards Abound. Who Benefits?

The internet generates other pressures that contribute to the economic squeeze that photographers experience. For example, once a photograph is published online, the original publisher loses control over it, most especially the ability to charge for its reuse. Inevitably, the photograph travels from the original website, through links to the website, to those who copy and repost the photograph, sometimes altering it in the process. That the photograph was copyrighted—authored and owned by the photographer and licensed to the original publisher—does nothing to prevent the photograph's promiscuity. This may create copyright liability for the publisher-licensee to the photographer if the publisher does not own all rights to the photograph. If the publisher licensed a single use for the photograph—for example, a one-time publication online for a month—and the photographer retained all other rights, later uses of the photograph that originated with the original online use might create thousands of dollars in copyright liability for the publisher. Instead of policing websites and locking down content—tasks that are easier said than done—wary publishers sought to minimize their potential copyright infringement liability by demanding "all rights" to the photographs in their freelance contracts. This is not an unreasonable business move, but as mentioned above, publishers did not want to pay more for "all rights" simply to cover infringement liability committed by others beyond their control.

Yet another pressure on the photographers' business model derives from a celebrated outgrowth of the internet: its capacity to generate and make accessible useful databases and compendia that can be updated in real time. Databases flourish on the internet thanks to effective scanning and search functions and low-effort reproduction and distribution of information and expression. Some of those databases are photograph databases, like those owned by Getty or managed by Flickr. These databases have depressed the price for uses of photographs through the stock photography model, to their users' benefit. Stock photography sites diversify options for clients and publishers by offering cheaper generic images. (Stock photography sites often diminish aesthetic quality and reduce expressive precision, as professional photographers explain later in this chapter.) Instead of hiring a photographer to make photographs of a client's bakery goods, for example, the client can license on favorable terms images of baked goods from a stock site that look close enough to their own cookies and cakes and thereby pay much less for their advertising and web design.

The dawn of the internet age inaugurated diverse and varied stock photography sites that initially benefited working photographers. But as Lou Jones explained, the payday from stock quickly dissipated. Originally, he earned "in the six figures" annually making photographs of "car manufacturing and biotechnology and computer industries and agriculture" because "people needed those pictures." Also, "everybody wanted, you know, naked girls . . . and fashion. Everybody wanted to shoot travel, and, you know, Paris, and . . . all that stuff." Professional photographers made lots of money filling the stock companies' photo banks. But now, Lou is lucky if he receives a monthly check for two hundred dollars from a stock site. He reminisced:

> We used to be with Image Bank. . . . So they made a lot of money from using our pictures. And . . . I was getting six figures. . . . [But] there's nothin' for the last ten years. Image Bank doesn't exist anymore. They sold to Getty. And Getty was giving me a little bit of money for a little while . . . twenty grand a year, maybe. . . . Now the stream is, I think I'd get maybe a hundred, two hundred dollars a month now. . . . The original agreement with stock was [a] 50/50 [split]. I produced the picture, got it to them, and they gave me half of what they sold it for. . . . [But] the industry eventually de-evolved. . . . The bean counters realized how much money was to be made, and they started giving the photographers smaller and smaller and smaller and smaller and smaller chunks, and my being the asshole that I am, I said [to my colleagues], "Mmm, no, guys. Let's all band together and sort of, you know, these guys are rippin' us off," but my spineless cohorts, you know. So then now, they're givin' the stuff away. So stock is a dollar, . . . and they're giving the photographer twenty percent of that.

When I asked Lou whether the stock companies were willing to negotiate better splits with better-known photographers, Lou laughed and said:

> No. No. No. When I was writing about it at the time, when it was all happening, and people were interviewing me, and writing, you know, I was saying,

you know, the mantra that they have is, "Here's our contract. A lot of people have signed, . . . it's a good contract, you can still make a lot of money, here, sign." "No." And they say, "Step aside." That was, you know—the person right behind you will sign.

Lou's story echoes throughout many other professional photographers' accounts. Few photographers I interviewed had anything positive to say about Getty's business practices. Today, more stock photography sites are owned by fewer companies—Getty, Shutterstock, Adobe, and Visual China Group are currently the global leaders—with photographers losing even more control over pricing and other contracting terms. To be sure, stock photography companies would make less money paying each contributing photographer more. But the stock sites' business model is to grow their databases to millions of photographs, made easily searchable and licensable through e-commerce efficiencies. They do so by purchasing photographs for miniscule sums from thousands of individual contributors. Photographers sign agreements (or "click" to agree to terms of use) and license all rights to their photographs to the stock site hoping for some revenue when their photograph is the lucky one chosen from among millions of similar photographs available for purchase. This is an excellent business model for the photography sites and platforms, much as Uber, Amazon, and YouTube are successful moneymaking businesses built on piecework or crowdsourced participation. But it does not serve photographers who hope to earn an independent living selling and licensing their work.

Other businesses benefit from the internet's capacity to build and use large databases as new revenue models. At the end of the last century, *The New York Times* compiled its content in a digital database to repurpose and sell, as did many other news and media organizations. This practice raised the question whether copyright law required authorization and payment from original contributing freelance authors to include their work in these new databases. *The New York Times* determined that copyright law gave it permission to use the original content without further payment to the original freelance authors and to license that content to LexisNexis. This led freelance authors to sue *The New York Times*, also naming Time Inc., Newsday, and LexisNexis as defendants. Chapter 2 describes this court case in further detail, emphasizing its ironic outcome. The freelance authors won, requiring *The New York Times* to seek permissions and make payments to republish the freelance authors' articles. But this led news organizations and database businesses to require, going forward, broader contract terms and a copyright transfer from freelancers without any further fees. The freelancers won the lawsuit but did not financially benefit from the expanded rights under copyright.

This result is one episode in a long history, as intellectual property scholar Jessica Litman wrote, of "copyright laws in fact giv[ing] [authors] little power and less money. Intermediaries own the copyrights and are able to structure licenses so as to maximize their own revenue while shrinking their payouts to authors."[13] Copyright is a tool to enable authors to negotiate with publishers for livable wages, but it becomes the basis on which publishers and other intermediaries accrue more wealth and power at the expense of most authors. As it turns out, this is an old story. Copyright historian Mark Rose provided a similar account of authors and publishing guilds in eighteenth-century England upon the introduction of the first copyright act that named authors as beneficiaries of the law, but that really benefited publishers who thereafter required transfers of authors' copyright to do business with them.[14] The story unfolds again in the Digital Age at the beginning of a new century amid further techno-logical revolution.

For the photographers I interviewed, these accumulated internet effects on fair contract terms and retention of copyright reduce their professional stature and their capacity to earn a sustainable living. To them, dwindling leverage in contract negotiations is a sign of disrespect, an interpretation orthogonal to the view that e-commerce click-contracts and boilerplate terms of service are admirably efficient and accessible. Photographers de-scribe inequality and abuses of power in business dealings with publishing intermediaries and clients, even though these are not the calculated effects of technological evolution and the Digital Age's staggering economies of scale. They describe as inequitable—disparate and imbalanced—the dis-tributions of wealth derived from their photographic work. Debates wage over the equities of that balance among small and giant internet companies, diverse publishers, and media organizations, from noncommercial blogs to Condé Nast, and among everyday authors, such as photographers. Left undisturbed is the consensus that photographs in the twenty-first century are indeed intrinsically valuable, even as their economic value in the marketplace is approaching zero.

This begs the question of whether something so valuable must remain protected through market mechanisms, such as copyright, or whether it can be protected and funded in other ways (such as taxes and grants), as are clean air, safe roads, and much university research. Linda, a documentary, fine art, and editorial photographer who still largely works with film cameras, explained the problem of the market in photographs with an analogy to perfume and pie:

> This new generation that grew up on Flickr think[s] that every photograph [is free] . . . as long as you give attribution and you don't make any money on it. . . . Where photography fits into people's idea, it's [as if photographs,] they're almost like perfume, like why are you wearing that perfume if you don't want anyone to smell it? Are you gonna charge me to smell it? It's just there. . . . Photography is like that. . . . People perceive that of photography, whereas if you're making pies, it's more like, well, sometimes people make pies to give, and sometimes people make pies to sell. . . . [If] you're a baker, . . . you . . . don't . . . [ever] question the business model.

Linda described the positive spillover effects of certain goods—what economists call positive externalities—for which there is not always an efficient or capturable market. Those who enjoy the smell of perfume when worn by others can enjoy that experience without paying. And if you shop at a bakery, you expect to pay for pie. People may give things away for free—free samples of pie!—but the baker's business model is typically to sell baked goods. Linda bemoaned the internet's transformation of photographs and photographic work from investment vehicles with rewards for professional photographers to a positive externality free to most of us who surf the web.

Photographers do not blame the internet. Most of their stories of authorship in the age of rapid digital reproduction concede the internet's vast opportunities for knowledge, amusement, and business. These opportunities appear to require a robust public domain to search, share, and communicate. Photographers further request respect for authors' contributions to the knowledge, amusement, and business of the internet by cleaving the owned and paid for, through copyright and contract, from what is free for all. In other words, photographers dispute the precise distribution of benefits of the public domain and the internet's marketplace.

We all rely on the internet's public-facing affordances, but those who produce some of its value hope to reap some of its rewards. Not all value-producing activity will or should be monetarily rewarded, of course. Doing so would produce an intolerable social system constrained exclusively by market exchanges. But as photographers tell the story, their valuable labor is unfairly exploited by those who wield inordinate market power. A skeptic might say "quit" or "change careers," and some photographers have done just that. But this is a less optimal answer when excellent photographs are still in demand. And thus perhaps a better response is "how can we support quality work with a living wage under fair conditions?" In this way, the photographers' stories also contest the nature of twenty-first-century postindustrial capitalism comprised of intangible assets, such as intellectual property and information goods, and founded on a dependable public domain. It is contested because the new twenty-first-century marketplace is tainted with bargaining hierarchies and inequitably distributed rewards. If the photographers are our canaries, they are warning us that exploitation in the internet marketplace is eroding some of our most fundamental values and hopes for civil society: equal treatment, dignity, and self-determination as well as a society in which people can expect a reasonable opportunity to thrive.

II. EVERYBODY'S A PHOTOGRAPHER

Contemporary photographers describe their creative practice as fraught with peril in the age of rapid reproducibility and scalable sharing platforms. But they also describe it as filled with opportunities to work with others in hopeful social structures that foster contemplative aesthetic practices. Photographers' stories about creativity in the Digital Age include abundant authorship and similarly situated authors who embrace the challenge of working with technological reproduction—photographic mechanisms—to build empathetic human relationships. As photographer and visual artist Sarah Newman says, "Everybody's a photographer now." This next story is about the challenges of maintaining quality and skill in the face of abundant production.

Abundance can breed diversity. Multiple perspectives of events and people can generate discussion, debate, and appreciation for truth in its iterative forms. With abundance of opportunity and output, however, photographers also lament what they perceive to be lax standards for the object of debate: the photograph that generates contemplation. Photographers describe the "good enough" problem, where the glut of photographs and other internet images, such as memes, lower the standards for excellent photography and professional output. This may sound like a critique of the democratization of photography and of the expanding opportunities of digital photography image-making in the internet age. But it is not. Photographers celebrate opportunity and access at the same time as they insist on aesthetic and procedural standards for work with the tools and subjects of photographic practice. As will be clear in the accounts below, photographers insist on quality standards for images to protect the integrity of the field and the status of the profession as based in expertise and ethics. This does not produce restrictive exclusivity, but it does rely on purposeful hierarchies. Anyone can be a photographer—just like any human can be a copyright author under copyright law.[15] But to be a professional photographer and make extraordinary pictures requires time, practice, cultivated relationships with subjects and teammates, and constraining disciplinary ethics—all of which the internet's pace and space can easily undermine.

The combination of photographic abundance and professional disciplinary constraints leads contemporary photographers to resist copyright rules that forbid all copying. Contemporary photographers embrace what is precious about the internet—its qualities of connectivity, network creation, and generativity—while they also insist on controlling some copying that embodies their distinctive creative contributions. Photographers combine the values of openness and opportunity with professional aesthetic and business practices of image-making to condemn *exact* copying of photographs (what in copyright law we might call "verbatim uses") that in pre-internet days would have been licensed and paid for. But most contemporary photographers I interviewed would also leave as free to others most uses of ordinary, everyday photographs—those not professionally crafted but that are part of regular digital communication. They would also tolerate uses of their photographs to promote artistic and cultural engagement, even uses that transform the original photograph if doing so would produce new images and art. As such, photographers broadly construe the public domain and rewrite the rules of copyright according to their own aesthetic and professional standards.

These adaptive professional norms better accommodate the values of equal dignity of all authors, privacy among authors and photographic subjects, and equitable resource allocation that enables earning a living making and using photographs. In the internet age, their version of "public" is broader than copyright law provides for because copyright law would protect all copies equally (ordinary everyday works of authorship and extraordinary ones) as well as all "derivative works" made from the underlying photograph (new versions and adaptations). Contemporary photographers are ambivalent about controlling new uses that materially change the underlying photograph, especially if new uses further authorship in some way. They are more tolerant of copying that precedes transforming the underlying work—for example, using a photograph as inspiration or motivation for another photograph or other art. And they also accept copying ordinary photographs (as opposed to those specially created and laboriously crafted). Professional photographers thus insert aesthetic discrimination—a doctrine that copyright law has flatly rejected since 1903—into their calculation of tolerated copying.

Contemporary photographers nonetheless assert stronger-than-copyright claims over exact copying of photographs, especially when the subsequent use and distribution decontextualizes the photograph, distorting its subject matter and message. They do this to protect the integrity of their subjects and of photography as a reliably communicative medium and also to maintain a revenue stream from the licensing and contracts on which they rely to earn a living. These assertions of hierarchy (both professional and aesthetic) sit uneasily along claims of equality and expressive freedom, which photographers also espouse as part of their practice. Problems of incommensurate values may have coexisted more comfortably in past decades of siloed practices when not "everybody" was a photographer and only professional photographers asserted copyright and entered into contracts concerning photographs. Today, when photographers negotiate potentially inconsistent fundamental values over the terrain of contemporary art and business practices, they highlight challenges of our Digital Age in which equality, privacy, and opportunity—all currently under siege—are as important as ever.

A. Opportunities of Abundance: Distributive Justice and
(E)quality Measures

Sarah Newman is an award-winning photographer and visual artist who started making photographs in high school in the 1990s. She attended college and graduate school, studying photography and philosophy. Afterward, she assisted professional fine art photographers and developed her portfolio. When I asked Sarah about becoming a professional photographer in the internet age and the transition from film to digital, she said:

> Everybody has a camera. . . . There's a shit ton of pictures, and . . . production of photographs and quantity of floating pictures, . . . everybody's a photographer now. . . . So there's that, and then in terms of the originality, or sort of making something new, photography's different than other media because it requires something to be existing in the world to base the photograph on, and in photography's history, it was kind of about copying the world. And for that reason, [it replaced] . . . other forms of copying representation. But photography's relationship, in my opinion, to those objects in the world is that [photography is] more closely tied [to the objects] than . . . drawing. Because it's a causal relationship, and I think that's different and important, in that the object is required in order for the subject to be depicted, . . . the light has to reflect off of it. So . . . people often mistake [the image for the thing] . . . [and] see past the surface of the photograph. [A] lot of people see the subject, [but] they don't see the photograph. They see—if there's a picture of a tree, they see the tree. They just kinda see past . . . [the] mediation of the world. It's like . . . . the Magritte [*The Treachery of Images,* which features the phrase "Ceci n'est pas une pipe"]. . . . It's kind of like that. What is [this]? [A] picture of a tree, it's a tree . . . no, it's a photograph. It's the same kind of thing, but it's even harder with photography.

Sarah's experience with and understanding of photography as an aesthetic practice articulate the tense relationship between mimetic representation and creativity. She described the making of photographs as a "causal relationship" but insisted that making photographs as an artist is the process of showing an audience more than the subject of the picture. She said, "If there's a picture of a tree, they see the tree. They just kinda see past . . . [the] mediation of the world." But she says, it's not only a tree, *it's a photograph.* Photographs are easily misunderstood as not reflecting aesthetic choices. Here, Sarah asserted the preeminence of the photographer, with their vision and authorship, whose skill is overlooked or misperceived as absent in a Digital Age overflowing with photographic images. One effect of this misperception is the erasure of the photographer from photographic practice.

Sarah's early experience with photography informs her understanding of how photography is an interaction with the world, not just a reflection of it. Learning to engage in this contemplative visual practice is, to her, part of what being a photographer is and what cameras can enable. She explained:

> There's all these layers of reality and . . . things we can perceive and experience, but somehow having a camera and . . . interacting with the world, in all these layers of experience, . . . gave me more agency . . . to . . . make creative expressions and interpretations of what I was seeing. So it was almost as if I were just starting to write poetry or something. I ha[d] this tool that I c[ould] use, and anything that would normally be kind of mundane became a lot more interesting, because I always had my camera with me. . . . Pretty much anywhere I went, I had a camera . . . so I wasn't just receiving and engaging. I was actually searching for meaning.

Sarah described the camera as a photographic "tool" and photography, like other forms of art (such as "poetry"), as a way to help us see the world in a new way. She said she personally experiences these new perspectives and aims to share them with her audiences.

Sarah's photographic praxis renders inseparable the human and their machine, in much the same way that the internet connects people technologically through personal digital devices. But Sarah prioritizes human agency as the will that generates and gives form to the art, demanding discipline in the use of cameras and the analysis of visual compositions that encourage contemplation. She explained how photographic art helps us to see things in the world differently and from new perspectives. It may also transform how we relate to the world. In this way, Sarah explained photographic art as quintessentially *original*—making something new from the photographer's intervention. The camera, like the internet, is a tool for human expression. To understand either as independent of human agency or as lacking fundamental human values such as self-determination is an error.

Lee Crosson and Ali Campbell are young photographers who devote substantial time and energy to making photographs. At the time I interviewed them, they shared aspirations to eventually make a living doing so full-time. Both are world travelers and use their photography to share those travels with others. Despite their professional youth relative to other photographers I interviewed, both Lee and Ali understand photography, like Sarah, as a craft that presents challenges of identifying and shaping what is made into photographs. Lee said that he thinks often about how "a photographer's job is to crop the world and prioritize . . . a certain set of images or an image in what is an infinite degree of, or an infinite number of perspectives. . . . It's more what a photographer leaves out than what they include." Ali offered a similar, albeit more overtly political account. She said she worries about the lack of visual literacy in the context of accumulating photographs on the internet and the unspoken cultural forces that shape what we see and what we don't see in photographs:

> There's this crazy proliferation of visual media, and I think a lot of people have this kind of antagonism, where it's like, "This is a photographer," "This is not a photographer," and for me . . . I think it's really good for people to be creating. I think by and large, . . . photography is such a fantastic thing, 'cause it encourages people to notice other things around them . . . that we're trained not to, right? . . . I think it's really nice that [the availability of cameras] gives people an automatic mechanism for doing that. I do think as well [that] . . . we don't have much visual literacy . . . [in] understanding what photos mean, . . . how they're taken, or how to interact with them.

Ali implicitly draws a distinction between *taking* photographs, which most of us say and do, and *making* photographs, which is how all the photographers I interviewed characterize their practice. When photographers *make* a photograph, they deliberately render the image from a particular perspective, with particular tools, making choices about composition and arrangement. This is a quintessential copyright story of originality and superintendence of the image.[16] Copyright authorship requires that photographers, not the machine or nature, constitute the origin of the photograph. This also tracks the difference between the skilled photographer and the amateur—what Ali identifies as an "antagonis[tic]" distinction—noting that visual literacy is important to "understanding what photos mean." Learning how to notice the world in a new way and become visually literate is part of becoming a photographer.

Despite insisting on certain hierarchies of photographic practice, Ali said that she would not want to deny anyone the opportunity to become a photographer. But she insisted that there are ethical implications that photographers should consider when making pictures, because the proliferation of picture-taking renders unremarkable and overlooked the resulting images and their possible meanings that circulate so easily today, with substantial effects on their subjects and audiences. She explained:

> We get so much of our information and so many of our views about the world around us . . . predicated upon the images that we see. . . . That comes from a certain perspective, and . . . there's motives behind how this information and this knowledge is produced. I think it's the same way with photos, right? . . . I think people don't necessarily understand the link between "OK, I'm going out, and I'm taking a picture of my coffee," . . . and [connecting that to] "what is the relationship between that process and what's happening in Syria" or "what's happening in this other part of the world," right? How are those parallel, and . . . you know, you're making choices about what you're sharing. . . . There's just so much horrific content out there, and I think so much of it is clickbait, and people are like, "Atrocity footage to share," [or] "Terrible news story to share" . . . and . . . obviously, there's really horrific things that are going on, that we have to . . . grapple with and fight against, but . . . culturally, we think in such binary terms, . . . "Everything is awful now," or "Everything is good now," and that's not how the world functions, right? There's nuance in everything.

For Ali, the photographer's practice communicates that nuance and shares responsibility for it. Lee confirmed that goal in his explanation of the selectivity and interpretation for each photograph that "crop[s] the world." Making photographs focuses the photographer's attention (and, one hopes, the photograph's audiences) on the many ways that images can be rendered in order to shift or make new understandings. To these photographers, making photographs is not merely mechanical but a deliberate practice that is part of a larger conversation they are having about their world.

The Digital Age has rendered more of us able to be photographers and participate in that conversation globally. And so more of us, as photographers, can add to the conversation that is more frequently conducted through images. We all have that opportunity, but not all photographs are made in that spirit. Photographers are not necessarily fearful of the automated digital technology that facilitates the making and sharing of photographs absent skill and practice. But they do worry that the ubiquity of photographs and photographic equipment, without attention to the practice of making and viewing photographic images, will dull the effect of the nuanced, novel, and critical perspectives that photographers generate to benefit cultural diversity and critique. Abundance demands some constraining practice—a disciplinary skill and ethic—that like all professions should be open to all equally but may be unevenly adopted to eventually create qualitative distinctions among Digital Age photographers.

B. Ordinary vs. Extraordinary Photographs: The Hierarchy of Practice and Discipline

Photographers celebrate the accessibility and openness of photographic practice for anyone with a camera—which is nearly anyone with a cell phone, approximately two-thirds of the world's population (or more than five billion people). The problem of "ordinary" or unremarkable photographs—if it is a problem at all—is not their lack of authorship or the difficulty in identifying the photograph's origin in a human but the imperceptibility of creative characteristics that shape the reality they are representing. When photographic skills of rendering reality become invisible or are effaced, as they often are in the ordinary photographs that crowd the internet, audiences no longer are asked to practice critical reception or question what they see. Photographs end up speaking for themselves, losing the anchor of the photographer and the context and history of the photograph's making. Photographic referents—people, interactions, events, facts, and natural phenomena—lose their footing; the stories the photographer tells with those referents seem to exist irrespective of a photographic author, who made choices about what to make visible and how. This erasure unintentionally devalues the disciplinary work of professional photographers and degrades self-determination over their art and business. It may also debilitate the appreciation for and practice of making photographs that aim to tell a trustworthy story about the world.

Rick Friedman, a longtime freelance photojournalist, explained what is misunderstood and complicated about making extraordinary photographs (as opposed to ordinary ones), specifically highlighting practice, skill, and time:

> People seem to have a lot less respect for a photograph, 'cause everybody runs around with their iPhone and does it. . . . I've actually had people say this to me: "I don't see what the big deal is. It's only a photograph." I've actually had people say that to me. And I have also had people say to me, when we've done a job, . . . "Your pictures look a lot better than our staff photographer's. Can you explain to him how you do it?" And I said, "I teach workshops. Would love to have him come to one of my workshops. But I'm not gonna get on the phone."

Rick relayed this story with some sarcasm and incredulity. Why was it so surprising to the client that the result of the in-house photography shoot was less impressive than that of the professional photographer with decades of experience? And why did the client think that professional skill and expertise can be taught with a phone call rather than years of training? Rick directed his client to the professional development seminars he conducts. He said that he believes in the importance of teaching aesthetic and business skills—he says teaching "forces him to be a better photographer." Articulating through teaching what makes a photograph extraordinary—or "better than," as his client said—can cultivate expectations for and understandings of exceptional photographs, encouraging audiences to contemplate the true and moving story it tells.

Contrast Rick's account with that of Lee Crosson. Lee, an aspiring landscape photographer, explained that time in the field and regular practice is essential to learning how professional photographers earn the attention of appreciative audiences:

> Most of the photographers that I know . . . all came up with film photography, so hearing them talking about the amount of hours that they spend, . . . the amount of money that they've spent on film, . . . the failures, and . . . getting back home with a roll of film that they were so excited about. . . . In

one way or another, that feeling of loss, and having digital come along, and suddenly . . . having infinity . . . at your fingers, but also seeing the transition, the change of that, and seeing their work that they had worked so hard to craft suddenly being right up against people who are just taking a phone out of their pocket, and clickin' somethin' and maybe getting lucky, maybe not, maybe having a great eye, maybe, maybe not. I feel like just the definition of a photographer . . . [is] a complex one. . . . It takes time to do anything. Like you [have to] . . . be in something for a while in order to figure yourself out, in order to figure the craft out, in order to figure the market out, [and] in order to figure . . . the community [out].

One might balk at the idea that to be a "photographer" requires time in the field, suffering through mistakes and losses, and that there are no prodigies, only hardworking artists. I understand both Rick and Lee as saying something else, however, and yet speaking from opposite professional positions—one from an established perspective and the other as a hopeful professional. They explained that making photographs worthy of broad audiences and critical contemplation requires an appreciation of photography's constructed form and technological affordances. Critical contemplation is challenging to learn because photography, like seeing, is something "everybody" does today without thinking. What is there to contemplate? But photographic form (its referential relation to reality) and its technological affordances (magnification, focus, lighting, etc.) relate to how we communicate on the internet today. Working photographers with years of accumulated practice and skill and an understanding of the medium and its tools have an important role to play shaping community norms of discourse and understanding in the Digital Age.

Carl Tremblay, a veteran commercial photographer, said that the ubiquity of digital cameras and the impatience they cultivate has diminished the aesthetic quality among the abundance of online photographs. Lower-quality photographs lower the quality of communication. He explained, "The digital, I think, . . . has brought in 'It's good enough. It's good enough.' And . . . I think it . . . steals better work from being done, because you have the ability to look in the back of the camera and say, 'We got it.'" Many of the photographers' accounts referred to the "good enough" problem, which is another way of describing the problem of "ordinary" photography.

Satisfaction with what is easy to produce sets a lower standard for quality, critique, and engagement.

To combat the lowering of aesthetic and communicative standards, Felice Frankel, a science photographer, described the importance of teaching the difference between good pictures and what she called "terrific pictures." Like Rick Friedman, Felice aims to help shape an appreciation of photography in the Digital Age through teaching, and she described the urgency of doing so in the age of the internet:

> I'm now making pictures on my phone . . . because . . . I now see that making pictures is democratic, you know? But . . . what I'd like to think is that [pause] you could tell the difference between a good picture, a good-enough picture, and a terrific picture. I mean, that's why I'm making this book. I want to raise the standards of what should be demanded . . . of images.

Felice is a science photographer in the vein of Berenice Abbott and Harold "Doc" Edgerton, photographers who explored the physical world unavailable to ordinary vision with special photographic equipment. Felice's photographs, like those of Abbott and Edgerton before her, are mysterious for their revelation of the physical world and stunning for the beauty of nature made visible through camera technology. Because she uses cameras to show audiences what they cannot see with their eyes alone, trust in her choices, process, and technique are paramount to achieving her goals as both a scientist and a photographer. Felice therefore puts a premium on accuracy, staying true to the science she is picturing with her camera, similar to how photojournalists worry about staying true to the events and the people whose lives they represent through photographs. With today's easy access to cameras, Felice aims to preserve the integrity of information conveyed through photographs by developing the awareness and skills of the growing multitudes of people who make and share pictures with digital equipment. This rising awareness and developing skill will distinguish the photographer and the photograph among a crowded field. It will also, she thinks, build stronger communities around shared expectations of effective, truthful communication and scientific principles.

Pre-shutter activity preparation, contemplation, and compositional choices informed by practice and experience distinguish extraordinary or "terrific" photographs from ordinary ones. The internet pirate who copies photographs without asking worries photographers, but more worrisome is the instinctive picture-taking and viral dissemination that minimize human input and individualized reflection. Photographers assert that self-reflection and attention should precipitate the act of photography in order to produce new and worthy images that enhance knowledge and understanding. Having standards for photography does not make it an exclusive field. But the hierarchies instantiated by professional photography assert the importance of certain qualities of photographic work, including an investment in the photograph's construction through practice, teams, time, equipment, and labor. Cultivation of diverse subject matter and multiple perspectives are also critical metrics of quality, as are trustworthiness and authenticity when central to the genre (such as documentary and journalism).

Consider, for example, Felice Frankel's photography practice. She works closely with other scientists, who trust her to render their experiments accurately through her unique camera equipment to illuminate central aspects of their research. For Felice and others, the difference between an ordinary photograph and an extraordinary one may be the effort to develop new equipment and build relationships with collaborators to explore and understand the scientific subjects together. For photojournalism and documentary photography, being in an unusual place with the ability to patiently carve out a unique perspective on an event or subject sets one's work apart. Lou Jones described a time when access to a shot during the Olympics required climbing through snow with heavy equipment and an assistant. "I remember . . . in Albertville, . . . Winter Olympics, . . . I was standin' there, and I was like knee deep, and it was freezing, me and my assistant had to literally dig out a ladder up the hill to be able to get [the shot]." Cultivating partnerships and perspectives and investing time and effort all facilitate exceptional photography.

Photographers also describe developing a distinct style—which takes experimentation and risk—that does not compromise the subject matter's authenticity. With help from assistants, photographer Mark Ostow combines portraiture lighting with photojournalism to make haunting photographs of contemporary politicians as well as everyday people. He described his process:

We . . . move the light constantly. . . . a mixture of photojournalism and portraiture. I think I came up with this hybrid thing. And I'm the only person at these events who has an assistant with them . . . I think it's unusual. 'Cause most people are using light that comes from the camera, or they're using available light in these situations, but I was trying to create a portrait version of reportage.

Distinctive styles contribute to the diversification of content, which can stand out in the sea of repetitious images and viral copying facilitated by the internet. Indeed, diverse and original content becomes rarer online when internet business strategies depend on the same photograph to circulate widely and repetitively. Dan, a veteran sports and news photographer, explained:

> [Today] the level of photographs [in news and general media] isn't as high. Bear in mind, they're reaching into a pool that everyone else is reaching into, so a lotta times you're seeing pictures you've already seen in other publications. Because they're not careful about having unique content. The death of every publication . . . *Saturday Evening Post, Life* magazine, . . . whatever the publication is, . . . has always been lack of original content. Original content always drives the wagon, . . . even in commercial [photography]. . . . I think one thing that's happened is that first off, resources are not as great, so they're relying on subscription services. . . . [And] that material . . . has often been regurgitated in the newspapers or websites.

Even worse than repetitive content is the distrust that lax photographic standards generate. Photographers I interviewed—even art and portrait photographers—condemn the staging or faking of images when audiences expect them to be true. As images circulate more widely than ever and with photographs significantly affecting politics and social welfare, photographers consider themselves internet ambassadors, setting standards of what should be expected from the medium: truthfulness, empathy, and respect. Together these metrics drive emotional impact. Indeed, emotional impact, authenticity, and aesthetic style are partners in professional photographic practice. As one photojournalist explained:

> We always try to . . . delve at what real photos [are], so the photos that you get are so emotional, you . . . really see the person's pain or whatever, and then hopefully the reader can connect at a higher level to the story. . . . We can't ask people to do anything, ever. You have to find out what they do and then kind of be there when they're doing it.

This same photojournalist explained that the newspaper she works for attempts to cultivate the expectation of accuracy in the Digital Age with a "rule . . . in terms of editing, cropping" of photographs, especially in the context of social media and online enhancements, that "we can only do things that you can do in the darkroom." This means no Instagram filters or overlays. Tying the photographic image to the capacity of people, not computer programs, is important for photojournalism's integrity, she explained. Audiences who learn that photographs of real places and people were changed or "faked" for whatever reason (be they aesthetic reasons, error, or lax journalistic ethics) will soon come to distrust all photographs. They may then also dispute the skill and labor that photographers expend to make extraordinary and truthful photographs, destabilizing this premium currency of online communication along with the ethical standards it upholds.

Quality metrics of photographs are reliably met by professional photographers through disciplinary learning and practice. They are described as a matter of domain specificity and field integrity central to community standards. Photographers describe their professional work as important because their standards establish the values of diversity of perspectives, commitment to community, and trustworthiness. Photographers are unafraid to assert artistic and institutional hierarchies within the field, as these hierarchies do not rank people but rather disciplinary skill and ethical commitments. They establish an integrity for professional work that includes specific expertise and a moral consensus concerning these values. Anyone can be a photographer. The equalizing force is (or should be) work and access to it. High standards are met with time, practice, mentoring, teamwork, and commitments to determining and testing the truth. This is an optimistic story despite being spun in the age of rapid, digital reproduction, when impatience for volume and abundance renders photographic work vulnerable to low-end production, easy copying, and distortion—all of which erode professional boundaries, aesthetic standards, and the moral values of truthfulness, empathy, diversity, and respect. Just at the moment in the Digital Age when photographs are critical internet currency, the photography profession seems to be facing an existential threat. And yet with their optimistic stories, photographers recast problems of inequality, distributive justice, and professional precarity in terms of the dignity of work, the importance of trust, and disciplinary standards grounded in both aesthetics and ethics.

C. Controlling the Copy, but Not the Conversation: Equal Dignity of Work

Professional photographers lament how exact copying of their photographs without permission or payment undermines professional photography and the standards it seeks to uphold. The exact replication of their photographs appropriates their individual identities and distinctive contributions, demeaning their effort and work. And the photograph's tangible transferability conveys value represented by the payment that is necessary to make a living as a professional photographer. Facilitating both permission and payment by controlling verbatim copying is therefore (to working photographers) essential to the production of skilled photography in its many forms today. Photographers describe their creative practice and financial well-being as relying on a functioning market in professional photography services and products with paying customers who respect contractual agreements and copyright law. But these business norms depart from copyright law in important ways. And so preserving them, by demanding conformity among newcomers among other means, is a challenge in the internet age.

Maintaining Business Norms of Mutuality and Respect. Alejandro is a commercial photographer with a growing fine art practice. Photography is his second career (the first was marketing and sales). Despite coming to professional photography late and without formal training, Alejandro's accounts of professional norms and aesthetic practices echo the other professional photographers I interviewed. When asked about his reaction to the copying of one of his photographs for the purposes of transforming it into another medium, for example from photography to painting, he gave the following response:

> I'd be like, "Wait a second, . . . you had to get permission from me first, to make your work." Because at the end of the day, even if they're saying they're not doing it for commercial purposes, it is commercial. . . . So I think there has to be some sort of permission there. Just like when I photograph something with a picture or painting in it. If I have to commercialize that picture, right, I have to get permission from the copyright holder. So to me that is, again, I come back to it, that is the most important thing is what I have inside of me.

Alejandro clarified the norms that he said guide the practice of exact copying for reuse:

> I think commercial use, . . . people taking my [work] and claiming it to be their own, would bother me the most. That would . . . most . . . annoy me and make me very mad. Whether commercial or noncommercial. Simple cheating. The second thing would be obviously usage, like if I were to find an image that was used for something that it was not intended for, and I never got compensated for it . . . by that client. [That] would really bother me.

This explanation articulates three harms of verbatim copying. The first is the injury of copying and selling another's image as one's own. This injury resembles the commercial and moral injury of unfair competition with its dimensions of fraud and diverted revenue. The second is a breach of contract or trust between photographer and client. Photographers describe a breach of agreement when clients reuse images in venues not designated by the original contract and fail to pay the extra fees. Although the agreement is anchored by copyright's exclusivity in the photographic author (with the right to transfer that exclusivity to licensees for limited purposes), the injury here is the contractual breach based on unauthorized reuse of photographs. The copying per se hurts less than the fact that the client broke a promise to the photographer. Economic loss is also a factor, but Alejandro's account highlights the offense of disrespecting an agreement between professionals. The third harm, from verbatim copying, concerns the emotional distress (and not the economic loss) of using a photograph without permission. Photographers describe this as a dignity harm, an act of erasure and disrespect. When Alejandro emphasized that "again, I come back to it, that is the most important thing is what I have inside of me," he was referring to the creative expression embodied in the photograph that represents his personality, which he maintains should not be appropriated without his permission.

As to this last point, photographers were remarkably consistent. Copyright law may be fraught with complexity and inconsistencies and many photographers do not understand it fully. But to them, the one sure thing that copyright should accomplish is connecting the photographer to the photograph. Most photographers adhere to this principle even in the context of a photograph to which they may not be particularly attached personally, aesthetically, or commercially, as with event or wedding photography. Josh Silk, an event photographer in New York, explained it this way:

> SILK: It's important [that I retain copyright] because it's just always, it's the school I come from. I come out of that school of thought of like, once you create, you created that image. If you weren't there with your camera, you know, making something happen or documenting that moment, it wouldn't exist. So therefore it becomes that photographer's image, from the second the shutter is pressed.

> INTERVIEWER: So is it . . . the symbolic meaning that's associated with it, or is it for practical uses that you want to make with these [images] that . . . means retaining the copyright is important?

> SILK: In the instance of event photography, I think it's symbolic. It's just what it stands for. I'm not gonna give you this for free, and you can say it's yours. That has . . . not only monetar[y] [value] but [also] has value in terms of being the creator, you know? If . . . you're the creator, that's what being an artist is all about, is being the person that's creating stuff, and when somebody takes your creation and puts their name on it and says it's their creation, that kinda takes the creator aspect out of the equation, which is kind of futile, I guess.

In the internet age, photographers fight against different forms of erasure: their identities as artists, as embodied in their aesthetic creations; and their labor and investments, as embodied in the payment for their time, skill, and photographs. Unauthorized exact copying involves all of these erasures. Professional photographers attempt to sustain norms of contracting and copyright retention to defend against them.

Although copyright law may theoretically help photographers protect their photographs from unauthorized exact copying, the reality of internet traffic is that most exact copies of photographs online are unlicensed. And many of those copies—such as search results and uses for news reporting or education—may be copyright "fair use." Fair use is one of the broadest exceptions to copyright's exclusive rights. It permits exact copying when doing so furthers copyright law's underlying goals of "progress of science" by facilitating research, education, journalism, and commentary and when the secondary use does not supersede the commercial market for the original use.[17] Photographers do not resist fair use as a concept, as the discussion below will explain. But they do worry that the avalanche of accessible digital photographs online and the internet norms of copy, paste, and send have devastating effects on sustainable professional photography practice that depends on licensing exact copies for commercial purposes. The proliferation of exact copying on the internet—the internet's generative engine—threatens the integrity and sustainability of professional photography.

Encouraging Conversation. Photographers' *in*tolerance of most forms of *exact* copying contrasts with their high tolerance for diverse uses of their photographs made into new images and used for alternative purposes than the original use. For example, professional photographers accept as part of aesthetic development and mass communication that photographs will be used or repurposed to maintain or evolve artistic and communicative norms. Indeed, some contemporary photographers grudgingly admit that copying may be an uncomfortable necessity in the ongoing conversation that relies on diverse artistic practices. Others describe being flattered by copying of their work when copying promotes conversations not only about the subject matter of the photograph but also about photography itself. As such, photographers compromise by objecting only to exact copies that circulate decontextualized and virally and by accepting a multiplicity of repurposed uses that are part of evolving and generative conversations that the internet has facilitated.

Two examples demonstrate broad copying tolerances outside the ambit of exact copying that photographers believe should be licensed. These forms of pro-social copying are perceived to promote creative freedoms and sustainable photographic practice. Both accounts demonstrate more flexibility than copyright law currently allows. These uses would unlikely be copyright fair use because they more closely resemble "derivative" uses, for which copyright law would require permission and payment. But photographers accept them as fair in their practice because the uses develop the field and the expression of other photographers. Alejandro, again, explained his tolerance for copying of his photographs in certain circumstances:

> There's only a couple of instances I came [across where] I kinda felt a little flattered. . . . They were good artists. . . . They took one image of mine, . . . said they were inspired by this image . . . and they took some other image, . . . and I'm like, "All right. . . . They're not selling it per se."

From Alejandro's description of this reuse, his initial photograph was used as inspiration and as raw material for a new work, although his photograph was recognizable as a component part.[18] This practice makes sense to him as an artist, and he considered the use of his photograph complimentary. From his caveat that the "good artists" were "not selling it per se," I understood Alejandro to mean that they were not copying his photograph and selling his photograph as such; Alejandro's photograph was not replaced in the market with the new artists' work. The new work was inspired by Alejandro's work, but it was not Alejandro's photograph sold by someone else without permission to do so.

Lee Crosson explained that sometimes the unauthorized part of copying is crucial to making art and that for this reason, in his view, one must be flexible when it comes to copying:

> CROSSON: I think it's a question of intent. . . . What is the person trying to do . . . ? In [the] case [of a student using a photograph in a Power-Point presentation], I would have no problem at all. That would flatter me and nothing else. . . . The thing is that it's not even just making the money. . . . I actually support this. . . . [The discomfort that accompanies unauthorized use] needs to be there. That's the art. Like we're saying, this is a conversation that needed to happen, and I think this is really the only way that it would've happened.

> INTERVIEWER: So what if [the copier] had asked permission and the photographer had said no, and then he went ahead and did it anyway?

> CROSSON: I think it would make it more powerful art. You know. I wouldn't wanna be that person. But it would make it more powerful art. . . . I don't know what I would say [if asked]. But that would destroy it . . . the conversation goes away. . . . F. Scott Fitzgerald has this great quote that I return to time and time again: . . . "The test of a first-rate intelligence is the ability to hold two opposed ideas in the mind at the same time and still retain the ability to function." And I think that's got applications everywhere. So . . . OK, I think it's almost necessary to be pissed about this [unauthorized copying], but . . . at the same time . . . I want to be able to say what I want to say and when I want to say it, and this is a consequence of it, you know. And the law . . . is, it's impossible for that to be made around one single person, and that is essentially the expectation

you're saying, like, "I don't want this to happen to me," but the implications of that not being able to happen I think are far more damaging and far more wide-reaching.

Without being aware, Lee's explanation of tolerating unauthorized copying rehearses the "breathing room" that copyright law intends to enact through its extensive statutory exceptions (such as fair use), but sometimes falls short in its formal applications.[19] Copyright law aims to promote free expression while at the same time protecting works from certain unauthorized copying and distribution—an opposition of ideas that Lee identified in his tolerance for unauthorized copying of his work. But interestingly, both Lee and Alejandro extend their tolerance for copying to derivative works and close stylistic similarities, which would typically be copyright infringement, not fair use.[20]

Both Lee's and Alejandro's accounts contain an implicit caveat in their forbearance. Sarah Newman made that caveat explicit when she explained that most forms of copying would be fine unless they were distorting the original work's meaning for ends with which she disagreed:

I think I generally tend to be in a pretty liberal camp for that sort of thing [unauthorized copying], but I think that there could be definitely situations. . . . Like, for example, if there was a right-wing political campaign . . . that was using it, then I would certainly have a problem with it. In general, I'd really like for people to be enjoying my work, and it makes me really happy when I go to people's houses, and I remember that they own a piece, . . . and I get to see it. It's nice for the work to . . . live in a place where people are getting to experience it [and] have their own experiences of it.

Sarah explained that most forms of copying would be fine because she aims for her work to travel and "live in a place where people are getting to experience it." Her approach focuses on human and artistic capabilities and flourishing—let the work be accessible for others to enjoy as a resource, either for free or for a workable fee. She said that she is "pretty liberal" when it comes to exclusive rights in her work because it is meant to be experienced by a wide audience. But, she explained, if the use implied her affiliation with a "right-wing political campaign" (a political ideology she rejects) or the use was distorting the photograph's meaning toward ends with which she disagreed, she might protest.

In other words, permissive critical engagement can go too far. On the one hand, reuse that is mildly transformative or derivative is okay—as Lee says, if it is in "conversation" with his work. On the other hand, reuses that are subjectively offensive in form or content and may be truly transformative (and are thereby usually exempt from copyright protection under the fair use doctrine) are preferably under the author's control according to these photographers. Reuses of photographs that are out of context and used to tell a very different story than originally intended—that change the nature of the photograph's reference or whose altered aesthetic features may threaten the photographer's reputation—are strongly disfavored. These unacceptable uses also may harm professional photography's integrity as a truthful form of communication on which we all rely. These are dignity harms, not economic harms. Photographers are appealing to a reduction in offense, not a reduction of speech.[21] This is a fuzzy line, to be sure, which chapter 4 discusses in significantly more detail in the context of distributive justice and human flourishing.

As ambassadors of photographic content, professional photographers consider control of the copy—but only some copies—to be critical to maintaining aesthetic and professional standards and to promoting dignity and trustworthiness in the Digital Age. Copying is essential to photography, however. Photographers make copies of the world with their cameras, and copying that keeps the conversation going is both tolerated and expected. As authors of images, photographers consider themselves fiduciaries of both the images they make and of professional photographic standards. This fiduciary role, developed more fully in the next section, explains reasons for and ways of controlling uses of their photographs. Fiduciary control is a far cry from IP law's purposes. However, moving from a property regime—ownership and control—to a fiduciary system that nurtures trust within a moderate hierarchy is a notable lesson that professional photographers provide for those of us hoping for equitable and flourishing communities in the Digital Age.[22]

III. WHO AUTHORS THE IMAGE? PRIVACY, SPEECH, AND CITIZENSHIP IN THE DIGITAL AGE

When professional photographers make photographs of other people, they negotiate a tense relationship between their own creative freedoms and the right of their subjects to control their images. This negotiation exposes competing values of the photographer's free speech and the subject's privacy. It also reveals the struggle to sustain trust among strangers and acquaintances, which is crucial for community resiliency. As a formal legal matter, this negotiation takes place over the terrains of copyright, right of publicity, privacy, and the First Amendment. But because most photographers and subjects are not legally sophisticated, this negotiation over photographs about fundamental values is informal. It is structured around implied understandings and aesthetic and business norms. This section describes those understandings and norms as features of the creative and civic-minded culture that photographers aim to cultivate and engage.

Photographers loosely understand that copyright law may provide them with control over their photographs—even those photographs that feature other people, whether or not they agreed to be photographed. Most photographers believe that, as the originators or creators of the work, they do (or should) have primary legal and moral authority over a photograph's circulation and subsequent uses.[23] Photographers also express empathy toward their subjects, who consensually or coincidentally become a photograph's focus, and thus they may have significant and sometimes competing interests in the photograph's composition, use, and circulation. How photographers describe the tension between authorial and subject control of a photograph resonates with fundamental values of liberty, privacy, and self-determination as well as aesthetic and expressive diversity. But photographers locate these values in their understanding of copyright authorship, not the rights of all individuals. And thus, their aesthetic and business practices—which they assert copyright governs—limit or subsume photographic subjects' rights. In this way, the concept of copyright does a lot of work for photographers, perhaps more work than copyright law in fact permits.

Photographers thus describe caring deeply about copyright, but not in the way that copyright is traditionally or formally analyzed. Copyright is an alienable right of control over works of authorship with significant exceptions and limitations built into its monopolistic structure. Copyright does not grant rights of attribution or credit to authors, nor does it contain rights of integrity to prevent mutilation of work, so-called "moral rights" that exist under other national regimes (in Europe, for example). And because copyright is freely alienable, photographers often lose (or contract away) control over works made for clients seeking maximum usage rights. As mentioned above, photographers rely on copyright as one of several mechanisms for payment for their work and services—a way to be remunerated for their labor and its output. But photographers also assert copyright as a way of connecting themselves to their work and their profession, as a measure of professional and artistic status, which is not part of copyright law's formal justification. Holding copyright in their images, even if they lose substantial control of the photograph's uses in some practical way, is to photographers symbolic of their standing as members of a professional class.[24] Copyright appears to serve a certification or status-enhancing role for photographers, which to them justifies their freedom and artistic choices and may overpower photographic subjects' own freedoms, self-determination, and privacy.

Formally, copyright law incorporates into its doctrine some fundamental rights, such as those embodied in the First Amendment, by excluding facts and ideas from protection and through flexible fair use.[25] But these limitations benefit *any* user of the copyrighted expression, without specific consolation for photographic subjects or subsequent authors. These limitations benefit those who engage in political speech, criticism, and satire as well as those reporting the news and otherwise transforming the underlying work. Reuse of photographs for criticism and commentary, as much as photographers may object, are typical fair uses permitted by law. But most of the photographers I interviewed do not understand copyright law at this level of specificity. And as already discussed in the previous section, they resist the breadth of fair use, especially as it applies to purpose and character of the use when the use is critical, political, or subjectively offensive.

Ironically, however, when photographers make images of people—to report, criticize, make art, or engage politically using images and events of the world—they describe limitations on their own subjects' rights of privacy or speech so that they may proceed to make photographs. In other words, photographers imagine limitations to subjects' fundamental rights to privacy and self-determination but not to their own rights under copyright law. Yet photographers do not describe these imposed limitations on subjects as a degradation of the subjects' rights or an assertion of unfair dominance but as a transfer of those rights to the photographer to protect and manage.

Indeed, photographers claim a strong form of copyright in their photographs—a stronger form than the law would provide—made stronger by their subjects' implied acquiescence produced through collaboration and trust with the photographic process and audiences. Photographers say that this acquiescence or submission is necessary to make photographs that are worth looking at. As such, photographers explain the interest they have in their photographs not only as a copyright interest to license or sell but also in terms of professional standards and personal expressivity critical to the art itself. Photographers' self-determination and autonomy as artists and authors take precedent over their subjects' rights of privacy and personal identity, but largely because that is the only way, in their view, that photographs can be made well.

Through a process of stewardship, relationship-building, and skilled photographic technique, the photographers I interviewed described the subjects' submission to the supremacy of the photographer's aesthetic vision. Either through implied norms or explicit consent, the subject's privacy, autonomy, and equitable rights in the image submit to the photographer's practice. This is a story of hierarchies among photographers and their subjects, but as the photographers tell it, those hierarchies are defined by trust and mutual respect. It is also a story about necessary governance structures in light of the twenty-first century's freighted and viral sharing platforms, which feel like chaotic free-for-alls and may require new rules for productive, peaceful ordering. The photographers' accounts in this vein are persuasive and empathic stories of relationships built not around formal copyright law but on trust and transparency, which are more challenging to maintain in the networked information ecosystems of the internet age.

A. Photographer as Lead Collaborator

Photographers describe working collaboratively with subjects. Photographers rely on consent and the independence of the subject but also on the eventual submission of subjects to the photographer's choices. The collaboration takes time, and sometimes photographers describe developing deep attachments to their subjects.

For example, Martha, a veteran photojournalist, describes sitting with people for hours or even days to make the necessary photos for stories on which she reports. She aims to build trust in order to produce photographs that are as authentic and accurate as possible. For one story on adult survivors of child abuse, Martha's boss at the newspaper told her, "We want real people. We want . . . to show real people," emphasizing the importance of representing realistic, unstaged emotions in the photographs. Martha explained:

> I think the obvious thing would be to go around and do portraits of these people that were named in the story, but I would go and meet them and talk to them, [and it was challenging. Then one woman said], "Well, you know, it's really difficult for me. This is what I do. I go to this therapy, and I end up like tearing up stuffed animals, and I tear up the couches," and [so I asked], "Is there any way I can go to this therapy with you?" and . . . then I could only stay for a few minutes, but . . . you get these intimate photos that you normally wouldn't get.

Many photographers described similarly intense relationships with their subjects in which they work together physically and emotionally to be comfortable with the picture-making.

This collaboration is rarely memorialized in writing as explicit intention or consent. In fact, photojournalists and documentary photographers rarely if ever get releases from their subjects to use their images. The photojournalists and documentary photographers I interviewed described confidently (and sometimes indignantly) how making pictures in public and of public people and events does not require permission. Yunghi Kim, an award-winning photojournalist and advocate for photographers in the Digital Age, explained:

> So, First Amendment, freedom of press . . . using it as reporting, you're protected, so that's what you use. You don't need a model release. . . . If I take a picture on the street now, . . . people are always like, "Don't take my picture, don't take my picture." So I spend a lotta time Googling . . . First Amendment, freedom of the press. . . . This is all legal. It's what you do with the picture that's another matter. . . . So this is where the social media is a little blurry, because, you know, my generation, we use photographs to report, for publications, whatever. Even if when you did the personal project, it was in the context of journalism or editorial, right? So you're protected.

Unlike photojournalists who rely on the First Amendment to make pictures of strangers in public, commercial photographers such as wedding and portrait photographers invoice their clients for a range of items, including equipment costs, travel, and assistant time, and for particular uses and forms of the delivered photographs. But even they rarely include in the contract an explicit release to make a photograph of a person with the right to control their image.[26] Instead, these photographers described having an implied understanding with the subjects they work with that subsequent use of their images on websites or promotional materials is broadly allowed.

In fact, most photographers who work closely with subjects to make photographs for editorial uses or personal uses (such as weddings or portraits) celebrate the collaboration that they believe obviates the need for explicit consent. This collaboration also justifies the photographer's authorship of the photograph because the photographer guides or frames the subject. One photographer said, as quoted in a photography journal, "Constant feedback is important with real people. Even if you want someone to be natural, you still have to guide them."[27] This guidance and direction has deep roots in copyright law, justifying photographers' authorship status with the original contributions that they bring to their images of the real world.[28] A photographer's superintendence of the photographic process—framing, cropping, lighting, staging, posing, conversations that put the subject at ease—reaffirms that, even in the age of hyperreality and the immediacy of internet communication, photographs (and videos) are crafted and shaped by their makers. Cameras, lenses, and filters are choices that direct the photographic subjects and shape the resulting images. For this guidance to be successful, subjects must willingly submit to the photographer's encouragement and control. A fine art and portrait photographer confessed to me, "I know [that when a potential client is] going to be incredibly controlling . . . they're really the wrong client for me. [This is why] I haven't built up much of a commission business. . . . There are very few people who are willing to give up that kind of control [to me]." In a successful collaboration, photographic subjects give themselves over to the process in an intimate and vulnerable way. The implied consent to use their rendered images reflects trust and the premise of equal dignity—but not equal control—between photographer and subject.

B. Photographer as Custodian

Sole authorship and control of a photographic image does not mean that photographers lack responsibility to the subject, however, or believe themselves to be the master of the image. To the contrary, photographers describe themselves as having significant responsibilities to subjects and the photographs they make of them. They invoke a shared fate and a mutual interdependence inherent in professional photographic practice.

Once the photograph is made, the photographers describe caring for the photograph and controlling its use as a matter of stewardship.[29] Photographers describe this stewardship as having three overlapping functions: protecting the photographic subject, protecting the photographer's relationship with the subject, and protecting the photograph itself (or the story the photograph tells). Ali Campbell, the young portrait photographer and photojournalist referenced earlier, described her awareness of this sensitive and complex relationship, saying:

> It's not just, "Oh, it's like my particular art form." . . . These are people with whom I have relationships and interactions, and I feel really lucky to be able to interact with people and to be able to take their photos. . . . I think it's such an intimate thing, right, to . . . take portraits, and have people let you do that?

Ali went on to describe how she accepts the hierarchy and power present in the relationship between photographer and subject while respecting the subject of the photograph she is making. "Whenever I'm shooting photos, I always give people the opportunity to see things on the other side of my camera." As she describes it, "I'm coming into these places, I'm this foreigner, with this camera, there's already all these dynamics of class and power involved. . . . It seems really . . . unethical to me to be like, 'Well, I'm gonna actually decide how you get to be shown to the rest of the world.'"

The power that photographers have over their subjects may arise from the foreign intrusion of the photographer, as Ali mentions, or it may arise from the situation of the subjects themselves. Lou Jones describes his justified strict control over his photographs of death row inmates and his distress at any unauthorized use of them. Only in very narrow circumstances would he give permission for those photographs to be copied and reused. He says about the photographs and their subjects: "These people entrusted me with their lives." This reflected a common sentiment among photographers, especially those who depended on their skill and expertise to make people feel comfortable in front of a camera and to build the trust needed for people to allow the picture to be taken in the first place.

The photographs rendered through trusting relationships with subjects enrich our understanding of the lived experience pictured in the photograph. The photographs reveal aspects of identity and experience otherwise invisible or incomprehensible. Thus, the unauthorized copying of the photograph may harm both the photographic subject and the photographer because it degrades the human relationships involved, interfering with the trust and transparency that fueled the photographic process. This was certainly true for photojournalists and portrait photographers. Noreen, a veteran and award-winning photojournalist, explained this harm and her distress at unauthorized reuses of her photographs of people as follows:

> You take an image of someone that you took months to gain trust from. Where you feel completely empathetic and compassionate to their story. And then someone, because that image is in the archive, and they couldn't care less [about] the context of that image, says, "She's hot-looking. Let's use her to sell this." . . . That's my problem.

Contemporary photographers emphatically lack tolerance for unauthorized uses when the subject of the photograph and the relationship the photograph helped establish are injured through decontextualization or reuse. Crucially, photographers describe themselves as sometimes the only defense against unauthorized reuses that harm the subject. This suggests that as authors, with relationships to their subjects, they feel responsibilities that publishers or internet intermediaries may not. Indeed, in the age of the digital archive, with millions of photographs that circulate on the internet without attachment to any photographer or context, photographers are reasonable to worry that the Digital Age default is to reuse without attention to attribution, subject integrity, context, or veracity. This uncontrollable promiscuity may fuel their righteous assertion of identity as "authors" of the image in order to control and defend the photographic subject and stories told with the photographs. The subjects' rights of privacy, already given over to the photographer or waived by appearing in public in the first instance, cannot protect against broad reuses. But authorship under federal copyright law (as chapter 3 explains in more detail), with legal remedies and scope that are stronger and broader than state-based privacy law, may serve photographers and their subjects well, albeit only as legal claims belonging to photographic authors.

Photographers experience their custodial role so strongly that few photographers I interviewed felt obligated to seek their subjects' consent to reuse a photograph, whether on a web page or social media or in a gallery show or book. While photographers who invoiced their services (for instance, for events or portraits) included in the invoice explicit permission for use on the photographer's personal web page, few were explicit about or even considered the need for permission for future artistic or expressive uses. This is because photographers take for granted they have nearly exclusive control over their photographs by virtue of the initial collaboration in which the subject submits for picture making.[30]

One interpretation of these accounts highlights the importance of protecting and honoring the relationship with the photographic subject. Photographers appear to believe that protecting the human relationships that facilitate flourishing of creative work is critical to contemporary communication in the Digital Age. The harm is personal and subjective, often described as a desecration. Stephanie Gomez, a young, emerging photographer in New York, explained that misuses of her portraits are "almost like defaming art." As parents protect children, artists protect their work and the subjects of their work with ferocity and a strong belief in the moral righteousness of their control.[31] They are "taking care" of the art, its purpose, its subjects, and the ability to make more.

A problem for photographers, however, is that many reuses that are offensive to them or their subjects may be legally protected under the First Amendment.[32] If the uses are critical, parodic, transformative, or otherwise in the public interest, such unauthorized uses are nonetheless fair uses, which means that they are permitted under copyright and privacy law pursuant to the First Amendment freedom of speech.[33] The inevitable injuries photographers and their subjects therefore face with Digital Age viral copying and recontextualization become the basis for acrimonious assertions of control rooted in privacy and dignity but fought over the terrain of IP. What follows from these disputes is a growing sense of institutional or community-based precarity, described in the final chapter of the book, as well as a lack of faith in the law's ability to protect photographers and their subjects from what they perceive to be cruelest reuses of their photographs.

C. Photographer as Citizen

Photographers assert exclusive control over their photographs to safeguard both the art and their relationships with their subjects. But not all photographic *subjects* concur with that hierarchy of control. Sometimes, the relationship between the photographer and subject degenerates or was never strong. Sometimes there is no initial meeting of the minds, or the implied consent for fiduciary control through copyright exclusivity was illusory. In these instances of conflict or absence of a relationship, photographers describe their authorial prerogatives as superior to their subject's interests.

Photographers describe subjects resisting subsequent reuses of their portraits or images for diverse reasons. Some were unhappy with the way the portrait looks—what it emphasizes about their image or reveals about their personality or relationships with others. Photographers recounted subjects who complained that their portraits make them appear unattractive or distant from their spouse, for example. Photographers also described celebrities who, in exchange for initial physical access to make the picture, demanded control over subsequent uses of the photograph in order to manage their ongoing professional personality. Some photographers described their subjects balking at the photographer making subsequent uses of the photographs for books and gallery shows because of the widened audience those new uses entailed.

When recounting these kinds of challenges, photographers sound wounded, as if to say: *why don't my subjects trust me?* At the same time, photographers sound slightly defiant, suggesting they believe that they have the freedom to make the additional work and to express themselves how they choose. As one photographer said, once the initial portrait was made and became part of her oeuvre, the story it told—of its making and its subject—was her "stor[y] . . . to tell."

I interpret the photographers' explanations of their ultimate control over the photograph to be a matter of professional ethics instantiating standards that produce authentic and aesthetically appealing photographs. Photographers expect to have the aesthetic and expressive freedom to make further uses of their photographs to protect their professional domain and the ethics of photographic practice. These explanations resonate with self-determination and autonomy as well as with deference to experts (the photographers) and their professional status.[34] If we consider photographers to be civic storytellers, these explanations also resonate with the importance of self-government and a diverse marketplace of expression and ideas in which photographers actively participate.

Photographers describe their freedom to reuse their own photographs without limitation and restriction by others, including their subjects, as essential to producing critical content and advancing aesthetic and expressive diversity. This was especially true of photographers who sought to convey messages about the world through their subjects that their subjects might reject. For example, Emily, an editorial and fine art photographer, explained how it can be difficult to make pictures that challenge stereotypes and show uncomfortable aspects of culture:

> So if I take the example of . . . wanting to make pictures that don't fall into stereotypical standards of beauty, or it's . . . not the traditional selfie picture that's . . . coming from a high angle, you know, . . . the lighting is perfect, everyone looks like a model, it's all great. And you think about how these images are being . . . perpetuated and spread around Instagram. Well, if you want to take a different type of picture of a girl or a woman, that picture might not be as welcome to be dispersed around the internet. . . . Is it good that only a certain type of photograph is allowed to be shared over and over and over? Isn't that . . . perpetuating a certain way of thinking or seeing?

Professional photographers embrace free speech for themselves, but less so for their subjects, who would restrict use of the photograph or for others who would use the photographs to speak in controversial ways.

These hierarchical assertions of aesthetic freedom, often overriding the photographic subjects' speech or privacy and the speech freedoms of other authors, illustrate the incommensurability of First Amendment's melting pot of values: liberty and autonomy, a marketplace of ideas, self-determination, self-governance, and intellectual privacy. Whose freedom counts? What if attending to diversity of ideas interferes with another's privacy? The tensions inherent in these combined values of equality and freedom are manifested in photographers' prioritization of their rights and control. These tensions, on which I elaborate in chapter 2's discussion of equality, may render the First Amendment a quaint constitutional provision for the twenty-first century that once aimed to promote a flourishing democracy but in the age of digital platforms, such as Facebook and Twitter, appears to be fomenting demagoguery.

Photographers' assertions of aesthetic freedom include several familiar but challenging tensions present in IP law that highlight new problems of the Digital Age. First, photographers make photographs from facts and events in the world, and most of what they photograph is "free" to make into pictures, even without permission, especially when photographing in public but even sometimes when doing so in private. This recalls the idea/expression dichotomy in copyright law and its nonprotection of facts and ideas.[35] Photographers rely on these principles—that they are free to make photographs of facts and things in the world—as a matter of mechanical necessity rooted in camera technology and developed through their practice. Photography, after all, mechanically reproduces the world. Were photographers limited in their reproduction to reshaping what they see, they would have no voice. So photographers are first and foremost copyists. They rely on the ability to make copies of the world in order to share their vision with audiences. And yet they also seek control over the copies they make. In an internet ecosystem whose primary benefits are freedom of access and copying, how do we balance the requirement of access and the desire for control without reproducing or exacerbating oppressive hierarchies of privilege and power that already exist?[36]

Another tension embedded in IP law that highlights Digital Age challenges is the growing need for trust and tolerance emanating from context in an age when context is almost always shifting and profoundly hard to determine. Photographers vary their practice of seeking consent to make photographs of people, places, or things based on their experience and professional norms. Consent is contextualized and adapted to particular situations and relationships. This is an important improvement to the Digital Age's norm of "click to contract," which too often leaves all the fine print with substantial waivers of rights and remedies unread and consumers at the mercy of platforms and merchandise sellers. For example, when photographers work in a business-to-business commercial setting, they often obtain releases or seek permission to photograph people or buildings when the photograph will be used in an advertisement. This is meaningful consent. In other situations, like many mentioned above, photographers who make images of intimate, private situations (such as in jail or in therapy) negotiate with their subjects and over time through conversation build mutual understanding. This too is meaningful consent. In both situations, consent is a feature of respectful relationships between photographer and client or subject, and it improves photographic aesthetic and business practice. It succeeds at establishing trust, allowing for more mature and perhaps even intense human relationships, which according to photographers will usually produce more evocative photographs. This kind of consent as building trust is rare and precious on the internet.

When the photograph is fine art, photojournalism, or documentary, photographers most often rely on their relationship with the subject, when one exists, or on practice norms that liberate photographers as free speakers to publish photographs without a subject's permission. Photographers claim that worthwhile photographs that tell important stories, which subjects are trusting them to make, are worth whatever invasive injury the image-making and circulation will cause. Asking permission of the public photographic subject to make or reuse the photograph disrupts the photographer's prerogative, which is based on professional norms of free speech through photography and custodianship. But a lack of explicit consent can cause significant pain if those professional norms and practice are underappreciated or rendered unclear. And they are rendered unclear in the Digital Age, in which viral sharing and display of images is endemic to all forms of communication channels, and permission and trust relationships among anonymous users and speakers feel both cherished and rare. Consent is critical to equal treatment, as chapter 2 explains, and also to protecting privacy, the subject of chapter 3.

A third tension embedded in IP law highlighting Digital Age challenges is the apparent trade-off between privacy and free speech. The photographers I interviewed adhere to a narrow view of privacy—for their subjects or any subject—in order to make the valuable work they do. Under privacy and right of publicity law, photographic *subjects* might have more control over subsequent uses of their images absent explicit consent limiting those uses, especially if the photograph was made in private, the subject is not a public figure, or the use is not in the public interest.[37] But photographers erode this privacy, trading it for a stronger view of copyright law that gives them control over the photograph and thus the subject's identity as represented by it. Insofar as the subjects lose anything, photographers appear to believe they are filling a gap through their custodianship of the photograph of the subject. Control shifts from the subject to the photographer, who might control the photograph for the subject's sake as well as their own. In the end, according to the photographers' accounts of their practice, photographers' speech supersedes their subjects' privacy. Theirs is an aesthetic practice that relies on a hierarchy of speakers but maintains equal respect through an assiduous attentiveness—a trusteeship of sorts—between photographer and subject. In the Digital Age, copyright is indeed stronger than privacy law, as chapter 3 demonstrates. Photographers' stewardship solution to the need for consent and control is a savvy response to the internet trend of waning privacy alongside the growing scope and strength of copyright.[38] Missing from the internet ecosystem and from IP law generally is the focus on strong professional norms that build expertise, develop solutions to fair resource allocation and equitable opportunity, and establish meaningful trust and community resilience, all of which photographers view as their moral duty to practice and uphold. Chapter 4's discussion of distributive justice delves into these norms; the final chapter of the book examines their breakdown and the institutional precarity that results.

One lesson from Digital Age photographers is that mistrust in media and communication is related to failing institutions, be they legal or business. Structures supporting photographers as journalists or other professional image-makers no longer exist or are not working well. And although the Digital Age has inaugurated what often feels like a wide-open public sphere for global participation in political and social debate, the experience of many, including photographers and their subjects, is that affecting that debate and its ecosystem in a positive way is difficult. Moreover, doing so risks humiliation and personal or professional injury. Instead of relying on voice and participation grounded in democratic rules of engagement, photographers, like many other people today, resort to private dealings. These are market exchanges buying influence and strong property or moral claims, such as copyright law or individual freedoms, that deal in individualistic concerns rather than shared interests. Do evolving digital technologies and networks contribute to the erosion of public trust in community infrastructure and institutions? The internet's potent combination of speed and virality certainly feels like an accelerant to social and political degradation. From this landscape, which to many resembles the nineteenth-century Wild West, defensive behaviors and responses emerge that deserve attention. Chapter 5 picks up this theme in terms of institutional precarity and resource scarcity.

*   *   *

Since its beginnings in 1830, photography played central roles in political and social change as both a technological practice and an art. As it spread from France to the United States, photography was an "art for all," as François Brunet wrote, "the cultural face of the political idea of equality, it heralded a democratic art."[39] Today, the challenges of this democratic art form play out in the professional photographer's struggle to preserve photography's valuable social, political, and economic practice as it evolves in the Digital Age alongside the internet's simultaneous democratizing and polarizing effects.

Photographers tell us contrasting stories. On the one hand, photographic storytelling and information transmission is at its apex in the internet age. Photographs are the most viral data packets on the internet.[40] They travel the fastest and the farthest. And for most people, photographs act on us, arresting or moving us to act or speak with an urgency that words alone seldom produce on such a scale.[41] Photographers assert that professional photography standards are critical to preserving free speech, equal dignity, individual and organizational trust, and truthful communication in an era awash with photographs. These civic storytellers conceive of their practice in these broad terms, but they nonetheless embrace disciplining effects and hierarchies of professional norms, which they fear are eroding or being eroded in an age when "everybody's a photographer." The norms of professional photography relate intellectual property to the fundamental values of equality, privacy, and human flourishing, heavily weighting copyright with these values, which many experience to be in short supply today. Whether copyright should or can sustain these values is beside the point if we are focusing on the values instantiated rather than the legal mechanisms for doing so. That photographers believe they have a role to play in amplifying these values through disciplinary practice and professional standards is noteworthy. Photographs are powerful fuel in an ecological age that is desperate for renewable resources and opportunities for empathetic engagement. And thus, how photographers produce and manage that fuel through standards of dignity, trust, fairness, and generative creativity is a story about the distribution of aesthetic and affective power.

On the other hand, photographers consider themselves insignificant and relatively powerless in the internet age because of the frequency and agility of digital copying and distribution and also because they see the standards of photography as gutted by impatience, venal market forces, and waning practices of self-reflection and critique. Nonetheless, photographers describe themselves as willingly shouldering significant fiduciary responsibilities on behalf of their images, subjects, and audiences. With this responsibility, like a professional code of ethics, photographers exercise control over both the stories told and the way that subjects are treated. They act as both gatekeepers and caretakers. We should pay attention to these roles and relationships if, as the audience, we care to encourage and enjoy truthful and remarkable photographs of our world and to understand the processes by which those images are made or corrupted. "Art as experience" may be a twentieth-century tagline,[42] but postindustrial, postmodern digital photographers remind us to measure progress not by the quantity of works created but by the qualitative manner in which their production and circulation engage us.

Photographers respond to the experience of powerlessness by adapting tools at their disposal. For example, photographers combat aggregation sites like Getty, Adobe, and Shutterstock, which depress photographs' market power and dilute image diversity, by founding their own image banks. In doing so, photographers collaborate to resurrect the cooperative, photographer-owned, and highly selective aspects of earlier syndicates, such as Magnum and Aperture. These twentieth-century image banks were elite photography licensing agencies in which curation, membership, and costs were tightly controlled by the artists themselves. Lost in the twenty-first-century aggregation sites housing millions of images is the quality control of images and photographers. Gained is market competition for the images themselves, which may benefit users, but at the cost (according to photographers) of lost revenue to invest in high-quality image-making of diverse subjects, a resulting lack of subject matter diversity, and ultimately, a glut of similar or generic images. New digital photographer-owned image banks, such as Stocksy United and NOOR, have not experienced the successes of their twentieth-century predecessor agencies. The ability to organize may be easier in the twenty-first-century internet ecosystem, but the incumbency biases and market domination of aggregation sites have professional photographers mourning the previously more equitable power balance between photographers and intermediaries.

Some photographers also respond to Digital Age virality and the feeling of precarity it produces by enlisting lawyers to file copyright lawsuits or send cease-and-desist letters. In previous decades, the circumstances precipitating these disputes were less common because the photographs (negatives and prints) were unavailable for use without permission and tangible access. Today, photographs published online, where most photographs circulate, are accessible to anyone with an internet connection. The right-click and copy function is the photographer's enemy. But lawsuits are rarely worth the time they take and the anguish they cause. And almost all the photographers I interviewed considered lawsuits too distracting in the context of a busy photography practice. Moreover, as a practical matter, the primary remedy for unauthorized online uses of copyrighted works on platforms like Twitter or Instagram is to take the work off-line. As Lou Jones explained, "All you're gonna get . . . if you pay somebody to chase them [the infringer], all they're gonna do is take it down. You're not gonna get a payment out of it."[43] Indeed, the law immunizes platforms like Twitter and Instagram from copyright liability if, when alerted to copyright infringement, they take the infringing work off-line immediately. Because of this law—the Digital Millennium Copyright Act of 1998 (DMCA)—most platforms with user-generated content have institutional mechanisms for responding to takedown requests. For a photographer to receive any remedy other than a takedown for the unauthorized use of a photograph, they have to sue the person who posted the photograph, which is much harder to do logistically: it entails locating the person and hiring a lawyer for whom it is worth taking on the case; meanwhile, the person sued must have the money to pay should they be found liable. Given these logistical challenges, realistically, an aggrieved photographer is left to file takedown requests with internet platforms like a game of whack-a-mole.

In recent years, however, some lawyers have had success filing lawsuits not against people but against websites and media companies who cannot shield themselves with the DMCA immunity because they are themselves the initial posters of unauthorized photographs online.[44] These lawyers have figured out that filing lots of small lawsuits against these defendants can be efficient and lucrative for both lawyers and photographers. Some file copious form complaints, mostly against media companies, and because it is rarely worth litigating the issue—either because the infringement is straightforward or because settlement is cheaper than mounting a legal defense—the vast majority end in private settlements. One lawyer, Richard Liebowitz, filed more than sixteen hundred copyright lawsuits between 2016 and 2020, prompting headlines like "Has This Man Sued You? A Copyright Troll Takes on Hollywood."[45] According to photographers, Liebowitz and other lawyers are paving the way for photographers to have some representation (and, they would say, justice) in a Digital Age in which giant internet and media conglomerates call most of the shots.

These so-called "trolling" tactics are highly criticized for the low quality of the plaintiff-side lawyering causing procedural dismissals and quick settlements. (Liebowitz has been sanctioned multiple times for his professional recklessness and legal errors.)[46] Media companies and websites often run afoul of copyright law unintentionally, and yet copyright statutory damages can be as high as $30,000 per accidental infringement. Suing individual people for infringement will hardly ever pay (although it may send a message), but suing media companies like CBS, Vice, iHeartMedia, and *The Hollywood Reporter* will most likely lead to a monetary damage award if copyright infringement is clear or even close.[47] These companies complain that such copyright lawsuits are a business liability and benefit only the plaintiff lawyers. Filing a lawsuit greatly magnifies costs to media companies who pay much more to settle than they would have paid had there been an initial license request under copyright law. Actual damages to the photographer are frequently the cost of a license, ranging from $500 to $3,000 dollars; file a lawsuit and the likely settlement begins at $3,000 and can run as high as $150,000.[48] Lawyers like Liebowitz who have figured this out consider it their calling to serve clients whose livelihood is threatened by the internet, which has simultaneously benefited defendants' businesses. Many of the media company defendants feel trapped by a copyright law that incentivizes lawsuits rather than private dispute resolution, especially when actual damages are so low. This situation illuminates how out of balance the intellectual property system has become for authors and publishing intermediaries and how much waste the law's imbalance produces. The profound power imbalance makes the prospect of earning a living as a photographer a growing challenge in the face of the media companies' leverage, which has led photographers to partner with lawyers to wield as weapons copyright law's most severe provisions: an eye for an eye—or so it seems. The breakdown of civility norms in IP disputes is part of chapter 5's discussion of institutional precarity.

Click, copy, paste, and send—the ubiquitous fuel of internet traffic, social media, and messaging—are frowned upon by photographers, who wish instead that users would simply link to photographers' professional websites or to the original location where the image was lawfully published. Google Images, the media giant's image search service that copies images on the World Wide Web for the purposes of search and retrieval, is a permitted transformative fair use of the underlying images under copyright law. Fair use also applies to the use of online images for facial recognition machine learning programs or other similar big data functions that use photographs but do not publicly display them. Affirming these new uses as fair is a sign of copyright law's adaptability to permit copying that helps the innovative and generative potential of the internet flourish and may help construct a different kind of public space that is less constrained and perhaps also more cutthroat.

Photographers' dissatisfaction with many of these and other uses and with the legal remedies available to them has led to complaints that the law does not serve them. This may lead to "trolling" by some copyright lawyers and potentially abusive business strategies ostensibly on behalf of aggrieved photographers. But these legal and business strategies have not helped to mitigate the battle among internet and media titans, contemporary creators, and internet users. IP law rejects the hierarchies that photographers assert as integral to their practice, such as distinctions between exact copying and iterative expressive transformation and between extraordinary and ordinary photographs. The new internet age nonetheless instantiates other hierarchies based in capital formation and information accumulation. New hierarchies experienced by many as abusive and ruinous—on and by platforms and internet giants that control search and identification—eviscerate the pro-social opportunities of the Digital Age grounded in public access and community-building, replacing these opportunities with firms and forces that are experienced as monopolistic, destabilizing, and unstoppable. The resulting precarity resounds in photographers' accounts of their losing battle with professional sustainability and maintaining community norms of equality and respect. In their stories of business depletion, contract usurpation, and aesthetic excellence driven by time, effort, and trust—all of which are in short supply—one can detect undertones of economic and social dejection and emotional and material harms experienced by many in the Digital Age.

Not featured in these stories are the everyday users of the internet—all of us who are not photographers—who need and rely on the internet's fuel to participate in the Digital Age bounties. Photographers have not forsaken us; indeed, they make photographs for us. But part of the discord in the internet age appears to be the foregrounding of IP owners and the ease of rendering invisible the everyday users whose beneficial relation to intellectual property is largely with IP law's limits and IP's spillover benefits. Photographers and platforms fight over the copyright status and use value of images. Intellectual property's public domain and its limitations and exceptions—such as fair use and first sale, which are fundamental aspects of its structure and of the progress to which IP aims—get lost in the fight over individual rights and remedies. This is yet another lesson from the photographers: as they fight for survival and we consider reforms to support the important work they do, what and who are potentially ignored or overlooked? How can we proceed to reconsider intellectual property as rooted in these fundamental values in ways that also preserve and protect the public domain on which all creators and innovators rely?

The next four chapters address these questions. They draw from court cases and more than one hundred interviews with creators and innovators. In them, I consider how these fundamental values are being renegotiated within the terms of intellectual property and Digital Age disruptions to it. The photographers' stories are a prelude to stark and categorical debates about equality and privacy within court decisions about intellectual property (chapters 2 and 3), which become more nuanced and complex when grounded in the everyday experiences of creators and innovators over distributive justice and institutional precarity (chapters 4 and 5). In the background of these debates is the presumption of a resource-rich public domain on which everyone can rely but that no one seems to explicitly defend or preserve. And thus, a central problem of fundamental rights informing IP disputes is the mistaken individualization and personalization of IP complaints. Remembering the vitality of the public domain for IP's structure and purpose clarifies the debates over equality, privacy, and distributive justice as highlighting a growing institutional precarity, arising from a fractured moral consensus about precisely these values, which threatens democratic self-governance and commitment to the common weal.

2 Equality

> The original agreement with stock was [a] 50/50 [split]. I
> produced the picture, got it to them, and they gave me half
> of what they sold it for. . . . [But] the industry eventually de-
> evolved. . . . The bean counters realized how much money
> was to be made, and they started giving the photographers
> smaller and smaller and smaller and smaller and smaller
> chunks. . . . So then now, they're givin' the stuff away. So
> stock is a dollar, . . . and they're giving the photographer
> twenty percent of that.
>
> —Lou Jones, commercial photographer and photojournalist

AS LONG AS THE INTERNET has existed, we have been debating what it
makes possible. Does it exacerbate crime or enable more crime detection?
Does it undermine fair bargaining but also facilitate purchases and sales?
Has the internet enabled more speech, or does its cacophony undermine
free speech benefits? It has a similarly fraught relationship with intellectual property. The internet is one of the most transformative inventions
of the twentieth century, and yet it makes the unauthorized copying and
distribution of other people's inventions and copyrighted expressions far
easier and much more likely. This chapter is about milestone intellectual
property U.S. Supreme Court cases since the internet became mainstream,
but it is not only about Digital Age challenges to IP law. It is also about
how those challenges at the Supreme Court feature debates about the nature of equality. The intersection of intellectual property, the internet, and
constitutional equality (or "equal protection") expose deeply rooted debates about U.S. law's fundamental commitment to equal treatment and
equal dignity.

Two Supreme Court copyright cases anchor this chapter's discussion
of intellectual property and equality. *Eldred v. Ashcroft* (2003) upheld a

twenty-year legislative extension of the copyright term under the principle that all copyright authors should be treated the same.[1] *Golan v. Holder* (2012) upheld the restoration of copyright to some works previously in the U.S. public domain as a form of affirmative action and anti-subordination for authors formerly and unfairly deprived of copyright protection under U.S. law.[2] Each case highlights a different form of equality—equal treatment and anti-subordination, respectively—that have been debated since equality first featured in debates over national values. Other Supreme Court cases in this chapter demonstrate how the reasoning in these milestone copyright cases extends and develops patent and trademark law, demonstrating the growing vitality of equality as a feature of intellectual property in the Digital Age. (For a fuller explanation of how I selected, sorted, and analyzed the Supreme Court IP cases between 1984 and 2020 as a textual data set, see the discussion of my digital humanities method in Appendix A.)

This chapter travels a narrow path of the U.S. Supreme Court's evaluation of intellectual property laws in light of the Constitution's commitment to "equal protection of the laws."[3] Before discussing Supreme Court IP cases, however, the chapter elaborates on the history of equality law in the United States. That history's core principles and problems form a backdrop for the specific contexts of Supreme Court cases debating copyright, patent, and trademark law.

In U.S. constitutional law, the origins of equality are limited to a small set of texts and juridical practices springing from broad philosophical traditions grounded in specific U.S. law and history. The first part of this chapter describes those texts and their interpretations, highlighting synergies with broader philosophical baselines. It navigates from the Declaration of Independence to contemporary "equal protection" doctrine in the twentieth century. The rest of the chapter discusses Supreme Court decisions about IP law, which at first blush may not seem to be about the philosophical nature of equality or the Constitution's promise of "equal protection of the laws." But on closer analysis, the picture changes, and deeply rooted, controversial debates over the purpose and structure of equality emerge even in the context of intellectual property.

As the Supreme Court's intellectual property caseload has grown, so too has the breadth of the justices' disagreements. On the surface, the justices seem split along consequentialist lines: whether the IP law at issue likely achieves its goal of promoting healthy market competition (trademark law) or "progress of science and the useful arts" (copyright and patent law). Only on closer look, comparing texts by the same justices, tracing phrases, structure, and influences in the opinions, does the ascendant significance of equality for its own sake—as a deontological justification for intellectual property laws—become clear. Whether sub silentio or overtly, the justices appear to be framing intellectual property debates in terms of equality's purposes and contours as they shift in the internet age. This chapter explores the entwining of intellectual property and equal justice under law as these legal and cultural concepts evolve together in the twenty-first century.

One goal is to open a new perspective into landmark IP cases at the Supreme Court as stories shaped by equality concerns. This is not to say that the Supreme Court is conscious of the equality frameworks shaping its reasoning. (I am not engaging in an exercise of authorial intent or motive.) If my interpretations are persuasive, then the rereading of these Supreme Court cases as shaped by equality modalities exposes what I describe as value choices about who should win and who should lose in this important intellectual property terrain, but without the court admitting (or perhaps even noticing) that it is doing so. Bringing the equality framework to the fore exposes its enduring importance as a concept within United States law. It also raises the possibility of its subliminal role, mediating winners and losers, when the explicit story is that equality is irrelevant to intellectual property or that equality is not bothered by the cases' outcomes.[4] Excavating the particular equality rationales of the cases also shows how IP disputes are settings for debates not only about equal treatment but related values relevant to the actualization of equality under new internet-age conditions— values such as meaningful democratic participation when access to informational resources is plentiful but access to material resources is scarce.

Amartya Sen's provocation "equality of what?" generates numerous variations on the nature and function of equality in a broad sense.[5] Is equality best understood as equal treatment, a kind of procedural fairness (procedural equality)? Is equality a matter of material welfare, providing each person at least those resources to enable a fair opportunity to flourish (resource equality)? If equality means equal treatment, then what procedures are due each person? If it means equal welfare, then what resources and how much are needed for a fair opportunity to flourish (and what does that mean)?

Human diversity, procedural equality, and equality of welfare are often in tension, leading to disagreements over the proper start and conclusion for the debate.[6] And then there is equal dignity: the principle that discourages or prohibits status hierarchies for their own sake, which exert unacceptable control over the lives of others.[7]

Despite these debates over the meanings of equality, general agreement exists that equality matters because it is a sign and function of human respect, a precondition to civil society in which people will inevitably disagree but have to cooperate.[8] Mutual human respect means that each person counts, indicating that *you, as a person, matter.* Treating people unequally therefore demeans them, and it may also disadvantage them. Avoiding inequality or its exacerbation also minimizes strife associated with social and economic hierarchies, which inevitably arise from the diversity of human differences and experiences. Equality is therefore a precursor to order and peace. An enduring commitment to equality assures that inevitable human differences and their stratification among society will not become justifications for the return of human caste systems from our past. These very general foundations for equality appear in specific and surprising ways in cases about IP at the Supreme Court. To notice them and understand the role they play in the decisions require close reading of cases as well as reading across cases. But once the various strands are unwound, they are unmistakable and provide a window into new issues that IP and the internet age raise for equality today.

This chapter also critiques how the court imports its equality principles into intellectual property cases. U.S. equality law is already a cramped rendition of broader philosophical debates. In the context of IP law, the discussion narrows further. The court's reasoning in these IP cases exposes not only the constrained origins of American equality from the Declaration of Independence forward, but its continued inadequacy when applied in new contexts that are nonetheless material to the public interest and common welfare in the internet age. Equality under law may have variable meanings, but its application regularly (and paradoxically) privileges certain people with certain characteristics. This puzzle at the heart of equality law, brought forward through centuries of constitutional doctrine, manifests in the IP cases debating who and what counts for resolving these disputes. This chapter shows how this troubling feature of equality law shapes the reasoning in intellectual property decisions without realizing its exacerbating consequences for the internet age, which has dramatically altered the nature of essential resources, the dynamics of access to those resources, and their allocative consequences for civil rights and liberties. In other words, a new look at these cases about intellectual property reveals not only how equality principles may unwittingly structure IP law but also how Digital Age changes to human organization, productivity, and affection—the subjects of intellectual property cases—force a reckoning with older and often cramped ways of thinking about what "created equal" and "equal protection" mean.

When read through the lens of equality, Supreme Court cases about authorship (copyright), inventors (patents), and brand identity (trademark) reorient our views about intellectual property *and* about equality. These cases are about more than market mechanisms promoting fair competition and progress of science and the useful arts in an individualistic and cumulative way, balanced and measured as if rights of equality and intangible properties are weights on a scale. As understood anew, these cases depict an interconnected and vastly expanding sociolegal landscape in which intellectual property concepts—free and fair markets, authors, inventors, creativity, and innovation—stand in for American identity, for which the idea of equality of persons is fundamental. American identity and equality have a timeworn relationship through centuries of debates,[9] but internet age affordances are reshaping the discussion, especially given intellectual property's rising relevance. As IP law grows in scope and strength in the Digital Age, more people and from diverse situations lay claim to it on terms that resonate with fundamental but contested equality standards.

The chapter begins with a description of the historical development of several strands of constitutional equality doctrine constrained by the particularities of political movements and entrenched socioeconomic power. It then discusses in broad strokes the evolution of Supreme Court cases about intellectual property over the past three decades. Generally, these cases reflect specific trends and growing conflicts in equality law brought into relief by Digital Age challenges, such as networked connectivity, amorphous public forums, global marketplaces, and shifting expectations of access and ownership. This sets the stage first for the discussion of *Eldred v. Ashcroft* and other cases about equal treatment. The chapter then turns to *Golan v. Holder* and other cases about anti-subordination. Both clusters of decisions highlight new ways to evaluate equality in the Digital Age, in which status, wealth, and equal treatment are connected in forms previous centuries of equality law could not have fathomed, bringing new attention to the importance of a revitalized public sphere. Disputes over IP therefore appear less about ownership and control as an individual and private right than about the preservation of public goods as a manner of protecting essential social, collective values. Close readings of these cases help unearth specific and sometimes contested values in the debates over equality—values such as democratic and diverse participation, privacy, and human flourishing—that are often left unvoiced and are thus underappreciated in contests over intellectual property. Later chapters will build from this one to explore these other values.

I. EQUALITY IN CONTEXT

A. "Created Equal" and Equal Protection

In 1776, American colonists severed political ties with England. In the Declaration of Independence, they claimed that "the king had placed his people under arbitrary power, reducing them to a state of slavery."[10] The ideas in the Declaration of Independence delineating the ideal relationship between a representative government and equality and freedom were not new. They came from earlier declarations of rights in the colonies and overseas. According to historian Jill Lepore, the Declaration of Independence was nevertheless "a stunning rhetorical feat, an act of extraordinary political courage," and its culmination in the new nation bound by the ratified Constitution in 1789 "a colossal failure of political will in holding back the tide of opposition to slavery by ignoring it, for the sake of a union."[11] This union, of course, broke apart eighty years later and had to be rebuilt.[12] Nonetheless, the Declaration of Independence is considered the origin of the American experiment, however flawed, asserting the equal moral worth of persons in a society where all should be free from the arbitrary and unaccountable will of others.

The American colonies abandoned their affirmation of the "self-evident" "truth" that "all men are created equal" upon ratification of the U.S. Constitution. Equality was omitted from the Constitution; inserted instead were hierarchies of persons rooted in protecting African slavery, isolating Native Americans as members of "dependent domestic nations," and protecting the property and civic freedoms of white men.[13] The promise of equality among persons in the United States was not renewed until the ratification of the Fourteenth Amendment in 1868, over the objection of the rebellious Confederate states. Not until the Northern Army won the Civil War were "equal protection of the laws" and equal citizenship explicitly inserted into the constitutional structure.[14]

The Fourteenth Amendment says that "All persons born or naturalized in the United States . . . are citizens of the United States and . . . [and that] No state shall . . . deny to any person within its jurisdiction the equal protection of the laws." These few words were meant to accomplish a lot. And yet because the Constitution originally permitted human enslavement, the specter of *in*equality shaped many of the Constitution's provisions and their subsequent interpretation by the Supreme Court. Despite the Civil War Amendments abolishing slavery, expanding voting access, and establishing equal citizenship, due process, and equal protection, the Constitution's promise of equality remained constrained by the persistence of White supremacy, territorial conquest, patriarchy, and economic class in exercising civil liberties in the United States.

Given the textual brevity of the Declaration of Independence and the Fourteenth Amendment, the Supreme Court has had to interpret the words "created equal" and (after the Civil War) "equal protection." The court's application of equality under law typically arose in the context of debates over rights or resources considered essential to citizens: voting, housing, contracts for labor and land, and process for criminal trials. Now, because of the internet's transformation of society, debates about equality are also being fought over rights and resources made consequential by the digital era, like intellectual resources and intangible property. And now the Supreme Court is getting involved.

Despite sowing the seeds of slavery and obfuscating Native American conquest, the Constitution is not devoid of anti-hierarchical sentiment. The Constitution prohibits titles of nobility and requires reciprocity of "privileges and immunities of citizens" among the states.[15] These prohibitions on specific forms of inequality, however, do not guarantee equality among citizens. They do offer clues to the kind of equality first considered essential to the American experiment: equality of station or status and the rejection of intrinsic hierarchies among human beings—at least among inhabitants who were white, male, and possessed some wealth. There was no express language in the original Constitution indicating that race, gender, or property mattered to equal status. But these small parts of the Constitution rejecting noble title and unequal state citizenship repudiated distinctions of moral worth based on inherited or accidental social status. Other more cancerous and persistently evoked sections of the Constitution permitted slavery, of course, an inheritable status turning on an accident of birth.[16]

Cancer is the word that many historians use to describe the constitutional provisions that permitted and protected slavery, because the persistence of slavery and the dehumanization it wrought ate away at the nation, eventually leading to war.[17] The contradictions between the founding principles of equality and the unfreedom and dehumanization of some people by law were unsustainable in a country growing in size, diversity, and global influence. Still today, substantial pockets of people mourn the "lost cause" of the Civil War. Lost was (in their words) the Confederacy's autonomy and self-determination given over to a federal government that demanded conformity to an amended Constitution that installed equal protection as a fundamental principle.[18] The "Lost Cause" ideology began soon after the Civil War as a response to the Civil War Amendments, which aimed to restrain the states' ability to reproduce slavery in another form.

The Civil War Amendments inaugurated a new era promising domestic, civil, and political equality, especially to formerly enslaved persons.[19] Of the three constitutional amendments (the Thirteenth, Fourteenth, and Fifteenth), only the Fifteenth Amendment directly mentions race by protecting the right to vote free from discrimination on the basis of race, color, or previous condition of servitude. The Thirteenth and Fourteenth Amendments are more general: The Thirteenth Amendment abolished slavery and involuntary servitude (except for those duly convicted of a crime). The Fourteenth Amendment granted citizenship to all persons born or naturalized in the United States and promised that no state would deny equal protection of the law, due process of law, or privileges and immunities of citizenship.

The Fourteenth Amendment mentions equality specifically, but its meaning and scope are more complicated. The first sentence of the Fourteenth Amendment declares all persons born or naturalized in the United States to be citizens of the United States and the states where they reside. This sentence overturns the Supreme Court decision *Dred Scott v. Sanford*

(1857), which interpreted the Constitution as denying to all inhabitants of African descent American citizenship and the privileges that citizenship confers.[20] The first sentence of the Fourteenth Amendment voids this heinous decision by declaring citizenship for all African-Americans born or naturalized in the United States.[21] Whatever the Constitution may have said before, this first sentence of the Fourteenth Amendment was a decisive step toward inclusivity and away from hierarchy.

The rest of the Fourteenth Amendment says, "No State shall make or enforce any law which shall abridge the privileges or immunities of citizens of the United States; nor shall any State deprive any person of life, liberty, or property, without due process of law; nor deny to any person within its jurisdiction the equal protection of the laws." These phrases were intended to guarantee civil equality to those newly freed from slavery by preventing states from erecting racial or other barriers to property ownership, employment, and associational or family freedoms that accompanied the privileges of citizenship.

"Privileges and immunities of citizens" and "equal protection of the laws" originally meant that no state was permitted to deny civil, political, and social rights on the basis of race or other arbitrary characteristics. And yet those "privileges and immunities of citizens" were gutted of this equality principle shortly after ratification. In the 1873 opinion called the *Slaughterhouse Cases*, the Supreme Court limited "privileges and immunities of citizens" to those few rights attendant to *federal* citizenship alone (such as being rescued on the high seas).[22] Historians attribute political backlash to the case's tortured reasoning successfully limiting "privileges and immunities of citizens" to largely inconsequential interests.[23] Having lost the war, men still fought and won limits to new constitutional rights of equality in order to maintain White supremacy.

Having gutted "the privileges and immunities" clause, disputes about equality of citizenship moved to the Fourteenth Amendment's "equal protection" clause. The clause's breadth and flexibility made it an easy target for all kinds of claims, not only those rooted in racial discrimination. The first major case interpreting the clause embodied the reason for the war. In *Strauder v. West Virginia* (1880), the Supreme Court explained the equal protection clause's purpose in the context of denying jury service on the basis of race. In its decision, the court said:

The very fact that colored people are singled out and expressly denied by a statute all right to participate in the administration of the law as jurors because of their color, though they are citizens and may be in other respects fully qualified, is practically a brand upon them affixed by the law, an assertion of their inferiority, and a stimulant to that race prejudice which is an impediment to securing to individuals of the race that equal justice which the law aims to secure to all others.[24]

In this early case, the Supreme Court recognized the harm of being "branded" as "inferior" because the law declares a person inherently unfit to perform civic duties. Mr. Strauder was the defendant in this case, not the juror, but the law judged him inferior as a Black man because it prohibited other Black men from sitting as jurors due to their race. The law created hierarchies with this categorical exclusion and offended the express promise of equality in the Fourteenth Amendment. This early case contained the seeds of both anti-subordination and equal treatment that were debated more robustly in the mid-twentieth century. Until then, however, Supreme Court cases from 1880 until *Brown v. Board of Education* in 1954 retreated from *Strauder*'s understanding of the Constitution's promise of equality among people without regard to race. Both women and racial minorities did not in fact benefit from the Fourteenth Amendment's equality promise until the civil rights victories of the 1960s.[25] Instead, a spate of Supreme Court opinions defined equal protection in other contexts and largely for business and commercial purposes—foreshadowing its relevance to intellectual property law.

The breadth of the Fourteenth Amendment's equality language—"no state shall . . . deny to any person . . . equal protection of the laws"—means that any person can claim its protection (subject to the jurisdiction of the United States). And indeed, business and property interests were first to broadly benefit from the Fourteenth Amendment at the end of the nineteenth and beginning of the twentieth centuries, often at the expense of the racial minorities for whom the amendment was actually written. In a case concerning the short-lived federal 1875 Civil Rights Act, which prohibited discrimination on the basis of race in theaters, inns, and transportation, the Supreme Court held that Congress had no power to pass the law because the Fourteenth Amendment did not regulate *private* commercial establishments.

The court said in the *Civil Rights Cases* (1883) that the Fourteenth Amendment by its language prohibits only state action, not private discrimination.[26] Private commercial amusements open to the general public were permitted to exclude or include whomever they chose. The court said that the equality promised by the Fourteenth Amendment prevented *states* from treating people unequally, not private citizens (and the businesses and corporations they organized) from arranging affairs however they preferred. This was a milestone of Supreme Court jurisprudence, protecting property and its private control at the expense of equal access to public life. The decision's influence permitting private discrimination absent a state or federal law to the contrary endures today.[27]

U.S. v. Carolene Products (1939) was another milestone equality case that protected business and commercial interests.[28] This case accomplished several things. First, it extended the reach of the Fourteenth Amendment's equal protection clause to disputes between business competitors. Second, it inaugurated judicial deference to congressional lawmaking and line-drawing. When laws are passed pursuant to constitutionally enumerated powers especially delegated to Congress such as regulating interstate commerce or intellectual property (in Article I), courts give Congress a wide berth. And third, it provided an exception to this judicial deference, and thus justified judicial oversight, when the democratic process ordinarily expected to generate rational legislation or repeal undesirable legislation appears unreliable, irrational, or corrupt. All three facets of the case have relevance for how equal protection analysis affects court decisions concerning intellectual property.

Carolene Products originated as a conflict between the incumbent dairy industry and innovative newcomers who made "filled milk" products such as margarine. The dairy industry prevailed in Congress to ban all filled-milk products in interstate commerce, significantly hampering competition from margarine producers. Carolene Products, which made oleo (or oleomargarine), claimed that prohibiting its product from shipment in interstate commerce was unconstitutional under the Fourteenth Amendment. One argument rested on the unequal treatment of filled-milk producers (singled out for the ban) as compared to pure-dairy producers (who were not so restricted). The other argument rested on a denial of due process by depriving the filled-milk producers the value of their business. The court upheld the law under both theories. Because the court found that the federal legislature was rational to conclude that the two commercial entities were distinct (one dangerous to the public health and the other not), treating them differently did not amount to a denial of equality. Different entities justified differential (unequal) treatment. There had also been no denial of process in this case. The democratic process provided both parties ample opportunity to air their concerns and have their interests debated by elected officials charged with enacting law. If it turned out that Congress drew the line incorrectly or if changes in circumstances required updates to the law, Congress—not the court—could strike a new balance.

Carolene Products is a blank check for Congress when legislating under its constitutionally enumerated Article I powers. The court approves legislation treating two entities differently if some rational basis exists for the law. As such, Congress draws all sorts of lines between people and entities that benefit some and disadvantage others, justifying the differential treatment with a plausible explanation to avoid the accusation of arbitrariness (which would make the law unlawful). Except for narrow exceptions to protect the democratic process, disenfranchised minorities, and fundamental rights (as described more below), this broad deference to the policy decisions of Congress persists today, especially in IP cases, and is celebrated as a form of judicial restraint.

Three narrow exceptions to broad judicial deference to democratic law-making was buried in what has become the famous "footnote 4" of *Carolene Products*.[29] That footnote reserves the power of courts to closely scrutinize the legislature's line-drawing or "unequal treatment" in three instances: when law itself restricts the democratic, political process on which the rule is based (such as a law restricting voting or speech); when the law implicates a right protected by the Bill of Rights, which is intended to be for individuals against the majority (such as freedom of religion or the right to be free from unreasonable searches and seizures); and when the law reflects prejudice against "discrete and insular minorities" such as racial, religious, or national origin minorities, "which tends seriously to curtail the operation of those political processes ordinarily to be relied upon to protect minorities."[30] Needless to say, the court does not exercise this power to closely scrutinize legislative line-drawing very often—these are exceptions after all. It took several decades after the 1939 decision about filled milk and a social, political, and legal revolution in equal protection law concerning race and sex equality for courts to implement this caveat and for "equal protection of the laws" to mean more than upholding the status quo. As we will see, however, what took decades to achieve in civil rights jurisprudence, especially concerning employment and public benefits, has yet to catch on in intellectual property law.

The epitome of the Fourteenth Amendment's initial failure to promote equality is *Plessy v. Ferguson*, the 1898 case in which the Supreme Court upheld a Louisiana law that racially segregated railroad cars. In that decision, the Supreme Court justified the segregation as rationally reflecting customary social separation of two groups of people who (the court said) choose to stay apart.[31] And because the segregated railway cars were otherwise the same and all riders were segregated, assigning seating on the basis of race was not a denial of equality.[32] This decision defining equality to include "separate but equal" eroded the anti-subordination rationale of *Strauder* that recognized how racial classifications brand Black people as inferior and are therefore per se denials of equality.

Plessy was overturned fifty-six years later, in *Brown v. Board of Education*. After several decades of litigation brought by the American Civil Liberties Union (ACLU), Thurgood Marshall, who eventually became the first Black Supreme Court justice, successfully argued that "separate but equal" violated equal protection in the context of racial classification in public schools. The court struck down the segregationist state laws as both arbitrary and invidious. *Brown*'s reasoning eventually also applied to classifications based on sex and alienage. Equal respect regarding these central markers of identity is today a deeply rooted constitutional commitment thanks to the social and political revolutions of the 1960s, but it took nearly a century to establish. Civil rights advocacy at the end of the twentieth century has recently expanded equal rights to LGBTQ+ identities as well.

When laws touch on wealth-based or property-based distinctions, however—for example, when the law concerns the scope of ownership based in authorship or inventorship—equal protection scrutiny is minimal, and the laws are usually upheld. Equal protection for corporate entities concerning commercial interests remains subject to the original rule of legislative deference regarding ordinary economic regulation (including intellectual property laws). Dissimilar treatment in the realms of copyright or patent law, when decided by legislatures for economic policy reasons, is generally left to legislative debate and rarely raises a recognizable equality concern.

Of course, the experience of equal treatment and dignity does not so easily divide between economic matters and invidious status-based hierarchies. Philosophers of equality, among them Amartya Sen and Elizabeth Anderson, have explained the interconnectedness of socioeconomics and politics as central to equality and its manifestation in everyday life.[33] The constrained origins of U.S. constitutional equality disassociating socioeconomic status and property from civil and social rights of equality and human dignity leave contemporary legal equal protection analysis with few analytical avenues to understand equality in its manifold complexity. Property and labor rights were deeply connected to concerns of people's equal moral worth at the founding—freedom from subordination and hierarchy required both fair opportunities to pursue a livelihood and a lack of degrading social norms that confined certain people to limited opportunities. But economic opportunity's connection to civil, political, and social status remained contentious well into the twentieth century, as evidenced by equal protection case law's forked path. Despite efforts during abolition and Reconstruction, the doctrine regulating economic opportunity split with those concerning social, civil, and political status, all of which courts would eventually scrutinize more closely. By contrast, most economic regulation would be subject to judicial deference and survive constitutional challenge even if it in fact exacerbated social, political, and civil inequality that the Civil War Amendments were meant to eradicate.[34]

Contrary to the ordinary economic legislation to which judges defer, laws that purposefully or explicitly create hierarchies or differentiate among people on the basis of race or sex are presumptively unconstitutional until the legislature provides better reasons than democratic process and rational bases. Wage, hour, and workplace laws protecting workers against exploitation or preserving public health are now also common among federal and state laws and are constitutional. But strong contractual freedoms enable employers and other hiring entities to avoid providing these protections. And because it takes a majority of business interests to pass labor laws in the first place, many laws contain exceptions (such as for religious freedom) or are minimally protective.

This is where the Supreme Court cases about intellectual property fit in, illuminating the challenges of combining analyses of economic equality (access to resources and a meaningful opportunity to thrive) with that of equal dignity concerning civil, political, and social matters in the twenty-first century. What we learn from this legal history interpreting equality under U.S. law is that what it means to be treated equally depends on the categories drawn and the rationales supporting them. How will the anti-discrimination and anti-subordination norms arising from the mid-twentieth-century civil rights movements mix with the increasing power of informational capitalism, corporate wealth and power, and intellectual property laws? If, as the cases below indicate, intellectual property is more than an economic resource in the twenty-first century and is also a measure of social and political status providing opportunities for self-determination and associational freedoms, then intellectual property disputes may be the new stage on which to debate the complex nature of equality and its relevance in the digital era in which informational goods and access to resources is the "new, new property."[35]

B. The U.S. Supreme Court and Intellectual Property Law

The Supreme Court is more often unanimous than divided in its decisions. The court nonetheless exhibits deep ideological division on issues about the role of government in ameliorating status inequality along lines of race, sex, or sexual orientation. Intellectual property cases tend to be much less contentious than those about affirmative action, reproductive choice, marriage equality, or voting rights. And when the court started taking more intellectual property cases in the 1990s, their decisions were largely unanimous.[36]

As the court's IP caseload grows, however, so does the level of disagreement among the justices.[37] On the surface, the justices seem split in their application of facts to traditional utilitarian calculations: whether the IP law at issue is rationally related to achieving its goal of promoting fair competition (trademark law) and progress of science and the useful arts (copyright and patent law). But dig deeper and the disagreements can be understood in terms more philosophically contestable and deontological, such as over the contours and substance of equality described above.

If intellectual property is an economic asset over which its creators have the liberty to exercise dominion in a traditional, property-like way, then the debate over its allocation may be uneventful and subject to ordinary judicial deference and a rational cost-benefit analysis. If, however, intellectual property rights affect a person's equal treatment and dignity—either by touching on procedural equality, equality of opportunity, or status equality—then the debate can become understandably contentious. And it may resemble the more deeply rooted disagreements over segregation, discrimination, and freedom to work absent the arbitrary and unaccountable domination of others. Rarely do private property or commercial interests outweigh the fundamental principle of equality when squarely facing off. But recent and controversial debates over whether private businesses can refuse services on the basis of religious objection—such as baking a wedding cake for a gay couple or dispensing birth control for a patient at a pharmacy—pit religious and labor freedoms against sexual orientation equality and gender justice.[38] Cases like these are evidence of the enduring unresolved conflicts between private property and equal treatment.

The presence of equality concerns in Supreme Court cases about intellectual property may arise from the new civil rights movements gaining traction, driven by digital communication and activism—namely, #MeToo, Black Lives Matter, and the LGBTQ+ equal rights movement.[39] Intellectual property also strongly influences everyday life in ways unforeseen in decades past. With copying and sharing technology at the fingertips of anyone with a cell phone, the Digital Age has changed how intellectual property regulation works—or does not. Control over intellectual property is more difficult. But the benefit of access to cultural works and useful inventions is potentially higher to consumers and users, who themselves are creators and innovators. The internet age has changed many of our baseline expectations regarding resource access and allocation as well as community formation and membership. Transparency, truthfulness, and accessibility of information on platforms subject to IP rules are also highly contentious. It should not be surprising, therefore, that the Supreme Court's resolution of issues concerning intangible goods and the communities and behaviors they enable grapple not only with market efficiencies and property rights but also with equality dimensions such as egalitarianism, anti-subordination, and pluralism.[40]

It may take time for the Supreme Court to squarely address equality concerns in the context of intellectual property cases. But *Plessy* came before *Brown*, after all. And for doctrine to evolve, it is imperative to pay attention to particular dimensions of equality that the justices discuss in these IP cases. Doing so highlights and explains the renewed urgency of the relationship between social and economic progress and our founding commitments to equality in the quickly maturing Digital Age.

*   *   *

What follows is an array of Supreme Court intellectual property cases that wrestle with the complexities of evaluating equality under U.S. law. Most arguments concerning intellectual property law in the United States derive primarily from theories of markets and personal property. As such, the cases disputing IP law's proper contours presume congressional rationality, because ordinary economic legislation is within Congress's core competencies. As long as there is some basis for Congress's categorical treatment, the law survives. In many cases about intellectual property, the law at issue extends protection on the basis of treating all copyright owners "equally" or all patentees "the same." Equal treatment itself is the rational basis for the expanding scope of intellectual property's exclusivity. As I argue later, this shallow formalist argument buries competing and complex concepts of equality that need more attention, such as equality of opportunity and equal dignity, which this chapter's analysis also foregrounds.

By critiquing intellectual property as ordinary economic or social policy and hiding the fundamental values at stake, I mean to make an argument in parallel with the undoing of *Plessy* by *Brown*. There is a growing and important debate about whether aspects of intellectual property law are better understood as involving the protection of vulnerable stakeholders and fundamental rights. *Plessy* did not simply approve a state law claiming to reflect ordinary social norms of railroad ridership; it entrenched White supremacy at the root of those "ordinary social norms" into constitutional doctrine holding that separate could still be equal. Similarly, when the court extends copyright for all authors national and foreign as "ordinary social and economic legislation" subject to legislative deference, a counterargument emerges that such copyright protection comes at the expense of other stakeholders who are unrepresented or unseen, such as readers, remixers, user-innovators, and the many other flourishing new creators or "prosumers," to borrow Alvin Toffler's coinage, in the Digital Age.[41] And, when the court expands rights "equally" to current and future copyright holders, lengthening the copyright term and shrinking the public domain, it threatens an already diminishing and inaccessible public sphere, limiting both freedom of speech and equality of resources for almost everyone else. The problem in both cases is the court conceiving intellectual property law solely in ordinary economic terms instead of as laws constituting civil rights and liberties.

The court's constrained equality reasoning grounded in an economic analysis of intellectual property often underappreciates the social and political changes wrought by the Digital Age. Doing so overemphasizes private rights and undercounts the public interest in the public domain that is essential to IP law and policy. Equality is not like property (or pie, as the saying goes), which is often a zero-sum negotiation.[42] The court's limited view of IP law and policy defines IP as property and not as an intangible, inexhaustible public good, and this limited view threatens to obscure and diminish IP's valuable roles building and sustaining flourishing twenty-first-century communities. The court's myopic focus on traditional authors, inventors, or trademark owners working within status quo economic structures—structures that the Digital Age has upended—renders less available an equality analysis of intellectual property grounded in anti-subordination and the protection of fundamental rights. It also surfaces a critique of democratic deference—the judicial act of deferring to the legislature—because without appreciating the breath of IP stakeholders, the court's analysis fails to promote political participation and an inclusive public sphere. Sometimes, however, debates within cases show signs of expanding and evolving arguments along these lines. Mapping the various arguments about equality in cases about intellectual property—whether they are dismissed, latent, or emerging—revives these arguments and demonstrates the growing stakes for IP law in our time when access to digital networks, resources, and platforms are essential to flourishing communities.

I divide the case analyses into two groups. One set of cases persistently analyzes intellectual property disputes largely as a matter of economic interests under the ordinary deference standard. As such, the equality analyses rest on the principle of democratic process and deference to it, with all the benefits and flaws described therein. The other set of cases combines the economic analysis with a concern that differential treatment undermines equal dignity and perpetuates inequality for its own sake.[43] Motivating this analysis is the disdain for caste systems, in which differences are really hierarchies that produce humiliation and shame for those with relatively little power or status. This kind of equality reasoning originates with *Strauder* and the dissent in *Plessy*, which called out racial segregation for what it was: a humiliating and oppressive practice implying the inferiority of Black people. *Brown v. Board of Education* declared racial segregation by law unconstitutional because it sanctions and reproduces hierarchy and subordination for its own sake. With *Brown*, equality law turned a corner in the United States, setting the stage for the civil rights movement of the 1960s. The second set of cases about IP law shows the court dabbling in anti-subordination arguments, signaling a shift in the perception of the stakes involved in cases about IP law today.

In all these cases, progress is promoted by bolstering equality as a matter of resources, opportunity, or status. And yet the outcome in many of them reinstates private property and exclusivity at the expense of the public domain and a sociolegal system whose ideal is inclusivity and democratic participation. This is perhaps due to inadequate attention to the internet's integration of social relations and economic opportunities. But that is changing. When foregrounded, the conflicting and interconnected equality concepts in these cases evidence how the Digital Age complicates what Elizabeth Anderson described as the evolving "social conditions of freedoms . . . . need[ed] to function as equal citizens."[44] This intellectual property debate is no longer simply about how much or how little intellectual property any one person gets in an oversimplified, bean-counting kind of way—some copyright for you, some copyright for me. These cases clarify both constitutional equality and intellectual property such that we can no longer understand intellectual property as mere market regulation and ordinary economic policy in the rapidly evolving internet era. These cases consider how IP law may produce and sustain equal respect and opportunity among strangers in common and for the public good as a twenty-first-century measure of progress.

II. THE PAUCITY OF EQUAL TREATMENT
A. *Eldred v. Ashcroft* (2003) and the Copyright Term Extension Act of 1998

Eldred v. Ashcroft concerns the rationality of congressional legislation called the Copyright Term Extension Act of 1998 (the CTEA), passed at the end of the decade that witnessed the mainstream onset of the internet and the World Wide Web.[45] The CTEA extended the copyright term twenty years, from life of the author plus fifty years (as enacted in 1976) to life of the author plus seventy years.[46] A central question in *Eldred* was whether Congress had a rational basis for adding the twenty years and, relatedly, whether the enlarged term could permissibly apply to existing and future copyrights alike.[47] Justice Ruth Bader Ginsburg, writing for seven justices, held that Congress did have a rational basis for the twenty-year extension and for its equal application to both existing and future copyrights.[48] The decision's theme is equal treatment of copyright authors, justified by a procedural equality narrative that idealizes deliberative democracy. But it obfuscates a system unevenly accessible to IP stakeholders and a legislative process that disenfranchises or disregards those most affected by the copyright extension.

The controversy around *Eldred* centers on the widespread disbelief that twenty more years of copyright protection adds any extra incentive to authors or owners to create or disseminate creative works, the incentive rationale being the primary basis for copyright exclusivity.[49] Those skeptical would be forgiven given that the Disney Corporation led the lobbying effort for this legislation in order to protect Mickey Mouse (in his earliest incarnation as Steamboat Willie) from falling into the public domain in 1998. Also, the legislation was sponsored by Sonny Bono, a man whose music made him wealthy. But rather than dig into the legislative history to discern whether the evidence and factual record supported a finding of sufficient incentives beyond those for the Disney Corporation and music celebrities, the court traveled its usual path when considering the rationality of what it deemed ordinary economic legislation: it deferred to Congress, the relevant democratic body, saying "it is generally for Congress, not the courts, to decide how best to pursue the Copyright Clause's objectives" of promoting progress of science.[50]

This is a correct statement of law and legal history. And there was some evidence before Congress—albeit self-serving and exaggerated evidence—suggesting that the extension of copyright by twenty years would benefit some authors and publishers and encourage both to invest in more creative work.[51] Musicians including Bob Dylan and Carlos Santana gave testimony before Congress that said an extra twenty years would assure "fair compensation for themselves and their heirs" and thus "was an incentive to create."[52]

The Motion Picture Association of America (MPAA), of which Disney is a member, said that the copyright term extension would "provide copyright owners [by which the MPAA means their studio members] generally with the incentive to restore older works and further disseminate them to the public."[53] And Senator Orrin Hatch advocated that given "increasing longevity and the trend toward rearing children later in life," copyright term extension would "provide adequate protection for American creators and their heirs," lest the "U.S. copyright term [fail] to keep pace with the substantially increased commercial life of copyrighted works resulting from the rapid growth in communications media."[54] Even without such evidence, however, the court regularly defers to ordinary economic legislation by *presuming* the existence of such facts. When there is no evidence of legislative irrationality (such as prejudice), targeting of a suspect class (race or gender), or burdening a fundamental right, the legislative power is at its zenith and courts demur.[55]

Another complaint arose about *Eldred* aside from the absence of sufficient basis for the twenty-year copyright term extension. The court's reasoning exposed the possibility of perpetual copyright protection that would violate the Constitution's "limited times" provision in the IP clause: Congress has the power "to promote the progress of science and useful arts, by securing for *limited times to authors* and inventors the exclusive right to their respective writings and discoveries."[56] If Congress could extend by twenty years both existing and future copyrights on the self-serving statements of select wealthy copyright owners who sit at Congress's bargaining table, what would prevent Congress from extending copyright indefinitely through a series of incremental extensions over time (which is precisely what happened to copyright over its two-hundred-year history).[57] To this, the court majority said little except that both it and Congress were aiming for "parity" and "evenhanded[ness]" in the application to future and present copyright authors alike.[58] This is where the equality rationale resurfaces in a surprising new formulation for intellectual property law.

The majority held that "in that 1998 legislation, as in all previous copyright term extensions, Congress placed existing and future copyrights in parity. In prescribing that alignment, we hold, Congress acted within its authority and did not transgress constitutional limitations."[59] By so stating, the Court sidestepped the perpetual copyright problem altogether, except to say that seventy years is not perpetual and that perpetual copyright would violate the "limited times" provision. It also justified its retroactive application of the longer copyright term with the moral force of the value of "equal treatment." As long as Congress acts to promote equality in the copyright field by treating existing and future copyright owners the same—or "alike," "evenhandedly," or "in parity," phrases the court repeated to describe equal treatment—the court trusts in congressional decision-making. Notably, Justice Stephen Breyer in his dissent accepted that "it is not 'categorically beyond Congress' authority' to 'exten[d] the duration of existing copyrights' to achieve such *parity*."[60]

One could understand the majority's decision in *Eldred* as both protecting a class of copyright holders equally and avoiding contravening formal equality by treating situated people (and things) the same. Indeed, long-standing copyright law dating back to 1903 prohibits discrimination among copyright holders, holding that "high" and "low" art are similarly situated with regard to copyright's exclusive rights.[61] *Eldred* may therefore be a straightforward extension of this century-old anti-discrimination principle. Simply counting the number of times the *Eldred* opinion used words synonymous with "equality" reveals the court's focus on similar treatment. The first paragraph ended with: "Congress provided for application of the enlarged terms to existing and future copyrights *alike*."[62] The third paragraph stated again that "Congress placed existing and future copyrights *in parity*," and then concluded by saying "in prescribing that *alignment*, we hold, Congress acted within its authority."[63] The opinion repeats the words *alike, parity,* and *alignment* or *aligned* nearly a dozen times. If we consider also references to *matches, equity, harmony, evenhandedly,* and *same/sameness,* which also pepper the decision, the prominence of equal treatment thinking in this copyright opinion emerges clearly.

Other than linguistic choices, Justice Ginsburg's majority opinion focused on the individual authors themselves and their expectations for equal legal treatment. She insisted throughout that current copyright holders are reasonable in expecting that they will be treated like future copyright holders should new legal benefits arise, because that is what has always happened.[64] She also explained that Congress's extension of copyright terms assures the equal treatment of American authors with regard to foreign authors under the 1886 Berne Convention for the Protection of Literary and

Artistic Works (which was adopted internationally in 1886 but which the United States did not join until a century later).[65] Personalizing the equal treatment—its present expectation and its future effect globally—paints this case not about monetary incentives to create or disseminate creative work but about the dignity of equal treatment as a social value absent a good reason to deviate. In other words, although the decision reads as the classic deference to congressional decision-making under Congress's plenary powers concerning ordinary economic legislation, the opinion evokes the deeply held principle of equal treatment under the law. The majority saw no plausible reason to treat some copyright holders differently from others, be it current versus future copyright owners or American versus foreign copyright authors. This was in part because of equal treatment's strength as a constitutional value.

This is a superficial analysis of equal treatment, however. It disregards the history of copyright legislation, its captured process subject to special interest lobbying, and the democratic principles of fair process and open institutions on which procedural fairness and equal treatment are based. The tortured history of special interest copyright legislation is well documented.[66] In her 2001 book *Digital Copyright*, Jessica Litman showed that twentieth-century U.S. copyright legislative reform was led largely by the advocates of strong copyright—the "big six" movie studios (represented by the MPAA), the music recording industry (represented by the Recording Industry Association of America, or RIAA), and the text publishing industry (represented by the Authors Guild).[67] Litman argued that the captured legislative process for copyright helps an elite group of copyright holders and harms the everyday audience of copyright users and creators. (In today's parlance, we might call the beneficiaries of these legislative reforms "the one percent.") This is a far cry from equal treatment, and it is camouflaged by democratic flag-waving.

Litman warned that if the past legislative process is predictive of the future, then copyright spoils will be only for the wealthy and powerful. Digital copyright's control will suffocate the constitutional mandate for "progress of science" that requires wide distribution of and access to information and expression. Justice John Paul Stevens's dissent in *Eldred* did not mention this legislative history but did say that "congressional action under the Copyright/Patent Clause demonstrates that history . . . does not provide the 'volume of logic,' necessary to sustain the . . . [CTEA's] constitutionality."[68] The dissents from Justice Stevens and Justice Breyer explained that the overly formalist logic of equal treatment appears to be a ruse benefiting only 2 percent of copyright holders.[69] Those beneficiaries' estates may profit fifty years after an author's death from the extended copyright term, but for the other 98 percent, the extra years of copyright will primarily sequester their work from the public.[70]

In this light, the equal treatment justification for the CTEA melts away. As it turns out, very few copyright authors actually supported the term extension. The CTEA was a compromise struck between digital platform intermediaries, which sought to build their commercial presence on the internet, and content companies such as those represented by the MPAA and the RIAA, whose copyright assets traveled farthest and fastest on those digital networks. In exchange for agreeing to the twenty-year copyright term extension, the digital intermediaries received immunity for certain kinds of unauthorized uses on their platforms pursuant to a law passed later the same year, the Digital Millennium Copyright Act of 1998 (the DMCA). Bill Herman summed it up in his 2013 book *The Fight over Digital Rights*:

> The motivation for record companies and music publishers was clear enough; the former wanted to reduce the number of illicit digital copies competing with their official recordings, and the latter wanted another source of licensing revenues. Technology companies supported the bill—not on principle, but because they wanted to design and sell their products without being sued.[71]

The result of a captured legislative process is copyright law that entrenches moneyed interests and benefits powerful companies.[72] Far from treating people the same, the CTEA and its sibling the DMCA were backroom deals between internet intermediaries and copyright owners (not authors), later justified by the court as democratic and reflecting equal treatment.

Justice Stevens's dissent was most vocal on this score. His critique of the parity argument shifted the focus on equal treatment from those seeking to protect their copyright (namely, content owners like those represented by the MPAA) to the public that the Copyright Act was intended to ultimately benefit. "*Ex post facto* extensions of copyrights," he wrote, "result in a gratuitous transfer of wealth from the public to authors, publishers and their successors in interest. Such retroactive extensions do not even arguably serve the purposes of the Copyright/Patent Clause," which, he explained, is "to allow the public access to products of [authors' creative activity] after the limited period of exclusive control has expired."[73] Justice Stevens argued further:

> The reason for increasing the inducement to create something new simply does not apply to an already-created work. To the contrary, the equity argument actually provides strong support for petitioners. Members of the public were entitled to rely on a promised access to copyrighted or patented works at the expiration of the terms specified when the exclusive privileges were granted. On the other hand, authors will receive the full benefit of the exclusive terms that were promised as an inducement to their creativity, and have no equitable claim to increased compensation for doing nothing more.[74]

The opinion unraveled the majority's parity argument with an expanded focus on *all* the beneficiaries of the Copyright Act, demonstrating how an overly formalistic approach to equal treatment can be easily manipulated by narrowing the relevant class. Treating "likes alike"—or "all" "authors" the same, in the majority's argument—ignored all those other people for whom copyright also exists as well as the flaws in democratic process that established the benefit. The equal treatment argument thereby perpetuates the exclusion of a vast public that should be included within the legislation's application of parity—as Justice Breyer named them, "movie buffs and aging jazz fans, . . . historians, scholars, teachers, writers, artists, database operators, and researchers of all kinds . . . who want to make the past accessible for their own use or for that of others."[75] By identifying flaws in the justification for the majority's equal treatment rationale, both dissents articulated additional, easily overlooked values for IP's constitutional implementation: a public and the public domain. The dissents did not reject equality as central to copyright law's structure but instead redrew the lines of class membership and asked explicitly, who else counts when considering equal treatment under law?

As the dissents explained, the category of "authors" varies depending on to whom the twenty-year extension applies. Most authors—98 percent of them, according to the dissent's calculation based on briefs filed in the case—would not materially benefit from the legislation. And future or aspiring authors who rely on previous work to create new works would be hindered by the extended monopoly. In 2003, the dissents foresaw the realities of today, when the category of authors to whom the equality principle should apply continues to expand and copyright's breadth is even more relevant to human relations and productivity. For example, in 2011, a successful grassroots movement of everyday internet users, authors, creators, and innovators shuttered major internet sites for a day in protest of the proposed Stop Online Piracy Act (SOPA), demonstrating their criticality and their power.[76] The law would have strengthened enforcement tools to combat online copyright infringement, including blocking user internet access. Movements like the SOPA blackout protest emphasize that twenty-first-century authors are not only those who succeed at earning royalties in exchange for licensed use by established intermediaries (a very small class of lucky authors). In the internet age, authors are everyday creators and users—or "prosumers"—who depend on access to the vast trove of expressive works now accessible through digital networks to produce and participate in our dynamic and industrious culture.[77] As the *Eldred* dissents explained, the court majority failed to recognize these other copyright stakeholders despite basing its decision on the value of inclusivity.

Civil rights advocates have long understood that mechanically reciting the benefit of "equal treatment" without investigating more deeply the relevant categories of people or things being compared will not create a more equal society.[78] This was one of the many failures of *Plessy*'s "separate but equal" doctrine.[79] The just application of equal treatment often depends on carefully defining the category of membership based on its history and social meaning as well as identifying a starting line to which everyone has similar access, in order to accurately evaluate social progress. Justice Ginsburg was no stranger to this critique; her leading roles in gender and racial equality cases debating special accommodation and affirmative action successfully interrogated *in*equality as a function of disparate origins and inattention to relevant differences. But her majority opinion in *Eldred* failed to recognize this argument's purchase. This failure may be explained by the strength of congressional deference, another constitutional principle that Justice Ginsburg championed. But that too would have rested on Congress deserving legislative deference in this case and on the court understanding intellectual property and the stakes of its extended term as just another ordinary economic policy. Whatever the failings of the *Eldred* decision, however, the debate between the majority and the dissents over equal treatment and the role of IP in the Digital Age illuminates new stakes on which the argument about intellectual property's future proceeds.

Eldred was decided in 2003. The Supreme Court decided other IP cases around the same time that also expose disputes about fundamental values in similarly split decisions. Two years earlier, in *New York Times v. Tasini* (2001), the court decided a case about newspapers, digital aggregators, and journalists, with the same 7–2 split (Breyer and Stevens also in dissent). I discuss *Tasini* in the second half of this chapter in terms of anti-subordination and the value of equal status. Two years after *Eldred*, the court decided *MGM Studios v. Grokster* (2005), a case about intermediary liability and peer-to-peer file-sharing.[80] Fractured in reasoning but unanimous in result, the *Grokster* case once again pitted Justice Breyer against Justice Ginsburg to debate the relative economic, political, and social benefits of digitally networked communication balanced against its heightened capacity to exacerbate copyright infringement. Chapter 5 discusses this case in the context of institutional precarity and twenty-first-century intellectual property harms from the perspective of everyday creators and innovators. Meanwhile, other unanimous IP decisions issue from the court that echo the equal treatment rationale of *Eldred*'s majority, celebrating the value of evenhandedness without adequately justifying the classification system that animates it. Close attention to these cases and their rationalizing threads illuminates the depth of the equal treatment principle at the heart of constitutional cases—even those about IP. The analysis also challenges the equal treatment rationale when applied superficially or formalistically, a problem from early constitutional history. As those cases evolved, so might intellectual property cases, suggesting that "equality" may need further reconsideration in the rapidly changing socioeconomic context of our internet age.

B. Trademark Law and Rewriting the Lanham Act

We now turn to trademark cases. *Wal-Mart Stores v. Samara Brothers* (2000) is a milestone trademark case in which Samara claimed trademark protection for its baby clothing designs, arguing that its design or "look and feel" acted like a logo, designating its source of manufacture as distinct from others in the marketplace.[81] Wal-Mart (officially renamed

Walmart in 2018) hired a designer to copy Samara's designs and compete in the children's clothing market. Samara alleged that Wal-Mart's close copy confused consumers into thinking its clothing was made by Samara. In the absence of trademark infringement, Wal-Mart's behavior had the laudatory effect of providing choice among manufacturers and lowering the cost to consumers of baby clothes. Samara argued that the harm of the plausible confusion, which it said amounted to a fraud perpetrated on consumers, outweighed any competitive pricing benefit to the consumer.

A unanimous Supreme Court interpreted federal trademark law (the Lanham Act, also known as the Trademark Act of 1946) to require product designs like Samara's to prove "distinctiveness" in the marketplace in order to be protected trademarks. In other words, the style or "look and feel" must be consistent and recognizable enough to identify the clothing as Samara's and not that of another merchandiser as a matter of empirical fact. This "distinctiveness" in trademark parlance can be difficult to prove with consumer evidence. Not all trademarks must prove distinctiveness, however. And whether Samara's particular kind of trademark—the "look and feel" of a product, or its design—had to prove that it was sufficiently distinctive was part of the issue in this case.

Wal-Mart's unanimous ruling requiring proof of distinctiveness in product design would be unexceptional except for the fact that nowhere does the federal trademark statute single out product design for this unique burden. Justice Antonin Scalia authored an opinion that imported an expensive and time-consuming requirement into federal law without evidence or legislative history. In doing so, he added trade dress product design to a special category of trademarks requiring proof of distinctiveness that until then had been reserved for color marks alone:

> It seems to us that design, like color, is not inherently distinctive. . . . Although words and packaging can serve subsidiary functions, . . . their predominant function remains source identification. Consumers are therefore predisposed to regard those symbols as indication of the producer, which is why such symbols almost automatically tell a customer that they refer to a brand and immediately . . . signal a brand or product source. . . . In the case of product design, as in the case of color, we think consumer predisposition to equate the feature with the source does not exist. Consumers are aware of the

reality that, almost invariably, even the most unusual of product designs—such as a cocktail shaker shaped like a penguin—is intended not to identify the source but to render the product itself more useful or more appealing.[82]

This kind of line-drawing by fiat—that product design is like color for trademark law purposes and unlike words or logos—is unusual for courts, which are supposed to interpret laws, not rewrite them. Here, moreover, the rewriting arose unmoored from consumers' lived experiences—experiences that Congress (not the Court) is tasked with understanding: consumers rely on brand identity in all its diverse forms, especially today in the Digital Age. And yet the court justified its decision by opining that some trademarks are not like others and that equal treatment is therefore unnecessary.

The court cited earlier cases to support the trademark categories to be distinguished, but until *Wal-Mart*, the case law was unsettled because the categories appear nowhere in the federal statute. The court was the only and ultimate line-drawer—distinguishing word marks from trademarks that are product designs—and yet the basis and scope of its line-drawing remained fuzzy. The court's determination of "like" and "unlike" on the basis of its view of "consumer predisposition" drove the *Wal-Mart* decision. This argument was especially strange coming from Justice Scalia, who ascribed to the judicial philosophy that federal judges should refrain from judicial interpretation that effectively rewrites federal laws. Lawmaking (adding or subtracting words in a statute, for example) is for legislators. But in *Wal-Mart*, Justice Scalia made an exception to his usual strict statutory construction and read language and categorical exceptions into the statute. The designation of trade dress product design as *special*—like the isolated case of color marks and unlike the more common use of words—functioned as a deus ex machina in the decision's story about how consumers behave. It drove the story about when and why to deviate from the equal treatment principle in the context of IP law.

Justice Scalia mentioned but did not fully explain the policy considerations underlying *Wal-Mart*'s departure from the logic of "all trademarks should be treated the same." The court explained that its burdensome rule requiring that only some trademarks show distinctiveness would enable competition for design in the marketplace. When product design is harder to protect because protection comes at a cost, competition for similar products may arise, benefiting consumers who seek choice and lower prices. The burdensome rule for product design enables a more open field—that is, more copiers of products—furthering consumer interests, which is what trademark law is supposed to do. This is a happy thought, but it is by no means a rule on which lawyers can rely when considering resolution of IP disputes at the highest court. Notably, this reasoning echoes the dissents in *Eldred* debating the rationality of copyright's extension by twenty years. The *Eldred* dissents cautioned that interpretation and application of IP law should err on the side of public not private benefits (less copyright, not more), especially when the evidence was at equipoise as to the incentives. That reasoning resembles the unanimous *Wal-Mart* opinion: err on the side of the public domain (no trademark) in contexts supporting competition and user access. How far does this rule take us? Without clearer guidance on the role of equality in either case, we are left to wonder.

I happen to agree with the result in *Wal-Mart* as a matter of policy, but the paucity of its equal treatment analysis leaves me wondering if it is repeating the errors of the past. There may be good reasons to require product design trademarks to clear the high hurdle for protection under the Lanham Act. But those good reasons must resonate with more than economic policy and market efficiencies for the court to intervene and rewrite a statute. If instead, the court meant to imply that economic policy affects equality among producers and access to resources for consumers and also that these equality concerns matter in this space, then that would represent a doctrinal innovation in IP law that would benefit from being made explicit. It would reflect equality jurisprudence from decades past that rejects formalistic equal treatment analysis and embraces substantive anti-subordination equality when a resource (e.g., education) or identity (e.g., race) are central to constituting an inclusive society and facilitating meaningful participation in it.[83] This is not to say that discrimination within trademark law is akin to segregation in education. But when intellectual property is considered sufficiently important to fret about its equal distribution absent clear statutory guidance, IP has been elevated to more than mere economic policy.

Indeed, in a 2017 trademark case, the Supreme Court held that trademarks are more than commercial signs, they are "private speech" and can convey "powerful messages."[84] In *Matal v. Tam*, the court held that the Lanham Act's provision barring registration of marks that "disparage" a person or group of people violates the First Amendment. The case was brought by members of an Asian-American rock band calling themselves the Slants when the U.S. Patent and Trademark Office denied their trademark application to register their name. The court explained that the name is a "derogatory term for persons of Asian descent. . . . But [that] the band members believe that by taking that slur as the name of their group, they will help to 'reclaim' the term and drain its denigrating force."[85] The court's decision was 9–0, albeit with some disagreement in concurrences about the necessary reach of the majority's reasoning. The agreement among the justices is noteworthy for the constitutional importance that it showers on trademarks. "In the realm of trademarks, the metaphorical marketplace of ideas becomes a tangible, powerful reality," Justice Anthony Kennedy wrote in his concurrence.[86] Justice Kennedy went on to say: "These marks make up part of the expression of everyday life, as with the names of entertainment groups, broadcast networks, designer clothing, newspapers, automobiles, candy bars, toys, and so on. . . . To permit viewpoint discrimination in this context is to permit Government censorship."[87] The majority opinion, authored by Justice Samuel Alito, explained that trademarks "do not simply identify the source of the product or service but go on to say something more. . . . The trademark in this case illustrates this point. The name 'The Slants' not only identifies the band but expresses a view about social issues."[88]

Judging from *Matal v. Tam*, the court seems to consider registered trademarks a limited public forum for vital and therefore protected individual speech. Citing a long line of cases dating from the 1920s that protect political and offensive speech, the decision reminds readers that the free speech clause is rooted in democratic self-government and the promotion of a robust public marketplace of ideas. In Justice Alito's words, "speech that demeans on the basis of race, ethnicity, gender, religion, age, disability, or any other similar ground is hateful; but the proudest boast of our free speech jurisprudence is that we protect the freedom to express 'the thought that we hate.'"[89] Trademark law should not be used to "prohibit the expression of an idea simply because society finds the idea itself offensive or disagreeable."[90] And so the Supreme Court struck down a one-hundred-year-old provision of the Lanham Act that prohibited registration of "disparaging" marks and cleared a path for brand owners who say that they use these disparaging marks for self-expression and self-actualization. These marks include swearwords and slang for people and acts as well as demeaning images of American Indians, other racial minorities, and women.[91]

It is tritely familiar for First Amendment cases to strike down speech laws that discriminate on the basis of speaker identity and speech content. Less familiar and more surprising is the elevation of trademarks from commercial devices to personal expression that is free from government control and "discrimination." Even more surprising—and paradoxical—is the *Matal* ruling's description of trademark law as a vehicle to promote anti-discrimination in a public forum when the function of trademark law is actually to *restrict* the use of speech and communicative devices by others who do not have rights in the mark—which is everyone but the owners and its assignees. Trademark law already restricts speech; granting broader trademark rights means more marks and less free speech for others, not the other way around. The surprise in this case is that the allure of the anti-discrimination principle was so strong that this basic trademark principle was forgotten.

In 2019, the Supreme Court decided a related trademark dispute, *Iancu v. Brunetti*, extending *Matal*'s ruling to "immoral and scandalous marks," such as the "FUCT" mark that Mr. Brunetti sought to register.[92] This time, there were three dissents and a concurrence, each worrying in its own way about the consequences of *Matal* run amok. The dissenters raised concerns about trademarks "further coarsen[ing] our popular culture" and the Government's lack of a statutory basis to "refuse . . . registering marks containing the most vulgar, profane or obscene words and images imaginable."[93] Their concern sent them searching for a principled distinction between "obscene, vulgar, or profane marks" that are not protected by the First Amendment (and thus may be banned by trademark law) and disparaging marks that under *Matal* may be trademarks because the First Amendment prohibits viewpoint discrimination. This is a topsy-turvy line of trademark cases. Their eventual resolution may require consensus on there being a difference between disparagement and vulgarity, which is hard to imagine under contemporary First Amendment law. But the point to emphasize is this: disputes over equal treatment and anti-discrimination in the context of trademark law are taking on constitutional importance. And despite lacking some logical clarity, these IP disputes concerning hierarchies of speech and equal dignity of speakers serve narratives reflecting deeply rooted American values of self-determination, individualism, and democracy; they echo historic cases about Fourteenth Amendment protections concerning legal regulations that are central to public life, just not intellectual property law.

C. Guilt by Resemblance and Treating "Likes Alike"

A patent case and a copyright case conclude this section's discussion of equal treatment in contested intellectual property cases, respectively, *American Broadcasting Companies, Inc. v. Aereo, Inc.* (2014) and *Bowman v. Monsanto Co.* (2013).[94] Their superficial reasoning and questionable limitations strongly suggest that something other than standard intellectual property law and policy provided their rationales. Both cases extended intellectual property protection, granting more protection for copyright and patent owners. And surprisingly, in both, Justice Breyer wrote for or joined the majority opinion despite usually expressing skepticism about IP's expanding scope. I suggest that the evolving arguments, attitudes, and approaches to intellectual property in these cases indicate IP law's intensified relevance to civil rights and democracy in the internet age, challenging the usual judicial alliances and policy preferences.

The question in *Aereo* concerned the newest iteration of DVR technology. Aereo was a startup technology company that sold a service allowing subscribers to watch free, on-demand, over-the-air broadcast television programs on internet-enabled devices. Aereo's unique business model leased tiny and individual antennae to each subscriber that could buffer, store, and retransmit television broadcasts to a subscriber's computer or tablet. A group of broadcasters, including CBS, NBC, ABC, and Fox, sued the nascent Aereo for copyright infringement. They argued that Aereo was no different from a cable company—a redistribution channel for broadcast television to the public—and thus, like cable companies, which pay compulsory licensing fees to carry television on their networks pursuant to a cable-specific section of the Copyright Act, must also pay to retransmit the television content.[95] Absent a license, the networks alleged that Aereo was in violation of the copyright owners' exclusive right of public performance.

Aereo argued that its service was more akin to DVR and VCR technologies that record and play television that was already free to users in the privacy of their homes. Aereo claimed that it was not at all like cable, nor was it "publicly" performing any of the content because each antenna buffered, stored, and transmitted content separately and uniquely to each subscriber when requested; the antennae were like mini television sets with DVR capability, just not in the home but in the cloud. As such, Aereo was more like a singular and unique form of cloud storage for each subscriber that produced one-to-one transmission, and thus it was not "publicly" transmitting at all. Under copyright law, private transmissions are exempt from a payment requirement.

The Copyright Act's definition of "publicly" and "perform" lacks sufficient precision to determine the case's outcome. Without textual clarity, the court interpreted and applied the Copyright Act's meaning and purpose with resort to superficial analogical reasoning, asking whether Aereo was enough like a cable company to be treated as one. Cable has its own statutory provision for compulsory licenses in copyright law—a statute-specific payment system. Aereo claimed that, like DVR and VCR makers, it provided subscribers with *equipment* to watch television programs at their own pace and thus they should be exempt from direct liability under thirty-year-old Supreme Court precedent. Its antennae were like VCR machines or DVR software, just not situated within the home. And any reproduction, distribution, or performance of broadcast content was done at the users' direction, not Aereo's. If VCR manufacturers were not liable for the copying and playback caused by their machines' users, then Aereo also should not be. In response, the plaintiff broadcasters said that Aereo was the next iteration of a cable provider without the cable infrastructure, enabling near-simultaneous play and record for diverse selections of content. In other words, Aereo's technology was not simply a VCR with a longer virtual cord to the internet cloud but a rebroadcast and retransmission system just like the cable companies, and thus likewise required to pay.

Aereo argued that critical distinctions between the two systems justified different treatment. Specifically, Aereo did not curate or create content like cable companies. It did not constantly transmit if subscribers were not watching, like cable companies. It *did* make unique copies of content for each subscriber and save each package separately, more like email systems, which cable companies did not. Whereas the Copyright Act has a section devoted to cable specifically (section 111: "statutory license for secondary transmissions by cable systems"), there is no such provision for startup technology companies like Aereo that do not fit neatly into the Copyright Act's categories. The question before the court was whether these differences justified dissimilar treatment of Aereo and cable.

Without clear statutory guidance, the court turned to the stakes in differential treatment. A six-justice majority held that Aereo was enough like a cable company in substance if not in form:

> Having considered the details of Aereo's practices, we find them highly similar to those of the [cable] systems in [prior cases]. And those are activities that the 1976 amendments [to the Copyright Act] sought to bring within [its] scope. . . . Insofar as there are differences, those differences concern not the nature of the service that Aereo provides so much as the technological manner in which it provides the service. We conclude that those differences are not adequate to place Aereo's activities outside the scope of the Act.[96]

The court ruled that Aereo's technical workaround did not absolve it of liability; exemption would violate the spirit of the Copyright Act, if not its literal provisions. The problem of course was that the Act speaks to cable specifically in its compulsory license provision, which was created decades earlier as a matter of legislative compromise to boost cable companies and incentivize cable infrastructure by ensuring predictable and low-cost business arrangements. The statute speaks to cable alone; it was special statutory treatment at a time when the early business model needed it. Now, according to the court, Aereo was too much like cable to be exempt from that cable-specific provision, despite it being absent from any legislative agenda and its technology being designed to avoid statutory liability. Left unexamined by the case was the fact that in the 1980s, when cable's statutory compromise was struck, no legislators imagined a system like Aereo's that was wholly disaggregated and modularized, operating on a wireless internet. For the court, it was enough that Aereo resembled cable to its users (even if the technology was as different as typewriters are from computers). Making cable pay and leaving Aereo free to operate was unfair.

With the decision rendered that it would have to pay something, Aereo sought determination by the U.S. Copyright Office that it should pay cable-like fees (a compulsory license). But in a brutally ironic twist of fate, the Copyright Office determined that Aereo's "*internet* retransmission of broadcast television [fell] outside" the compulsory cable license in the 1976 Copyright Act. In other words, the Copyright Office said that Aereo was not enough like cable to pay the statutory fee. The Copyright Office may have had to acquiesce to the Supreme Court's determination that Aereo resembled cable, but it had the final word on whether Aereo was eligible for a statutory license. Such a license would have kept Aereo's costs in check. Ineligibility meant that any license to carry broadcast television had to be individually negotiated, which was sure to be much more expensive. Caught in this double bind, Aereo went bankrupt. The demise of new technology was, of course, what the cable-specific provision in the Copyright Act was trying to avoid. The result of the Aereo decision was that cable's special treatment in the Copyright Act, originally intended to protect a newcomer, became a hammer by incumbents to suppress upstarts. What kind of equal treatment is that?

The dissent in *Aereo*, written by Justice Scalia, predicted this killer squeeze and Aereo's demise. The dissent charged the majority with accusing Aereo of "guilt by resemblance." Justice Scalia wrote that the majority created an "ad hoc rule for cable system lookalikes [that was] so broad" that it rendered much of the majority's reasoning "superfluous" and unworkable, threatening with overwhelming copyright liability the newest of digital content systems that many take for granted (such as cloud computing, remote DVR storage, YouTube, and Amazon).[97] The dissent's critique is of an equal treatment analysis whose superficiality renders the relevant categories unintelligible and thus cannot serve as a predictable rule of law on which to rely going forward.

First, the dissent said that "guilt by resemblance" sounded a lot like "guilt by association," the opposite of individualized treatment that equal justice requires. Second, housing all broadcasters under one roof without accounting for new technological differences that affect access, usability, and content curation—the differences that distinguished Aereo from cable networks—undermined equal treatment by limiting opportunity and distorting a fair playing field. This points to equal treatment's role in the context of intellectual property law: its application should encourage the emergence or use of diverse or innovative technologies by facilitating predictability and fairness. Instead, the equality analysis here promotes incumbents and squashes newcomers. Third, the "looks like cable" rationale was an unworkable rule because its intelligibility depended entirely on justifying the categories of "like" and "unlike," which the majority could not. How could a future cutting-edge technology company decide whether its newest invention infringes with the relevant test being "am I more or less like a cable company?" when cable is unique under the Copyright Act? Law must be predictable, nonarbitrary, and rational to be fair. This is a cornerstone of the rule of law (alongside accountability and transparency) and justifies subjugation to it. From a predictive and logical standpoint, the *Aereo* dissent argued that this equal treatment rationale simply did not compel consistency—and therefore was not the rule of law at all.

With this biting critique of the majority's equality analysis in the context of copyright law, the dissent exposed the stakes in the case:

> I share the Court's evident feeling that what Aereo is doing . . . ought not to be allowed. But perhaps we need not distort the Copyright Act to forbid it. . . . [W]hat we have before us must be considered a "loophole" in the law. It is not the role of this Court to identify and plug loopholes. It is the role of good lawyers to identify and exploit them, and the role of Congress to eliminate them if it wishes. . . .
>
> We came within one vote of declaring the VCR contraband 30 years ago in [the "Betamax case"]. The dissent in that case was driven in part by the plaintiffs' prediction that VCR technology would wreck all manner of havoc in the television and movie industries.
>
> The Networks make similarly dire predictions about Aereo. We are told that nothing less than "the very existence of broadcast television as we know it" is at stake. . . . We are in no position to judge the validity of those self-interested claims or to foresee the path of future technological development. Hence, the proper course is not to bend and twist the Act's terms in an effort to produce a just outcome, but to apply the law as it stands and leave to Congress the task of deciding whether the Copyright Act needs an upgrade.[98]

This honest and revealing statement admitted to the shared concern that Aereo was benefiting from broadcasters' content without paying for it but also that doing so is not automatically illegal. IP law provides innumerable benefits to those who do not pay IP owners directly or at all. That is the purpose of the public domain, and why the limitations and exceptions to intellectual property's exclusivity are so crucial to it functioning well. As originally intended, IP is a public good. Spillover benefits from all sorts of public social goods—roads, clean water, national defense, vaccines, and so forth—go unpaid for by the majority of beneficiaries. That does not make beneficiaries thieves. They are called "public" goods for this reason. The problem is *funding* public goods, not whether they are in fact public. The *Aereo* dissent did not raise the public goods problem but instead defined the debate as who would decide whether Aereo should pay in the first instance (courts or Congress). It was (and is) a question of governance, not of payment. The majority stretched the statute to reach Aereo's conduct using a vague equal treatment principle that, while fundamental to legal reasoning, was flawed in this context of copyright law. The dissent said that it was Congress's job to fix the statute if the Copyright Act needed an "upgrade" for the internet age, even if leaving it to Congress would have let Aereo off the hook.

Beneath the equal treatment argument in both the majority and the dissent lay a governance issue rooted in democratic theory and the role of courts. Both majority and dissent worried that the case would effectively discourage innovation and embolden incumbents. The majority wanted to level up—all broadcasters, broadly defined, should pay when delivering content on demand, even if the statute speaks to cable alone: if cable had to pay, then Aereo should too, even though Aereo designed its system to avoid a payment requirement. The dissent wanted to level down—cable had settled expectations built into the statute, and Aereo was a misfit and an upstart, growing with significant uncertainty in an unsettled technological ecosystem. If IP law aims to facilitate business predictability, grow nascent fields, and incentivize investment in costly infrastructure, then leaving Aereo alone until Congress (the ultimate policy decider) determined that it should pay left the law's accountability more directly in the hands of the people. The majority's superficial invocation of equal treatment hid this deeper value of democratic representativeness and inclusivity on which equality jurisprudence is based.

Justice Breyer favored leveling up and raising the compliance standards, even at the expense of consumers and new technologies. Perhaps this made sense when we consider that he and other justices in the majority tend to believe that courts—distant from the messy, conflicting policies and special interests—are better than democratic bodies at evaluating the stakes of inequality. And this gives us a clue that despite the rule of deference to congressional line-drawing in the context of ordinary economic policy, Justice Breyer and his majority may have been thinking that this was no ordinary situation; it was a case of statutory interpretation in view of copyright policy, to be sure, but the conspicuous theme of fairness reconfigured the usual legal argument into something stranger and less familiar in the context of copyright law. Perhaps intellectual property was no longer ordinary economic policy, or perhaps the majority saw an opportunity in the statute's ambiguity to extend equal treatment principles into it. The dissent called out this strangeness by saying that the principles of ensuring equal treatment or preventing "free riding" (benefiting without paying) did not make sense as applied in this context.

The issue from an equality perspective was that the majority acted as if, in view of statutory ambiguity, it could avoid picking winners and losers at all. To this, the dissent said, in effect, "Don't be naïve." A ruling for the broadcasters would hurt emerging technology companies and their diffuse consumer base and favor traditional broadcast companies and copyright owners, the latter of whom had enough power and prestige to affect the law should it have gone against them. An interim ruling for Aereo, on the other hand, would have kept content flowing and technology progressing and would have put the ball in Congress's court to decide through evidentiary hearings and lobbying efforts if "filling the loophole" was necessary to protect broadcasters and content creators from devastating revenue losses against the public interest. The dissent accused the majority's equal treatment rationale of obscuring what was inevitably a hierarchy of values (content providers over consumers and incumbents over newcomers), suggesting that the better thing to do was defer to democracy, which was the argument in *Eldred*. By rewriting the statute to plug a "loophole," the majority disrupted the democratic default in our constitutional system, replacing Congress's view, however dated, with its own.

To be sure, legislative choices usually favor incumbents, who often have many seats at the bargaining table, as cable did. In this case, however, the ambiguity in the copyright law as written favored the upstart, giving it more freedom to maneuver. Absent fraud in the legislative process or suspicion of irrational prejudice, democratic choices are typically left to be revisited in further deliberative sessions and not to be rejiggered by courts. Given

Aereo's underdog status, it would seem especially critical to apply this deference to the Copyright Act absent a good reason to deviate. In what was apparently a fit of fairness, however, the majority tried to make Aereo pay its fair share, which ended up putting it out of business. Neither Justice Breyer nor Justice Scalia expressly suggested that Aereo purposely took advantage of the broadcasting companies or that copyright law must provide revenues (or exemptions) in a proportionate fashion, but these equal treatment concerns lay beneath the motivation for holding Aereo's feet to the fire. And it was the majority in conversation with the dissent that surfaced this debate over equality's role in deciding cases about IP law against a backdrop of rapid technological change.

Breyer's opinion in *Aereo* resembled the court's unanimous reasoning in *Bowman v. Monsanto Co.* (2013) a year earlier. *Bowman* concerned patented seeds and their interference with farmers' long-standing practice of saving seeds from their harvests for subsequent planting. Indiana farmer Vernon Hugh Bowman argued that because he bought the patented seeds, he had the right to use them as seeds—to plant them and to use what they produced, be that soybeans or more seeds—the same way that someone who buys a golf club or a cell phone containing patented components can use the device or resell it without patent liability. This principle is called "exhaustion" in patent law. (It exists as the "first sale" doctrine in copyright law as well.) It applies to terminate or "exhaust" the patentee's right to control use and sale of the product after a lawful first sale transfers the physical product and the right to use and resell it to the purchaser.[99] Despite this long-standing limitation on the patent holder's rights in favor of the public domain, the *Bowman* court held that patented seeds, once purchased, planted, and cultivated, *cannot* be lawfully replanted, even though producing more seed is what seeds do. This was surprising not only because it caused significant harm to farmers by reducing critical access to seed storage and grain facilities but also because only a decade earlier, a divided Supreme Court in *J. E. M. Ag Supply v. Pioneer Hi-Bred International* (2001) had debated whether seeds are exceptional commodities that should be subject to alternative intellectual property rules.[100] Could a growing focus on equality principles explain unanimity on this issue a decade later?

Bowman argued that cultivating seeds to both sell as soy and use as seed are typical uses and thus "copying" the seed by planting and using it as seed should be lawful. But the court (and the Monsanto Company) claimed the opposite, that farmers may lawfully use the purchased seed by planting it and can lawfully sell the harvested seed from the first planting as soy, but they cannot plant the seed they harvest from the first planting in lieu of purchasing more soybean seed from Monsanto. In other words, Monsanto argued that the right to use and resell the purchased seed is exhausted by the first lawful purchase but that the right to make more seed from the first planting to use as seed remains with the patent holder. How does this make sense?

Justice Elena Kagan, writing for the court, said that seeds are not special. Sure, they self-replicate in a way unique to seeds. But according to the court, all patented inventions (even self-replicating ones) should be treated the same: using the invention to make copies of it is not permitted under patent law, even if that is the natural and foreseeable result of their use. In other words, all patented inventions should be treated the same, even if they self-replicate. The court said that it was Bowman, not Monsanto, who was asking for special treatment in the form of an exemption from the rule that no patented inventions may be copied without permission from the patent owner, even if the invention functions by making copies of itself: "It is really Bowman who is asking for an unprecedented exception—to what he concedes is the 'well settled' rule that 'the exhaustion doctrine does not extend to the right to make a new product.'"[101]

But is not the reverse also true? Monsanto was the party seeking an exception to farmers' long-standing practice. Yes, all patents are subject to exhaustion, including seed patents. And Bowman's ordinary and inevitable use of lawfully purchased seed to produce seed (and soybeans—*which are the same thing*) exhausted Monsanto's claim on Bowman's reuse and resale of the seed as soy or as seed. Seeds are not special, as Bowman agreed. And just because Monsanto's invention regenerates itself did not mean that its use in the intended seed way was unlawful. It was not Bowman but Monsanto who should be prohibited from claiming a special exemption from application of the well-settled rule of patent monopoly's exhaustion over the invention's intended use after a lawful first sale.

Faced with parallel arguments about the equal application of patent law's exhaustion doctrine, the court adjusted its focus on the specific invention in which Monsanto's right of reuse had been exhausted. The court said that exhaustion applied to the purchased seed but only as to *resale* of the *original* product, not to the resale of a new seed made with the purchased one. Farmers could use the purchased seed however they wanted (plant it or resell it), but once the seed had been planted, its offspring were a new (albeit identical and foreseeable) product not yet exhausted of its patent limitations. This confounding reframing demonstrates the slipperiness of equal treatment arguments that we have seen before.

Recall that in *Plessy v. Ferguson*, the analysis began as an argument about how differential racial treatment (segregation on train cars) perpetuated inequality because the law was intended to maintain White supremacy. The court transformed the argument into a conclusion about how segregation that treated both Black and white passengers the same—each was separated from the other—comported with equal treatment. To accomplish this turnaround, the court had to assume away differences among the train cars and occupants and ignore the social meaning of distinct racial identities as perpetuating social hierarchies, those differences being the basis of the segregation law. In *Bowman*, the court followed a similar strategy, erasing differences between relevant categories to justify their equal treatment: seeds, like golf clubs, are equally subject to patent exhaustion upon the first sale, meaning that further sales of that seed or golf club are lawful, but making copies of those seeds or clubs is not. If the court instead understood seeds to be unlike golf clubs precisely because seeds naturally self-replicate upon their proper and lawful use and golf clubs do not, then treating seeds unlike other patented objects for exhaustion purposes would be justified. One of *Plessy*'s errors was seeing sameness where there was obvious difference—the train cars were not the same, and segregation on the basis of race was not equal treatment but was intended to maintain differential social statuses of Black and white people. Another error was locating the source of differential social status in culture rather than in the law. The majority said in *Plessy*, "We consider the underlying fallacy of the plaintiff's argument to consist in the assumption that the enforced separation of the two races stamps the colored race with a badge of inferiority. If this be so, it is not by reason of anything found in the act, but solely because the colored race chooses to put that construction upon it."[102] The *Plessy* court assumed away the social differences as irrelevant to law's application, thereby exacerbating those differences by treating everyone as if they were the same.

Bowman repeated these problems. Seeds and golf clubs are not the same, even though the court effectively said they are. Treating them the same perpetuates differences between the ordinary behaviors of farmers and golfers that lead to substantial hardship for the former and not the latter. It is the court's superficial equality logic, not the behavior or attitudes of farmers or golfers, that exacerbates this hardship. The court could have remediated that hardship and appealed to equality by distinguishing seeds as a class of inventions. But instead, the unanimous *Bowman* court aligned seeds with most other inventions, justifying the equal application of patent law to them regardless of the negative effect on farmers. Ironically, the justices left open the rule's application to other self-replicating products (such as computer programs), claiming to be deciding only the limited case before them.[103] Unlike a decade prior in *J. E. M. Ag Supply*, there was no dissent to push against the formalistic logic that begs scrutiny of the original "like" categories in the first place (be they seeds or other patented products). And one wonders if the critique from a decade earlier asserting seeds' difference from other inventions has fallen to the force of Justice Kagan's formalist equal treatment logic here.

Plessy, like *Bowman*, ascribed a limiting principle to its empty equal treatment analysis. When asked whether the "separate but equal" doctrine could lawfully extend from trains to sidewalks and from race to hair color, the court had two responses. The first was that "such laws [are constitutional only if] . . . enacted in good faith for the promotion for the public good and not for the annoyance or oppression of a particular class."[104] Second, it said that the legislative power had to be "reasonable," which was established "with reference to the established usages, customs and traditions of the people and with a view to the promotion of their comfort and the preservation of the public peace and good order."[105] *Plessy* honored both of these limitations in the breach, as the dissent forcefully argued. The dissent's emphasis on segregation's purposeful oppression of Black people became the center of *Brown v. Board of Education* sixty years later. Can we apply *Plessy*'s dissent to *Bowman*'s superficial equal treatment logic? Does the farmer's liability for saving seed oppress "a particular class" and ignore the "reasonableness" of "established usages and customs"? For sure, Monsanto's monopoly over seed (it controls 92 percent of the U.S. soybean market) and patent law's sanction of that monopoly sabotages farmers' sustainable and customary practices of saving seed for their risky late-harvest crops. Unfortunately, the civil rights revolution that overturned *Plessy* has not come for IP cases yet.[106] But debates about equal treatment and social welfare that unravel the narrow logic of IP cases create opportunities for change. Strategic and persistent civil rights litigation over the twentieth century by the ACLU charted opportunities for racial justice and sex equality. The growing relevance of creativity and innovation to the exercise of fundamental rights in the Digital Age may yet provoke a cyber civil rights movement. Indeed, the ACLU's first involvement in intellectual property cases was in the recent 2013 patent case *Association for Molecular Pathology v. Myriad Genetics, Inc.* concerning the patenting of human genes. Cases related to Myriad are discussed in Chapter 3.[107] But first, we move to intellectual property cases that address subordination and oppression as a different dimension of equality law.

III. ANTI-HIERARCHY, ANTI-CASTE: REJECTING DOMINANCE AND IDEALIZING CONSENT

The equal treatment principle is a pliable reed. Diverging circumstances, resources, and freedoms lurk beneath its application, leading to inequitable results despite similar treatment. These other considerations animate anti-subordination and status equality. Intellectual property cases at the Supreme Court do not overtly manifest these values in the way that disputes about race or sex equality do. But critiques of hierarchy and caste are nonetheless present and do work toward resolving intellectual property disputes. For example, *Golan v. Holder* (2012), the first case in this section, exhibits a layered equality jurisprudence by dismissing a superficial equal treatment analysis in favor of copyright "affirmative action" to remedy status hierarchies and prevents the perpetuation of denigrating castes. *Golan* rejects a formal equality analysis ("all authors") and looks instead to promote equality by treating some authors differently ("foreign authors" alone) in order to undo injustices of prior differential treatment that the court characterized as a form of subjugation.

At first glance, *Golan* and other cases in this section may resemble typical analyses of intellectual property policy. But on further reflection, narratives of power imbalances, unequal resources, and equal dignity arise. Treatment of these other themes may be underdeveloped or fail to consider variables fundamental to equality—including institutional constraints, contractual freedoms, market conditions, baseline resource allocation, and a stable, robust public domain—that are rapidly shifting in the Digital Age. Nonetheless, the cases' equality analyses reflect current cultural debates about persistent inequality and solutions to it in the new era of the internet.

In typical disputes analyzing equality as anti-subordination, courts describe the harm of hierarchy or caste in terms of their opposite: the abolition of dominance and undue influence in order to achieve transactional and relational freedoms within society. This kind of equality celebrates (and may also idealize) choice and consent, describing a fair legal regime as one that buttresses both. In the racial segregation context, "freedom of choice" meant that law cannot mandate segregation—it cannot force people to segregate— but neither does it force integration. "Choice" was the mantra after *Brown v. Board of Education*, leading to decades of disputes over "freedom of choice" school integration plans that failed to achieve diverse classrooms and mandatory busing and school assignment plans that succeeded.[108] Choice and consent remain the optimal status quo for achieving diversity in educational contexts, and mandatory busing and school assignment eventually fell out of favor and were limited under law.[109] One reason for this may have been that *Brown v. Board of Education* was notably ambiguous on the nature of equality that the Fourteenth Amendment demands.[110] Interpreted narrowly, *Brown* only invalidated racial segregation in K–12 schools, reasoning that racial classifications operationalize racial hierarchies. Interpreted more broadly, *Brown* also required race-conscious affirmative action measures to integrate education in order to achieve equal access to opportunity and equal dignity in educational settings.

In the intellectual property context, affirmative action and equal dignity debates focus on whether the law discriminates and therefore symbolically creates oppressive hierarchies. This would follow the narrow reading of *Brown*. Some of the IP cases discussed below also debate whether the optimal status quo is integration (more mandated access for all) or freedom of choice (promoting contractual norms of bargaining and marketplace freedoms). This implicates the broader reading of *Brown*, which current cases about affirmative action still debate. And like these ongoing disputes about the proper basis and scope of educational affirmative action, these IP cases debate the proper basis and scope of IP protection in order to render accessible on an "equal" basis the benefits of the digital era. The internet age pits extensive network access, which we understand to be a basic resource for everyday life, against "click to contract" terms that farcically presume equal bargaining power and limit or condition internet access. We may believe that oppressive hierarchies are easy to identify in the context of race or sex (although persistent assertions that affirmative action oppresses white men question that clarity). In intellectual property cases, oppressive hierarchies may be less obvious. Nevertheless, in these IP cases, ideals of anti-subordination and equal dignity emerge with the moral force of earlier civil rights cases, while also bringing along the unresolved issues from that era. In my view, they are therefore even more complicated than canonical civil rights cases. Add to this the complexity of IP's underexamined integration of economic opportunities with social relations (integration and connectivity being defining features in the internet age), and analysis of these intellectual property cases advance deliberations about the nature and stakes of equality in the Digital Age.

A. *Golan v. Holder* (2012) and the Affirmative Action of Copyright
 Restoration

The 2012 *Golan v. Holder* decision upheld as constitutional section 104A of the U.S. Copyright Act.[111] That section was added in 1994 as part of the United States' accession to the international Berne Treaty. Section 104A grants copyright protection only to certain preexisting works of Berne member countries previously in the public domain in the United States. These foreign works lacked U.S. copyright protection and were in the U.S. public domain because either the United States did not protect works from that country at the time of their publication, or because authors of those works failed to comply with U.S. statutory requirements. Section 104A's restorative effect gutted the U.S. public domain of hundreds of thousands of works—canonical works such as Sergei Prokofiev's *Peter and the Wolf* and Edvard Munch's painting *The Scream*—and brought them under U.S. copyright protection for the remaining portions of their exclusive terms.

Some considered section 104A a violation of the First Amendment and beyond Congress's power under the intellectual property clause because it substantially shrank the public domain on which innumerable people rely for education, speech, entertainment, and commerce. The petitioners in *Golan* argued that "removing works from the public domain . . . violates the 'limited [t]imes' restriction by turning a fixed and predictable period into one that can be reset or resurrected at any time, even after it expires."[112] Shrinking the public domain presented new challenges to freedom of speech. Those opposed to section 104A drew on the Supreme Court's statement a decade earlier in *Eldred* that altering the "traditional contours of copyright protection" warrants heightened scrutiny under the First Amendment.[113] "Heightened scrutiny" means that a court demands more than a rational justification for the law. The justifications for democratic deference and mere rationality no longer exist when a fundamental and individual right is affected. The *Golan* petitioners appear to have learned a lesson from *Eldred*'s submissiveness to congressional line-drawing for ordinary economic policy issues: if the court defers to Congress's *ordinary* copyright legislation based on economic policy, then the *Golan* petitioners had to show how 104A qualified as *extraordinary* legislation because it interfered with the fundamental right of free speech. As such, Congress would have to justify 104A's copyright restoration with a more rigorous showing that it promotes the "progress of science"—a challenge the petitioners thought Congress could not meet.

As it turned out, the petitioners focused on the wrong fundamental right. In *Golan*, as in *Eldred*, the court was less concerned with free speech than with equality. The decision began with familiar language about equal treatment—"sameness" and "reciprocity"—stating that section 104A gave to foreign works "the same full term of protection available to U.S. works" because "members of the Berne Union agree to treat authors from other member countries as well as they treat their own."[114] Justice Ginsburg, for the majority, explained the United States' acquiescence to Berne as a "reciprocat[ion] with respect to . . . authors' works."[115] The laudable effect of section 104A, despite its diminution of the public domain, is a "restoration plac[ing] foreign works on an equal footing with their U.S. counterparts."[116]

The *Golan* decision went beyond equal treatment, however, and relied on an anti-subordination principle.[117] Commitment to anti-subordination reflects a belief that certain distinctions reproduce or enforce inferior social status, especially of historically oppressed people. As Reva Siegel and Jack Balkin wrote, anti-subordination theories "contend that guarantees of equal citizenship cannot be realized under conditions of pervasive social stratification and argue that law should reform institutions and practices that enforce the secondary social status of historically oppressed groups."[118] In contrast to equal treatment, the anti-subordination rationale allows—and even encourages—the government to prefer or benefit some groups over others to remedy past conditions of subordination or deprivation. Rather than seeking "sameness" and avoiding "difference" as measures of equality, anti-subordination logic justifies treating people differently to undo hierarchies that enact and reinforce both privilege and stigma. The Supreme Court's equality jurisprudence embraces both anti-subordination equality (affirmative action) as well as anti-discrimination equality (equal treatment). These doctrines co-originated after the Civil War when the Freedman's Bureau provided benefits only to newly freed slaves at the same time as the new Fourteenth Amendment required "equal protection of the laws."[119] Constitutional affirmative action extended into the twentieth century with programs in education and employment that remediated systemic discrimination and disadvantage by selecting for and protecting certain identities and traits historically targeted, such as race and sex. These two theories of equality sometimes appear to conflict and require deeper investigation of their purposes, mechanisms, and effects to identify the shortcomings of equal treatment and to justify anti-subordination equality in a particular context.[120]

Consider the case of gender inequality. Under the equal treatment model, women and men are both persons and thus equal (as in "the same") and should be judged by the same criteria, for example, when applying for jobs.[121] Conversely, they may also be "different" in some capacity and thus need not be treated the same, for example when assessing leave after childbirth.[122] Neither approach considers how gender as a social category constrains or provides opportunities for and access to social, political, and economic benefits on the basis of sex.[123] Job criteria may be the same, but fewer women may be hired because they experience less access to opportunities that prepare them for the job market because of gender stereotyping and differential social roles (of childcare or career expectations). Similarly, providing more leave for women after childbirth may make sense because their physical experience of childbirth may require more recovery time, but granting more time to women than to men may encourage more mothers to stay home with newborns than fathers and discourage equal parenting and equal opportunity to return to and advance at work. "Same" or "different" treatment without regard to existing gendered social stratification and the reasons for it reproduces inequality through powerful male-dominated institutions (the paid workforce) at women's expense. By contrast, an anti-subordination approach to gender inequality identifies the power instantiated in the labels "male" and "female" and asks whether the maintenance of these labels "participates in the systemic social deprivation of one sex because of sex."[124]

What does all this have to do with the *Golan* decision and copyright law? As literary historians and copyright scholars recount, the U.S. copyright system was rigged against foreign authors from its earliest days on behalf of the American publishing industry.[125] Foreign authors were disadvantaged in relation to domestic authors regarding copyright. U.S. copyright was riddled with technical traps unfamiliar to foreign authors. And U.S. copyright law in large part failed to protect foreign authors who first published overseas and later sought to publish and sell their works in the United States.[126] This disparity led to profound imbalances in the United States of the relative cost of works by foreign and domestic authors: foreign works were cheap to publish because copyright licenses were not required. These market asymmetries skewed the perceived value of, and access to, foreign and domestic works. Foreign authors were the "women" in this social hierarchy limiting access to economic independence and career opportunities. Congress enacted section 104A to remedy those imbalances—only for foreign authors. It was enacted, according to Justice Ginsburg's majority opinion, as affirmative action to undo or reverse the harm caused by decades of copyright deprivation for foreign copyright holders.[127]

The *Golan* majority provided two justifications for fixing the anti-foreign bias in the U.S. copyright system by reserving benefits only for formerly deprived foreign authors. International harmonization assured better treatment to U.S. authors abroad. It was also a targeted remedy for the purposeful deprivation of foreign authors' copyright by restoring their exclusive rights in the United States. Section 104A did in fact harmonize the U.S. copyright regime: it placed foreign works in the "position they would have occupied" if a nondiscriminatory U.S. regime had been in effect when those works were first published. As the court stated, "authors once deprived of protection are spared the continuing effects of that initial deprivation; [section 104A] gives them nothing more than the benefit of their labors during whatever time remains before the normal copyright term expires."[128] Restoring works to the "position they would have occupied" and "spar[ing]" authors any further "deprivation" unmistakably echoes the language of affirmative action and remedying past unjust discrimination.[129] In a footnote, Justice Ginsburg's opinion accused the unreformed copyright law (and Justice Breyer's dissent) of American exceptionalism and isolationism, a critique resonating with concerns of cultural dominance (status and stigma) that animate antisubordination equality in its more typical applications.[130]

The *Golan* decision further stated that restoration of copyright and a focused shrinking of the public domain was a modest reform. Far from making foreign authors whole (it did not add all the years they had lost), it raised those "deprived" foreign authors to the current status of the U.S. authors.[131] Like the affirmative action doctrine in the gender or race contexts, the bestowed "benefit" on the select class—here, copyright authors of foreign works whose protection was unavailable under the older regime—was something that should have been conferred previously and was unlawfully or wrongfully withheld. The wrong was the denial of copyright to foreign authors, which benefited U.S. authors by providing them with market leverage. Because foreign authors were unrepresented in the U.S. legislative process, their denial of copyright, which enriched the U.S. authors without any obvious connection to copyright's "progress of science" goal, smacked of abuse of power.

Of course, the U.S. public domain did benefit from the surfeit of uncopyrighted foreign works under the previous regime. Those works could be disseminated without license, making them cheaper and more available to readers (albeit without remuneration to the original authors). Some historians suggest that this fact alone explains the prevalence of the modernist European authors in U.S. public school curricula for much of the twentieth century.[132] Would U.S. students have read James Joyce to the same extent had his books been more expensive to print and publish? Justice Breyer's dissent in *Golan* developed this theme, focusing on the public domain's indispensability to education and national culture.[133] He also ridiculed as wishful thinking and irrational the majority's argument that rescuing lost copyright and harmonizing both foreign and domestic rights "promotes the diffusion of knowledge" (a copyright goal) by incentivizing the republication and restoration of those works in the public domain.[134] The dissent argued that restored copyright for these foreign authors would not in fact

promote their wider distribution. Empirical evidence supports this assertion: copyright disappears all but the bestsellers worth the investment to
reprint and republish, leaving the majority of books invisible until they
become public domain material and free to all.[135] This suggests that section
104A's restoration or affirmative action did more harm than good from a
copyright perspective (building readership and revenue) and that attention
should be paid when concerns of status and stigma anchor IP policy, which
is typically geared to progressing economic and cultural production, not
ameliorating social stigma or hierarchy.

The *Golan* majority decisively rejected the public domain benefits of the
previous U.S. copyright regime that left so many foreign works unprotected
because, the court argued, equality is worth the costs to users. In making
this argument, the court analogized to a well-understood equality harm of
pay discrimination. Ginsberg wrote:

> The question here . . . is whether would-be users must pay for their desired
> use of the author's expression, or else limit their exploitation to "fair use" of
> that work. Prokofiev's *Peter and the Wolf* could once be performed free of
> charge; after § 514 [section 104A] the right to perform it must be obtained in
> the marketplace. This is the same marketplace, of course, that exists for the
> music of Prokofiev's U.S. contemporaries: works of Copland and Bernstein,
> for example, that enjoy copyright protection, but nevertheless appear regu-
> larly in the programs of U.S. concertgoers.[136]

This analogy resonates with the rhetoric of "equal pay for equal work," the
slogan used for the Equal Pay Act of 1963 that continues to be marshaled
in support of the Paycheck Fairness Act, which was first introduced in
1997 and has been reintroduced every two years but has never passed. On
the surface, the *Golan* argument makes sense: why value Copland's work
higher than Prokofiev's? If there is no difference between the works by
copyright standards, why must one be paid for while the other is free? Absent a rationale for the differential treatment, the possibility of irrational
or invidious purposes arises. Indeed, Justice Ginsburg's opinion criticized
the unreformed U.S. copyright law as xenophobic and U.S.-centric, purposely devaluing and marginalizing foreign works in order to enrich national authors. To her, there was no suitable justification for the stigmatic
and material harm arising from the exclusionary scheme.

But contrary to equal pay laws, which have no losers except the employers for whom anti-discrimination policies may be expensive, the *Golan* dissent argued that section 104A causes real harm to a diffuse and vulnerable public. Those who rely on the stability and existence of public domain material, such as educators, researchers, and fledgling artists and authors, would now be forced to pay for material they had previously used freely. The *Golan* majority and dissent disputed the relevance and importance of the existing public domain to cultural production, expressive freedoms, and community development. The dissent claimed the existing public domain (and its stability) to be a resource relied on as if a right with constitutional importance. As already mentioned, some literary historians contend that the U.S. publishing industry's "piracy" of European works shaped American and European literary culture.[137] Without the "burden" of copyright protection, authors such as James Joyce, Ezra Pound, Djuna Barnes, and even Gilbert and Sullivan evaded U.S. government censors and enriched their celebrity through lower prices and saturated U.S. markets, which led the global market for these works.[138] Because many of these works were intellectually challenging or even obtuse to American readership, their prevalence in the U.S. marketplace given their affordability and lack of regulation very likely facilitated their widespread acceptance and celebration. Whether this justifies the "subordination" of foreign authors to U.S. authors in the national copyright marketplace is an important question that the *Golan* majority did not address, instead sidelining the U.S. public domain as "unowned" and thus less protected or important than intangible, personal property such as copyright. This left equality and anti-subordination of foreign authors as the dominant concerns.[139] According to the majority, there was no public good at stake other than that produced by copyright ownership. As such, equality concerns regarding that ownership could take priority.

The majority's equal pay argument would be laudable in the context of pay discrimination cases in which similarly situated workers are paid less because of irrelevant differences (such as gender or race). But in the copyright context, this argument spoke past the dissent's belief that the public domain should remain constant or grow and that a shrinking public domain thwarts copyright's progress goals measured by access to and opportunities for creative expression. The majority's argument assumed a financial benefit for authors whose copyright was revived under 104A, which might encourage further publication and dissemination of those works. To the dissent as well as to many commentators, this position was laughable. For the most part, works not under copyright disseminate freely and are widely accessible.[140] By contrast, works once in the public domain and now under copyright due to *Golan* would likely less frequently disseminate precisely because permission was now required and could be made expensive. The majority and dissent were debating what "progress" meant in this case: equal status under copyright law (but without any guarantee of financial returns) or a stable and nourished public domain, albeit with diminished control by copyright owners.

The *Golan* majority's unconvincing reliance on copyright's financial benefit to justify foreign copyright restoration belied its true focus—the dignity deprived European authors due to their exclusion from the U.S. copyright regime.[141] Foreign authors lacking U.S. copyright and seeking publication in the United States with the hope of copyright-like revenue had to devise creative business solutions. Some issued alternative versions of their work to assure "first publication" of this "new" work in the United States.[142] Others struck precarious publishing deals on handshakes without legal enforceability. These additional hurdles required for foreign authors simply to participate in the same market as U.S. authors were insulting and degrading. Working twice as hard for less control or pay is a professional affront in other contexts (such as in gender or race discrimination situations). Indeed, authors such as James Joyce, Ezra Pound, and T. S. Eliot were vocal about the unfairness of U.S. copyright law to non-U.S. authors.[143] They joined together to challenge the law as a means of controlling the manner in which their work was published in the United States.[144] These and other authors signed Joyce's "protest" accusing certain American publishers of being "get-rich-quick promoter[s]" by benefiting from "the innocent connivance of American law."[145] The *Golan* majority echoed these sentiments, without dwelling on the literary characters or history, and characterized the foreign authors' experiences as dignity harms owing to the unreformed U.S. copyright law.

In other contexts, the harm of anti-subordination is obvious. Typically, women who cook do so as wives and mothers without pay. Men who cook do so as chefs to fame and fortune. Formerly, mostly men were doctors and women nurses, with the former being high-paying and providing more autonomy and prestige.[146] Doing laundry and changing bandages is not inherently "beneath" a person—the vast majority of us do both—but over the centuries, those who did so for others came to be perceived as part of an underclass of maids, servants, and even enslaved persons. As T. M. Scanlon described:

> The evil involved in such arrangements is a comparative one. It is not the tasks themselves that are demeaning—they may be necessary tasks that someone has to perform in any society. What is objectionable is being marked as inferior to others in a demeaning way. The remedy is to abolish the social system that defines and upholds these distinctions between superior and inferior.[147]

The identity and status of "author" is subject to the same structural analysis: when are authors valued under copyright and when are they excluded despite doing the same work? The *Golan* majority and other Supreme Court opinions from the recent past appear to draw on this equality critique, identifying unjust hierarchies in the distribution of IP benefits and burdens anchored in status and subordination. Their underlying effect is to elevate the status of authorship in the Digital Age. But doing so without concern for the public domain's critical function for all people, especially subsequent and developing authors who rely on it, may miss an opportunity for larger structural reform.

When amplifying anti-subordination causes and remedying past discrimination, it is often too easy to reinstate property relations that oppress those who are absent or less visible. Such was the case in *Golan* regarding all who routinely rely on the public domain. Failing to account for absent and diffuse stakeholders who rely on access to a public domain that is vastly improved by the digital era doubly oppresses them in today's networked society. The majority's bean-counting copyright solution—simply give more copyright to more people to undo the subordination—triggered the dissent's response that the public domain has value too. Fair enough, but that imagines the copyright pie as a zero-sum resource, balancing allocations like a finite amount on a scale. That is not how copyright works. It is not how anti-subordination equality works, either. Describing copyright exclusivity and the public domain as opposites of the IP coin characterizes the public domain as copyright's negative instead of a fundamental baseline for all intellectual property regimes.[148] A different solution to those injured by the unreformed copyright law would have been reparations to the injured class paid for by those who became rich from the free foreign works and a declaration requiring fair treatment going forward. Shrinking the public domain and hurting all who rely on it in order to pay authors aggrieved by the public domain's prior contours perpetuates the injury of exclusivity and hierarchy under the guise of inclusivity and equality.

The risk that affirmative action aiming to undo past unjust discrimination may paradoxically perpetuate inequality of status and opportunity is the reason the Supreme Court strictly reviews such plans when they are based on race and gender.[149] When they are based on copyright, however, as the legislation in *Golan* was, the court is not doctrinally required and thus misses the chance to ask the hard questions of legislative rationales. When importing commendable equality jurisprudence into copyright law, the court did not go far enough with its anti-subordination logic. Doing so would have exposed and thus more ably considered copyright law not only as market regulation producing economic chits and fungible assets but also as legislation advancing social and civil rights by sustaining a public resource that protects speech for all.

Equality law, be it based on anti-discrimination or anti-subordination, is complex and contentious—especially at the Supreme Court—for a reason. It is rooted in deeply felt convictions based on centuries of historical experience about what equal treatment and equal dignity mean and what is required from individuals and government to promote both. As the Supreme Court begins to weave more of this equality reasoning and history into its intellectual property decisions, we may see more contentious disputes reconceiving IP in the new century as central to progressing human welfare and promoting fundamental rights. The Supreme Court traditionally protects those rights against a tyrannous majority and legislative overreach. It may be no surprise, therefore, that it has begun to do so in terms of the Constitution's "progress" mandate and in the context of our irrevocable, bittersweet Digital Age.

B. *New York Times v. Tasini* (2001) and Digital Age Journalism

The Supreme Court's analysis of intellectual property and equality fails to connect social status with economic opportunity, reflecting a doctrinal cleavage born of traditional equal protection law. And yet IP's place in the Digital Age is at the intersection of social and economic status, the combination of which affects equality of opportunity and equal dignity in a complexly integrated legal culture. The 2001 case of *New York Times v. Tasini* highlights the importance of this intersection and the law's failure to address it.[150] The case concerned news databases and the market for republication of news, a phenomenon that has substantially transformed journalism in the twenty-first century.

At issue in *Tasini* was whether freelance writers, when granting publishing rights to newspapers and periodicals, also grant the right to republish the newspaper and periodical in an electronic database such as LexisNexis. Section 201(c) of the Copyright Act extended the transfer of copyright from an author to a publisher of a collective work to "any revision of that collective work, and any later collective work in the same series." *Tasini* concerned whether an electronic database counts as "any revision of that collective work" because it does not always preserve the original form of the newspaper. (Within databases such as LexisNexis, news articles are identified, read, and distributed in isolation from their placement in the original collective work published as a unique whole.)

Freelancers sued to require the *New York Times* to relicense their work for digital databases that disaggregated the collection in which they were published. The *New York Times* defended by interpreting the Copyright Act to include in the original license the right to publish the freelancers' work in the digital database. The court majority sided with the freelancers, interpreting section 201(c) to strengthen authors' rights and concluding that "the 201(c) privilege [granted to publishers] does not override the Authors' copyrights."[151] Section 201(c) thus limits the copyright transfer from authors to publishers to the reproduction and dissemination of authors' work *as part of a collective work*, which a database is not.

In ruling for the authors, the court relied on the history of the 1976 Copyright Act. The legislation aimed to "enhance the author's position vis-à-vis the patron."[152] Several provisions of the Copyright Act were intended to upend the publishers' "superior bargaining power over authors."[153] For example, publishers often fail to put copyright notices on individual contributions to collective works, inadvertently placing those individual works into the public domain. Congress fixed this problem in 1976 with a new section that made "a single notice applicable to the collective work as a whole

... sufficient" to protect the rights of freelance contributors.[154] Another part of the 1976 legislation intentionally gave authors (and their heirs) a chance to renegotiate bad bargains through a clawback or "reversion" provision. This provision accounts for typical relations between authors and publishers: first-time deals tend to undervalue authors' work because authors are eager to be published and publishers claim that first-time publications are risky investments. But the new Act's reversionary "termination of transfer" provision allows authors after several decades to renegotiate those first deals in light of changed circumstances and the passage of time, should they wish to. Publishers get the benefit of the copyrighted work for the first several decades at a low price, and authors (or heirs) many years later can benefit from the increased value of their work (if that occurred). Many of these 1976 revisions to the Copyright Act were meant to "clarify and improve" authors' rights with regard to "frequently unfair legal situation[s] with respect to rights in contributions" and other publishing deals.[155]

The court's persistent and repetitive description of the publishers' statutory benefit as a "privilege" in *Tasini* reminds readers that the case concerned the preservation of "authors' rights," created to be distinguished from monarchical privilege and power. The term *privilege* dates from before the first "copyrights" in England, when they were instead called "privileges" granted by the Crown to printers and booksellers to copy and vend books.[156] The *Tasini* majority used this language presumably because it is part of the ambiguous statutory section at issue in the case. But it is hard to avoid hearing echoes of the conflict between the "privileges" of earlier times granted by the monarch and the individual "rights" now inhering in everyday authors. "It would scarcely 'preserve the author's copyright in a contribution' as contemplated by Congress if a newspaper or magazine publisher were permitted to reproduce or distribute copies of the author's contribution in isolation or within new collective works."[157] The majority's statutory interpretation preserved demand for the authors' work, whereas a contrary reading that includes a publishers' "privilege" of republication in a database would limit authors' ability to charge for additional reproduction and dissemination. The court quoted a 2001 report from the Register of Copyrights as support for the author's rights approach that "freelance authors have experienced significant economic loss" due to a "digital revolution that has given publishers [new] opportunities to exploit authors' works."[158] The majority therefore read section 201(c) in light of Digital Age challenges to labor equity and publisher (and platform) domination to restrict publishers' "privilege" and benefit authors through republication rights. This interpretation has been described as a thumb on the scale for authors when bargaining with publishers over contributions to collective works—an affirmative action measure for authors who struck unfair bargains in the past and are uniquely suffering in the internet era.

The dissent disagreed, chiding the majority for its failure to apply the Copyright Act's "media neutrality" principle, which prohibits the Copyright Act from being interpreted differently with regard to diverse media (such as film, photography, text, and images) absent specific exceptions. By excising electronic databases from 201(c)'s general "collective work" language to help authors control their republication rights, the dissent claimed that the majority violated an anti-discrimination principle at the heart of the Copyright Act, thereby subordinating the primary interests of the reading public, which benefits from the completeness and accessibility of databases, to authors' interests in being paid extra for inclusion in a publisher's electronic database. Should authors be preferred to publishers in the interpretation of the Copyright Act's progress goals? This is a point on which the dissent was agnostic as compared with the majority's fundamentalism. But the dissenters firmly believed that readers' interests deserve equal consideration under the Copyright Act and that readers should prevail in this case (even if that meant publishers do too).

Quoting Thomas Macaulay that copyright is "a tax on readers for the purpose of giving a bounty to writers," the dissent (written by Justice Stevens) explained that:

> [The] tax restricts the dissemination of writings, but only insofar as necessary to encourage their production, the bounty's basic objective. . . . The primary purpose of copyright is not to reward the author, but is rather to secure the general benefits derived by the public from the labors of authors. . . . the majority's decision today unnecessarily subverts this fundamental goal of copyright law in favor of a narrow focus on "authorial rights." Although the desire to protect such rights is certainly a laudable sentiment, copyright law demands that private motivation must ultimately serve the cause of promoting broad public availability of literature, music, and other arts.[159]

With the public interest in mind, the dissent pointed to further harms suffered by authors and readers alike. First, Justice Stevens wrote, the majority's rule might disadvantage freelance writers by inducing the "purge [of] freelance pieces from ... databases," making their work more obscure rather than more noted and available.[160] And second, "today's decision in favor of authors may have the perverse consequence of encouraging publishers to demand from freelancers a complete transfer of copyright. If that turns out to be the case, we will have come full circle back to the pre-1976 situation."[161]

To the majority, preserving the breadth of authorial control rested on anti-dominance and equal dignity theory. The dissent did not disagree, but it had a more pessimistic view of author-publisher relations given social and economic structures that form an inevitable background to copyright law. The majority claimed to protect authors in the copyright system from voracious publishers by buttressing authors' status and control and restricting publishers' privilege. The dissent's response was that complete databases might actually help authors in the long run (to be read, known, and compensated) and would certainly help readers. But was it the court's job to decide what's best for authors, when by filing suit they had named their injuries and desired remedies? The majority dismissed the dissent's concern as paternalistic, contending that freelancers sued to allege harm and that "we [the court] may not invoke our conception of their interests to diminish [their] rights."[162] The court should support authors' choices and assertions as a matter of respect. The majority concluded its paean to choice and autonomy—traits of the idealized "romantic author" to be sure[163]—by asserting that "it bears reminder here and throughout that these Publishers and all others can protect their interests by private contractual arrangement."[164] Reverting to private ordering and consent (the ability for authors and publishers to individually protect their interests) described authors as having and deserving equal power in future negotiations with publishers. The *Tasini* majority's was an idealized world, to be sure, but one that it believed copyright should instantiate. The dissent warned that relying on choice and consent as a matter of statutory interpretation to protect authors' equal dignity would more likely—and unhappily—reinstate publishers' power in the future. If authors' rights under section 201(c) precludes incorporation into a database without their consent, then publishers would seek that consent. And if history is a guide, publishers would not pay any more for it. The dissent maintained that authors do not magically have more bargaining power by interpreting section 201(c) in their favor.

The fundamental disagreement between the majority and dissent concerned the source of equal dignity. The majority considered the leveling up of rights between authors and publishers essential to the actualization of exercising those rights in the manner one may choose. The dissent, however, saw leveling up as only a small part of a larger and more complex socioeconomic context that determines power and control. Simply leveling up and then relying on contract negotiations to actualize individual needs and desires would likely reproduce the same imbalances that the majority had sought to eradicate. A broader context would consider the public interest and the digital domain as inseparable from authorial prerogatives. The dissent wrote:

> It simply begs the question for the majority to argue that the right not to have a work included within [an electronic database] is an "authorial right" that "Congress [has] established," or that . . . a decision allowing such inclusion would amount to "diminish[ing] authorial 'rights' on the basis of 'our conception of their interests'" . . . [given that] copyright law is not an insurance policy for authors, but a carefully struck balance between the need to create incentives for authorship and the interests of society in broad accessibility of ideas. . . . The majority's focus on authorial incentive comes at the expense of the equally important (at least from the perspective of copyright policy) public interest.[165]

The dissent embraced the principle of anti-subordination in the copyright context and appreciated that distribution of statutory rights might mitigate domination of authors by publishers. But the dissent objected to the majority's reasoning because it shortchanged (or even ignored) the public interest, creating a more loathsome hierarchy stacking authors above audiences and denigrating as inessential the public domain's "accessibility of ideas."[166] The dissent reminds us that "authors' rights" depend on the public domain and that prioritization of authors' rights misunderstands what Abraham Drassinower calls the "correlative equality" of copyright law.[167] There is no hierarchy of rights in copyright; authors and the public domain are part of a larger symbiotic whole. Leveling up unhelpfully promotes equality of status between authors and publishers by neglecting the correlative equality of the public regarding both. The majority's prescribed leveling up in fact subordinates the public to copyright ownership. And that is exactly backwards. The majority's anti-subordination approach, laudable in its balancing of power between authors and publishers, nonetheless remained stuck in an individual rights regime that considers a market-based consent and choice framework as neutralizing domination. But outsourcing morals to markets only reinforces the status quo. Instead, the dissent urges us to recognize copyright in the Digital Age as supporting an integrated system of readers, writers, and publishers as part of the public interest in accessing diverse authors' work. The private exploitation of an expected copyright for authors or publishers may in fact be incompatible with the freedom for all who "need to function as equal citizens" in the internet age.[168]

Tasini's majority opinion failed to strengthen authors' rights or enlarge their purses in the long run because the future became what the dissent predicted. The photographers' stories from chapter 1 describe this future in some detail, epitomized in this chapter's opening quote from Lou Jones. Publishing contracts demanded more rights for the same price from freelancers, including rights to include freelancers' work in electronic databases. Recall photographers' complaints about coercive contract terms that were necessary to maintain media clients when the World Wide Web became an everyday destination. Putting more beans in the authors' proverbial bucket did not give them more bargaining power in the Digital Age, even if the *Tasini* majority said that the 1976 Copyright Act should be interpreted to grant authors more respect and status vis à vis publishers' privilege. *Tasini* may have been right to demand equal dignity for authors versus publishers regarding the value added to the broad terrain of expressive works from which we all benefit. But the majority's approach to copyright that asserted authorial dignity as a matter of anti-subordination without ensuring equal opportunity to exercise that status or consider the effect on the public interest in access to copyrighted work was an incomplete solution to the problem of inequality in copyright law. *Tasini*'s reasoning left authors to negotiate on their own without real bargaining power against aggregators and publishers. And it left no one representing copyright's public interest or reinforcing the system and institutions that connect us all, obscuring if not also minimizing our shared fates in the internet age. What good is equal dignity and the right to freely consent and contract with background rules that have everyone fending for themselves?[169]

C. Patent Law, Academic Publishing, and Private/Public Partnerships

Patent cases fall into similar traps of elevating the status of authorship at the expense of its pragmatic exercise. Several key patent cases highlight choice and consent as a measure of equal dignity and anti-subordination, romanticizing self-determination and individualism and minimizing each person's reliance for that autonomy on equitable background conditions and a system that protects the public interest. The 2010 case of *Board of Trustees of the Leland Stanford Junior University v. Roche Molecular Systems* concerns patent licenses between inventors and their employers, particularly the relative control that employee-inventors may wield when contributing inventions to their employers' assets.[170] *Roche* explicitly continued the conversation in *Tasini*.

The court in *Roche* held that the so-called "Bayh-Dole Act" (or Patent and Trademark Law Amendments Act) of 1980 did not change the underlying default in the Patent Act that vested inventions initially with inventors. That default gave inventor-employees initial control and preserved inventors' rights in their inventions unless and until they deliberately contracted them away. The Bayh-Dole Act aimed to incentivize universities to patent faculty inventions by enabling the inventions' commercialization even when developed with federal funds. But when the university does not receive a contractual assignment from the faculty-inventor, the effect of *Roche* is that the university owns nothing to commercialize. In *Roche*, the faculty-researcher signed an agreement with a private company preceding any valid assignment to Stanford University. This meant that the inventor and the private company controlled the invention and that the university was unable to profit from its employee's invention.

The court's reasoning relied on the myths of the independent inventor who transfers his rights by contract in an exercise of mutual, knowing consent between inventor and licensee. The majority rejected an interpretation of the Patent Act that "moves inventors from the front of the line to the back by vesting title to federally funded inventions in the inventor's employer—the federal contractor [here the University]."[171] And "for Congress to supplant one of the fundamental precepts of patent law and deprive inventors of rights in their own inventions . . . would be truly surprising."[172] The language of pecking order and priority—like the language of rights and privilege in *Tasini*—laced this opinion, reminding the reader that patent inventors are special and deserve respect. If Stanford failed to receive a clear assignment from its faculty-researcher, that was Stanford's problem. Or if, as the dissent maintained, the public has to "pay twice for the same invention"[173]—once through federal funds to the university and once more for the invention from the private party that purchased the assignment from the faculty-researcher—then that is a failure of contract, not patent law. In protecting the inventor's priority and title to the invention, the majority in *Roche*, as in *Tasini*, mitigated harsh IP rules with appeals to the ideals of consent and contract. "Universities typically enter into agreements with their employees requiring the assignment to the university of rights in inventions. With an effective assignment, those inventions—if federally funded—become 'subject inventions' under the Act, and the statute as a practical matter works pretty much the way Stanford says it should. The only significant difference is that it does so without violence to the basic principle of the patent law that inventors own their inventions."[174]

As in *Tasini*'s dissent, the *Roche* dissent worried that the "contract solution" was no solution at all. Moreover, it protected the wrong party. The Bayh-Dole Act intended to protect the *public* (not patentees) from lopsided deals by preferring nonprofit research universities (Stanford) to private third parties (Roche Molecular Systems) in the bargain. Under the "majority's [reasoning] . . . the individual inventor can lawfully assign an invention (produced with federal public funds) to a third party, thereby taking that invention out from under the Bayh-Dole Act's restrictions, conditions, and allocation rules" meant to avoid a double tax on the public to use the invention.[175] But being an inventor does not make one magically able to protect oneself (or the public) in the contractual negotiation any more than being an author (in *Tasini*) enables one to strike a better bargain in light of generously interpreted statutory rights. Inventors routinely assign their rights for very little compensation or benefit, causing significant long-term consequences for themselves and the public, which likely has the least access to and will pay the most for the invention if it gets to market.

The Bayh-Dole Act was meant to avoid these problems by restructuring the baseline bargaining for universities and inventors. Instead, the *Roche* majority, as in *Tasini*, interpreted the statute through the frame of equal status between inventors and assignees, omitting the public altogether, and assumed that inventors are capable of exercising fortitude in the face of business negotiations with their employers. The expressive force of this image amplifies its equal dignity approach. But it made the mistake of assuming that fair bargaining and free consent follows from independent contracting between parties, preventing the mismanagement of rights and their public benefit. The *Roche* dissent, as in *Tasini*, embraced the ideal of anti-subordination equality but recognized the distance between ideals and equality-in-fact given disparate circumstances. Moreover, the dissent emphasized that however consent is reached between individual parties, private ordering is unlikely to protect the unrepresented public interest at all. Progress for the court majority was exclusively a private affair. And the anti-dominance fixes in both *Tasini* and *Roche* did no more than symbolically lift the status of authors and inventors, granting equal dignity under the law without economic power or institutional leverage and ignoring the public benefit entirely. This reading reveals the underlying debate in both cases as less about the status that IP rights confer as a comparative matter and instead about the relevant weight to accord the importance of the public interest when assessing status claims. This critique understands intellectual property not as a right for any single individual concerning their human worth or wealth (who and how much counts) but instead as a system that assesses and calibrates productivity and accessibility as a whole (what counts and why).

Kirtsaeng v. John Wiley & Sons, Inc. (2013) reversed course with a ruling favoring the public interest.[176] *Kirtsaeng* concerned copyright's "first sale" doctrine, a corollary to patent law's exhaustion doctrine discussed earlier in *Bowman v. Monsanto*. After the first sale of a lawful copy (e.g., a book), the author's right to control the copy's distribution ends, and the purchaser can resell it or otherwise distribute it without permission from the copyright holder. The first sale doctrine facilitates the market in used books and is a cornerstone to copyright's dissemination function. The dispute in *Kirtsaeng* originated when a Cornell University student, Supap Kirtsaeng, learned that Wiley textbooks assigned in U.S. colleges sold in his home in

Thailand at significantly lower prices than in the United States. He asked friends and family in Thailand to buy the books there and ship them to him in the United States. Kirtsaeng then resold the books in the United States for a considerable profit. Wiley sued, claiming that the lawful purchase of the textbooks overseas did not count as a "first sale" under U.S. copyright law and that importation into and sale of the books in the United States was therefore a violation of Wiley's copyright.

The *Kirtsaeng* majority held that if the book was lawfully made and sold overseas but protected by U.S. copyright, then the copyright owner's exclusive right of distribution terminates and the book can be imported into and sold on the secondary market in the United States free of authorial or publisher control. The practical implication of this ruling is that books first sold overseas and imported into the United States will be substantially less expensive than if a U.S.-based first sale is required to create a used market in the books. *Kirtsaeng* sounded the death knell for international "price discrimination," which, based on copyright control over first sales (but not subsequent ones), enables copyright holders to segment the globe into various markets and vary the price of copyrighted goods within them. As Justice Ginsburg complained in her *Kirtsaeng* dissent, international exhaustion eradicates price discrimination among distinct global markets, which she claimed is essential for authors (and their publishers) to earn sufficient revenue.

Interestingly, *Kirtsaeng* was just a year after *Golan*, when Justice Ginsburg's affirmative action rationale justified the special benefit of restoring copyright to foreign authors to resurrect their U.S. market leverage. But a year later, she failed to convince a majority of the same court that copyright's first sale doctrine should be interpreted to protect authors' (and publishers') initial monopoly in the U.S. market. This may be unsurprising given that her argument in *Kirtsaeng*, taken to its logical extreme, would encourage U.S. companies to send their manufacturing of copyrighted works overseas in order to preserve market segmentation, likely to the detriment of state and national economies. But she nonetheless embraced a segmented international marketplace and its opportunities for developing countries as benefits worth pursuing, as she did in *Golan*. She argued for freedom—freedom of authors and publishers to choose their markets—and criticized the abdication of control over price and distribution that a global used-book market creates. By contrast, Justice Breyer, writing for the *Kirtsaeng* majority, described the benefits of first sale accruing to consumers who would have a global market in which to shop with competitive (lower) prices. He also identified benefits to the authors and publishers: they would receive the price of the first sale somewhere, after all.

Justice Breyer's majority opinion also identified rank geographical discrimination in the dissent's argument. The dissent's view depended on the illusion of national boundaries in what is in fact a global digital marketplace with consumers all over. The majority justified its international exhaustion rule by embracing "unified" markets and "equalize[d] treatment of copies manufactured in America and those manufactured abroad."[177] It declared that "it is particularly difficult to believe that Congress would have sought this unequal treatment while saying nothing about it and while, in a related clause (the manufacturing phase-out), seeking the opposite kind of policy goal."[178] Even though publishers might subsequently find it "more difficult to charge different prices for the same book in different geographic markets," the majority celebrated the result of this ruling:

> We can find no basic principle of copyright law that suggests that publishers are especially entitled to such rights. . . . [T]he Constitution's language nowhere suggests that its limited exclusive right should include a right to divide markets or a concomitant right to charge different purchasers different prices for the same book. Neither, to our knowledge, did any Founder make any such suggestion. We have found no precedent suggesting a legal preference for interpretations of copyright statutes that would provide for market divisions. . . . To the contrary, Congress enacted a copyright law that (through the "first sale" doctrine) limits copyright holders' ability to divide domestic markets.[179]

As this language demonstrates, the majority heavily relied on equality and unity tropes to justify international exhaustion, assuming the righteousness of leveling up: this time raising *consumers* and *secondary distributors* to the level of authors and publishers in terms of marketplace competition. Justice Ginsburg's dissent called again for special treatment for authors and publishers on the theory that doing so would level a smaller, more critical playing field of just authors and their partners, in order to protect creation and its profits in the first instance.

Four years later, the Supreme Court applied the holding and reasoning in *Kirtsaeng* to patent law in its *Impressions Products, Inc. v. Lexmark International, Inc.* (2017) decision, authored by Chief Justice John Roberts.[180] *Lexmark,* our last case for this chapter, concerns patents for components of printer cartridges that would prevent their resale and refilling by competitor cartridge companies to generate a competitive market for printer toner. The *Lexmark* decision is a straightforward adoption of *Kirtsaeng*'s reasoning in the patent context, except that the Patent Act does not contain explicit provisions limiting rights to the first sale the way copyright law does, and here, the purchaser promised not to resell. Nonetheless, Chief Justice Roberts easily extended the exhaustion doctrine in this case based on the deeply rooted principle in the United States of the alienability of property and its public benefits.

Chief Justice Roberts imagined a nightmare in which "automobiles, microwaves, calculators, mobile phones, tablets and personal computers" could not be repaired, refurbished, and resold to purchasers because of patent law restraints and global markets[181]—which cannot be what patent law intended. The majority opinion appeared to elevate the public interest in competitive markets over intellectual property. But its reasoning resonated more with the common law of private property and idealized individual freedoms (rights in one's labor and its fruits) than it did with equality principles that demand geographic nondiscrimination and the equal dignity of consumers and patent holders. Chief Justice Roberts wrote:

> More is at stake when it comes to patents than simply the dealings between the parties, which can be addressed through contract law. Instead, exhaustion occurs because, in a sale, the patentee elects to give up title to an item in exchange for payment. Allowing patent rights to stick remora-like to that item as it flows through the market would violate the principle against restraints on alienation.[182]

This opinion praised individually negotiated and consensual bargains, which, as we saw in *Tasini* and *Roche,* are considered evidence of freedom and respect. But this time that praise justified a reduction in the IP holder's rights. The "more at stake" was consumer welfare in the competitive market for printer cartridges, just as it was in *Kirtsaeng* for the market in textbooks. But the *Lexmark* decision further justified its ruling by "the common law's refusal to permit restraints on the alienation of chattels," which "makes no geographical distinctions."[183] Patent exhaustion's "roots in the antipathy toward restraints on alienation" means that Congress could not have intended "to confine that borderless common law principle to domestic sales. In fact, Congress has not altered patent exhaustion at all; it remains an unwritten limit on the scope of the patentee's monopoly."[184]

The *Lexmark* decision further supported its argument by conjoining patent law and copyright law. Chief Justice Roberts wrote:

> [D]ifferentiating the patent exhaustion and copyright first sale doctrines would make little theoretical or practical sense: The two share a "strong similarity . . . and identity of purpose." . . . There is a "historic kinship between patent law and copyright law," and the bond between the two leaves no room for a rift on the question of international exhaustion.[185]

Equality between copyright and patent doctrine does the most work here, not the equal opportunities of patentees and the public, who seek inventive, competitively priced goods. In recent cases, Chief Justice Roberts has continued to express skepticism of intellectual property's broadening reach in the Digital Age as well as its anti-competitive effects, which he sees as undermining older, more fundamental common-law principles.[186] The rhetoric of equality in these decisions follows rather than leads the arguments, which are framed in terms of individualism, personal property, and free markets. Systemic equality and market regulation to promote fairness and opportunity, and structures or institutions to sustain these values, remain unexplored subtexts.

This would make sense given that U.S. equality doctrine follows—albeit long after—the declaration of individual freedoms and the fundamental right of private property ownership (for some). The equality doctrine that began with the Declaration of Independence and was replanted in the Fourteenth Amendment remains limited by the post–Civil War doctrinal schisms distinguishing economic regulation from political and civil rights. As the cases in this chapter demonstrate, intellectual property in the Digital Age increasingly blurs the line between economic interests and regulation that affects equal citizenship. Indeed, arguments after the Civil War and during Reconstruction about rights in labor and land connected economic with civil equality.[187] For good or for ill, debates over the immorality of slavery and the necessity of remediation and reparation did not disaggregate economic interests from those of equal treatment and equal dignity.[188] These recent cases about intellectual property, which raise allied concerns about the interrelatedness of economic regulation with civil, social, and political rights, provide new opportunities to evaluate the fundamental promise of equality in all its contours in U.S. law in the internet era.

*   *   *

This chapter aimed to demonstrate how the nature of equality animates decisions about intellectual property at the Supreme Court. By debating intellectual property's goal of "progress of science and the useful arts" in terms broader and more complex than simply "more" IP, these decisions center intellectual property within fundamental discourses of equality and in doing so reshape both IP and equality for the twenty-first century. These are contested cases, and I disagree with many of the majority opinions. But their internal debates reflect our nation's commitment to and ongoing struggles with equality, its admirably expanding application, and the pressures of information capitalism on intellectual property and other fundamental rights, to which we now turn.

3 Privacy

> You take an image of someone that you took months to gain trust from. Where you feel completely empathetic and compassionate to their story. And then someone, because that image is in the archive, and they couldn't care less the context of that image, says, "She's hot-looking. Let's use her to sell this." . . . That's my problem.
>
> —Noreen, award-winning photojournalist

PRIVACY IN LAW AND CULTURE has evolved significantly over the last century. Some may say that privacy is the right most important to personal and social well-being, but also the one most under attack today. Privacy's evolving critical contours are a challenge to identify and navigate among the abundant virtual and physical communities that our internet age makes possible. Over the past decade alone, extensive and diverse debates about the value of privacy and the harms from its violation demonstrate its contemporary consequentiality.[1] Privacy is everywhere disputed in terms of shifting definitions, trade-offs, and differential benefits to particular communities in specific places and times. "Privacy is a concept in disarray," Daniel Solove wrote in 2008, echoing Judith Jarvis Thomson in 1975.[2] Privacy may feel like a shape-shifter that evades sufficient demarcation to apprehend and defend.[3] But privacy is no chimera; it is inexorably real, especially for those who seek it or allege injury from its invasion.

Privacy's elusiveness as a concept and diversity as an experience mean that privacy injuries are often alleged alongside more concrete claims, such as copyright and trademark with their well-established and deeply rooted legal frameworks. Copyright and privacy are especially fruitful collaborators because copyrighted expression embodied in a tangible object, such as a photograph, missive, or manuscript, often contains personal information, describing intimate relationships, events, or circumstances. And like the unauthorized publication or distribution of a copyrighted work, which is often characterized as "theft,"[4] unauthorized exposure of private facts, behavior, or relationships through publication of copyrighted expression feels like a personal—even physical—incursion.

The idea of privacy may have existed since humans lived in populated societies. But the right of privacy with a legal remedy against both governmental and individual actors did not exist in the United States until the twentieth century.[5] The apocryphal story of privacy's birth as an independent legal right starts with an 1890 *Harvard Law Review* article titled "The Right to Privacy" by Samuel Warren and Louis Brandeis. Allegedly, the fear of paparazzi photographers at Warren's daughter's wedding provoked the article's writing.[6] Like most origin stories, this one may be more mythic than true, but its influence nonetheless has shaped privacy law ever since.[7]

Warren and Brandeis framed "The Right to Privacy" through the rapid evolution of new technology that facilitates information dissemination in the 1890s:

> Instantaneous photographs and newspaper enterprise have invaded the sacred precincts of private and domestic life; and numerous mechanical devices threaten to make good the prediction that "what is whispered in the closet shall be proclaimed from the house-tops." . . . The press is overstepping in every direction the obvious bounds of propriety and decency. Gossip is no longer the resource of the idle . . . but has become a trade. . . . When personal gossip attains the dignity of print, and crowds the space available for matters of real interest to the community, what wonder that the ignorant and thoughtless mistake its relative importance.[8]

Cameras and new forms of journalism were encroaching on expectations of privacy. Warren and Brandeis described harms arising from escalating privacy invasions, such as the degradation of the public sphere, an ineffective marketplace of ideas, and the personal injuries flowing from exposure, misuse, and distortion of private facts and personalities. The personal harms eventually formed five new privacy torts that became tools to protect against privacy invasions in the twentieth century: public disclosure of private facts, misappropriation of private facts, false light (or "publicity") claims, breach of confidence, and intrusion upon seclusion.[9] Handing personal privacy harms over to the domain of tort law made sense at the time. Tort law addresses personal injuries or "wrongs" between individuals based on norms of reasonable expectations to avoid hurting others.[10] The limitations of the approach were twofold, however. Most personal injuries arise from a breach of a duty to take *physical* care and to avoid unreasonable physical risks toward others. Warren and Brandeis described *nonphysical* privacy torts. These new torts also challenge the stability of the concept of "reasonable" behavior rooted in established norms given fast-evolving communication practices, both then and now in the context of technological evolution.

Warren and Brandeis recognized and addressed both these limitations. They agreed that the established "law gave remedy only for physical interference with life and property, for trespasses."[11] But, they argued, new times call for new legal contours. A new right to privacy "entail[s] the recognition of new rights . . . to meet the demands of society."[12] In the 1890s, the demands of society were responding to the new technologies of photography and the penny press. Today, society's demands depend on the ubiquity of communication technology and the internet's networked connectivity. In addition to inserting adaptability into the concept of privacy, Warren and Brandeis hinted in their opening paragraph that another solution to new demands for privacy protection was to recognize that property invasions can be to "intangible, as well as tangible" property.[13] Enter intellectual property's support of privacy interests.

There was a third problem with a new "right to privacy"—the First Amendment. The First Amendment's free speech and press clauses protect taking unauthorized photographs of people in public and disclosing true (albeit private) facts about a person that are in the public interest. Preventing the dissemination of public images of private people or true facts through a new right of privacy created a back door to circumvent the First Amendment and undermine the democratic values and institutions it sustains.

To address the first two problems, Warren and Brandeis's innovation was to extend existing and established rights against physical invasion (trespass), false statement of fact about a person (defamation), and relationship transgression (breach of confidence) to a "more general right of the individual to be let alone."[14] In the context of the penny press, yellow journalism, and the new "snap camera" that inaugurated amateur photography,[15] this more general right "to be let alone" was rooted in early copyright concepts and cases describing intellectual or "intangible" property that inheres in a tangible copy:

> [It would] secure to each individual the right of determining, ordinarily, to what extent his thoughts, sentiments, and emotions shall be communicated to others. Under our system of government, he can never be compelled to express them (except when upon the witness stand); and even if he has chosen to give them expression, he generally retains the power to fix the limits of the publicity which shall be given them. The existence of this right does not depend upon the particular method of expression adopted. It is immaterial whether it be by word or by signs, in painting, by sculpture, or in music. Neither does the existence of the right depend upon the nature or value of the thought or emotions, nor upon the excellence of the means of expression. The same protection is accorded to a casual letter or an entry in a diary and to the most valuable poem or essay, to a botch or daub and to a masterpiece. . . . No other has the right to publish his productions in any form, without his consent. This right is wholly independent of the material on which, the thought, sentiment, or emotions is expressed.[16]

In this passage, as with the article's opening incantation of "intangible" property, we see the roots of the copyright in privacy. The authors footnoted this passage with a citation to an influential eighteenth-century copyright case, *Millar v. Taylor* (1769), writing that "every man has a right to keep his own sentiments, if he pleases. He has certainly a right to judge whether he will make them public, or commit them only to the sight of his friends."[17] Warren and Brandeis also cited an 1849 literary property case, *Prince Albert v. Strange*, in which etchings made only for the royal family's private enjoyment were printed and sold to the public without permission.[18] The decision in *Strange* punished the unauthorized publication of the etchings as a breach of the right of first publication by the copyright owner. But the court also explained its decision as adjudicating a breach of confidence claim (by the holder of the etchings) with the additional injury that a "man may employ himself in private in a manner very harmless, but which, disclosed to society, may destroy the comfort of his life, or even his success in it."[19] Copyright and privacy were effectively connected in these cases to explain the importance of the new "right to be let alone."

Warren and Brandeis did not *fully* elide the right to be let alone (privacy) with the right to control first publication (copyright). Had they done so, both doctrines may have developed differently over the past century.[20] Instead, "The Right to Privacy" distinguished the legal right to privacy from copyright and extended the right to privacy beyond intellectual property to "the right to one's personality."[21] The "protection afforded to thoughts, sentiments, and emotions, expressed through the medium of writing of the arts, so far as it consists in preventing publication," Warren and Brandeis wrote, "is merely an instance of the enforcement of the more general right of the individual to be let alone. . . . The principle which protects personal writings and all other personal productions, not against theft and physical appropriation, but against publication in any form, is in reality not the principle of private property, but that of *an inviolate personality*."[22] Copyright may be a part of privacy, but privacy is not always a part of copyright.

Much of the argument in "The Right to Privacy" depended on successful claims for relational harms: established cases for breach of confidence, contract, and trade secret misappropriation.[23] But as Warren and Brandeis explained, these claims require a legal duty arising from preexisting relationship obligations and could not prevent publication of a letter by a casual recipient or the publication of a photograph taken in public—both copyright harms that may or may not be privacy violations.[24] Warren and Brandeis sought a stronger privacy right as "against the world,"[25] unlimited by preexisting relationships, and thus they conjured a new, controversial right "to be let alone." Fast-forward to the early twenty-first century, when the "right of privacy"[26] or a "reasonable expectation of privacy"[27] as debated and shaped by common-law torts and constitutional law is no less controversial than it was in the 1890s. Against whom may we assert the right of privacy? Must there be a promise not to disclose personal information to enforce privacy? Can we prevent strangers from posting our images or words from social media elsewhere online? These privacy claims are alleged with increasing frequency against acquaintances and strangers. And they are becoming more robust, as Warren and Brandeis imagined. Privacy's more frequent entanglement with intellectual property disputes adds dimensionality and strength to contemporary privacy claims, illuminating the stakes of both. These shared stakes may seem mutually exclusive, but their interaction is the root of the puzzle. The stakes include personal interests in self-determination over our private expressions, lives, and identities—essential features of democracy and civil order—and the public interest in disseminating expressive works and truthful information to enrich the public domain and promote science and the useful arts.

In their article, Warren and Brandeis did not resolve this standoff between "public welfare [and] . . . private justice," except to provide general suggestions for limiting the right to privacy when matters concern the "public or general interest."[28] The vagary of this phrase has generated more questions than answers. But when privacy claims attend intellectual property contests, such as when a newspaper seeks to publish a photograph of a private moment of a public figure, three factors focus the "public or general interest" to address the puzzle at the center of "The Right to Privacy": (1) intellectual property's goal of "progress of science and the useful arts," (2) the constitutional "limited times" provision requiring that all copyrights and patents eventually enter the public domain, and (3) the First Amendment's free speech limitation on all intellectual property claims. As it turns out, however, these factors, although much debated, have not coalesced around a sufficiently clear principle to resolve contemporary debates that pit privacy against intellectual property. But the debates nonetheless helpfully illuminate features of social progress, such as the public interest in the public domain, access to information and other expressive resources, and the positive and negative consequences of free speech for contemporary society immeasurably transformed by its digital manifestations.

It turns out that contemporary invigoration of privacy interests also has roots in the 1890 "right to [protect] one's personality."[29] Warren and Brandeis described privacy as establishing and maintaining trust among people, which strengthens social arrangements. They described privacy as protecting vulnerability and preserving dignity, making people fit for essential personal relationships as well as social participation. They implied that privacy is also indispensable to curiosity, innovation, and eccentricity.[30] Today, we tout these same benefits of privacy in the face of privacy's erosion from comprehensive digital connectivity and irresistible technological convenience.[31] And, perhaps alarmingly, we deny privacy as a form of punishment or to those deemed unworthy of the benefits it makes possible.[32] All these privacy values can be found animating intellectual property disputes today. Whether copyright (or other intellectual property) *should* be leveraged to protect these interests "of personality" or identity in the twenty-first century is a separate question. That it *is* marks a turning point, as did Warren and Brandeis's article.

"The Right to Privacy" both descriptively and normatively announced a new right born of converging trends in technology and expression. The rising tide of privacy claims now brought through intellectual property complaints provides a similar opportunity to better understand the problem of privacy today in relation to copyrighted works primarily, but also concerning distinctive commercial signs (trademark's domain) and patented inventions in terms of personality, reputation, and identity. This chapter first describes the twentieth century's evolution of privacy's dimensions. It then explains how those privacy dimensions frame twenty-first-century intellectual property disputes, eliding their objects as legal regimes when previously they may have been doctrinally and culturally separate. Their overlap and sometimes partnership in contemporary cases brings into relief new challenges for protecting both intellectual property and the fundamental value of privacy in the internet era.

I. PRIVACY DIMENSIONS

Intellectual property interests substantially overlap with four developing dimensions of constitutional privacy: spaces and things, bodies, beliefs and relationships, and information.[33] As these four privacy dimensions evolve through common law and statutory development in response to the stochastic evolution of technology and its impact in our internet age, they intersect with intellectual property law aiming to control dissemination and publication of works and inventions by and about people and relationships. However, intellectual property's goal of public dissemination of expression and inventive knowledge through limited market exclusivity also clashes with privacy's protection of seclusion and obscurity. This clash sometimes generates unsatisfying compromises for both intellectual property and privacy disputes. The disputes nonetheless delineate the contested values most at risk today and in their resolution help identify contexts in which the disputes are most likely to occur.

Most literally, the Constitution preserves privacy over a person's spaces and things as against governmental intrusion.[34] This is the Fourth Amendment's contribution to privacy (as well as that of the Third Amendment), which includes one's person, home, papers, and "effects."[35] Today, this spatial and personal property dimension of privacy includes cars and cell phones, although these were not uncontroversial extensions of privacy in spaces and things.[36] Copyright (which protects a "work of authorship" embodied in a "copy") may be used to protect one's privacy in the contents of the copy by preventing the dissemination of papers and effects.[37] As described more fully below, these claims arise most often when the papers are unpublished, such as manuscripts, diaries, letters, and private photos, and have remained private or semiprivate during the author's lifetime. These claims resemble protection from intrusion into seclusion and trespass and present the strongest justification for control by the copyright author to prevent dissemination of unpublished work. Along with bodily privacy and autonomy, these claims also most resemble the personal property claims and assault torts that Warren and Brandeis's "The Right to Privacy" inaugurated.[38]

Constitutional privacy also extends to bodies and persons, protecting against government-forced medical treatments, bodily searches, and reproduction or sterilization. This web of privacy rights in one's body derives from common law and natural law as much as from the Constitution's Bill of Rights.[39] The right to bodily autonomy has corollaries in informed consent doctrines, the right to self-defense, and the right to be free from assault by others.[40] It applies with ease to prevent forced feedings and unwanted medical procedures and more controversially to laws criminalizing reproductive choice and body searches.[41] As copyright and trademark law extends to images and representations of people, claims arise to suppress publication or dissemination of copyrighted material and trademarks as a way to seclude one's body (via the image) from intrusion and scrutiny by others, not only from the government. These cases concern: the dissemination of photographs or trademarks that place the subject in a false or unappealing light; the commercial, parodic, or critical expression of a subject seeking privacy; and the nonconsensual dissemination of intimate or sexual images by ex-lovers whose goals are to threaten, shame, or humiliate. There are even some patent cases in which medical patients are unwittingly trapped between healing their bodies and capitulating to patent infringement. For reasons that may already appear obvious, these are emotionally charged cases with claimants (and lawyers) seeking quick resolutions rather than legal clarity. Privacy's fuzzy common-law contours and robust First Amendment exceptions make federal intellectual property claims more appealing avenues for redress, given their relative clarity and statutory penalties.[42]

Legal protection of privacy also extends to thoughts, beliefs, and relationships through the Constitution's First Amendment and its penumbra.[43] With surprising ease, courts apply the First Amendment to preserve spiritual and intellectual autonomy—a version of privacy of the mind that relates not only to thoughts but also to personal choices.[44] Courts declare the state's intrusion into matters bearing on religion and political association especially detestable. Our constitutional democracy relies on intellectual freedom to strengthen self-government and as a "critical check on totalitarianism."[45] With more difficulty (but not without success), courts apply the First and Fourteenth Amendments together to protect privacy in intimate relationships, both publicly sanctioned and domestically enacted. Only recently has it become illegal to criminally sanction same-sex marriage and consensual sexual adult intimacy because doing so "demean[s] [a person's] existence or control[s] their destiny by making their private sexual conduct a crime."[46] The Supreme Court recently explained in *Obergefell v. Hodges* (2015)—the case that confirmed the constitutional right of marriage equality—that marriage is essential to personal dignity and that it is considered one of the "great relations in private life."[47] The court also reaffirmed that what goes on in the bedroom is protected by privacy "in the most basic sense."[48] It is unclear whether marital privacy is more firmly grounded in law by the private space of the home (and bedroom) or by the personal and independent choice of a marriage partner.[49] But both the home and fundamental life choices (such as whether to be married or become a parent) are part of constitutional privacy's established legal dimensions.[50]

Intellectual property claims may resemble disputes concerning intimate choices and private thoughts when they seek to prevent the publication of expressive works in order to protect the author's intellectual serenity and personal or intimate relationships. As discussed below, these claims most often arise in copyright, but some also arise in trademark and patent contexts. This form of IP/privacy overlap interferes with other strong, constitutionally protected individual rights, such as free speech and the intellectual autonomy of other speakers, authors, and inventors. These disputes pitting privacy against free speech reflect an enduring challenge for privacy law identified in "The Right to Privacy" and thereafter.[51] Some contemporary copyright cases reflect a possible compromise by preserving to the author or originator the right of *first* publication in order to protect intellectual privacy and relationship autonomy that inheres in the expressive work. Trademark and patent law are more challenging for privacy seekers, as both legal doctrines begin with public dissemination, not private creation.

Generally, intellectual property has solicitude for first movers by protecting the first to use or invent and works that are original or novel.[52] Within copyright law specifically, control over *first publication* has been a cornerstone of the author's prerogative. However, copyright law does not protect the facts and information contained in the work, even if it is unpublished.[53] This is true even if first publication is saved for the author (or originator) and the facts or information are private and intentionally sequestered. Under copyright fair use and its fact/idea exclusion, copyright law expressly permits the critique, publication, or transformation of parts of copyrighted works even if doing so reveals private information. This kind of permissible reuse and critique may threaten spiritual and personal self-determination, extinguish personal relationships due to the content of the critique or transformation, or savage precious memories and beliefs. Derogatory use of a trademark—sometimes called "tarnishment" when the mark is famous—may stir the same pot and reflect similar injuries.[54] Although trademarks are by their nature always already public and published, their reuse in this way can affect private relationships and interests. Trademark law also has a free speech limitation built into its framework.[55] But this does not prevent plaintiffs from bringing sincere claims alleging that private and personal relationships suffer from the trademark's misuse. We will see similar complaints with patent infringement claims later in this chapter.

A typical IP problem requires balancing the private incentive to produce expression and knowledge with the public interest promoted by the goods produced. The injection of relational or intellectual privacy interests into this balance is especially jarring and may seem anomalous when compared with disputes over physical seclusion, bodies, and private effects.[56] Nonetheless, when disputes raise this privacy dimension, they also concern intellectual property's constitutional purpose to promote progress of science and the useful arts by addressing authors' and inventors' evolving needs and norms. Battles regarding already disseminated work and intellectual and relational privacy turn on revised understandings of public interests in the Digital Age, the subjective severity, and the objective consequences of the harm from unauthorized use of another's intellectual property in the internet era.[57]

Common-law privacy has a fourth dimension that has not yet reached a constitutional tenor despite its being the primary subject of "The Right to Privacy" in 1890: privacy over the collection, processing, and dissemination of personal data.[58] Of the five privacy torts that arguably address informational privacy, all but the breach of confidence tort are recognized in the vast majority of the fifty states.[59] Although slightly over a century old and not yet constitutionalized, the "right to privacy" in personal information is deeply embedded in twenty-first-century society. We are preoccupied with concerns over the compulsive collection of personal data, constraining and invasive algorithms programmed on the collection and analysis of that data, government and private surveillance empowered by the data, and the data breaches that compromise sensitive information but today seem part of the cost of doing business and engaging in ordinary commercial transactions.[60] In 1890, Warren and Brandeis wrote about "instantaneous photographs and newspaper enterprise[s] [that] have invaded the sacred precincts of private and domestic life; and numerous mechanical devices [that] threaten to make good the prediction that 'what is whispered in the closet shall be proclaimed from the house-tops.'"[61] They were not only lamenting the spread of "idle gossip" but also the "perver[sion]" of little things (think birth dates, children's names, illnesses, faces, gaits). "Thus harvested," they become "the seed of more, and in direct proportion to its circulation, [result] in a lowering of social standards and of morality."[62]

In the twenty-first century, these cries of "standards and . . . morality" may sound quaint. But who has not experienced the "creepiness" of automated data processing's online precision targeting?[63] More malignant but perhaps no more insidious are the dignitary and welfare consequences of big data aggregation: algorithmic discrimination; systematic, institutionalized disadvantage; and diminished well-being.[64] As Julie Cohen has written, "privacy is about boundaries and boundary crossings" in the context of the inevitable social construction of selves through our myriad daily interactions.[65] Thus, the "condition of privacy entails dynamic maintenance of breathing room" so that we may "engage in the processes of boundary management .

. . [to] define and redefine" ourselves and our life circumstances.[66] Whether this requires "semantic discontinuity"[67] or "desirable inefficiency" in the flow of information,[68] fundamental to privacy and freedom is control over the collection, processing, and publication of facts about ourselves.

Intellectual property does not protect for our own use facts and information about ourselves, be it facts about our face, our locations, our phone use, or our genes. And although intellectual property regimes are designed to focus control in the owner of expressive works, trademarks, and inventions, all of which may contain facts, all intellectual property laws (except trade secret law) leave facts and information open to public knowledge and use.[69] Nonetheless, the deeply felt desire for informational privacy directs complainants to IP law as an additional aid to suppress the work, mark, or invention containing the information. The disputes discussed in this chapter demonstrate the risks of this approach. But their many occurrences demonstrate intellectual property's growing centrality to the public debate about informational privacy as a fundamental value. This contributes to the contemporary development of theories of privacy harms and justifications for their reprisal.

As Helen Nissenbaum wrote, privacy is a fundamental value because it protects the "diversity of personal choices and actions."[70] When we protect private conversations and spaces, we also protect the ability to think and develop ideas without concern for social and political constraints.[71] Social media battles, created by relentless sharing—not privacy—have been accused of accelerating the polarized political discourse instead of helping us appreciate difference. When we are assured privacy over our minds, bodies, and spaces, civil order and crucial personal relationships remain stable and are able to develop progressively. Friendships, families, and intimacies—the bonds of civil society—are unimaginable without these critical dimensions of privacy, which are threatened by our networked communications and internet platforms. As Charles Fried wrote about privacy decades ago, privacy is essential for respect, trust, friendship, and love.[72] Privacy promotes the production of aesthetic and scientific goods, the flourishing of creativity and eccentricity, the binding of communities together around shared interests despite individualized differences, and the flourishing of respectful debate that is essential to democratic self-government.[73] In this way, privacy as an individual right and a fundamental element of personhood is a critical public good and societal value.

Intellectual property law may seem only tangentially related to these lofty concepts and interests. Copyrights, trademarks, and patents are perceived generally as assets in need of protecting because they lose market value when copied and disseminated without restraint in the age of rapid digital reproduction. And yet privacy claims have lingered on the periphery of copyright cases since the British Statute of Anne in 1710 (the precursor to the U.S. Copyright Act of 1790). And today, many copyright disputes—and a growing number of trademark and patent cases, too—resonate with the above-described privacy values and harms that are far afield from usual economic-based claims grounding IP law. Intellectual properties of copyright and patent aim to promote progress of science and the useful arts. Trademark law promotes fair competition and consumer clarity in commercial markets. And yet, when network capabilities of the internet age threaten privacy with extinction, these broad progress mandates become even broader, to guard against privacy's erosion in all its dimensions.

II. PRIVACY DISPUTES AS INTELLECTUAL PROPERTY CLAIMS

Until the late twentieth century, intellectual property cases brought to protect privacy were mostly copyright claims used to protect unpublished work from public dissemination. These isolated cases described debates over private letters, unpublished manuscripts, and personal portraits or photographs.[74] But the internet and associated late twentieth-century digital technology transformed these cases from special to mainstream, and they now reach beyond copyright law.

IP cases in which privacy-like claims arise reflect the early twentieth-century privacy dimensions described above. They take the shape of particular story forms that draw from familiar plots of privacy deprivation or intrusion. As such, they communicate normative values similar to older privacy complaints, but they also frame the problem largely in terms of copyright law (or sometimes trademark or patent law). Framing the problem as primarily about intellectual property rather than privacy may imbue the complaint with more force or significance, as property often trumps privacy in the legal balance. Intellectual property is also largely federal law (whereas privacy is state by state), which helps a plaintiff's case in terms of predictability and rhetorical force. Despite differences, the two fields seem to be merging in the public and legal spheres as creative and innovative work are felt to embody both an aspect of one's personality and a business asset. The discussion below explains in more detail the circumstances of and possible reasons for the merging. But whatever the explanation, that IP is fodder for a late twentieth-century story about the importance of privacy shapes policy choices for IP in the twenty-first century. These cases also demonstrate how plaintiffs exploit popular narratives of privacy and intellectual property to challenge those with wealth and power—those with substantial capital assets that increasingly take the form of intangible property in the Digital Age.[75] This is therefore also a story about how privacy meets twenty-first-century capital and sometimes even prevails.

In terms of copyright, there are two kinds of cases that raise privacy interests: those concerning unpublished works and those about published works used without authorization. The trademark and patent cases fall into the latter category, as all patents and trademark are public. The copyright cases concerning unpublished works date from the earliest of copyright disputes and resonate most directly with secrecy and creative autonomy interests.[76] They revolve around the publication of private letters or unfinished manuscripts. Although these kinds of copyright cases are not new to copyright law, their contemporary manifestation as privacy claims as well as copyright claims may be new. And their challenge to the First Amendment, whose importance and breadth has mushroomed in the internet age, is more significant today.

Cases about the unauthorized use of already-published work are also not new; that is what IP infringement cases tend to be about. But complaints that these unauthorized uses of already-published work are derogatory or offend authorial dignity are in sharper focus and intensify with the internet's facility to decontextualize, recontextualize, and broadly disseminate subject matter.[77] These cases contrast with more typical complaints over market control and the right of first publication or sale, which is what IP law traditionally enabled. Using copyright (or another IP regime) to protect privacy makes sense today when the internet's infinite capacity for remix and dissemination disrupts market exclusivity, control over one's identity (or "personality"), and privacy. Looking more closely at how and why IP claims overlap with stories about privacy invasions encourages us to rethink intellectual property's roles in the evolving dimensions of and need for privacy in the Digital Age.

A. Unpublished Works, or Privacy as Access to Spaces and Things

There are many examples over the years of authors (or owners) seeking to enjoin the publication of unpublished works. Famous authors and authors' estates, such as those of J. D. Salinger and James Joyce, asserted copyright to control access to drafts, journals, and notes.[78] Litigated on the public stage, often between scholars who seek access to archives and heirs who seek to honor the wishes of deceased relatives, these cases pit the dissemination of expression and the knowledge it contains against the control copyright provides to restrict any dissemination at all. Unlitigated but still debated, Willa Cather directed her estate executors and trustee not to license her work for anything but reproduction of the books she wrote (that is, no dramatizations, films, or other derivatives) and also not to allow publication or use of any part of her letters.[79] To some, the lack of dramatization of Cather's work led to its squandering as a cultural jewel. And as Eva Subotnik wrote, "Cather's instructions were given effect for six decades to prevent even scholarly quotation of her letters, leading to much paraphrasing—some of it divergent from the original text."[80] The embargo lasted until 2011, when Cather's nephew and executor died. In another case, Vladimir Nabokov requested that his unfinished manuscript, "The Original of Laura," be destroyed when he died. It sat unread from 1977 until 2008, when Nabokov's surviving heir, Dmitri, decided to extricate it from a Swiss Bank vault and publish it.[81] Brought as copyright cases, these disputes—or the desires that underlay them—were motivated by interests in seclusion and intellectual privacy.

Although the Digital Age may exacerbate the tensions between copyright's dissemination function and privacy's promise of seclusion, these kinds of cases date from the beginning of copyright law. In one of the first copyright cases brought under the Statute of Anne, the parties disputed the unlawful publication of Alexander Pope's private letters to Jonathan Swift (among others) by bookseller Edmund Curll. Pope filed the lawsuit pursuant to what has been described as the world's first copyright statute. But that complaint and the drama that surrounded it were as much about privacy as control over works of authorship.[82] A contemporary pamphlet that Pope published to contest Curll's surreptitious publication was titled "A Narrative of the Method by Which the Private Letters of Mr. Pope Have Been Procur'd and Publish'd by Edmund Curll, Bookseller."[83] That pamphlet aimed to prove that Curll's publishing of Pope's private letters was "flagrant enough as an Example, to induce the legislature to prevent for the future, an Enormity so prejudicial to every private Subject, and so destructive of Society itself."[84] It did not matter that Pope orchestrated the letters' publication to strategically manipulate the market in his works, exact revenge on Curll, and curry favor with the legislators debating copyright reform.[85] Privacy and copyright have overlapped since copyright's origins.[86]

And yet, the contemporary manifestations of copyright disputes describing privacy injuries are now clearer than ever. Starting in the late twentieth century with claims by authors over their unpublished letters and manuscripts, this dimension of privacy asserts an interest in preventing intrusion into seclusion of both a spatial and intellectual dimension—the right to one's home, effects, and mind free from the oversight of others. Characterized in this way, it is one of the most fundamental and established of constitutional privacy rights, only growing more insistent in the Digital Age of omnipresent surveillance.[87] When authors tell their survivors to burn their letters and manuscripts, as Franz Kafka famously did,[88] or tell their heirs to keep their unpublished writing and letters private, as Willa Cather did, audiences may feel deprived of great work or deep understanding. But the requests are understandable as expressions of desires to write from a place of freedom and to think and explore without interference from prying eyes (or today, webcams). These interests also concern public reputation—the "inviolate personality" that Warren and Brandeis described. Authors may hope to protect their established reputations built on prior works while alive and not risk reputational injury with unfinished works or private writings that can alter people's perceptions. Reports documented this latter concern for Cather, Nabokov, and Kafka. As Dmitri Nabokov reported, his father "did not want unfinished bits [of his work] trailing behind him after his death."[89]

Unpublished manuscript and letter cases project two established privacy dimensions (spaces and things) and one newer one (thoughts and beliefs, or intellectual privacy). The internet age exacerbates all of them, however, as spaces and things are today more virtual than tangible and thus harder to control. And intellectual privacy is more of a challenge in a digital world where to be secluded in one's thoughts requires disconnecting from all ordinary and everyday interactions, such as e-commerce, email, and cell phones. Are these interests still paramount, then, when the Digital Age has eroded them or made them quaint? In the twenty-first century, can we unplug entirely? If privacy interests remain strong despite their elusiveness today, why not withhold sending letters, emails, photographs, and texts? And for Cather and Kafka in another time, why not destroy the manuscripts and letters themselves rather than direct their destruction after death?

The answer from an author's perspective is straightforward: one writes or creates for oneself, not just for an audience.[90] For many artists and authors, expressing oneself in writing and creating works of authorship, which requires producing drafts in various stages of unfinishedness, is synonymous with thinking. To them, this practice is essential to processing the world and one's experiences in it.[91] Fixing those experiences as writing (or digital traces) marks their life, helping them to understand it; destroying such writings prematurely—that is, before one's life is over—diminishes the quality of living every day. Withdrawing from communicating with others for some may be necessary for productivity, but total withdrawal is a form of emaciation and decay. More so, destroying work has often been analogized to suicide or death.[92] We are glad that Max Brod (the friend to whom Kafka gave the destroy directive) did not burn Kafka's manuscripts, and that Willa Cather's heirs eventually released her letters. Those letters and manuscripts would have entered the public domain eventually, but if destroyed, no one would benefit from them at all.[93] And so the peace of mind that Cather and Kafka sustained in view of copyright's control over their private effects and intellectual works may have facilitated both living and writing as well as they did. One would be forgiven for thinking that copyright's term (life plus seventy years) is too long to wait to accomplish the goal of copyright: enabling the making and disseminating of creative work. But that is an argument about copyright's duration, not about whether copyright should protect against the premature divulgation of works of authorship, especially when protecting privacy might facilitate creative expression in the first place. If the extended duration of copyright concerns us in the Digital Age, when abundant works are created, disseminated, and orphaned, we might shorten copyright to the life of the author— coincident, as it turns out, with privacy claims, which still today in most jurisdictions expire upon a person's death.[94]

It bears reminding that statutory copyright did not extend to unpublished works until the passage of the 1976 Copyright Act, which took effect in 1978. So how did these complaints about unpublished manuscripts and letters sound in copyright in the first place? Today, copyright attaches to original works when fixed in a tangible medium whether or not the works are made public. All post-1978 works privately held in drawers, computer files, or email servers are automatically protected by copyright and, if quoted or distributed without consent, a copyright lawsuit may follow. Before 1978, manuscripts, letters, or photographs that were sequestered from the public and remained unpublished were subject to the law of unpublished manuscripts (tangible property) and sometimes also to state common-law copyright. Both of these legal domains may be importantly distinct and independent of federal copyright law, but not of privacy. They are the domain of personal property, chattels, and private land, residing most clearly in the Constitution's Fourth and Fifth Amendments. (For example, "Hands off my diaries!" "No trespassing in my home or bedroom drawers!") And they are also the domain of privacy torts—intrusion on seclusion, public disclosure of private facts, and breach of confidence— which common-law and state-based copyright was previously "enlisted" to protect, as the Supreme Court explained in a famous copyright case called *Harper & Row Publishers v. Nation Enterprises,* which cited the Warren and Brandeis article.[95]

When law decides the fate of an unpublished work as a personal "effect" (a letter) or to protect privacy (seclusion), the law's interest in them is not as a "public good" such as copyright. Public goods are by definition enjoyed by the public, which is why copyright *fair use* is an anchor of federal copyright law. Fair use (upon a balancing of four statutory factors) protects the right of *other* authors and audiences to quote and refer to works of authorship to promote progress.[96] Crucially, copyright law protects rights in original works of authorship for *both* authors and audiences, even concerning unpublished works. However, not until 1992 did Congress amend the Copyright Act's fair use provision to say that "the fact that a work is unpublished shall not itself bar a finding of fair use."[97] And so until then, unpublished copyrighted works, even post-1978, were practically off-limits to anyone but their authors and possessors. After 1992, unpublished work—at least according to the statutory admonition—became fair game.[98]

Privacy may serve the public interest, but it is not a public good. The "right to be let alone" may congeal civil society and help it prosper, but by definition there is no sharing of privacy with the public. We may protect each other's privacy through mutual restraint, but again, the internet age makes that increasingly difficult. And thus adding privacy to that which copyright might support, even unpublished works, "introduces a potent incoherency," as Robert Spoo wrote.[99] So what happens today, in our internet era, when copyright protects all tangible works of expression including the voluminous digital works that proliferate in quantities impossible to count, and privacy is more important and elusive than ever? When private thoughts or personality are sequestered from the public (or "unpublished," in the copyright sense) and also eligible for copyright protection, privacy and copyright become partners in a defense against Digital Age intrusions.

Abraham Drassinower resolved the tension between copyright (dissemination) and privacy (seclusion) by rejecting the "bifurcation of the unpublished or published status of the content of the work."[100] He wrote that this tension exacerbates "privacy-imperialism in respect of unpublished works" and instead favored describing the right as "the author's irreducible prerogative whether to publish."[101] As Drassinower explained, copyright protects the originality in works of authorship, not the personality of the author. He distinguished between "the meaning of publication in copyright and the meaning of publication in privacy,"[102] writing that whereas "the privacy analysis . . . target[s] the defendant's unauthorized dealings with personal information, the copyright analysis . . . target[s] the defendant's unauthorized dealings with a work of authorship."[103] Sometimes these analyses overlap, but often they do not:

> Unauthorized publication infringes copyright even in the absence of any breach of privacy. This is because the infringed right is not a right to privacy but a right of first publication. The author's complaint is not that his privacy has been violated [although it could be that too] but that his autonomy as a speaker—his right to speak or not to speak—has been ignored.[104]

By describing unauthorized publication (of published or unpublished work) as compelled speech that interferes with the autonomy and dignity of the author, Drassinower, perhaps unwittingly, flirted with the U.S. Constitution's First and Fifth Amendments, which shape contemporary privacy dimensions. In doing so, he called into service the autonomy and self-determination interests that privacy and copyright explicitly serve.

In the internet age, it is too easy to say that privacy is about "personal information" (namely, facts), which is unprotected by copyright law. Copyright only protects original works of authorship—their expressive form but not the facts or ideas the expressions contain.[105] This long-standing fact/idea exclusion in copyright law is essential to its facilitation of free speech and new works of authorship. But the cases mentioned above are not only about personal information kept secluded from the public and divulged without permission. They are about the *forms of expression* that authors chose to keep from the public eye.[106] The deliberate choice to refrain from making one's expression public at present or at all is an act that copyright law robustly protects.[107]

Practically speaking, anything secret embodied in a writing is protected as any other secret or private concern—to the extent of its effective seclusion. Copyright fair use and the fact/idea exclusion are not tools to open up a bedroom drawer or to unlock a diary. Copyright protects secrets embodied in tangible works of authorship that are sequestered from the public eye; it also protects one's privacy in seclusion and in those personal effects. In other words, when copyright law protects works of authorship, the privacy concerning those works in view of their secluded physical location is also protected. Storing a manuscript in a vault keeps it from being viewed as a thing and a copyrighted work; sending an email, though less private, makes it no less copyright-protected. And so copyright law survives when privacy claims diminish—another reason for their partnership in privacy battles.

B. Limited Publications, or Privacy as Control over Our Bodies and Minds

The looming problem in the internet age is not the difficulty of protecting actual seclusion and preventing trespass to things or "chattels," as they say in property law. Keeping a manuscript in a vault remains possible, however inconvenient and unlikely. In the Digital Age, the problem is that all digital works, even when shared privately, are *publi*cations in effect.

Private emails reside on servers uncontrolled by sender or receiver and are owned or accessible by third parties or employers. Messages sent over social media, despite being labeled "private," travel over platforms accessible to and hackable by people with rudimentary computer skills. This fact of life in the twenty-first century renders outdated the published/unpublished difference in copyright. And it brings to the fore the challenge of self-determination and autonomy—what some would call the problem of privacy as *control*.[108] Participating in civil society and being an author or innovator today demands engagement with the internet.[109] Public spaces are (and will remain) surveillance-capable, collecting and transmitting image and video of movement, faces, and sounds. Although methods exist to embolden privacy as seclusion and protect access to our "papers and effects," these dimensions of privacy are becoming less realistic. Privacy over our bodies (faces, fingerprints, DNA), our minds and relationships (decisional privacy), and our personal information is increasingly at risk. Disputes over these forms of privacy are not only about control but also about *context*. And they arise alongside intellectual property disputes because copyright, trademark, and patent law give their owners control over many contexts of use.

In copyright law specifically, early cases about "limited publication" artificially hardened the distinction between published and unpublished works, assuming away the challenges of the internet age to come. In those cases, a general publication occurred if a performer or politician presented to "the general public in a manner as allows the public to exercise dominion and control over the work," or if the "work is exhibited or displayed in such a manner as to permit unrestricted copying by the general public."[110] Prior to 1989 in the United States, this kind of general publication without proper copyright notice and registration could have resulted in losing copyright protection. This harsh consequence led many courts to hold that the publication was "limited" and the copyright preserved within the author's control.

The doctrine of "limited publication" became less relevant for works created after 1978. Under the new Copyright Act, all works, whether published or not, were protected if original and fixed. Then, by 1989, when the United States became a signatory to the Berne Convention, copyright notice and registration were also no longer required for copyright protection. The practical effects of these legal changes were that nearly everything was copyrighted and also that sharing of one's own work, whether in a limited or a more general manner, did not eviscerate copyright protection. However, significant consequences did arise for unauthorized copying and sharing of another's work. Copyright *protection* (due to publication or nonpublication) was no longer the issue, but copyright *enforcement* would be. In 1989, the World Wide Web was new, and the widespread use of email was only a few years away. Changes to copyright law making copyrighted works more promiscuous and democratically attainable arrived right in time for the internet's seemingly infinite copying and distribution capacity. These changes brought an explosion of copyrighted works—nearly everything on the internet today—and the potential for viral and infinite infringement.

Before email existed, when parties fought over unpublished letters, the law was that the owner or addressee of the physical letter had no copyright interest to publish the content of the letter further.[111] According to courts, the letter writer and copyright author had a right to control the expressive work (the content of the letter and thus the thoughts expressed in it) if not the actual letter itself (the thing or "effect").[112] Authorial control also relied on the right of first publication, as mentioned above, defined as a general publication to a broad public, not to a single recipient.[113] The eighteenth- and nineteenth-century court cases concerning private correspondence made these points clear, easily blending copyright and privacy interests in their analyses.[114] These issues are not as easily resolved in twenty-first-century copyright cases about similar forms of private writings. These cases concern the lawfulness of leaked email, conference call recordings, and transcripts; the publication of purloined or surreptitiously made photographs and videos; and the distribution of "revenge porn" by scorned lovers. (Revenge porn is sometimes also known as "nonconsensual pornography"—videos or images made between intimate partners that are later used to harass, intimidate, or embarrass.) These are Digital Age versions of eighteenth- and nineteenth-century copyright disputes that raise newer and perhaps more acute privacy concerns than those from centuries past.[115]

The concept of "limited publication" loses coherence in the internet age when almost anything is accessible on the web. We can assert our intention to limit publication of our email or text message to only the private recipient. We can claim that web postings protected through passwords are private (as in "secluded") with an intention to keep the expressive work from the general public. But in truth, these works are sent over platforms that are unreliably leaky, and their formal terms of use put users on notice of that leakiness.[116] For this reason, privacy claims usually fail. But many of these copyright claims fail as well. When they are brought to enjoin the further dissemination of photographs, correspondence, or videos, two factors contribute to defendant wins: the inevitable publicness of everyday life and copyright's status as a public good promoting "progress of science."[117] Copyright fair use and the First Amendment prioritize information dissemination and openness over secrecy, and these cases turn on these bedrock principles. Only in the rare cases concerning severe bodily intrusion and intolerable interference in the privacy of mind and personality do plaintiffs prevail; some of these cases are discussed later in this chapter. These cases do not really concern protecting the original work of authorship as such (arguably copyright's purpose) but instead adjudicate breaches of confidence and trust—an ancient and rarely used tort today.[118]

Swatch Group Management Services v. Bloomberg (2014) and Online Policy Group v. Diebold, Inc. (2004) are two "limited publication" copyright cases that masqueraded as privacy breach of confidence claims.[119] In both cases, private or semiprivate communications were shared more widely than their original senders intended. In Swatch, the Swatch company held a conference call discussing financial analysis and future strategy that included hundreds of investors. Swatch recorded the call but asked the listeners to refrain from further recording. Nonetheless, a Bloomberg employee on the call made an unauthorized recording and shared the entire transcript with Bloomberg subscribers. In an effort to retract the dissemination because of its sensitive content, Swatch registered the audio recording with the copyright office and sued Bloomberg for copyright infringement.

Both the district court and the court of appeals determined that Bloomberg's use of the transcript was permissible copyright fair use because the use was reporting what Swatch said on the call. News reporting is quintessential fair use under copyright law because it transforms the original content created (here, to demonstrate Swatch's financial strength) into a new work with a new message (here, about Swatch's behavior and statements). Transformative uses under copyright law are presumptively fair without evidence of injury to the market for the underlying work (and there was no such market for the conference call transcript). Additionally, the courts explained that Swatch had no legitimate copyright interest as an author in the audio recording of the call because it "did not seek to profit from the publication of the . . . call in audio or written format. The copyright-protected aspects of the earnings call—that is, the manner by which the facts were expressed—thus were of no value to Swatch or Swatch Group except insofar as they served to convey important information to the analysts in attendance."[120] This may have been true of Swatch, but it is not usually true of most authors who have multiple legitimate interests in their work, some of them unrelated to their market value.

Reproducing and widely disseminating the entire confidential transcript in written and audio form may seem like an egregious case of breach of trust and implied contract. But it is not a difficult copyright case. Usually, when "too much" of a work is copied, the fairness balance tilts toward the copyright owner. And surely Bloomberg could have conveyed the information contained in the call without reproducing the entire call verbatim—that is, without clearly committing copyright infringement. But the court did not think that mattered in this context:

> In the context of news reporting and analogous activities, . . . the need to convey information to the public accurately may in some instances make it desirable and consonant with copyright law for a defendant to faithfully reproduce an original work without alteration. Courts often find such uses transformative by emphasizing the altered purpose or context of the work, as evidenced by surrounding commentary or criticism. . . . Here, Bloomberg provided no additional commentary or analysis of Swatch Group's earnings call. But by disseminating not just a written transcript or article but an actual sound recording, Bloomberg was able to convey with precision not only the raw data of the Swatch Group executives' words, but also more subtle indications of meaning inferable from their hesitation, emphasis, tone of voice, and other such aspects of their delivery.[121]

In other words, this work of authorship was only marginally protected by copyright law because of its densely informative content, and because Bloomberg's news reporting use of the work was a classic exception to copyright exclusivity to serve the public interest in the dissemination of truthful information about a matter of public importance. Despite a straightforward case on the law, the copyright claims were thoroughly and expensively litigated in the federal trial as well as twice in the appellate courts. The case was an important victory for fair use and news reporting. It is nonetheless troubling if one wants to reasonably rely on maintaining confidentiality amid participants in closed conversations.

The case's resolution would likely have been the same had Swatch Group litigated it as breach of trust or implied contract. The group on the call was too large to reasonably imply confidentiality or mutual assent to the call's confidential terms. Nonetheless, that it was a fiercely argued and contested case, even on copyright grounds, signals the focused attention on the privacy interests at stake. Those interests center on control over expressions to manage one's reputation, identity, and relationship with others. Sharing work with the understanding that one's private audience will stay private is critical to forming and developing one's identity and supportive relationships with others. We may scoff at this description applying to the Swatch Group. But imagine the Swatch call as instead a confidential online support group for small businesspeople, single mothers, or alcoholics. The privacy harm and the stakes in avoiding it become clearer.

At issue in *Online Policy Group v. Diebold* were private emails internal to the Diebold company, which manufactures voting machines.[122] Individuals unaffiliated with Diebold accessed the company's email archive and made it public, revealing defects in the voting machines. The company claimed that accessing and reposting the emails violated copyright law because the emails were copyrighted works. But the court disagreed, explaining that many of the emails were not subject to copyright protection. (Generally, emails are copyright-protected as original works of expression fixed in a tangible medium. These emails largely contained facts, which are unprotected, and thus their copyright status was "thin.")[123] Even if the emails were protected by copyright, however, their unauthorized use was not copyright infringement because of their unambiguous public value: "It is hard to imagine a subject the discussion of which could be more in the public interest. If Diebold's machines in fact do tabulate voters' preferences incorrectly, the very legitimacy of elections would be suspect."[124] Touted as a win for fair use and for copyright law generally, *Diebold*'s unfortunate underside was the reality of insecure email systems and the inevitability of privacy breaches. We may agree that information of faulty election systems should be publicized and fixed, even at the cost of a company's reputation and the limitation of copyright's scope. But we might also worry that these breaches are part of the new normal of social and business relationships and that legal redress for the breaches may be elusive.

Both *Swatch* and *Diebold* develop the expectation of broken or breakable electronic communication systems and the shrinking of opportunities for reasonably reliable private correspondence and communication. For example, we might simply expect that email communication, online commerce, and password-protected platforms are public, whether or not they are asserted to be private. Shifting expectations massively shrink the world of truly private spaces, relationships, and expressions. But this is not how we live, nor is it how privacy law at the Supreme Court and elsewhere is being shaped. In 2014, the Supreme Court held that cell phones and their contents are private personal effects that require a warrant for search.[125] And in 2018, the Supreme Court held that cell phone data shared with cell phone providers (required for the phones to function) is likewise private information subject to Fourth Amendment requirements.[126] Our expectation of privacy—at least according to the Supreme Court—is expanding, not retracting. Thus, the injury described in both *Swatch* and *Diebold* is not copyright's failure to protect the original works of authorship. The harm is the degradation of relationships formed through digital communication because of the privacy breach, even if the breach is authorized by copyright law itself. As Ari Waldman wrote, treating breach of confidences "as theft of property gives copyright law too much credit."[127] This is true, but it does not stop people and organizations from using copyright law (or intellectual property generally) to protect those confidences when they are embodied in tangible form and are copyright-protected. The expectation of privacy is so critical for generating and sustaining important social relationships and associations that it becomes an acceptable legal argument to assert copyright in email and conference calls.

We may be understandably skeptical of the privacy injuries in *Swatch* and *Diebold*. Copyright law's failure to recognize the privacy interests in these cases may on balance be good for copyright law's constitutional goal of promoting the progress of science (here, of market transparency and election accuracy). My point, however, especially for the next set of cases about unauthorized use of semipublic copyrighted photographs, is that "progress" in the Digital Age is broader and untethered to knowledge in a disciplinary or institutional sense. Recall that "progress of science" in the Constitution originally concerned the classical "sciences"—the study of geography, politics, war, and the like.[128] Copyright law has evolved over centuries, and now it protects all works of authorship without discrimination as to subject or person, and thus progress of "science" means much more. Many celebrate this expansion (even as it extends to conference calls and emails) because in our digitally enabled creative culture, copyright may foment inclusive authorship and promote values of diversity, access, autonomy, and free speech. By serving non-elite authorship and these democratic values, however, copyright interests may partner with privacy to encourage initial production but also may limit dissemination. The eventual copyright goal may be to promote the progress of public enlightenment through widespread dissemination, but copyright's privacy dimension—especially in the Digital Age—increasingly postpones that possibility. "Progress" thus paradoxically means both control for seclusion and also dissemination. Digital Age affordances of copy, remix, and share run headlong into privacy's expansion of copyright protection.

1. The Special Case of Limited Publication Photographs: Privacy over Body and Mind

Some limited publication cases have combined copyright and privacy to favor the plaintiff. These are the more severe cases of intrusion mentioned earlier. Under copyright law, cases involving photographs and videos, even those that include violence or sex, should be analyzed like any other. And yet, in these particular cases, courts struggle to remain consistent and neutral. Understandably, plaintiffs seek quick relief from unintended internet dissemination of humiliating or revealing photographs or videos. Also weighing in plaintiffs' favor, the social meanings and consequences of embarrassing photos or videos meant to remain private are usually very different from the array of social meanings of already-published works by authors.[129] Images circulate more widely and rapidly on the internet than written text.[130] Subjects may therefore experience these kinds of visual disclosures as particularly harmful. Indeed, in the early days of privacy law, under the burgeoning right of publicity, lawyers and commentators compared the unauthorized dissemination of a person's likeness as an "act of invasion of an individual's privacy . . . possibly more formidable and more painful in its consequences than an actual bodily assault might be."[131] In "The Right to Privacy," Warren and Brandeis described "the mental pain and distress" of privacy invasions, which are akin to unauthorized publicity, as "far greater than could be inflicted by mere bodily injury."[132] Privacy invasions concerning one's body and image are intimately tied with identity and thus can feel like a physical assault or bodily intrusion.

The reasonable extent of body searches by safety and security professionals, and our loss of control over choices concerning our bodies—be it in terms of medical care, reproduction, or sexual intimacy—are at the center of public debate today. Fighting for and demanding bodily autonomy has roots in the abolition and suffrage movements, which are formidable national narratives attesting to fundamental values of equality and freedom as essential to dignity. Today, those fights continue most notably regarding voting access and discrimination, racialized police brutality, the weakening of women's reproductive rights, and a heightened awareness around sexual harassment and abuse. When private or semiprivate photographs or videos circulate publicly for profit, attention, or spite, nothing less than bodily integrity and physical liberty is at stake. Ari Waldman explained that victims of revenge pornography surely "object to their images being 'taken' and 'misused' in a harmful, unexpected way. But that concern is, at best, secondary to the victim's and society's chief objection . . .: it invades victims' privacy and transforms them into sexual objects for others."[133]

Revenge pornography is a significant social problem, which some seek to combat through criminal and civil sanctions and others through copyright law.[134] But many challenges exist to punishing nonconsensual pornography with copyright law. One is that victims are rarely the authors (or owners) of the photographs and thus lack standing under copyright law. Another is that copyright law cannot pick winners and losers in the marketplace of speech and expression; like all laws regulating expression, copyright law must be content-neutral or else be narrowly tailored to achieve the highest of governmental purposes.[135] Hate speech, intimidation, and harassment are unprotected under the First Amendment, and preventing or punishing nonconsensual pornography (a form of intimidation and harassment) might be a noble governmental objective. But copyright law's broad protective brush tends to be insufficiently precise to filter consensual from nonconsensual pornography.[136] Distinguishing consensual from nonconsensual pornography, just like high art from low art, is a mislaid task for copyright law, whose chief purpose is protecting original works of authorship without discrimination.[137]

These doctrinal (some would say legalistic) hurdles to using copyright to prevent or punish certain forms of privacy-invasive publications—such as nonconsensual pornography or the unauthorized dissemination of personal photographs—resemble those described in "The Right to Privacy" over a century ago. When copyright and tort laws were insufficient to address the proposed need for protection from invasive photography and yellow journalism in the early days of mechanical reproduction, lawyers and courts birthed a new legal right. The privacy interests were so significant and the cultural context so changed that legal limitations in statutes and common law presented new arguments. These same innovations (others may say sleights of hand) have arisen in recent court cases not only about revenge pornography but also about more quotidian photographs of semiprivate weddings and barroom antics. Such cases force judges to address hard questions about whether copyright can or should care more about the frequent losers in its regime (namely, victims of privacy invasions) and whether such preferences are consistent with our constitutional values of free speech and procedural fairness.

Monge v. Maya Magazines, Inc. (2012) concerned a celebrity couple who sued a gossip magazine over dissemination of wedding pictures leaked by an assistant.[138] The plaintiff and subject of the photographs, Noelia Monge, did not take the pictures (she was not the copyright author), and yet the court nevertheless allowed her to bring the copyright claim to suppress the photographs' publication.[139] This is the first strange aspect of the case. The second is that the appellate court (reversing the trial court) held that the gossip magazine's news reporting was not fair use, even though news reporting normally qualifies as such. The court reasoned that although the purpose of disclosure and secondary use (news) was different from the reason the photos were originally made (to document a wedding), this fact was insufficient to transform the photographer's work under copyright law. The appellate court also based its reversal on the defendant's "undisputably commercial" use and the plaintiff's intent to keep the wedding and the photographs secret.[140]

To many copyright lawyers, the *Monge* outcome was surprising. Indeed, the combination of a lengthy appellate decision accompanied by a dissent demonstrated a close case on the legal issues. One possible explanation for the plaintiff's success in this case is that the photos remained unpublished prior to their being leaked to the press by a turncoat confidant. The photos were secluded "effects" (to use the privacy parlance of the Fourth Amendment, protecting the "right of people to be secure in their . . . papers and effects"). The court explained that the copyright holder's right of first publication—an ancient and formidable right under copyright law—may be stronger than the public's "right to know" about the wedding as depicted in the photographs. The likelihood that the first publication of celebrities' wedding pictures would be especially valuable did not help defendant either.[141]

The legal wrinkles in the plaintiff's case—the plaintiff's dubious copyright ownership in the photographs and the fact that a secret wedding between two celebrities is news—did not convince the majority to rule for the news organization. *Monge v. Maya* resembled the formative Supreme Court copyright case of *Harper & Row v. Nation*, in which the court held that first publication of a purloined manuscript detailing critical historical events—President Gerald Ford's pardoning of Richard Nixon—was not fair use.[142] *Harper & Row* turned on the fact that the manuscript was soon to be published by Harper & Row and *The Nation* scooped the story, usurping plaintiff's licensing revenue. The privacy interest in *Harper & Row* was meager compared with *Monge*, but the secluded character of the eye-opening and newsworthy content was similar.

Curiously, the *Monge* court explicitly but unconvincingly disclaimed the privacy interest at the center of Ms. Monge's case:

> Although the published photos were not highly artistic in nature, they do have a defining and common characteristic—until [the magazine] hit the stands, they were unpublished. We pointedly note that we address the unpublished status of the photos only under copyright principles, not privacy law. . . . Maya's publication undoubtedly supplanted Plaintiffs' right to control the first public appearance of the photographs.[143]

Cloaking privacy in intimate portraits with a copyright claim for the right of first publication of those images did not fool many plaintiffs; the case was an invitation to bring more such claims on the basis of copyright law. The decision may have been on copyright principles, but it was brought not for reasons of protecting a work of authorship and the originality that inheres in that work. (And it was not brought by the photographer himself!) It was brought to protect the *subject* of the photograph—her personality and her self-determination in her presentation to the public as a married person. It was an old-style privacy claim based on seclusion of one's body and intimate facts. It was also a new-style privacy claim based on autonomy over personality and intimate relationships in the Digital Age, in which autonomy and personality are harder to manage. And yet the case was won on copyright grounds.

A wedding photo may not be embarrassing, although wedded couples may still wish to keep the intimate moments of their event private. Drunk and sexualized antics in a bar are by contrast likely to be embarrassing, made worse if captured on camera and widely disseminated. In *Balsley v. LFP, Inc.* (2012), the plaintiff was a newscaster who engaged in a wet T-shirt contest in a bar. Without her consent, a bar patron took a photograph of the contest and published it online.[144] The photograph was posted first on Lenshead.com, an adult website, and later in *Hustler*, a monthly pornographic magazine. After the photograph posted, the newscaster lost her job. To control the photograph's further distribution, the plaintiff acquired rights to the photograph from the bar patron and sued *Hustler* for its publication of the photograph, claiming copyright infringement as well as violations of privacy. Only the copyright claim survived to a jury verdict; the privacy claims were dismissed. Finding no fair use (that is, no newsworthiness and no transformative use), the jury awarded the plaintiff copyright damages of $135,000 plus attorney fees.

The appellate court affirmed the jury verdict. As with *Monge*, in *Balsley* the plaintiff was uninterested in the photograph as an author of an original work or as an owner of valuable copyright. Nonetheless, the appellate court accepted as plausible the jury's finding that the commercial use of the photograph by others depressed the plaintiff's opportunities to market it *should she have so chosen*. This justification rings hollow given that the plaintiff sought to suppress the photograph's publication and keep it from the marketplace entirely. A more honest analysis would have acknowledged that the copyright claim protected the plaintiff's near-naked body from ridicule and objectification on the internet.

It is easy to imagine that the jury was motivated to help the plaintiff and "reached" to do so. They were left only to decide a copyright issue because the privacy claims were dismissed under the First Amendment (which does not so easily limit copyright claims).[145] The photograph's dissemination caused the plaintiff significant career damage, which was exacerbated by *Hustler*'s combined sexual objectification and commercial exploitation. And it is likewise hard to avoid reading sympathy for the plaintiff and disdain for *Hustler* into the appellate court's opinion when it recounts *Hustler*'s "Hot News Babe" labeling of the contest and the magazine's description of the plaintiff as a "tasty talking head" alongside photographs of her exposed body. Stylized as a copyright case because the privacy claims failed, this was really a case raising privacy claims, but for the event having taken place in public. The plaintiff's lawyer persisted even after the privacy claims were dismissed for First Amendment reasons ("newsworthiness" and her behavior having been in public). He believed, correctly, that if the case ever got to a jury on the copyright claim, the jury would be moved to help the plaintiff given the harmful effects of internet dissemination to which anyone could be subject. To be sure, the sexualized images, the aggravated context of the photographs, and the network effect of the internet made this a particularly sympathetic case for the plaintiff.[146] But photos of public figures in public are usually fair game for the purposes of news, even the salacious type. That the plaintiff won here demonstrates the pull of the privacy interests in bodily autonomy and the strength of copyright doctrine to compensate for privacy law's limitations.

One way to think about *Balsley* is as a limited publication case, in which there was no implied permission to make or distribute the photograph from the limited public sphere of the bar. This makes it a spatial privacy case, like *Monge*, protecting intended seclusion of places and things. But a public bar is a far cry from a private wedding, and without more to establish a reasonable expectation of privacy, the plaintiff waived her interest in seclusion when she publicly performed in the contest. Her privacy interest lost, copyright law was brought in to resurrect it.

A different way to think about *Balsley* is that the surreptitious and demeaning uses of the plaintiff's image were forms of bodily appropriation, an "ancient" harm (to quote Paul Ohm) deeply rooted in the Constitution.[147] As such, the case resembles revenge pornography, for which advocacy around specially crafted laws is gaining traction.[148] To be sure, revenge pornography tends to be defined as a violation of trust between intimate partners, and *Balsley* does not include that critical feature. But the nonconsensual publication of sexually graphic images that produces grave emotional and dignitary harms, increases risks of physical assault, and may chill self-expression and even ruin lives is certainly at the heart of this case and others concerning nonconsensual photographic copyright.[149] Unlike *Monge*, the plaintiff in *Balsley* acquired copyright in the image to properly initiate the copyright lawsuit. But like *Monge*, she did not have an authorship interest in the photograph, and the lawsuit was not brought to protect or sequester the work of authorship for later dissemination and commercial exploitation. Like the concerns animating "The Right to Privacy" a century earlier, the *Balsley* plaintiff brought her lawsuit to protect her personality and private identity.

In this case, like others, we witness the power of copyright law in contemporary society because only the copyright claim survived when privacy was really at issue. The privacy claims based on bodily appropriation, intrusion into seclusion, and misappropriation of identity all failed under a doctrinal legal analysis. We might explain the strength of the plaintiff's copyright claim on the basis of the "propertization" of IP.[150] Property tends to win over other less concrete injuries, and privacy is neither property nor a concrete concept. Moreover, privacy claims wither in the face of the First Amendment, whereas intellectual property is more resilient because it is said to already incorporate First Amendment safeguards. As the Supreme Court has said, copyright is not opposed to free speech but an engine of it.[151] The fair use doctrine, first sale principle, and fact/idea exclusions preserve the breathing room for free speech in copyright law. (Similar limitations also exist in trademark law.) In the internet age, however, it may be time to reconsider how well digital copyright integrates First Amendment freedoms, just as it may be time to embrace privacy's evolving contours in light of its increased urgency in our technosocial and networked twenty-first-century culture. When privacy and intellectual property claims are brought to address the same harm, the First Amendment as a categorical limitation should similarly cut through both.

Privacy is as much a fundamental right as its sister right of free speech. Yet the two are often exercised in opposing directions. And the First Amendment is, well, first. When copyright can serve privacy interests, as in *Monge* and *Balsley*, plaintiffs and courts chart a path forward that they may perceive as harmonious with free speech. This path may require willfully ignoring inconsistencies in legal doctrine. But those inconsistencies are precisely what pushes law reform to address new challenges of contemporary culture.

2. The Special Case of Inventions: Privacy over Bodies and Minds

In the patent context, inventions regulating or monitoring bodies, such as digitally connected pacemakers or health trackers, raise issues of users' privacy. Patented medical treatment or devices often require information or mechanical inputs from natural bodily functions to produce the innovative outcome. This was the case in a 1994 lawsuit brought between two drug manufacturers over a patented antibacterial medication. Zenith Laboratories made a product competitive with Bristol Myers Squibb's patented formulation of cefadroxil (a treatment for antibiotic-resistant bacterial infections).[152] The allegation of infringement required comparing Bristol Myers Squibb's drug and the *digested* form of Zenith's drug. In other words, the unlawful making and using of Bristol Myers Squibb's patented medicine occurred as part of the normal function of the patient's digestive tract. In its pre-ingested form, Zenith's drug did not infringe Bristol Myers Squibb's patented medicine. When patients ingested Zenith's drug, however, it transformed into the same chemical composition of Bristol Myers Squibb's drug. In this case, Zenith was accused of "contributory infringement" because, as the new drug's maker, it was inducing patients who took the medication to "make" or "use" what resembled exactly Bristol Myers Squibb's drug in their stomachs. The patient was the direct infringer, although for public relations and reputational reasons, Bristol Myers Squibb sued Zenith alone.

The appellate court decision in this case did not dwell on the patient or the patient's body, except as a site of experiment and evidence.[153] It talked about "x-ray diffraction patterns" of crystals in a patient's stomach and the "in situ or in vivo conversion" through the digestive processes of the patented medicine.[154] Left unaddressed was whether Zenith could defend the lawsuit by insisting on the patient's privacy—her right to be left alone (both the body and images of it). This is surprising because in an earlier, more famous case involving proprietary interests in one's body (and the profits made from it), a court dismissed the conversion claim and held for the patient on privacy alone.

That case is the now-famous 1990 dispute between John Moore and the University of California Board of Regents, when cells from Moore's spleen were used without his consent to produce lucrative medical research results.[155] Moore was treated successfully for leukemia by doctors at the UCLA Medical Center. Over the course of his treatment and without clear consent, doctors and researchers harvested cells from Moore's bone marrow, semen, and spleen because his cells proved to have special immunity-boosting properties. The Board of Regents received a patent on a use of the special cells, and Moore sued seeking to share in the profits, which he argued were derived from his body and thus his property. The California Supreme Court eventually ruled that patients have no rights in their blood and tissue that are voluntarily discarded, and thus they also have no interest in the commercial products derived from them.

The California Supreme Court took Moore's privacy and personality claims more seriously, however. It asked, "if the courts have found a sufficient proprietary interest in one's *persona*, how could one not have a right in one's own genetic material, something far more profoundly the essence of one's human uniqueness than a name or a face?"[156] The court directly compared bodies and identities, their invasion being a harm that both property and privacy can address. This analogy is at the heart of evolving intellectual property claims today, combining personal privacy with intangible property. To its own question, the court had several responses, one directing us to the patented invention, another distinguishing property (and intellectual property) from privacy:

> As the defendants' patent makes clear . . . the goal and result of defendants' efforts has been to manufacture lymphokines. Lymphokines, unlike a name or a face, have the same molecular structure in every human being and the same, important functions in every human being's immune system. Moreover, the particular genetic material which is responsible for the natural production of lymphokines, and which defendants use to manufacture lymphokines in the laboratory, is also the same in every person; it is no more unique to Moore than the number of vertebrae in the spine or the chemical formula of hemoglobin.[157]

In this analysis, the California Supreme Court erased Moore's identity from his cells by describing their transformation into the issued invention at issue. This denied Moore any inventor status in the patent, which might be uncontroversial because his role was simply as a patient who acceded to the ordinary discard of his bodily tissue. But it also denied him any profits from the invention, which is perhaps more controversial given the defendants' enrichment at the expense of Moore's privacy. Moore was not an inventor, the court said, despite the invasion of his privacy being central to the invention.

The court next addressed Moore's right to refuse medical treatment in terms of unlawful bodily intrusion. Moore cited as support an earlier California Supreme Court case that the lower court had relied on to rule in Moore's favor, which stated that "every human being of adult years and sound mind has a right to determine what shall be done with his own body."[158] Agreeing with Moore, the lower court had said that "a patient must have the ultimate power to control what becomes of his or her tissues."[159] The difference between informed consent (which Moore gave to be treated) and the conversion of his discarded body parts into research specimens (for which he did not give permission, not having thought it necessary) made no difference to the lower court. "To hold otherwise would open the door to a massive invasion of human privacy and dignity in the name of medical progress."[160] But the California Supreme Court disagreed, driving a wedge between property rights (in the form of the aforementioned conversion) and privacy in one's body:

> [O]ne may earnestly wish to protect privacy and dignity without accepting the extremely problematic conclusion that interference with those interests amounts to a conversion of personal property. Nor is it necessary to force the round pegs of "privacy" and "dignity" into the square hole of "property" in order to protect the patient, since the fiduciary-duty and informed-consent theories protect these interests directly by requiring full disclosure. . . . [A] fair balancing of the relevant policy considerations counsels against extending the tort [of conversion].[161]

The court appeared to believe that Moore (or any patient) could maintain his dignity through informed consent to be treated, even as his proprietary rights in his body were diminished. The court asserted that the latter is unrelated to the former, while forgetting that standard property rights in land, personal belongings, and tenancies require the protection of a person's space, things, and labor—all central to individual dignity and indeed to privacy.

On the one hand, John Moore's case is praised for promoting new life-saving medicines by preserving access to vital biomaterials, while at the same time recognizing the importance of informed consent as a feature of doctor-patient relationships. On the other hand, the case has been widely criticized. Moore's treatment has been compared to "bioslavery" and the court's celebration of doctor-researchers an example of a misguided romance with the myth of the romantic author and inventor.[162] Today, the legal status of bodies and body parts remains contested among bioethicists and lawyers, with the courts debating most recently whether DNA traces inadvertently left on a police chair or water glass are voluntarily relinquished and thus "evidence" free for authorities to take and search.[163] Behind these debates is the increasingly fraught distinction between public and private— what is relinquished and what is retained. These debates are escalating given developing technologies that scan a person's face, voice, or movements in public without their knowledge and recreate their private identity, locations, and habits in order to store, share, and analyze along with like data from millions of other people.[164]

Many of these debates momentarily resolve in terms of informed consent and choice (discussed in the equality context in chapter 2). This reminds us that property and privacy are waivable assets rather than inalienable rights. Indeed, John Moore's only surviving claims were a breach of fiduciary duty and a lack of informed consent regarding his treating physicians. Thus, unlike the copyright decisions described earlier, in which the copyright claim remained the only chance to vindicate privacy interests, in the patent context, the facts supporting harms to relational privacy and bodily autonomy are sufficiently strong to keep common-law torts alive. Either way, the intersection of intellectual property and privacy related to our bodies and identities seems inevitable and increasing. That intersection also focuses attention on how our technology-saturated society elevates and reconfigures both intellectual property and privacy for our changed world.

C. Reuse, or Privacy as Safeguarding Relationships ("Privacy in Context")

Most intellectual property infringement actions arise because an author (or owner) voluntarily disseminates a work and then later objects to subsequent unauthorized reuse. IP and privacy interests clash when objection to the reuse is not to protect the work's market value or its reauthorization in various derivatives to reach additional markets but instead to protect the private identity and personal relationships of the author, owner, or subject.

Typically, IP owners complain that an unauthorized copy (of a book or an invention) will undercut the owner's controlled sale of copies. Competition from copies lowers the cost to purchasers. IP owners have the right and often the desire to control exact copies for the purpose of earning revenue from their work. For example, unauthorized digital file-sharing of music is said to interfere with the music copyright owner's legitimate expectation of revenue from copies of that music. Unauthorized copyright derivatives, such as sequels and translations or patentable improvements and related inventive spin-offs, are also typically licensed or made with IP owners' permission and are an expected part of the revenue from their work. For example, Lucas Industries owns and licenses uses of *Star Wars* characters and plots. J. K. Rowling owns and licenses Harry Potter universe costumes and merchandise as derivative works. Improvements to patented gadgets—new materials or parts—are incorporated into original patented inventions with original patentees' permission. These are considered typical uses of IP's exclusive rights.

Less typical but growing in frequency are lawsuits over unauthorized copies used not to compete in the market for copies or derivatives but to parody, comment on, or critique the copyrighted work or trademarked goods. When a Missouri teenager's T-shirt company printed "South Butt" on T-shirts alluding to the brand "The North Face" and included a reversal of the company's triple arc logo on the merchandise, The North Face sued not to prevent consumer confusion or control copies of its goods but to end the ridicule.[165] Suits like this have been frequent in the late twentieth and early twenty-first centuries, in part because copying and manufacturing expressive works and consumer goods are easier than ever before. These are lawsuits not to control the market for one's work or its legitimate derivatives but to defend identity and personality in increasingly frenetic and chaotic public forums.

The diverse cases in this category of reuse center on reputation and relationships that inhere in the intellectual property itself. These reuses are objectionable recontextualizations from an owner's point of view (the original owner or heir) or from the subject of the work's point of view. None of these objections are based on intrusion into seclusion, protecting sequestered things or effects, bodily autonomy, or private, personal information, because all the work and inventions at issue are already public. These disputes concern the control of identity and relationships through their public manifestations in copyrighted works, trademarks, or inventions. A private relationship's significance—like that of a romantic partnership—often rests on public acceptance and avoiding public denigration. Similarly, one's identity as a creator or innovator is intimately bound with the public presentation of one's work, its recognition, and its celebration and critique. Intended for public audiences, creative expression and scientific achievements are predictably targets of disagreeable attention such that creators and innovators and their heirs harness IP law to control negative treatment.

1. Owner Objections

In a copyright or trademark context, parties fight over the recontextualization of published work. Authors or owners bring these cases because the reuse offends them or demeans the work or brand. (In the few patent cases noted below, the issue manifested as a desire to disassociate from the invention, despite having been a collaborator.) In the copyright and trademark context, these cases nearly always turn on fair use and the weight of the First Amendment to protect the secondary user's speech from the author's or owner's claims of expressive integrity, intellectual privacy, and creative control. It may seem a stretch to describe these cases as protecting privacy, but they resemble the privacy tort of "false light." A false light claim contests the placing of information or expression in a false or misleading context such that its portrayal is highly offensive or embarrassing to a reasonable person of ordinary sensibilities.[166] These IP claims allege unlawful interference with professional identity by distorting reputation and personal expression, taking place over the terrain of one's "assets" or "persona" (such as authored books, photographs, artwork, brands, or inventions).[167]

Federal trademark law explicitly contains a reputation-protective cause of action. The Lanham Act prevents "dilution by tarnishment," described as an "association arising from the similarity between a mark or trade name and a famous mark" that harms the reputation of the famous mark.[168] This cause of action was added to the federal trademark statute in 1996 and further clarified in 2006. It was intended to protect the investment in the famous brand's positive identity by prohibiting use that puts the mark in a disparaging context and degrades consumers' positive associations with it.[169] Exceptions to this legal claim are broad, however, and they weaken the dilution claim. These exceptions include "any fair use" (other than use as a mark) that may be comparative advertising, parody, criticism and commentary, or news reporting. Examples include when Louis Vuitton and Tiffany sued a pet toy manufacturer who called its stuffed dog toys and beds "Chewy Vuitton" and "Sniffany"[170] and when Starbucks sued a local Vermont coffee roaster for naming one of its darkest roasts "Charbucks."[171] These would be weak trademark claims on the basis of consumer confusion: few consumers would believe that Louis Vuitton is in the plush pet toy business or that Starbucks is making fun of its own reputation for strong coffee. But as dilution cases they are stronger, alleging that disparaging use of the famous marks negatively affects the companies' reputations in consumers' eyes. But in both cases, the courts found these uses to be nondilutive and fair. The suits were failed attempts to stifle commentary and parody about the products in an effort to manage consumers' positive associations with the luxury fashion brands and the global beverage company.

Legal debates rage over the propriety of and evidentiary support for claims of trademark dilution.[172] The point here is not to recite those arguments but instead to highlight Congress's recent creation of dilution in parallel with the rise of the internet. Prior to dilution, federal trademark law protected trademark owners only from confusing uses of their trademarks by others that were likely to divert consumer purchases. Trademark law is primarily fair competition law and protects trademarks to the extent that their distinctiveness and source-designating function facilitates consumer choice and information clarity among goods and services. Trademark dilution, a new kind of trademark harm, does not require consumer confusion. It arose on the federal stage in the form of the Federal Trademark Dilution Act of 1996 (modified a decade later in the Trademark Dilution Revision Act of 2006) and is available only to "famous marks" for the reputational injury caused by "non-confusing" uses of similar-looking marks or symbols that render the famous mark less unique or tarnished in the marketplace. Famous trademark dilution cases include those mentioned above, as well as many others, such as Victoria's Secret against Victor's Little Secret (a sex toy shop) and ToysRUs against a firearms store calling itself Guns Are Us (and

We Are Guns).[173] The indefatigable circulation of images and information on the web escalates the need for reputation management. Intellectual property claims are strong tools in the arsenal for defending against the internet's ills, and trademark law's expansion to include dilution is a new weapon.

Is it appropriate to compare the reputational injuries of companies such as Louis Vuitton, Starbucks, and Victoria's Secret to the privacy harms of individual people in *Monge* or *Balsley*? One objection to describing trademark dilution by tarnishment as a privacy harm is that companies do not have privacy rights at all. But this is a very narrow view of privacy—one in which Swatch loses on the breach of confidence complaint described earlier not because the communication was in fact public but because Swatch as a corporation is incapable of experiencing privacy in the same way an individual can. Whether or not we are ready to expressly limit privacy protections of this kind to individuals only, it bears noting that the Supreme Court has extended freedom of speech and religion to companies.[174] Other "individual rights" housed in the Bill of Rights have also been extended beyond individuals to companies, institutions, and organizations (such as the Fourth Amendment right against search and seizure, the Fifth Amendment right to due process, and the Seventh Amendment right to a jury trial).[175] Corporations also have equality rights under the Fourteenth Amendment's equal protection clause.[176] If Louis Vuitton and Starbucks have no privacy rights in the Digital Age, it is not because they are companies instead of people.

The line between a person and a company blurs as brands form around celebrities and companies develop consumer followings by portraying themselves "as people too." Taylor Swift, for example, is both a person and a brand.[177] Insurance companies and banks raise brand awareness by appealing to personal trust relationships based on privacy and confidentiality.[178] This blending further undermines the contention that companies cannot be bearers of individual rights like privacy. Intellectual property is traditionally a corporate or business asset, but it is evolving as a legal and cultural regime from one that regulates market behavior to one that regulates public relations. In each of the following cases, plaintiffs assert trademark, copyright, and patent rights to protect or manage their identities in terms of their public and private associations.

Scholz v. Goudreau was a 2015 dispute among members of the 1970s rock band Boston.[179] After breaking up in 1981, the former band members fought over who could properly use the trademarked band name "Boston" to refer to themselves. The issue was lawful use of the trademark "Boston" without confusing audiences about who was and was not a "founding" or "former" band member. Tom (Donald Thomas) Scholz and other Boston band members sued Barry Goudreau, their former bandmate, to prevent him from describing himself as an "original founding Boston member," harnessing trademark law to do it. Negotiations lasted years in the context of a trademark lawsuit.

Scholz sought to limit Goudreau to the self-designation of "formerly of the band Boston" and to censor him through the use of trademark law from any other way of describing his affiliation with the band. Under trademark law, could Goudreau be prevented from referring to himself instead as a "founding Boston member"? The plaintiffs alleged that the latter phrase would confuse the public as a "false designation of origin, false or misleading description of fact" or "deceive as to the affiliation, connection or association of such person with another person, or as to the origin, sponsorship, or approval of his or her goods, services, or commercial activities by another person."[180] The federal trademark statute contains these descriptions of harm, which are most often used to combat false advertising and consumer confusion in the marketplace for goods based on the misleading use of trademarks or trademark-like expressions. Trademark law is not usually used to negotiate breakups.

This unusual trademark case went to trial, and Goudreau won the ability to designate himself as he pleased. In August 2018, a federal appellate court affirmed the jury verdict.[181] Spanning three decades and costing hundreds of thousands of dollars, the dispute confirms that intellectual property is an imperfect but alluring framework in which to negotiate the terms of affective relations.

David Anasagasti, also known as Ahol Sniffs Glue, is a twenty-first-century graffiti artist and muralist whose work appeared in the Wynwood area of Miami. Wynwood is a tourist destination known for its exquisitely colorful and imaginative graffiti. Artists' creations cover whole sides of city buildings throughout the neighborhood, at first made without permission and now sometimes by commission. When the clothing brand American Eagle Outfitters staged an advertising photo shoot in the Wynwood neighborhood, Anasagasti and his work inadvertently (or so American

Eagle claimed) became part of an advertising campaign. Anasagasti hired a lawyer to file a copyright lawsuit, who explained the following in a press release:

> Mr. Anasagasti has never permitted his work to be used to advertise or sell commercial products[.] . . . Given that he hails from the counter-culture world of underground street artists, Mr. Anasagasti's reputation as an artist has been founded, in part, on a public perception that Mr. Anasagasti doesn't "sell out" to large corporate interests. Yet ironically, in today's fashion market-place, affiliation with artists bearing such "street credibility" is highly sought-after by retail brands for the cultural cachet and access to the profitable youth demographic that it offers.[182]

Public support for Anasagasti was strong. As one supporter and fellow artist told the press, "if American Eagle was truly interested in becoming authentic by affiliating its product with a street artist and tapping into a creative vein, they should have approached Ahol for permission and compensated him for his work. And if he didn't want to work with them for whatever reason, they could go fuck themselves and find someone else."[183] That's one way of putting it; another is that the company copied and distributed Anasagasti's creative expression without permission and for commercial, advertising purposes; if American Eagle was making money from near-exact copies of Anasagasti's work, the company should be required to compensate him under copyright law.

The problem with Anasagasti's copyright claim, however, was that it was really a claim for disassociation and not for market exclusivity. The background images of Anasagasti's mural in the American Eagle advertisement did not compete with copies of Anasagasti's work, which might deplete his expected revenue from his art (a typical copyright harm). The advertisement was not a "superseding work," which in copyright law means that it interferes with an artist's expected earnings. Also, graffiti originates with a trespass and therefore already has a contested copyright status.[184] Nonetheless, a recent case brought by the 5-Pointz graffiti artists, whose work was destroyed when a building on which their artwork was made was razed, ended with a jury verdict in the artists' favor and a damage award of $6.7 million dollars.[185] And other graffiti artists are following Anasagasti's path. After Jason "Revok" Williams illegally painted a handball court in Brooklyn with his "original works of authorship," and clothing retailer H&M used the courts as a backdrop for an ad campaign, Williams sent them a cease-and-desist letter on the basis of copyright law. H&M retaliated by filing a federal lawsuit, but the public backlash against the company was so strong that H&M dropped the suit and the advertising campaign.[186] Graffiti artists' use of copyright law to protect their aerosol art—even for reasons of disassociation and identity management—is gaining traction.

These copyright cases could turn on the interesting legal issues of whether graffiti is copyright-protected in the first place or whether its unauthorized use in the background of advertising campaigns is permitted as copyright fair use. But at their core, these cases are not about the scope of copyright protection per se, with its policies of protecting originality, remunerating copyright authors for their work, and promoting progress of science. These graffiti artists brought copyright claims because they did not want the public to associate them with particular forms of mainstream commercial culture. They successfully asserted copyright to manage their private identities and public reputations through relationships they choose to reject. In doing so, they affirmed that their work represents them and that the reuse of their work by others affects their identities in harmful ways for which they felt confident seeking redress through law. Judging from the public support for their complaints, their confidence was well founded. The outcry concerning these lawsuits was not because they used copyright as legal leverage to manage boundaries between private and public identities but because audiences supported their attempts to control their artistic identities and reputations—an increasingly bewildering challenge in the internet age.

To be sure, we can trace relationship and identity-based privacy interests to nineteenth-century copyright cases fought over private, unpublished letters and drafts. But contemporary artists are further reshaping copyright law beyond its traditional and usual boundaries to protect current identity-based privacy claims in the internet advertising age. Trademark law may seem like a better fit, as it is more directly attendant to advertising and managing public relationships with consumers and competitors. It too is broadening and being harnessed with increased frequency. Patent law, by contrast, presents unique problems for relationship-based privacy interests. But in the Digital Age, where public reputation and private relations are more readily discernable, even patent law and subject inventions are the focus of lawsuits brought to manage private identity.

Courts are seeing a growing number of patent cases brought under the Patent Act's Section 256 for "change of inventorship."[187] These are cases in which inventors allege to have been wrongfully left off a patent and thus suffer reputational, professional, and pecuniary harm. In most of these cases, such as *Shukh v. Seagate Technology* (2015), the court permits omitted inventors to sue only if they can allege "concrete and particularized reputational injury."[188] The primary injury of incorrect inventorship is loss of patent royalties. But increasingly, these claims sound also in reputation harm for being omitted as a named inventor and lack quantifiable monetary damages. Other cases predating *Shukh* debate the issue of bringing patent claims for reputational injuries alone without financial loss.[189] But these other cases concern being erroneously left *off* a patent and suing to be named as an inventor. *Pedersen v. Geschwind* (2015) is the rare case in which a named inventor advances associational privacy and public identity interests for having his name *on* the patent.[190] In *Pedersen*, the plaintiff filed a patent lawsuit to have his name taken off a patent. He alleged injuries not of lost royalties or reputational benefits from omission, but the harm of commission: being named a co-inventor on the patent of a research group with a tarnished reputation. The court struggled with this concept new to patent law, although as a demand for disassociation, it resembles the lawsuits brought by Boston band members and aerosol artist David Anasagasti.

Dr. Peter Pedersen worked at the Johns Hopkins University School of Medicine and engaged in a research collaboration with Dr. Jean-François Geschwind and a research partner named Young Hee Ko. The results of the research were two patents directed toward the treatment of cancerous tumors, and the patents were assigned to Johns Hopkins University to commercialize as part of routine university procedures. Only Drs. Pedersen and Geschwind were named on the patents, however; Ms. Ko was not listed as an inventor, although she did not sue to correct inventorship. It was Dr. Pedersen who filed the lawsuit "to enforce his right not to have his name used in a public way to promote the commercial activities of" Johns Hopkins University and to protect his reputation as a "fair and honest academician" worthy of collaboration and respect.[191] A central allegation in the lawsuit was that Ms. Ko's omission from the patent was unfair and that

Dr. Pedersen did not want to be publicly associated with that injustice as a named inventor on the patent.

The federal court ruled against Dr. Pedersen, writing that "simply because he is unhappy with the manner in which a bona fide assignee of a patent chooses to deploy or license its interest" cannot confer standing in a patent suit.[192] If such were the case, "disaffected scientists" would have "near-limitless standing" undermining federal jurisdiction's requirement for particularized injuries.[193] You can almost hear the court scoff at Dr. Pedersen's complaint that his reputational injury "is particularly acute with regard to [his] potential colleagues—young researchers who are trying to determine which lab they should join . . . who are particularly attuned to a potential supervisor's reputation for accurately attributing discoveries made by subordinate researchers."[194] Unlike the previous cases described, there was no public outcry supporting Dr. Pedersen's effort to right a wrong done to Ms. Ko. And perhaps the experience of harm was too subjective or unfamiliar for the court to understand it without better evidence that "young researchers [would avoid] employment in his lab . . . because of the inventorship discrepancy."[195]

There was more to the story, however. In a not-so-subtle footnote, the court hints of a "domestic arrangement" between Dr. Pedersen and Ms. Ko, which suggests that there was more at stake than professional reputation and "taking credit where credit is not due."[196] Dr. Petersen and Ms. Ko had apparently been lovers. The subtext of the case concerned private reconciliation and a public apology for emotional injuries suffered in a romantic relationship among coworkers. Dr. Pederson sought to promote through patent law a form of affiliative privacy by asking that patent law enable his reconciliation with Ms. Ko by disassociating from the other research collaborators. Only recently has the constitutional right to privacy protected marriage equality and relationship autonomy.[197] Dr. Pedersen sought a similar privacy right through patent law to protect his intimate and professional relations free from interference by others.

To the *Pedersen* court, however, the subtext of harm to private affiliations only made Dr. Pedersen's patent case weaker. As the court wrote in conclusion, this was a case where the parties had years of "bad blood between them." It was not a case about promoting the progress of science and useful arts by rewarding people a patent for their creations:

> Plaintiff's theory here would turn that law on its head, redefining a patent not
> as a badge of professional and intellectual honor but as an albatross around
> the neck. . . . [T]he Court holds that Plaintiff has failed to allege an injury
> redressable through the [Patent Act] section 256 relief.[198]

This court had no patience for the attempt to expand patent law's function,
and so it cleaved patent law from the personal interests in preserving or
ameliorating private relationships, even those publicly acknowledged. It
left Dr. Pedersen on the patent and Ms. Ko "bound by any decision rendered in th[e] action on the merits"[199]—a very different result than those
in the Boston trademark case and the graffiti copyright cases. But the attempts to control private relations through public recognition of intellectual property rights ring the same.

Despite these kinds of patent cases being rarer than similarly motivated
trademark and copyright claims, once the search begins, claims asserting harms from compelled associations and loss of control over intimate
or personal relationships are legion. Most plaintiffs have well-established
public reputations in their professional fields. As a general matter, however,
famous brands and public authors or inventors have less recourse to privacy
claims regarding their public personae. And yet, famous plaintiffs more
frequently sue than private citizens. In 2019 Louis Vuitton sued to bar the
use of an image of one of its notorious handbags on down-market canvas
bags parodically called "My Other Bag" that made fun of the luxury brand's
elite status.[200] Louis Vuitton also recently sued political artist Nadia Plesner
for depicting the same Vuitton handbag in a mural to critique luxury in
a world of food scarcity.[201] The Mattel company sues frequently to contest
the reimagination of its iconic Barbie dolls in contexts that critique Barbie's objectification of women, such as artworks with titles like "Dungeon
Barbie" and "Food Chain Barbie."[202] Even the world-renowned *New York
Times* sued to prevent republication of its photographs by photojournalist
David Shields, who used them to critique the newspaper's war coverage.[203]
Famous plaintiffs tend to lose these kinds of conflicts because they are so
often transparent attempts to quell speech and political debate. These claims
by public figures and companies are the weakest kinds of affiliative privacy
claims. The public nature of the original expression succumbs to the strong
First Amendment values protecting counter-speech (e.g., more and diverse

speech as opposed to censorship or silence).[204] Nonetheless, these claims are brought more frequently in the age of digitally networked communication, and they are expensive to litigate, which plaintiffs know and use to their advantage. This trend fuels the use of intellectual property as a tool to bolster and protect reputational harm and associational privacy in the internet era.

2. Subject Objections

Some cases are not brought by authors or inventors but by the *subjects* of works, who also turn to intellectual property law to protect their privacy. These cases resemble *Monge* and *Balsley*, except that in those cases, the female plaintiffs never consented to the dissemination of their photographic images. In these new cases, the subjects agreed to the publication of their image in one context but then sought to use copyright law to prevent their reuse in others. These are therefore not intrusion on seclusion or limited publication cases, as were *Monge* and *Balsley*; these disputes assert control over the contextual use of one's image already permissibly and publicly circulating. These plaintiffs seek to control their public personalities and private relationships by controlling the use of images of which they are the subject, not the author. In the most extreme case, they may also assert bodily autonomy claims insofar as threats to safety and bodily integrity arise from the unauthorized recontextualization of an image. None of these cases dispute authorship, however, although they involve authored works and their misuse.

Hill et al. v. Public Advocate (2014) concerns a conservative anti–marriage equality advocacy organization that featured an engagement photo of a gay couple in an anti-gay political campaign.[205] The professional photographer who made the photo and from whose site the photo was copied joined with the married couple to sue an organization called Public Advocate of the United States for copyright infringement. (The subjects of the photograph had no standing to sue for copyright infringement otherwise.) The lawsuit also included a misappropriation of likeness claim, which is a privacy tort. The court dismissed the privacy claim on First Amendment grounds because Public Advocate's use of the photo "reasonably relates to . . . a matter that is newsworthy or of legitimate public concern," even though the subjects themselves were private figures.[206] But the copyright claim survived and provided the relief that the plaintiffs sought. The court determined that the photograph's reuse may be infringing and not fair, despite its arguably trans-formative use as political commentary. In other words, the newsworthiness extinguished the privacy claim but not the copyright claim, which was surprising because fair use requires consideration of four statutory factors, and three in this case favored the defendant—namely, purpose of the use, nature of the work, and market harm.[207] After the court's ruling keeping the copyright claim alive, Public Advocate settled the copyright infringement claim enjoining further use of the work and paid $2,501 in costs.[208]

This was an unusual outcome. Cases of this ilk may be upsetting (see, for example, the epigraph to this chapter about a similar circumstance), but they often favor defendants rather than plaintiffs. Non-author plain-tiffs who are *subjects* of the work and have allowed its dissemination in one context tend to lose their lawsuits when they contest its circulation and reuse in another context. But because these cases are time-consuming and expensive, plaintiffs have both an incentive and the confidence to use copyright for privacy purposes, hoping that a settlement will prevent their images' ongoing use by others. For example, in *Katz v. Chevaldina* (2015), the plaintiff-landlord Raanan Katz sued Irina Chevaldina, a tenant, for posting an unflattering photograph of Katz on a blog critical of his business practices.[209] The photo of Katz with his tongue "protrud[ing] askew from his mouth" had been previously published in a foreign newspaper.[210] At the time, Katz was a well-known real estate magnate in Florida and owned part of the Miami Heat, a professional basketball team. Unhappy with the critical blog post and especially his photographic image, Katz acquired copyright in the photo from the photographer and sued Chevaldina for copyright infringement.

After nearly four years of litigation, the case finally ended in the defendant-tenant's favor. The court held that Chevaldina's unauthorized publication of Katz's photograph was copyright fair use, and it awarded Chevaldina over $150,000 in attorneys' fees. In ruling for the defendant, the court highlighted Chevaldina's laudable purpose to inform readers of Katz's business practices. The court also noted Katz's "highly unusual step of ob-taining the copyright to the Photo and initiating this lawsuit specifically to prevent its publication . . . [an] attempt to utilize copyright as an instrument of censorship against unwanted criticism."[211] Katz was a public figure and was the subject of news before Chevaldina wrote about him, which further strengthened the fair use of his photographic image and diminished the strength of his privacy interest in his public persona.

There are many copyright cases like *Katz v. Chevaldina*, all of which resemble the false light tort. Originating with Warren and Brandeis's 1890 article, the privacy tort protects a person from being placed "before the public in a false light" in a way that is "highly offensive to a reasonable person."[212] Such cases include *Dhillon v. Does* (2014), in which California Republican Party vice chairman Harmeet K. Dhillon sued an anonymous blogger over the use of a five-year-old campaign photo that accompanied a critical post on a political website.[213] The court held that the reuse of the photo for this purpose was fair and not infringing. In *Scott v. WorldStar-HipHop* (2012), a student recorded on his phone a classroom brawl involving Robert Scott and his current and former girlfriends and then posted the recording to WorldStarHipHop, a user-generated content video website similar to YouTube.[214] The posting was titled "Disgraceful: College Fight In NYC Breaks Out Between A Guy, His Girl & Another Girl In Class! (Man Strong Arm's [*sic*] The Student. Hitting Her With Body Shots)." Scott acquired the video's copyright from his classmate and sued the platform for copyright infringement, privacy violations, publicity rights violations, and negligent infliction of emotional distress. After four years, only the copyright claims remained and the parties settled on confidential terms.[215] In another case, *Caner v. Autry* (2014), the dean of Liberty University's theological seminary sought to suppress dissemination of YouTube videos depicting him at public events and establishing that he had lied about his upbringing.[216] The videos demonstrated that the plaintiff, Ergun Caner, had fabricated aspects of his background, and the court held that dissemination for these purposes was fair use. All these cases privilege speech over privacy when the subject of the speech is already a public figure. This is a predictable result under privacy law, but it is a surprising trend for copyright law that grants control to copyright owners regardless of their public or private status. What is really at stake in these copyright cases is the relevance of privacy to copyright's public-interest goal of progress of science.[217]

The disturbing case of *Garcia v. Google* (2015) followed a similar pattern of asserting copyright to redress the privacy injury of "false light."[218] *Garcia* involved a movie titled *The Innocence of Muslims*, which was disseminated on YouTube. A movie producer retained actress Cindy Lee Garcia

originally to appear in a video called "Desert Warrior." The producer ver-
bally misrepresented the nature of the final video to Garcia; instead of being
a story about life in Egypt two thousand years ago, the producer made a
video with an offensive and racist anti-Muslim message. The final video included a five-second clip of Garcia's performance, but the producer dubbed
anti-Muslim phrases over her voice. As a result, the public film included only
Garcia's physical likeness and movements. Garcia received death threats
for her role in the film and filed a copyright claim against Google to take
the film off YouTube.

Garcia had originally and unsuccessfully sued YouTube in state court
for a variety of privacy torts. But these state claims were preempted by the
federal Communications Decency Act of 1996, or CDA, which provides
substantial immunity from state law claims, such as privacy torts, to platforms hosting user-generated content. When the state court denied Garcia's privacy complaint seeking to take the video off-line, she sought legal
alternatives that would avoid the pitfall of federal law's immunity. Garcia
recrafted her complaint as a violation of a *copyright* in her acting performance and requested a takedown from YouTube on that basis. Copyright
claims survive immunity defenses under the CDA. But YouTube nonetheless
refused the takedown request on the basis that the filmmaker, not Garcia,
was the lawful copyright owner.

This case produced three federal court decisions, demonstrating both
the complexity of the legal issues and the severe harm that Cindy Garcia
suffered. A federal trial court sided with YouTube, dismissing Garcia's claim
because she had no copyright in the film. But then a three-judge panel of
the U.S. Court of Appeals for the Ninth Circuit ordered YouTube to take the
movie down, largely because of the death threats against Garcia:

> Garcia has shown that removing the film from YouTube will help disassoci-
> ate her from the film's anti-Islamic message and that such disassociation will
> keep her from suffering future threats and physical harm. Although Google
> asserts that the film is so widespread that removing it from YouTube will have
> no effect, it has provided no evidence to support this point. Taking down the
> film from YouTube will remove it from a prominent online platform—the
> platform on which it was first displayed—and will curb the harms of which
> Garcia complains. It is not irrelevant that the harm Garcia complains of is

death or serious bodily harm, which the dissent fails to mention. Death is an "irremediable and unfathomable" harm . . . bodily injury is not far behind. To the extent the irreparable harm inquiry is at all a close question, we think it best to err on the side of life.[219]

Raising the specter of bodily assault and privacy intrusion, the federal appeals panel sided with Garcia despite the weakness of her copyright claim.

In close or controversial cases, parties often petition for a rehearing by the federal circuit's appellate court, which is what happened here. The en banc U.S. Court of Appeals for the Ninth Circuit (eleven federal judges) reheard the case and ruled in a 10–1 decision against Garcia, reinstating the film to YouTube and overturning the original federal appellate decision. The new majority based its decision on the principle of copyright law that movie actors do not have copyright interests separate from the movie itself, which are owned by the filmmaker or producer. In other words, Cindy Garcia had no authorship interest in the film. And thus, despite suffering very real privacy and assault-related harms, Garcia had no standing to sue under copyright, which protects works of authorship, not bodily integrity. The court said that because "Garcia claims that she never agreed to the film's ultimate rendition or how she was portrayed in *Innocence of Muslims*, . . . she can hardly argue that the film or her cameo in it was fixed 'by or under [her] authority,'"[220] a requirement of authorship and ownership under the Copyright Act. The court concluded that "Garcia's harms are too attenuated from the purpose of copyright" to sustain a copyright claim.[221]

Had Garcia been a coauthor of the film, the privacy interests she sought to protect through copyright law would have been covered. However, without copyright, Garcia was left without a legal remedy. The *Garcia* court explicitly addressed the collision of copyright and privacy, rejecting using the former to protect the latter:

Privacy laws, not copyright, may offer remedies tailored to Garcia's personal and reputational harms. On that point, we offer no substantive view. Ultimately, Garcia would like to have her connection to the film forgotten and stripped from YouTube. Unfortunately for Garcia, such a "right to be forgotten," although recently affirmed by the Court of Justice for the European Union, is not recognized in the United States.[222]

The court then criticized the earlier decision's takedown order:

> [The order] gave short shrift to the First Amendment values at stake. The mandatory injunction censored and suppressed a politically significant film—based upon a dubious and unprecedented theory of copyright. In so doing, the panel deprived the public of the ability to view firsthand, and judge for themselves, a film at the center of an international uproar. . . . The panel's takedown order of a film of substantial interest to the public is a classic prior restraint of speech.[223]

This appellate court distinguished privacy from copyright on the basis of a constrained view of authorship (which regularly attaches to film producers and rarely to actors) and elevated free speech over privacy. It further suggested that protecting the privacy interests of seclusion and bodily autonomy would require a coincident authorship claim, which Garcia did not have, and that in any case, First Amendment values overcome a claim to suppress politically relevant speech. This is a fairly typical legal argument, but it understates the challenges of the case.

The first appellate court's decision to enjoin the film in light of threats to Cindy Garcia's life privileged her privacy claims over the film producer's authorship interests, over YouTube's interest as an internet platform, and over the public's interest in viewing the film. The subsequent appellate decision weighed these considerations differently. But why? The facts had not changed—Garcia's life was still in danger and the film producer was still out of jurisdictional reach. Moreover, as we have seen, copyright is shot through with reputational and relational privacy concerns when authors sue to prevent dissemination of their work, even when it has already been published. Courts sometimes stretch to allow non-authors to sue when they partner with authors (as in *Hill*) and sometimes even when they do not (as in *Monge*). Other times, authors acquire copyright (as in *Balsley* and *Katz*) to pursue privacy claims through copyright law. The result in *Garcia* was one possible result among many in the evolving internet terrain mixing intellectual property and privacy. Possibly, the doctrinal and policy issues in *Garcia* were too complex and fraught given the highly motivated film industry and giant internet company stakeholders, all located in California, where the case was litigated. This made it difficult to transform a privacy case concerning a single person and her bodily integrity, seclusion, and false light claims into a successful copyright case about authorship and expressive works. Although Cindy Garcia was unsuccessful in the end, copyright proved itself a formidable defense of privacy against Google and YouTube, two titans of the internet age.

3. Heir Objections

Intellectual property, unlike privacy, is alienable. That means that a person can transfer the legal claim to another, as certain of the above-described cases make clear. It also means that copyrights, patents, and trademarks can be inherited. And like authors and subjects, heirs often sue for privacy-related reasons. Copyright has an express postmortem term: as mentioned previously, works of authorship originating from human authors last the author's life plus another seventy years. The only privacy-like interest that is both transferrable and can endure beyond a person's life is the right of publicity, which has recently evolved into an alienable and postmortem right in several jurisdictions.[224] As such, the right of publicity is sometimes referred to as a quasi-property right because it is inheritable and transferrable. But most heirs claim copyright, not publicity law, on behalf of deceased authors to protect a family member's work that is (to them) being misused by others or at risk of such. And yet through these copyright claims, heirs allege a kind of privacy claim rooted in care for intimate associations and relationships that they wish to keep protected from public distortion.

Some heir lawsuits concern unpublished works (such as letters or drafts), in which case the interests previously discussed about preventing dissemination of unpublished work predominate. But the vast majority of these disputes brought by heirs center on preventing the *reuse* of already-published works in order to preserve the reputation of the deceased author or artist. These are cases such as the one by Marcel Duchamp's heirs over the 3-D printing of Duchamp's chess set, or the many recent literary and music estate cases (such as those concerning the works of J. D. Salinger, Martin Luther King Jr., and Marvin Gaye), in which the recontextualization of the creative work is considered anathema to the artist's identity and legacy.[225]

In recent years, the award-winning hip-hop band Beastie Boys sued the toy company GoldieBlox for the parodic reuse of its song "Girls" in an advertisement for an engineering toy directed at young girls.[226] One might think that an irreverent and edgy band would embrace the critical reuse of its song for a progressive purpose. But because deceased Beastie Boy Adam Yauch's last will and testament required that none of his music be used for "advertising purposes," the remaining band members sued to honor that request.[227] The lawsuit settled for a million dollars, which went to a charity of the band's choice. A similar purpose motivated Marvin Gaye's heirs to sue Robin Thicke and Pharrell Williams for their 2013 song "Blurred Lines," which allegedly copied part of Gaye's 1977 song "Got to Give It Up."[228] Gaye's children explained that "through [their father's] music . . . we find our compass and our paths moving forward. We are his children, but we too are his fans and we hold his music dear."[229] Their vigilance in protecting their father's musical work took the form of "caretakers" with "an obligation to . . . preserv[e] the integrity of the music so that future generations understand its origins and feel its effect as the artist intended."[230] These cases dispute claims over work already published and widely circulating in culture. Their privacy dimensions aim to preserve not public consumption but private memories and "reinforce family ties" through ongoing but controlled circulation of the deceased's work.[231]

These cases often include complex copyright fair use assessments. They also chill well-meaning creativity and secondary speech. The secondary uses of these famous works are often homages made by admirers without intention to derogate or demean the first author or their work. Costly lawsuits against fans or other artists can therefore undermine copyright's goals of progress of science and the useful arts. Nonetheless, heirs' copyright claims remain durable—as durable as those brought by authors and the original copyright owners—because unauthorized copying occurred and fair use remains an easily contestable doctrine.

Heirs often cast these claims in terms of artistic integrity, which has only limited purchase under U.S. law given the narrow application of moral rights to only certain visual works.[232] But heirs are nonetheless strongly motivated to preserve family honor and precious relationships. As Andrew Gilden and Eva Subotnik have written, these cases describe attempts by remaining family and friends to preserve memories of relationships and loved ones as they wish them to be remembered without interference by other people who remain alive.[233] Most sympathetically, we may describe these claims as sustaining cherished private affiliations and honoring intimate relationships beyond the grave. The U.S. Supreme Court has reaffirmed privacy law's extension to parent/child relationships and relationships between sexual partners and to an expanding view of marriage.[234] And yet these kinds of constitutional privacy claims attach only to and among living people;[235] a dead person no longer has a legal claim to their reputation or privacy, making copyright claims that extend beyond death more vital than ever.[236]

These cases protect family relationships by controlling other people's speech and artistic expression. They necessarily take place over the terrain of published works already in the public sphere, involving adverse parties with legitimate claims to their own speech and affiliations. Robin Thicke was inspired by Marvin Gaye and was grateful for his music. Thicke reasonably relied on the ability to listen to and learn from a widely published author who came before him in order to make his own. This is precisely how copyright law imagines progress to occur. Similarly, GoldieBlox was indebted to the Beastie Boys' song to make the important point that once-derogatory and once-demeaning connotations (specifically, "Girls" objectified because of gender) can be appropriated and transformed to empower those who were once so targeted. Copyright law enables building upon earlier work to foment new understandings of it. But, in these cases, heirs weaponize copyright to freeze or stultify the meaning of the original work to preserve their cherished memories and private relationships with the deceased and with each other.

Like copyright claims, the familial relationship dimension of privacy claims is structured bilaterally.[237] One's claim inevitably implicates another with a plausibly equal and opposite claim. Control over published works implicates the speech (and copyrights) of others, just as claiming privacy in one's relationship implicates third parties who are asked to refrain from interfering. Claiming copyright in a published work, like claiming privacy over a relationship that is public, does not entitle the claimant to prevent all unwanted attention. Public policies determining regulation over both copyright and privacy are subject to constitutional limits. State-based privacy claims are heavily limited by the First Amendment, and constitutionally derived privacy claims are limited by the slow evolution of constitutional common law. But copyright law, subject simply to congressional oversight and rational review by the Supreme Court, has become an open back door to circumvent privacy law's contours, which is evolving to balance the substantive private and public interests under pressure in the Digital Age.

*   *   *

This chapter makes clear that personal history and public identities are mutually constitutive, underscoring how privacy concerns shape public interests. This bilateral nature of privacy reflects qualities of other fundamental rights too, such as equality, distributive justice, and liberty, in which the contours of one person's fundamental right inevitably shapes the enjoyment of another's. The freedom to attend a single-sex public school affects another person's freedom to attend that same public school as a coeducational institution.[238] Similarly, one person's privacy claim to prevent disclosure of private facts is another person's claim to speak the truth about those very same facts. One person's right of non-association and bodily integrity (to prevent dissemination of a compromising photograph, for example) is another person's right to express themselves as a reporter, critic, or comic about that very situation. This bilaterality is sometimes described as maintaining an essential balance between private and public interests in both fundamental rights and intellectual property contexts. But this misconceives privacy and intellectual property as embodying competing interests and values. The bilateral nature of fundamental rights and intellectual property more accurately describes the inseparability, not the balance, of the interests at stake.[239] Privacy is unthinkable without some intrusion by government to protect it. Authorship, inventorship, and even trademark rights are unthinkable without the existence of the public domain.

The puzzle remains that most state law–based privacy claims resolve with disclosure if a strong public interest exists. And yet many related IP claims that allege privacy interests err on the side of seclusion and protect intellectual property. To be sure, the deeply felt commitment to privacy may explain why one might desire vindication any way one can get it. In other words, if copyright or other IP claims fit the facts, then have at it. As already mentioned, one way to explain this inconsistency is that property (as in intellectual property) trumps privacy, especially in the age of postindustrial capital in which intangible assets rule the roost.[240] The mainstreaming or "domestication" of IP is another explanation. As IP absorbs into our everyday commercial, political, and technosocial culture, it develops roots that become as foundational as other areas of law. But IP has not yet evolved doctrinally or culturally, as other fundamental legal fields (like constitutional privacy and equality law) have, to develop a deep bilateral or relational structure binding private interests with the public good. IP's ascendance is too recent. Perhaps with these new kinds of intellectual property cases, its common-law evolution and contextual complexity will occur.

The cultural and legal domestication of intellectual property documented so far through equality and privacy signals discursive shifts as IP mainstreams into our legal system. This shift implies broader relevance to wider constituencies than ever before. Intellectual property's discursive domestication appears to develop and debate a moral narrative around intangible but highly prized aspects of culture: speech, aesthetic forms, inventions, and the everyday creative and innovative practices that produce and sustain primary human relationships. As we learn to understand the centrality of these aspects of our cultural life and their relationship to our flourishing within society, we may consider regulating them as we do other fundamental values and behaviors—as public and common goods rather than personal assets to be hoarded or rationed. Distinguishing between intangible goods as commodities (like financial assets) or as priceless aspects of meaningful existence (such as privacy) is central to the law's reasoned and effective functioning for all. Words like *equality, privacy, discrimination,* and *fairness* were infrequently marshaled in favor of stronger or weaker IP rights until the twenty-first century. And yet, close analysis of Digital Age disputes reveals disagreements about precisely these concepts in the context of IP. Paying attention to this language of fundamental values in intellectual property disputes—language that is otherwise deeply rooted in other areas of law—serves the diverse peoples for whom the IP regimes are newly relevant: everyday creators and innovators. We must understand this evolution if intellectual property is to achieve the progress it seeks.

4   Distributive Justice (or "Fairer Uses")

> I'm now making pictures on my phone . . . because . . . I
> now see that making pictures is democratic, you know? But
> . . . what I'd like to think is that you could tell the difference
> between a good picture, a good-enough picture, and a
> terrific picture. I mean, that's why I'm making this book. I
> want to raise the standards of what should be demanded . .
> . of images.
>
> —Felice Frankel, science photographer

THE NEXT TWO CHAPTERS explore different terrain with the same
aim—to show the relevance of fundamental values to intellectual property in the internet age. Instead of looking to court cases and official
legal rhetoric, these chapters rely on accounts from everyday creators
and innovators whom I've interviewed over the past decade. This chapter begins with a singular account from a hearing in 2014 to introduce
the theme of distributive justice as a fundamental value challenged and
undermined by certain legal arguments justifying exclusive intellectual
property rights today. An outline of various distributive justice frameworks follows and becomes the foundation for many other creator and
innovator accounts. I call these accounts "fairer use" stories, as they
build on principles of copyright fair use to explain how sharing, borrowing, and a vital public domain are essential to creativity and innovation in the internet age. These fairer use stories are about all sorts of
creators and innovators, copyright authors and patent inventors. They
reflect core principles of distributive justice and resist the exclusivity and durations of intellectual property rights rooted in twentieth-
century legal logic.

* * *

In March 2014, the Library of Congress hosted a roundtable series to discuss the problem of "orphan works" in copyright. This problem arises when someone seeks to use a copyrighted work but cannot find the author or owner to ask permission. The problem of orphan works exploded in the twentieth century thanks to the digital access the internet provides and the lengthening copyright term (old works dating from the 1920s and 1930s remain under copyright today). The orphan works problem compounded in 1989 when the United States became a signatory to the Berne Convention, making copyright notice on and registration of authored works optional and thus tracking authors more difficult.[1] Moreover, after 1976, all original works of expression—published *or* *un*published—were protected by federal copyright law, vastly increasing the total number of copyrighted works.[2] The combination of time's passage, the lengthening copyright term, and these legal changes meant that many millions more federally copyrighted works existed and that fewer were traceable to authors. Then in the 1990s, with the popularization of the internet, copyrighted works spread virally, with abandon, and without regard to owner or author. By some accounts today, 25 percent of core library books and an even greater share of visual artworks are orphaned, although data is notoriously challenging to collect and analyze with reasonable certainty.[3] In the case of photographs on the internet, only a tiny fraction (some estimate 1 percent) identifies the author or rights holder.

Trademarks and patents suffer a slightly different fate. Trademarks by their nature identify their source. And patents must be registered with the U.S. Patent and Trademark Office (PTO) to be valid. But both trademark and patent licensing are burdened by the complexity of chains of control and the reality of obscure holding companies that manage vast amounts of intellectual property. And yet we do not talk about the problem of orphaned trademarks or patents the way we do with copyright. Nonetheless, the Digital Age has disrupted the control of copying, exclusive use, and distribution of trademarks and patented inventions to an extent not experienced since the invention of the printing press in the fifteenth century and the rise of the manufacturing factory system in the nineteenth century. When the Library of Congress convened the 2014 roundtable series, titled "Orphan Works and Mass Digitization," its concern was orphaned copyrighted works, but its larger framework was the problem of runaway copying and distribution combined with (and compounded by) the internet's anonymity.

At one of the roundtable discussions, a National Press Photographers Association (NPPA) representative took aim at mass digitization of the kind undertaken by the Google Books project. Since its origin, the Google Books project has digitized and made available all or a portion of forty million of the world's books (out of an estimated total of 135 million titles). The NPPA representative also criticized the HathiTrust Digital Library, a similar project that links directly to academic libraries, which to date has over seventeen million titles in its digital library, many of which are available for reading by registered users. The NPPA representative and others attended the roundtable to support photographers and other copyright authors who considered the Google Books and HathiTrust projects a form of theft, despite having been blessed by a federal court as "fair use" under copyright law. In two thoughtful and widely watched decisions, federal appeals courts held in *Authors Guild v. HathiTrust* (2014) and *Authors Guild v. Google, Inc.* (2015) that the kind of mass digitization undertaken by Google and HathiTrust was permitted as fair use under the Copyright Act.[4] Fair use is a First Amendment anchor in copyright law (and in trademark law) that permits as non-infringing certain forms of unauthorized copying, reuse, and distribution. Copyright law is meant to prevent copying and distribution of an author's work that supersedes the use of an author's work in its existing or expected market. Fair uses are non-infringing uses that tend, generally speaking, to be transformed uses (for example, for scholarship, criticism, parody, or conversion into something new). As such, fair uses rarely interfere with the predictable or foreseeable market for an author's work and a reasonable return on their investment. The court adjudicating the dispute over the Google Books project held that the form of digitization it performed in particular—scanning whole books but displaying only a snippet of those still in copyright—did not cause market harm to the works in copyright. (These snippet views actually grow the market for books and even renew the market in some out-of-print books.)[5] Furthermore, the court held that the copying Google Books engaged in produced a transformative search of millions of the world's books—an undeniable benefit to the progress of science and the useful arts.[6]

But the aforementioned NPPA representative participating in the round-table discussion considered this federal court decision a travesty. And in so saying, he drew a comparison that elicited gasps from the participants of the roundtable. He compared the Google Books project and its affirmation under federal law to the despised *Plessy v. Ferguson* "separate but equal" doctrine from the Jim Crow era, which was infamously and embarrassingly held constitutional by the U.S. Supreme Court in 1894, not to be overturned until 1954 in *Brown v. Board of Education*:

> I think part of the mass digitization problem is that . . . it only adds to the fact that much of the public believes that the internet is the public domain and that anything there is there for the taking. I think really one of the un-derlying themes here is, at least from the Google aspect, this is more like mass monetization. They figured out a way of taking all this content. And it's a word that I truly dislike. Content[.] . . . In terms of addressing some of the cases, *Plessy v. Ferguson* was the law of the land for a hundred years [*sic*] but that didn't make it right. So, just because we can look at these things as courts deciding what is right now, I think the bottom line is really if we expect to have a culture, then the creators now somehow need to be com-pensated in a way that they can earn a living. And that is really all we are asking for here.[7]

The Supreme Court's *Plessy v. Ferguson* decision upheld a Louisiana state law that racially segregated passenger railroad cars. *Plessy*'s logic justifying racial segregation rested on social norms celebrating White supremacy as a form of natural law and willfully ignored slavery's long, traumatic history as the source of racial inequality and sociopolitical dehumanization of Black people in the United States. It was not only misguided but coldhearted to compare the court decision blessing the Google Books and HathiTrust projects—which as innovations opened millions of the world's books to anyone with internet access—to the decision blessing White supremacy as a natural order.

But *Plessy*'s evocation in this context is nonetheless worth contemplating because it suggests deeply felt personal anger and hurt directed at copyright court rulings (*Google* and *HathiTrust*) akin to the anger and hurt that *Plessy* generated. The depth of emotion merits exploration. At the root of the anal-ogy are disputes about the personal and financial stakes in an internet age that makes access to creativity and innovation easy and risks fostering the perception of creativity and innovation as expendable or worthless.

The NPPA representative seemed to suggest that as *Plessy* was wrong when it was decided and eventually overturned by *Brown v. Board of Education*, the *Google* and *HathiTrust* decisions declaring mass digitization copyright fair use were also wrong. He implied that as with *Plessy*, with *Google* and *HathiTrust*, we will eventually recognize the profound error of our ways—that courts blessing a behavior made that behavior neither moral now nor legal in the future. But what is the "error" to be fixed? "Separate but equal" perpetuated racial castes under the perverse argument of "freedom of association" and "local tradition and custom," ignoring the political, social, and economic dominance of the white ruling class that controlled exclusive associations, traditions, and custom through law, state-sanctioned force, and threat of violence.[8] It seems manifest today how *Plessy* was wrong even when it was decided. But how is the application of fair use in these mass digitization cases anything but a leveling mechanism, undoing hierarchies and promoting inclusivity? *Google* and *HathiTrust* reaffirmed fair use as a principle central to intellectual property law's overall structure: that the right of public access for specific uses of copyrighted works promotes progress of science as a necessary limitation on the privilege of copyright protection. *Plessy* instantiated hierarchies on the basis of arbitrary difference such as race and called it constitutional. By contrast, *Google* and *HathiTrust* remind us that the progress contemplated by the Constitution sometimes demands access to sufficient cultural resources without regard to status or property. The two situations could not be more different.

But digging further, the NPPA spokesperson seemed to be suggesting that the fair use doctrine as applied in *Google* especially demeans the rights holders at the expense of fair users, creating unjust hierarchies just as *Plessy* did. He complained about the cheapening of copyright through mass digitization and thus of the dilution and devaluation of creative culture and of those who produce it. He worried that the internet has generated the false belief that everything on the World Wide Web is in the public domain and free and thus (by his own erroneous logic) also worthless.[9] He asserted that the primary beneficiaries of this "freedom" are not working artists and authors but aggregators like Google. And he bemoaned that where once there were authors, whose work was paid for to earn a living, now there is only "content" to be "monetized" by internet giants like Google:

> [Google] figured out a way of taking all this content. And it's a word that I truly dislike. Content, to me, is something that settles in the bottom of macaroni boxes. . . . I mean, we create works. It is not just content. But unfortunately, that is what it is being seen as these days. It is just more and more, and more content going out there.[10]

The NPPA spokesperson insisted that at stake is "culture"—the production of creative and novel work from which we all benefit but which also will dissipate if authors (and presumably inventors also) do not get paid. But by comparing the application of fair use in *Google Books* and *HathiTrust* to *Plessy*'s "separate but equal" doctrine, he exposed beliefs about whose culture matters and which creators and curators deserve protection and special treatment under copyright law (or IP law generally). Present at the roundtable to protect professional photographers and other traditional authors under the Copyright Act, he would seek to do so at the expense of everyday readers, writers, artists, and educators. He was not representing all authors—that is for sure. Contrary to vindicating *Brown* and its principle of equal status and access, the NPPA spokesperson's comments reinforced as justifiable the principle of status hierarchies within creative industries— status hierarchies that were also at the heart of *Plessy*. He implied that not all users of the copyright system deserve equal access to resources. His comments exposed resistance to equitable access and to distributive justice principles aiming to reduce resource scarcity in order to promote collective flourishing. His position therefore undermines the heart of intellectual property's purposes and policies.

The scarcity that the NPPA spokesperson feared is lost wages produced by the internet's complicity in diminishing payment to authors for uses of their works. As a consequence of this scarcity, he argued, fewer works get made and "culture" suffers. This view rehearses the narrow economic analysis that justifies IP's exclusive control. Under this view, the public domain is invisible as a force that contributes to the production and sustenance of creative cultures. Economic incentive plays the star role. But this interpretation fundamentally misconstrues IP law (and copyright law specifically). The public domain is vital terrain—it is the clean air and water of culture.

And we rely on it every day to communicate and innovate. We rely on the public domain's existence and growth through unencumbered resources of culture and innovation. Doctrinally, in the public domain are facts, laws of nature, abstract ideas, the alphabet and other systems of communication, expired IP, and the many other statutory exceptions to IP's exclusive rights.[11] As already mentioned, authorship, inventorship, and even trademark rights are unthinkable without the public domain.

The NPPA spokesperson represented distressed professional photographers who are admittedly hurting in the Digital Age, as chapter 1 describes in detail. Low-end competition, the ease of copying on the internet, and the plethora of photographic options on the web make earning a living as a photographer harder today than ever. In this context, he explained that *Plessy* was wrong because all people are owed equal treatment as a matter of fundamental law, and *Google* was wrong because all authors should own the fruits of their labor, also as a matter of fundamental (or "natural") law. But constitutional lawyers will explain that the word *equal* was added to the Constitution only after a civil war and as a condition of surrender; it was left out of our fundamental law until a war ripped the country apart, and its meaning remains contested and far from self-evident, as chapter 2 explains. Similarly, copyright law is a reflection not of natural rights but of centuries of legislative craft and bargaining.[12] There is no "natural" understanding of "copyright" as a reward for creative labor.

Copyright, like all federal intellectual property, is a creature of statute, evolving in response to social and technological changes and political bargains. It is a human fiction that has been shaped and reshaped over centuries. Fair use is central to those years of compromise and cultural development. Our historical and cultural baseline for how to generate and protect creative work is not, in fact, through copyright but through its absence.[13] This is not a chicken/egg problem. The public domain came first, along with thousands of years of cultural production before copyright existed.[14] The same is true for patents and trademarks. Congress could repeal any of the federal IP statutes tomorrow, denying the "right" to all future intellectual property owner-wannabes, and there would be no constitutional problem or moral injustice. The Constitution gives to Congress the power to grant for limited times to authors and inventors rights to their writings and inventions, but Congress is not obligated to do so. And if it does, the contours of those rights are entirely up to Congress in compliance with other provisions of the Constitution.

Remembering that intellectual property protection is the *exception,* not the rule, inverts contemporary and common conceptions of its purposes as a property right justified by "natural law." We accept all too easily that property rights are *necessary* to incentivize the production and dissemination of creative and innovative work, which is clearly overstated to the point of being false.[15] One might say, however, that the accumulation of intellectual property signifies status and well-being because it signals opportunity, productivity, and prosperity—all signs of progress. This is one way to interpret the NPPA spokesperson's statement about the internet's effect of cheapening culture and producing "content." He suggested that facilitating free access to authors' copyrighted works dishonors and degrades their contributions, born of sweat and creative labor, and diminishes their opportunity for further productivity. He could not have been suggesting that only degraded or demoralized people work without pay, because of course that is not true: many people volunteer or choose to work for less than a competitive wage without impugning their humanity. His fair wage argument nonetheless resonates with many artists and authors in light of rising competition from platforms and the internet's ocean of opportunity driving down prices for creative and innovative goods. And in this competitive environment, which is often stratified on the basis of race and gender, one must critically inquire whether there is injustice in who is being paid (or getting rich) and who is not. Nonetheless, his account was an exaggeration of property law's natural law justification. He failed to consider the central role of the commons and an essential, sustainable, and growing public sphere (think roads, public education, and yes—fair uses of copyrighted work) on which all healthy and productive work practices rely. In the natural law account that John Locke codified late in the seventeenth century, owning the fruits of one's labor comes with the critical proviso of leaving "at least . . . enough, and as good, . . . in common for others."[16] The NPPA representative left that part out.

This singular commentary at a 2014 copyright roundtable discussion thus traces an ancient debate relating property to justice and the public good. Some philosophers have argued that protecting property rights as exclusive entitlements is the central job of the state, with a duty to its subjects to promote justice and common welfare.[17] This claim relies on some notion of merit or desert: only those with property (those who have earned or in-herited it) benefit from the state's power. Other philosophers have argued that justice requires all people to be supplied with or have access to sufficient levels of property or resources to meet material needs. This more modern principle, often associated with John Rawls, requires property distribution or access to critical resources independent of merit or desert: simply by being human and living under a just state's governance, a person should have their basic needs satisfied and live a life free from unnecessary suffering, which may require giving them resources for free.[18] By minimizing fair use and rendering invisible the public domain, the NPPA spokesperson rehearsed the first account and the importance of merit in a system of exclusive intel-lectual property rights. He implied a rejection of the more modern theory of distributive justice that demands access to cultural resources, including those authored or invented by others. Underlying the more modern the-ory is that free or subsidized access to resources minimizes physical and emotional suffering as well as acrimonious inequality, with the greatest up-side being productivity and prosperity.[19] Contrary to undermining culture and creating injustice, a robust public domain and limitations on exclusive property ownership provide essential cultural resources to current and future generations of artists and innovators, facilitating common welfare and community-wide justice for more people.

In the specific context of intellectual property, these ancient debates materialize in the scope of limitations on rights, such as with fair use and first sale, and also in the scope of subject matter debates. We ask: Do more exceptions to and limitations on copyright and patent promote progress of science and the useful arts? Does generous access to creative and innovative works through digitization and the internet facilitate more creativity and innovation? Or is more perfect control and uncompromising requirement of payment for intellectual property's use the best way to optimize its pro-duction and distribution?

IP's exclusivity can stifle collaboration and follow-on innovation, thwart partnerships and relationships, and restrict capabilities in its requirement of permission or payment to proceed.[20] It has always been true that fair use and other IP limitations and exceptions such as the first sale doctrine are essential to the "breathing space" that all intellectual property regimes claim to provide.[21] And yet with more work digitally available and digital access dissolving geographic, institutional, and political boundaries, that "breathing space" expands by virtue of our Digital Age technologies. Copying and distribution is the heartbeat of the internet, and it is what IP aims to control statutorily with significant financial (and sometimes criminal) sanctions. Insofar as access to the internet and its resources are critical to sustaining meaningful existence in twenty-first-century everyday life, so are its essential mechanisms of copying and distribution that IP law regulates. This IP function creates scarcity where the internet would generate abundance.[22] And this means that IP protection, if as broadly enforced as the NPPA spokesperson sought, is lethal to the benefits that the Digital Age has so far provided. It might also be lethal to the view of distributive justice that assures to all sufficient access to creative and innovative work in order to thrive.

Whether intellectual property law stifles or enables creativity and innovation surely depends on context and community. This chapter builds on the NPPA representative's account with many more and diverse accounts from creators and innovators describing how IP works and does not work for them in terms of their particular communities and practices. We learn from these accounts that "progress" for creators and innovators is not predominantly measured by financial growth or gross wealth. Creators and innovators instead describe progress more broadly in terms of opportunities and freedoms that enable them to be or do what they have reason to value, such as participating in a particular kind of work or building sustaining and sustainable relationships with others. They rehearse the second and more contemporary form of distributive justice that expects mutual sharing of private property in order to develop and grow resources in common. These sharing practices assume and instantiate what I call "fairer uses."

The diverse but distinct categories of tolerated, unauthorized copying and distribution of and access to creative and innovative work reflect the more modern view of distributive justice. In it, baseline resources are anticipated and celebrated as a condition of virtuous living together in society. Based on my accumulation and analysis of these varied accounts, the NPPA spokesperson's comments are unrepresentative (or at least present an extreme version) of the views and practices of everyday creators and innovators. Nonetheless, his commentary's lucidity and its contentiousness help identify the terms on which an agreeable resolution of distributive justice claims may turn.

Before delving into the "fairer use" accounts, I describe underlying values that these fairer uses both stimulate and sustain. As in previous chapters discussing other fundamental values, I highlight the contours of distributive justice generally and its place in intellectual property specifically. This aims to be a basic framework through which to interpret the specific and more nuanced accounts from creators and innovators that illuminate these fairer uses in practice. Thereafter, I dig into themes and details of the data to illustrate three patterns in fairer use stories built on the framework of distributive justice and drawn from the lives of everyday creators and innovators.

I. DISTRIBUTIVE JUSTICE DIMENSIONS

A. IP's Distributive Justice Justification

Intellectual property's limited exclusivity aims to facilitate the production of new resources and materials to promote science and the useful arts. Patents and copyrights also generate a public domain through their limited terms: when they expire, they are free to all. And all federal intellectual properties contain substantial limitations and exceptions to their exclusivity to enable meaningful access by others. What is meaningful access, and why hard-wire access to the public domain into intellectual property law? The answer for both is the same. Intellectual property law's conceit is that every person is or can be creative or inventive if provided with sufficient cultural and scientific resources. An unjust or malfunctioning intellectual property system therefore impedes everyday creativity and innovation, hobbling the hands and minds of aspiring authors and inventors. IP requires access to essential cultural and scientific resources to realize the virtues achieved through them. As such, IP law demands (some would say is defined by) a theory of optimal resource allocation—a form of distributive justice—grounded in human capability and flourishing.[23]

Most theories and applications of distributive justice principles presume exhaustibility, depletion of resources, and some measure of inequality; indeed, modern theories of distributive justice presume the existence of poverty and the compulsion to minimize it.[24] Because basic material resources could be scarce, expensive, or wasted if left unregulated, decent and virtuous societies require a distributive agenda in order to provide those essential material resources. This is true of clean water, food, and shelter and of services such as health care and education. But is it true for cultural and intellectual resources? Why create limitations on cultural and intellectual resources through IP, producing scarcity and resource allocation problems, when so much creativity and invention is born free and absent IP protection in the first place? All IP systems generate fences around cultural and intellectual goods that otherwise are inherently sharable and inexhaustible—ideas are not depleted when used; played music or copied art does not disappear, it propagates. IP's exclusivity and artificial scarcity demand justification.

The economic explanation is that without the incentive of strong property rights, we would be plagued by underproduction of cultural and intellectual goods, especially those that are expensive to create and distribute. This economic explanation dominates IP law's justification. And yet this incentive story is insufficient to justify the extent to which intellectual property law has over decades evolved to swell in subject matter and usage scope to the detriment of a shrinking public domain and access to cultural and intellectual resources.[25] IP's incentive story of economic necessity is simplistic and overdetermined as well as undermined and contradicted by empirical, philosophical, and humanistic interventions.[26] And yet this story persists in describing necessary and strong forms of exclusivity to promote progress of all kinds of science and the useful arts.

For most of the twentieth century, the view of scientific and aesthetic "progress" was accumulationist, aiming for more inventions, more authored works, more trademarks.[27] During the early decades of the twentieth century, the explicit goal of economic policy and the nation's political agenda was to grow capital assets regardless of how they were distributed.[28] Indeed, under the rubric of liberty to contract, the U.S. Supreme Court issued several decisions (since discredited and overruled) enforcing the principles of unregulated markets and laissez-faire capitalism as constitutional mandates.[29] The faulty assumptions underlying these decisions included that freedom to contract and laboring without minimum wages or safe working conditions would grow opportunities for everyone.[30] At the same time, IP laws reflected a similar laissez-faire regulatory policy.[31]

As the introduction mentioned, at the beginning of the twentieth century the Supreme Court issued a now-canonical decision about copyright law and its nondiscriminatory application to all forms of authored work, be they fine art or circus posters. In that decision, *Bleistein v. Donaldson Lithographic Co.*, the court rejected the argument that circus advertisements are of insufficient "artistic merit . . . value and usefulness to be entitled to copyright."[32] Justice Oliver Wendell Holmes wrote the following in the majority opinion:

> A picture is none the less a picture and none the less a subject of copyright that it is used for an advertisement. . . . It would be a dangerous undertaking for persons trained only to the law to constitute themselves final judges of the worth of pictorial illustrations, outside of the narrowest and most obvious limits. At the one extreme some works of genius would be sure to miss appreciation. . . . At the other end, copyright would be denied to pictures which appealed to a public less educated than the judge.[33]

What justifies copyright protection, then, if not the application of some standard of aesthetic progress under the constitutional provision? There are two answers: authorship—the human act of authoring an original work of expression; and the demonstrated commercial value of the work. Justice Holmes continued:

> Works are not less connected with the fine arts [and therefore uncopyright-able] because their pictorial quality attracts the crowd and therefore gives them a real use—if use means to increase trade and to help make money. . . . [I]f they command the interest of any public, they have a commercial value— it would be bold to say that they have not an aesthetic and educational value—and the taste of any public is not to be treated with contempt.[34]

The *Bleistein* decision rehearsed a rhetoric that survives today—one of the common-man author's and inventor's opportunities in a young, industrious nation and the liberalizing laws that would facilitate (not frustrate) those hopes for prosperity. By the late twentieth century, patentable subject matter expanded to include "anything under the sun made by man" as long as it remained novel, nonobvious, and useful.[35] And trademark subject matter scope also grew, to include not only words and symbols but as the federal statute now says, any "trademark by which the goods of the applicant may be distinguished from the goods of others."[36] The possibility of massive IP accumulation from these lowered bars and broader scope form part of the same story tying capital accumulation to social progress. Its origins in *Bleistein*'s anti-hierarchical and populist sentiment are laudable in principle. But the march of capitalism through the twentieth century into the twenty-first demonstrates that unregulated markets and populist politics do not necessarily follow fair procedures or produce fair outcomes.

Canonical philosophers have disagreed about what "fair" looks like under conditions of scarcity.[37] And yet, regarding intellectual property, it is hard to imagine the constitutional goal of progress of science and the useful arts demanding anything but substantive, qualitative outcomes. Intellectual property aims to improve society, not just to promote the production of *more* intellectual property separate from the things or experiences to which the intellectual property label is attached. Indeed, when considering the fair distribution of cultural and intellectual resources, special and substantive preferences are baked into the IP laws themselves.[38] These preferences include consumer access and choice; free speech and critical dialogue; resource-strapped follow-on creators and innovators; specific users such as educators, religious organizations, small businesses, and the hearing and visually impaired; and rare disease patients (to name just a few).[39] Despite these preferences, intellectual property laws aspire to be technology- and content-neutral to avoid the specter of ideological or partisan bias in the judicial evaluation of creative or innovative work. As Justice Holmes said, "it would be a dangerous undertaking for persons trained only to the law to constitute themselves final judges of the worth of pictorial illustrations." This aspiration is not only to protect the judiciary's reputation but also to promote diversity of productive means and output—diversity being a key value.[40] Implicitly—and my goal here is to make the proposition explicit—intellectual property rules have long been internalizing varied and sometimes conflicting distributive justice concerns.

B. A Contemporary Agenda for Distributive Justice

Intellectual property law describes itself as balancing access and exclusivity to promote progress for all.[41] By contrast, creators and innovators describe IP laws that limit access frustrate progress. And so they routinely avoid the constraints of IP regulation and err on the side of more promiscuous sharing—what I call "fairer uses." They resist IP law's production of cultural and intellectual scarcity through its exclusive rights. And instead, their accounts of creativity and innovation describe practices that enable, expect, and tolerate diverse forms of unauthorized uses of their own and other people's intellectual property. Grounded and situated practices of indulgent sharing undermine the dominant legal narratives of necessary exclusivity. Creators and innovators often work without regard to specific legal and technological constraints when possible. Rather, they rely on norms and affordances of their specific practices and communities to generate or maintain access to cultural and intellectual resources that feed their work. The variations of everyday behaviors described below express values in tension with IP's traditional doctrines. Nonetheless, they support the work of and sustain creator communities by producing intrinsic satisfaction and extrinsic social benefits. In other words, the permissive sharing of cultural and intellectual resources, which IP ostensibly constrains, actually affords fruitful opportunities for and freedoms in creativity and innovation. In breaching IP rules, creators and innovators practice their own distributive agenda.

Making one's own rules for exclusivity and sharing may be necessary given how the Digital Age facilitates more perfect enforcement of intellectual property with regard to copying, surveillance, and use. It may seem that the opposite is true: that the internet enables instantaneous copying and distribution without permission or payment. But already present are digital fingerprints, block chain–enabled unique identifiers, and ubiquitous surveillance of search queries and web browsing, all of which enable hypercontrolled use of resources that previously flowed more freely.[42] Digital rights management systems lock down information and expression that would otherwise be unprotected by intellectual property law and would be likely to circulate unrestrained. Automated content management systems take down or disable music videos and images from internet platforms before a determination of protectability (or even a desire for protection).[43] An abundance of material on the internet used to be free and legally unprotected but is now tolled or restricted due to technological advances in digital locks and the proliferation of "walled gardens."[44]

My aim is not to question whether payment should be made for uses, or whether access to cultural and intellectual resources on which creativity and innovation rely is more or less flexible today. These are enduring debates with analogies in the material world. (Should clean water and air be free, subsidized, or tolled? Who pays for clean water and air, how much, and under what conditions? Today, is access to clean water and air easier? For whom and at what cost?) My point is to demonstrate how today, those who generate and exploit cultural and intellectual resources are more nuanced and flexible in their distributive rules and practices than is the law, with its property-guided expectations for exclusivity management and payment. Everyday creators and innovators articulate in their accounts and instantiate in their behavior a distributive justice agenda that is in many ways more generous ("fairer") than the law's formal application, despite—or perhaps because of—the Digital Age's new risks and opportunities.

In more than one hundred interviews that I conducted with a range of creators and innovators, I sought to understand the effects of the internet and digital technologies on creative and innovative practices.[45] In particular, I was interested in opportunities for earning a living and developing productive partnerships. How does the generativity of our internet age facilitate or frustrate working creators and innovators? What helps manage the internet's opportunities and drawbacks? Interviewees came from a broad range of creative and innovative professions—fiction writing and journalism, visual and fine arts, designers of services and goods, photography, filmmaking, advertising, software and hardware engineering, e-commerce development, chemical engineering, and the medical and pharmaceutical industries. Reading across the accounts and citing to many as illustration, the discussion below explores themes of sharing and borrowing ("fairer uses") within and among these professional communities in the Digital Age. Interviewees described sharing and borrowing practices that the internet makes easy—and IP law would prohibit—as critical to sustaining good work. But the described practices and values also have roots in creative and innovative communities that predate the internet, anchoring these distributive justice themes and their variations on fairer uses in intergenerational, field-specific practices. These intergenerational practices of fairer uses, adapted for the internet age, enable learning, mentoring, and evolution that promote and sustain the arts and sciences.

As a general matter, the creators and innovators I interviewed did not describe accumulationist goals. They do not aim to collect things or money for their own sake. They also seemed to reject the idea of maximizing consumer preferences and leaving markets to decide successes and failures. Their goals are substantive and discriminating and include protecting certain processes and outcomes over others. Within this framework, three specific themes arise—or, as I call them, "stories," given their narrative form, moral points, and multifaceted actors and motivations. These stories reflect central features of well-worn theories of distributive justice.

The first story describes a process of human flourishing over the terrain of a fertile public domain. Its central elements are play and self-determination in that play.[46] The public domain is described as a critical watering hole on which all of my interviewees rely to pursue and realize creative and inventive work. This play inevitably involves working with or borrowing from other creators and innovators, either explicitly or implicitly. Being influenced by and drawing precedent from those who work nearby or in the past is necessary for creative and innovative practices, both for skill development and success. Access to and use of this rich public domain that originated with and includes the work of others is expected and assumed.

The second story centers on human dignity, with characters who insist on mutual respect and reciprocity regarding resource use and sharing. Dignity demands attribution and credit—a form of recognition that creators and innovators describe as deeply rooted in their practice norms as a condition of drawing on the work of others. Common practices of recognition, which among some may reflect homage and implicit or explicit citation, help sustain communities by distributing market prospects and credit. These credit practices also help maintain a history of the fields by referring to past participants and the development of work over time, thereby generating a sense of belonging by locating people within these practices and their evolution. Credit practices also enable critical engagement with the work of the creative and innovative communities when conditioned on respect for the intrinsic value of each person's contribution. These attribution practices are not without tensions around the subjective evaluation and experience of critique as gainful and dignified. But their aim is to sow conditions to grow meaningful activity. This includes engaging cognitive capacities and developing an audience of supporters defined and celebrated as diverse. Human dignity has varied meanings. But these are some of the characteristics of dignity anchoring a just distribution of resources in these accounts.

The third story features intellectual autonomy as a cornerstone of collective well-being and a just society. Creators and innovators seek freedom to develop domain knowledge and expertise, and they expect that doing so will facilitate not only their own welfare but also democracy and self-government on local and larger scales.[47] For everyday creators and innovators, this includes the freedom to make improvements and to iterate existing work by themselves or in collaboration with others. Central to this account of intellectual autonomy as a distributive justice variant is that exclusive rights are awarded only to the truly new and not to what is derivative or additive. More is left in the public domain for exploration and play. A higher bar for what is new or creative drives exclusive ownership into a narrower category and may return smaller earnings from exclusive rights to creators and innovators. But they ascribe benefits—including more intellectual autonomy—to this higher bar, as well as multiple and diverse opportunities to earn a living doing their work, not only from intellectual property rights. They assume that the socioeconomic contexts in which they work can sustain their particular creative or innovative practices and anticipated resource needs. In other words, they find that by following these norms and practices (often in defiance of IP rules) the pie is usually big enough for them to pursue their creative and innovative work without interference. This assumes the absence of abusive or unjust practices—an important and hopeful assumption.

What is the relevance of these stories of a grounded distributive justice agenda to the NPPA spokesperson's statements at the orphan works roundtable? His comments about the injustice perpetrated by Google Books reflect a perception of resource scarcity (of payments and revenue), a threat to the recognition of quality work, a critique of the consolidation of control over resources, and a lack of respect toward authors and artists akin (in his eristical analogy) to the dehumanizing effect of racial segregation. His telling was an extreme read of some of these stories' elements.

But his account omitted two key factors present in all three distributive justice stories: the structural anchor of a public domain and a broad view of the essential components for a sustainable future in creative or innovative fields. These are fatal omissions, and they are related: an absence of precarity and the presence of trust in institutions or organizations underlie these distributive justice stories. Chapter 5 describes how both institutional precarity and distrust unsettle the creative and innovative ecosystems that are grounded in distributive justice values. In this way, the NPPA spokesperson's commentary explains the imperative of distributive justice for sustainable well-being and the corrosive effects of its extinction.

II. FAIRER USE STORIES ABOUT CREATIVE AND INNOVATIVE PRACTICES

Most creators and innovators must copy from and build on others' work to do their own work. Despite IP's anti-copying principle, artists, scientists, engineers, and their business partners flout strict anti-copying enforcement, instead habitually under-enforcing their own IP. They do not describe their practices in this way, however. Most are unfamiliar with IP law; what their accounts convey are various forms of generosity and sharing (or "tolerated uses")[48] that they assume form parts of a legal system meant to be reasonable. They insist on this reasonableness as a matter of self-determination and community sustainability within their particular fields.

The fairer use stories of human flourishing, dignity, and intellectual autonomy share three common features, in addition to all being conceptually anchored in theories of distributive justice: they each highlight a rich public domain, respect for creators and innovators, and domain expertise that generates broad opportunities to refine creative and inventive practices. In other words, these fairer use stories have context, characters, and plot. The context of the public domain focuses on the individual playing in a big sandbox (or a "big pool," as one person described it) in order to participate, work, and learn. The characters (the creators and innovators themselves) develop relationships and communities through mutual obligation and respect to facilitate both dynamism and sustainability. The plot combines the first two in the pursuit of high quality and meaningful activity. It celebrates the creative and innovative work produced as improving prior experiences or producing truly new experiences and expanding access to both. Although the interviewees' accounts are specific to each person and their practice, their stories all reflect what these fairer uses make possible—productive, self-directed work, broad access to its fruits by others, and individual and community flourishing. These are portraits of justly distributed creativity and innovation, made and shared under conditions that everyday creators and innovators describe as fair and worth maintaining.

A. The Context: Reconceiving the Public Domain

Copying and being strongly influenced by others' work are inevitable features of creative and innovative practices. Forms of copying and influence vary, but the creators and innovators I interviewed mostly explained it as a way of learning from each other to develop field-specific skills. Building from others to make one's own way is a well-worn and accepted path. It reinforces community through reliance and common ties. It also generates competition and productive interactions, which are embraced as progressing science and the useful arts.

A photographer, David, with a past commercial practice in fashion photography who now mainly works producing fine art photographs, explained that he would be fine with someone copying his style or artistic perspective because "they would be doing something that is [in] their own experience, . . . that is what being an artist is. Picasso did that, too." Other interviewees drew this same distinction between troublesome copying—exact or verbatim reproduction—and acceptable, expected copying that is influenced by and borrows particular styles or aspects from another's work. The former is a step too far; the latter is something that all artists and innovators do. Mary, a singer-songwriter and musical performer, explained this sentiment and practice:

> A total copy rip-off, you know, [is] not so great. But if someone's just taking parts, I mean, and being influenced by it, that's totally great—or inspired in some way by it. . . . It's all this big pool, and we're throwing stuff into it. So if someone is being inspired to write something by it or stealing an image . . . yeah, that's unavoidable.

The sense that being influenced by others and that borrowing from the "big pool" is inevitable and accepted implicates a discourse of self-determination and play. How else is one supposed to speak the language of and participate in the domain they inhabit? Restrictions on this kind of borrowing or influence are like shackles, objectionably constraining the pursuit and realization of one's creative goals.

Some creators and innovators explicitly described the skill transmission that arises from borrowing styles and features of another's work. A children's book author at the end of her career, Barbara described mentoring many aspiring writers seeking careers similar to hers. She specifically recalled one young writer she worked with:

> [She] would submit an outline, and then . . . I'd call her and she'd say, "Oh, goody, goody! Now we get to do the Barbara's School of Plotting." . . . She was

really, really learning from me. . . . She has gone on to have a very nice career. In fact, a couple of them have. And I feel like—I feel sort of like a proud
grandmother or something.

Grandchildren do not have to resemble their grandparents, but Barbara's
metaphor explicitly celebrates the idea of familial traits—here, creative
practices and skills—passed from one generation of writer to the other.
Mark, a Cambridge-based photographer, described a similar situation,
but one that produced some competition, which is also inevitable among
members of the same field. He described how his mentee's work resembled
his own to the point of confusion:

> I had an assistant who was my third, I've had so many assistants, and they've
> all been wonderful in their own way, but I had one who I got along with well,
> her work was . . . good, and I finally said, "You should go out on your own,"
> and I helped her get a job . . . and it turns out that she was a better photog-
> rapher than me in some ways, and she started taking on some of my clients,
> and I don't think she aggressively did that. . . . Every time . . . I'd see a photo-
> graph, I'd almost thought I shot it, kind of thing.

Not all borrowing or influences will be embraced, especially when they
too closely resemble their precedents. But teachers (and parents) understand that students (and children) learn by copying and emulating men-
tors—the first step toward independent thought and practice.

Bob, a copyright lawyer with a long career in the field, explained that
lawyers and businesspeople know that borrowing and being influenced are
the norm for their creator and innovator clients. He invoked the cliché of
"standing on the shoulders of giants" to explain that fair use is contextual
and depends on specific industry practices:

> Sampling [practices in music] are . . . ordinarily going to be appropriate fair
> uses of material. I realize there's lots of close lines. I absolutely understand
> that. I don't get involved with music in part because it's too hard for me. But
> having said that, I do believe that we stand on the shoulder of giants. Stuff
> that's in the—what's in the air that helps you create the next thing is—and
> that's the way life has gone.

The "stuff . . . in the air that helps . . . create the next thing" resembles
the "big pool" described by Mary, the musician. Together, both metaphors

reflect the ubiquitous fact of simultaneous invention in science and technology.[49] Everyday creators and innovators cannot but help influence each other and build toward similar goals in related ways. They do so both consciously and unconsciously and without surprise. But intellectual property law does not comfortably allow for it.[50]

Andrew, an internet entrepreneur who develops data management and storage systems and has successfully built several companies, explained how his first big idea "never got executed by *us*. It got executed by [another company]—it was in the air, you see. It was just a matter of time." He went on to explain how simultaneous invention works in his experience: "You know, there are always many smart people that are exposed to the same conditions, and they will come up—I actually believe there are very few ideas that are such breakthroughs that you won't have, over a period of two years, many people come up with the idea." Kevin, a telecom investor and former software engineer, was more explicit about paying attention to what's "in the air" as a strategy—a way of capitalizing on the "big pool." He described how "very little entrepreneurship, in fact, is about developing really fundamentally new things. . . . You don't fund a startup to do new . . . solid state device physics. It's too risky; it's too expensive. It takes too long. Usually, it's people taking an existing thing, reconfiguring it." Innovation happens incrementally, Kevin said, and relies on common ground.

Some interviewees described feeling flattered when confronted with this inevitable or natural copying. Melanie, a documentary filmmaker, said that "everything's derivative. Like art in general. You know, people are always emulating. . . . I would be flattered." Lisa, an award-winning novelist, echoed this sentiment:

> I would be flattered to be quoted. I mean, it's very flattering and pleasing to think that something that you have written has kind of entered the public domain. . . . I think that probably what enrages people [is] the failure to ask permission. I bet if people asked permission, a lot of writers would either charge a small amount of money, or they would say, "Sure." You know, it could be free. "Take it, and I'm glad."

For Jennifer, a journalist, a rich public domain is essential for work like hers to be done well. And that means that drawing from it and copying others' work is part of how news is written:

> Once my story is out there with its copyright, I just think, "Oh, that's kind
> of obnoxious" if somebody copies it. But my story is already out, so I have
> performed my function. I mean, everyone kind of draws on each other. . . .
> The truth is . . . the copying would have to be pretty egregious for me to care
> about it, because so much of what we do is kind of in the public domain, you
> know?

Both Lisa and Jennifer expressed limits on celebrated and permissible copying, but both also understand that an open and active public sphere is necessary to produce work in the first place. They also said that they believe they are contributing to that public sphere with their work as much as they are borrowing from it to do their work. These creators and innovators described the "social conditions conducive to flourishing lives."[51] They and others reflected a belief that intellectual property rules preventing copying should not interfere with their art and science.

This fairer use story relies on an abundant public domain—a "big pool" and work that is "in the air"—to promote play and participation within creative and innovative communities so that its members may pursue what they value. It features more flexibility than IP law usually allows, embracing situations that resemble derivative uses in copyright law and the making of equivalent inventions in patent law that would ordinarily require permission and payment. Constraints exist, to be sure (and will be described more below). But tolerance is high for copying and borrowing to sustain and grow a public domain that enables self-determination to learn and work.

B. The Characters: Expecting Respect

Authors and inventors are even less concerned with copying and borrowing when other community norms are followed, such as attribution, homage, and avoiding derogatory reuse. Values underlying these norms include respect for diverse creative and innovative practices and mutual obligations of credit and forbearance. Attribution includes credit and name recognition practices that respect the intellectual and physical work of others. Homage entails the perspective of history and changing practices over time, projecting a sense of precedent and evolution. Creators and innovators develop their identities and work over decades, expecting that what counts as meaningful activity within their fields evolves and that their practice communities provide room to reflect on and critique these changes. Authors and inventors define derogatory responses as norm-violating behavior resembling defamation or assault, which they experience as dignitary and bodily autonomy injuries such as those described in chapter 3.

Community norms are distinct from intellectual property regimes. Attribution is not required in copyright, and it is practiced in patent law only through the congested process of prior art claiming in patent applications. Trademark law formally eschews giving credit to others because trademarks amplify distinctiveness and identification of the owner's mark; giving credit to others arguably undermines this goal.[52] Derogatory use, on the other hand, is expressly allowed in all IP regimes as a feature of critical fair use in copyright law, First Amendment expressive uses in trademark law, and first sale freedoms to reuse, disassemble, or destroy your owned property (such as electronic devices, machines, or consumers goods) in patent, copyright, and trademark law. But everyday creators and innovators relate shared expectations to avoid derogatory use to further community well-being and mutual respect. Although critical engagement is encouraged, uses or copies that subjectively degrade the work, its originator, or its subject are not. Drawing the line between subjectively derogatory use and critical use, however, remains subject to ongoing negotiation and dispute.

1. Name Recognition and Credit

Attribution features so centrally in the tolerance for fairer uses that many creators and innovators mistakenly believe that intellectual property law requires it. Those I interviewed described attribution's importance in several ways. Some recalled awkward but necessary interactions to clear the air after instances of non-attribution among acquaintances. Mary, the musician, described addressing a subconscious copying incident with directness, collegiality, and mutual respect:

> There are a couple awkward moments where one person will have worked on a song for a while, but then another person puts out a record and there's imagery from that song on their record but the record comes out first so it looks like the other person is copying. . . . [A fellow songwriter] came up to me and was like "Oh my God, I think I stole a line from you for this song." So

we just chat amongst ourselves when we notice that stuff, it clears the air. But no one's ever a creep about it.

Not being "a creep" and tolerating the inevitable copying that occurs is a cornerstone of fluid, productive creativity and innovation. And according to copyright historian Peter Decherney, intolerance for copying leads to stylistic anachronisms.[53] He explained that "both the way that we make and experience art change over time. And creation and consumption are inflected with cultural norms about borrowing and influence."[54] Authors and inventors avoid anachronistic behavior by following cultural norms of borrowing and credit, drawing on each other to participate in cultural and scientific exchanges. When those norms are violated, even if a law has not been broken, anger can lead to lawsuits. Ann, an award-winning documentary filmmaker with her own film production company, said she accepts that copying norms shift with rapid technological change but worries that the ease of internet-driven copying and distribution debilitates her business model:

> The Napster model is happening to film. . . . No matter how much technology we invent and reinvent [to prevent unlawful distribution of copies and derivatives], . . . basically technological distribution will always be ahead of us, and basically we will be distributing our films for free. I mean, we might get a dollar here, a few pennies there, but . . . as long as it's attributed, you know, I think that's the trend. So I expect that more and more that will happen. I don't like it, because when you cut and paste and mash up, it's very hard to tell what is yours and what isn't, and so there's a slippery slope in the claim of ownership. But I'm not gonna go crazy about that.

While accepting copying, which is all but unstoppable given the internet's lifeblood of networked dissemination, Ann said she draws the line at lack of attribution or misattribution. Recall Lisa, the novelist, who said she was "flattered to be quoted" and called it "pleasing to think that something you have written has . . . entered the public domain." Lisa also said that "the failure to ask permission" angers her. Like Ann's attribution expectation, Lisa explained that asking permission shows respect for the author and that failure to do so is impertinent and also usually unnecessary. She said, "I bet if people asked permission, a lot of writers would either charge a small amount of money, or they would say, 'Sure.' You know, it could be free. 'Take it, and I'm glad.'"

The creators and innovators I interviewed consider failure to credit profoundly insulting. Karen, a visual artist who does installation work and complex ink drawings, likened the anger and agitation around misattribution or lack of credit to the fear and anxiety that a burglary or other personal invasion would generate: "The bottom line with a lot of this stuff, is that if somebody—if they—if you have communication with them, and you are asked [permission], and you are part of the process, then it's not like somebody just walking in, robbing something, and you don't see them in the dark of night." These fervid sentiments cross domains and professions. Some interviewees recounted failure to properly attribute causing deep rifts in working relationships. Robert, an academic chemist and cofounder of a company that develops clinical trial improvements, vividly described fights about attribution in his field:

> I mean, there's people who are just hysterical about citation and about "I did it first." ... The competition for credit is vicious ... for most people. It's pretty horrible. I mean, I find myself wanting to throw up in half the conversations because it's so ferocious.

Professionals practice careful attribution strategies to avoid violating this important norm of giving credit where due. One interviewee, a web designer and information architect, explained his attitude as follows:

> I am really anal about both references that I give and also referring to my own work—what my role was and how collaborative or not it was. So if there was an overarching idea that I came up with on my own, I will say that. If it was something that came up in collaboration, I say that. There are a lot of people that claim authorship over work over which they were collaborators. ... It's just unethical.

Attorneys and business managers are especially careful about attribution practices because they facilitate the collegial functioning of companies. And in the case of patents, misattribution can mean legal liability if inventors or prior art are left off patent filings. Any mistakes of inventorship invalidates a patent, whether they are errors of over-inclusion or omission. Several attorney-interviewees described how they have to "indoctrinate" their clients or in-house scientist colleagues about the proper legal standard for credit on patents because the scientific norms of over-inclusiveness and hierarchy within their fields are out of sync with the legal rules. Ted, a lawyer and vice president of a high-tech energy company, explained that the problem "is far bigger . . . when you set up inventorship so that it excludes an external collaborator or something like that. . . . But you still want to do the right thing." Carol, who was previously a university biologist, described a sincere attentiveness to accurate attribution among her clients:

> I have some applications with solo inventors. And when I see that, I tend to ask questions, because if you are an academic scientist, I find it hard to believe you're the only one that invented—because they talk, you know? . . . I think that the way that science goes now is you really need collaboration in order to build scientific programs. And with collaboration is going to come joint inventorship, because you sit in a room and you talk. And joint inventorship is a tough . . . because like I tell inventors, you know, you don't know who thought of it first in their head. . . . I think generally speaking, most inventors want to get it right. They don't want to exclude people.

Attribution and credit involve recognizing and not devaluing or ignoring another person's commitment and contribution. Attribution affirms belonging, representativeness, and inclusive collaboration. Authorship and inventorship are not ranked in law. One is either an author or not, an inventor or not. Some creative and innovative fields have developed more nuanced naming practices (for example, first authors on scientific journal articles, and split sheets in music to divide royalties according to contribution to the songwriting). But most creators and innovators give credit and name contributors in a general and generous way. From the interviews I conducted, it seems that the motivation for this attribution norm is its instantiation of respect for creators and innovators and for the mutuality and reciprocation that is modeled and learned in the professional communities in which they work.

2. Homage and Critical Engagement

Not all attribution is welcome, of course. Some people may wish not to be affiliated with expression they dislike or oppose. Transgressing the line from homage to derision is a risk attendant to borrowing and attribution. Critical, cutting-edge art for one artist or fascinating technology for one inventor may to the original author or inventor be devastating or dangerous work from a reputational, aesthetic, or practical standpoint. Everyday creators and innovators negotiate this important line between homage and critical engagement on one side and defamatory or dangerous derivatives on the other. Those I interviewed described the permissive side of the line as good faith borrowing, which, as already discussed, may be accompanied by a request and a modest payment. They also described unauthorized borrowing as an often-acceptable part of critical work because it is compelled by the art or science. The accounts below relay subjective (and some might say moralistic) gatekeeping of this line between permissive and derisive uses that is common in practice but controversial in law. Intellectual property law's application is supposed to be ideologically neutral. These examples of permitted homage or critical engagement flout that neutrality and serve what creators and innovators consider "worthy" and mission-aligned practices and projects.

Melanie, a filmmaker and film producer, described negotiating use of archival photographs for a project between two relatively budget-constrained entities:

> I would be willing to give things for free if it was a worthy project, you know? . . . I've learned this with every negotiation. . . . I would tell a historical society, "This is a PBS project, and we have the money and the budget, and you should charge us $100 a picture." Like I know what I think is a fair price, and [instead the historical society is] . . . giving it to us for free? "You guys need the money. We *have* the money. We should give you the money!" So I wouldn't say to them, "Give it to us for free." I mean, I guess I have a feeling of what's fair, and so we sort of feel like these little nonprofits, they should definitely charge if they have these things they are offering. But I would say if they said to me, "We want to charge you a $1000 for a picture," I would say, "You are crazy! Even a commercial place doesn't charge me that much money, and I can't use your material. That will bust my budget. But you won't bust my budget if you charge me $100, and if I use more than 30 pictures, you'd knock it down to $50 per."

Notice how Melanie had internalized a fair price, which was not free and included permission, but was affordable and relative to the organization's means. She also internalized the expectation of sharing among those with shared missions of collecting and producing historical work. These kinds of value judgments about the nature of the use and the entity seeking to use the material permeate assertions of "fairer uses," including the project being a "worthy" one. Interviewees described deferring to high-quality work (as understood in disciplinary terms), admirable reuses, and the importance of reciprocity in their tolerance for these fairer uses. In law, the ability to pay is irrelevant to the legality or illegality of the use. And quality, worthiness, or reciprocity of uses are antithetical to copyright law's commitment to aesthetic nondiscrimination and patent law's technology neutrality principle. Nonetheless, interviewees described the values of quality work and ability to pay as explaining these fairer uses in their fields.

Of course, artists and innovators understand that judgments of work quality can be subjective, and thus on balance they are flexible arbiters of this standard. Leo, an artist who works primarily with paint, explained that he "can't be too possessive" about uses of his work, even if it is copied and put on T-shirts to sell on a street corner—a question I asked many artist-interviewees to test their tolerance for unauthorized commercial uses:

> Look, ultimately . . . I paint because I want to share, you know, my visual— my sense of how I see the world, how I see color, with other people. I think I've got to . . . not be totally possessive about that. So . . . as long as someone was doing it in a way that I felt was up to the quality, you know? . . . But if you think they are degrading your work, that's [another] thing. Right?

Interviewees described considering quality, aesthetic value, and freedom for other artists, balanced against the possibility of offensive copying. Dan, a theatrical and orchestral composer, reflected these considerations, adding an expectation of revenue sharing:

> If someone wants to see [my production] differently in a different venue and that makes them happy, that's great. If they were doing it and not making any money, I wouldn't care if I didn't make any money either. If they were doing it and bring[ing] in a profit, I would like a piece of it. So in terms of what would I want in a way of a licensing fee, I mean, it's all depend[ent] on how much money they are making from it. . . . As long as it's not defamatory of

the original, they can do whatever they [want]. . . . And if somebody wants to reinterpret a character . . . which is in a non-offensive way, it's a slightly different interpretation, that's great. But to make it something which would be offensive and then put my name on it would be a problem.

These are value-laden judgments about acceptable reuse, but they reflect a desire for shared respect for the work (the original and the copy) and a belief in mutuality of authorship. The default tends to be permissive use as long as the second work's critique or reuse is made in the same spirit as the first—as an authentic aesthetic practice that continues or "reinterprets" the conversation and is not "defamatory." A belief in common purpose, and sometimes the shared upsides of the creative and innovative work, pervaded the interviewees' accounts. These fairer use stories imagine sympathetic characters with gracious attitudes toward creativity and innovation that drive community well-being.

Scientists and engineers, as well as many of their business partners, described similar reasons for widespread permissive copying: an ethic of sharing that includes presumed good faith that the downstream use conforms with the original human welfare–oriented purpose of their work. Susan is a director of technology licensing at a major university. Her practice of working with commercial entities aims to promote more science by making the tools accessible on a reasonable basis while also monitoring the quality of the tools' uses. She described negotiations around "co-exclusivity" as a way of accommodating commercial pressures, promoting accessible and progressive science, and fulfilling the university's mission of open research. Susan recounted a negotiation that included these variables:

We have this buddy who has this company . . . and he's only going to [invest] if you give . . . an exclusive license. So we decided we were going to give four licenses to suppliers, and . . . there would be an ability to audit them for quality [as a compromise]. So that would keep the price down so that it would be available, because this rapacious guy, if I'd given it to him [exclusively], nobody would have been able to afford it. . . . Now, that story went on quite happily, . . . and four or five years later, it was so evidently useful that everybody and his cousin . . . [was] just infringing like mad. And we promised the co-exclusive guys that we won't have more than four licenses. It's a mess. We're dealing with it.

Faced with having to enforce her deal and protect the relationship with her four licensees meant having to pursue those who saw the invention's value but were not paying for its use (those who were "infringing like mad"). Having started with what she thought was a sufficiently accessible supply chain, Susan realized that many more needed the tool; she wanted to provide access to it but had an obligation to her commercial partners, who wanted (and rightly expected) some exclusivity. The dispute eventually resolved with the infringers paying under-market royalties for their past uses and reasonable royalties for their future uses; and the university-licensor monitored the proliferating uses and selecting licensees to help control quality in collaboration with the original licensee-commercial partners, who continued to see revenue growth. The aim was for end-users (patients) to benefit from these multiple, semi-monitored uses of the invention, which was a hard-fought negotiated compromise managing many stakeholders. The deal took a long time to hammer out, but Susan described its compromises and reciprocity as exemplary of her office's work.

Susan's account is an example of these fairer use stories' baseline of respect and reciprocity among participants in the creative and innovative communities. Even when the copying or borrowing is uncomfortable, if creators and innovators perceive an alignment of interests and goals, they tend to accept the copying, which a strict application of IP law might not. Recall from chapter 1 how budding photographer Lee Crosson tolerated unauthorized copying of his photographs when it continued conversations that "needed to happen." Quoting F. Scott Fitzgerald, he said that while anger about the copying may be inevitable, letting the anger go was essential to the art's momentum—both his art and the work of the artist who copied him without permission. Lee's explanation of tolerating unauthorized copying rehearses the "breathing room" that copyright law provides through its extensive statutory exceptions and limitations (such as fair use), allowing for transformations of others' expression to create new meanings and messages.[55] And yet the kind of copying Lee described tolerating appears to be a derivative work—less transformative than the law demands—which would typically not be fair use and would require payment and permission. Like many similarly situated authors, Lee's tolerance for unauthorized copying is therefore broader—*fairer*—than the law allows and is based on a respect for the community and its continued vitality.

3. Justifiable Limits on Breathing Room and Bad Faith

What happens when respect or mutuality is missing? Or when financial or resource precarity threatens to stifle productivity, or infringements represent a risk to productivity and sustainable industry? These are circumstances when authors and inventors (or owners) may object to unauthorized copying. While acknowledging the importance of letting others critically engage their work, everyday creators and innovators also want to retain some control over their professional identity and the future life of their professional output. It may be difficult to draw lines between good and bad faith and between tolerated uses and personally or financially degrading ones. For IP law, these lines are especially fraught due to the law's consistency requirement and the First Amendment's viewpoint neutrality mandate. Creators and innovators navigate these challenges in order to continue their work and support the work of others. That these are hard lines to draw does not mean that they should not be insisted on. For many interviewees, bad faith or degrading uses are personal affronts or attacks on the community itself, undermining productivity. For them, fairer use stories are shaped by a professional ethic in which the community supports its members, prioritizing ongoing creativity and innovation and minimizing offense.

Ali Campbell, the portrait photographer from chapter 1, explained how she draws this line in her work:

> I think . . . if someone were to lift my photos and use 'em in . . . a Breitbart News article, I'd be livid, like, right? Because I'd be like, "I don't want to have any association with that." If someone were to do something . . . disparaging or really bigoted, I'd be really, really upset, whereas if someone's like, "I included this in a painting," or like, "I drew somebody from one of your photos," it doesn't really bother me. . . . Because I think if it's encouraging other people to do creative work, that's good, that's . . . fine with me.

For Ali and other interviewees, the tolerance limit for homage and critique is when the work offends the artist personally, professionally, or politically. The numerous recent cease-and-desist letters sent and lawsuits filed by musicians protesting politicians' use of their music in campaigns confirm this sentiment as common.[56] These are weak intellectual property claims because U.S. law privileges viewpoint neutrality and criticism as part of the First Amendment's breadth. And yet for many interviewees, this is where fairer use ends, because these uses are not perceived as continuing a conversation or making new work. They interpret these uses as disrespectful and exploitative because they neither relate to nor support creative or innovative practices and appear to undermine the original author's personality or integrity.

As chapter 1 described in detail, photographers explain how reuses of photographs that are out of context or retouched without permission threaten the integrity of the professional photography field. If, for example, people cannot rely on photojournalism to tell a truthful story, then what happens to the profession of news reporting and image-making? Pharmaceutical executives describe a similar tension. Medicine and medical devices are designed generally to improve people's health. The field suffers if off-label or infringing uses injure patients, or if beneficial uses are inaccessible due to pricing decisions beyond scientists' control. In these situations, withholding permission is motivated by recognition of and respect for the inventive communities and the good they do. Uses that degrade the field and corrupt its purposes undermine support for art and science, and everyday creators and innovators think that they should be preventable.

It seems clear that personality and professional identity are at stake in stories about fairer uses. And yet the speed at which communities and their behavioral standards evolve in the internet age challenges the stability of individual identity and community norms, making an identifiable community ethic sometimes hard to identify. Also, online communities may lack leadership or direction and resemble amorphous herds or flocks. It therefore makes sense for everyday creators and innovators to rely on professional practices and to insist on field-specific norms and ethics, such as in photojournalism or laboratory science. It is hardly novel to suggest that professional communities and cultivated institutional norms play strong roles in developing and sustaining creativity and innovation.[57] But the interviewees' emphasis on community ethics and professional identity as a feature of fairer use stories bears note. In their stories of fairer (and unfair) uses, the practice-based community helps constitute the characters who are owed and expect respect for their commitment to the work and other community members. Professional ethics are therefore a component of distributive justice and central to the progress of creativity and innovation.

And, as chapter 1 discussed, professional ethics are under siege in the Digital Age.[58] (Chapter 5 will continue this theme.)

IP "trolls" are high-profile examples of professional ethics violations that implicate distributive justice values. Instead of promoting work through community resilience, they stifle it by siphoning resources. An IP "troll" is an IP owner whose primary business model is to collect money from others' alleged infringement and who does not otherwise sell or promote the invention or creative work.[59] IP trolls are often holding companies that have a straightforward money-generating objective and no intention to practice the invention or reuse or circulate the creative work. They lie in wait—much like the troll under the bridge—and demand payment when an unsuspecting passerby crosses over. The troll did not build the bridge, nor does it maintain the bridge or even use the bridge; it just owns the bridge. As Donald, a general counsel to a software company, explained to me, "Trolls always work the same. They identify unsophisticated small companies that don't have a lot of patent experience, haven't been involved in a lot of suits, and they go in." The ethical violation, he explained, is not just the element of surprise and the exploitation but that these kinds of lawsuits go against the spirit of the Constitution and its mandate for promoting science and the useful arts by conferring benefits on authors and inventors. "So patents lawsuits among *competitors* is really what I think the Constitution envisioned when it gave these monopolies. You know, it's the right—for twenty years, you get a monopoly to your invention. But what this [troll] is doing . . . I think is very different. He does not conduct any business at all. He is not the inventor."

Trolling is not illegal, but it feels unethical and wrong to many who spend funds to settle lawsuits that could otherwise be put to productive and creative uses. In the patent context, the patents asserted by trolls are often weak or invalid, but it is cost-prohibitive to challenge them in court. In the most egregious of copyright cases, plaintiff-trolls produce or distribute low-value content (such as pornography or low-quality video), hoping to entice its unauthorized copying and further distribution in order to then collect money from infringement lawsuits, not from use licenses.[60] Settlement is the fastest, most efficient solution. Quick settlements for relatively low-dollar amounts (usually several thousand dollars), when aggregated, become millions of dollars for trolls and a huge transfer of wealth from actual creators and innovators or from benign users. Another general counsel, Jacqueline, put it this way: "The patent trolls have really taken control over . . . litigation, and it's extraordinarily painful for companies to pay extortion in order to basically just make the litigation go away." Trolls are the quintessential bad characters in the stories of fairer (and unfair) uses. They amplify through contemptuous disregard the values of sustainability, mutuality, and respect that are celebrated by everyday creators and innovators.

IP law justifies troll suits as examples of IP investments earning revenue for investors. The investors may be holding companies who invest in latent patents waiting to see if they are useful, or they may be streaming platforms or digital archives that collect unused or uncapitalized content (videos, photographs, or other creative works), waiting to see if their use grows. This behavior is analogized to investing in vacant land and waiting for it to become valuable before insisting on being paid for its use—much to the surprise of past and present users who thought the land was open to roam. These holding companies directly challenge the notion of what is or should be for public use and undermine established expectations of exclusivity's benefits. Lying in wait and then filing hundreds of lawsuits for small amounts of money to extract rent from unsuspecting users is a business model with no regard for public welfare and certainly no respect for community development or enhancement; it seeks only to aggrandize the wealth of those who already have sufficient wealth to collect low-value properties and sit on the investment.[61] Trolling is understandably criticized by creators and innovators whose primary goals are to promote art and science and the sustainability of their fields. Though it is not illegal, it is welfare-depleting (except from the point of view of the trolls), and it undermines the distributive benefits and breathing room that everyday creators and innovators incorporate into their practice.

C. The Plot: Enriching Work and Culture

Another theme of fairer use stories is that iterative improvements are welcome and not restricted. Creators and innovators express this expectation in various ways. They criticize claims to exclusivity of work that they believe is not original or novel and is simply derivative. They also explain that their own creative or inventive practices rely on others' work as a matter of skill-building until their work reaches the new or novel stage (when it is then off-limits to others, absent permission). And they contend

that true novelty and originality are rare and require significant investment of time and skill, which then justifies some limited protection. These
baseline expectations and practices deepen the pool of accessible tools
that creators and innovators have at their disposal, constituting broader
breathing room than copyright and patent law formally afford. They also
create a more limited normative scope for exclusive rights in final work
product. But creators and innovators act as if these practices will produce
sufficiently sustainable revenue over time in their fields and communities.
The point of fairer uses is to sustain creative and innovative work, and
the problem (or plot) of this fairer use story is that too much exclusivity
restricts all sorts of iterative and incremental creativity and innovation.
Exclusive rights should be reserved for the truly new or novel.

1. True Novelty Is Rare

Elizabeth, a novelist, described the higher standard of novelty for creative
works by explaining her practice of writing as starting off drawing from
the pool and then eventually reaching the point where she has created
something original. She recalled one particular instance:

> I based [my character] on somebody I met. And then as I was thinking it
> through . . . I thought . . . this is kind of like [Jane Austen's] *Emma*! That
> gives me confidence! . . . I think it gives writers . . . confidence when you can
> say, . . . "This book is just like this other famous book that . . . has lived in the
> public mind since . . . 1797 ." . . . I think it's very easy . . . to feel like human
> nature has been pretty stable for a long time, and we have probably said ev-
> erything there is to say about it.

Elizabeth said she justifies her borrowing and use of precedent in two
ways. She said that it builds confidence, which propels her own writing.
She also explained that the limited ways to effectively convey basic aspects
of human nature demand broader access to language on which all can rely;
otherwise, one just reinvents the wheel or is misunderstood. However, she
said, there is a line between what is acceptable borrowing (or copying) and
what is not:

> Conditions . . . of human nature . . . do change, have changed. . . . There are
> always these specific details that are new. So come up with a new story to tell
> me about those things. . . . I think . . . using people as models . . . to comfort

yourself and . . . feel like you have the confidence to do this thing [is fine], because it can be done. . . . And I think there's a line between that, imitating the masters until you find your feet, and just taking somebody's scaffolding for your own.

Elizabeth's distinction between "imitating the masters" and "taking somebody's scaffolding" is an important principle for her. We imitate to learn and to build confidence, and that should be allowed and encouraged, but taking that which is fundamental to another's work (the "scaffolding") is a step too far.

Creators and innovators simultaneously celebrate the hard work of everyday labor and insist on a high bar for the newness or novelty that justifies exclusivity. Together, these elements afford the freedom to work in one's field—to develop skill and capacity—from which likely arises works of diverse quality and usefulness. Outcomes range in quality and substance, and only some merit or capture an appreciative audience. The sentiment that true novelty is rare arose frequently among interviewees, notably in conversations with scientists and engineers and their lawyers or business agents. These professionals in particular often downplayed discoveries as insufficiently inventive and only small steps in science's progress. Dennis, an IP lawyer for a pharmaceutical company, elaborated:

> It's really rare to have true innovation, right? Steve Jobs and Wozniak created the personal computer, all right? Cohen and Boyer created biotechnology. . . . But most of the rest of us mere mortals just learn from other people and then the frontier of science [is] pushed back . . . gradually through similar ant-like persistence by scientists.

Dennis did not intend to demean the hard work that produces innovative goods to be sold in a competitive marketplace. He was celebrating the collaboration and collective work in the scientific community, assuming that the work inevitably builds on other work and that true innovation or originality worthy of exclusivity is special or otherwise extraordinary. He therefore assumes a much broader range of resources on which one can freely draw to contribute to knowledge and a diverse culture.

Accordingly, some interviewees expressed surprise at how IP law easily protects discrete and often minor features of inventions and creative work.

Leora, a mechanical engineer who later became an attorney working in-house with IP and contracts, described her surprise at learning this fact of IP law during an early experience patenting an invention she developed with a colleague:

> [My colleague] took a feature that was there, that really wasn't the sexy part of the invention, or anything, but he said, "You know, this is happening. And it doesn't always happen, but it's happening in this case. And yeah, it has some effects, some of which are not that interesting, but maybe some of which are, and that has potential to be interesting." . . . It was a complete revelation to me how . . . we spun it, you know. So getting a patent is different or can be different from the actual thing that you have [invented]. We had a light bulb that turned on and off with daylight, but we got a patent on a feature of that, that was enough.

Leora was not necessarily denigrating the patent system for its protection of incremental innovation. But she was describing how as an inventor and engineer, what she thought was novel and interesting was more significant and complex than what the patent system protects. That aspect of the law was "a complete revelation" to her.

Many creators and innovators adapt within these different legal standards, maintaining high standards for their own work and playing along within an ill-fitting IP system that may either under- or overprotect the work they produce.[62] As chapter 1 described, photographers acutely experience this misalignment in the internet age, and yet many also adapt, honing the skill they bring to the art of photography to maintain their reputation and livelihood. Photographers are an example of a professional class of creators who embrace amateurs in their field—and thus the possible disruptive influence of low-end competition. They also encourage people to make and share photographs and to learn how to make better photographs. But the professional photographers also insist on high standards for professional photography, both to justify the prices they charge and to distinguish their work as reliably, expertly, and beautifully made.

Recall Felice Frankel, quoted at the beginning of this chapter, who works as a science photographer rendering microscopic natural phenomena both visible and beautiful. In the Digital Age, Felice said she worries that republication or unauthorized use of her photographs will diminish her goals of scientific explanation and accuracy. But she understands that "making pictures is democratic" today. She embraces the easy access to camera equipment and the widespread practice of photography in the Digital Age, sometimes even making pictures on her own phone. Nonetheless, she champions a high standard in photography—one that distinguishes "a good picture, a good-enough picture, and a terrific picture." And she sets goals to differentiate herself in terms of her skills as a scientist, an educator, and a photographer; to use her digital photography practice to preserve the integrity of information conveyed through photographs; and to assist in developing skills and critical awareness for those who make and share pictures with digital equipment.

Felice is not alone in embracing amateur creators and hoping to train them to distinguish the excellent from the ordinary. Her account of her field today assumes without being explicit that a sustainable business model requires paying for making and copying photographs of high quality (even if it may not always be easy to discern the line between what is free to share and what uses demand payment). Like Felice, today's creators and innovators act as if, contrary to IP law, establishing a higher standard for protectability—and respecting professional artistic and business practices to define that standard—is the better and "fairer" way.

2. The Pie Should Be Big Enough for All

Implicit in "fairer uses" is a belief that revenue from a broad enough audience will support a diversity of creators and innovators. Develop amateurs into professionals within these sustainable practices, and everyone thrives together. I heard this theme echoed throughout the interviewees' accounts. For example, Barbara, the children's book author, described a situation in which she believed her works were used without permission as the basis of a less successful writer's work but did not object:

> I remember running into one of the people who copied me . . . at a local stationery store. And I said hi, and I said, "I understand you have got a new series coming out." And he blushed. . . . He said, "Well. . .yeah." I said, ". . . you know, it's the sincerest form of flattery." . . . It didn't bother me. Not at all. . . . You know you have succeeded when somebody tries to copy you. . . . Oh, I'd be annoyed if theirs succeeded more than mine did. But mine went into a television series. Theirs was optioned.

Tacit in Barbara's assessment is her own continued success; she would be able to continue working despite the unauthorized copying. Similarly, Steve, a media consultant and marketing executive, belittled as inconsequential and shortsighted complaints of lost revenue from unlicensed copies or derivatives. He discussed how his clients have come around to tolerating infringements and mash-ups on the internet to embrace a bigger picture of diversified benefits:

> As a general policy, they are starting to say, "Look, if we have got a fan out there who has taken all of our stuff and made some YouTube video out of it, that's great for us, right? That's not bad. That's good." . . . I do see media companies embracing the technology a little bit more, and saying, "Look, OK, it's infringement, probably, by the letter of the law. But I am OK with it, because it's not really hurting; it's actually helping me, right? I mean, it's actually getting my message out."

Both of these examples demonstrate that "free riding"—often negatively characterized as benefiting without payment—is in fact mutually enriching and should be encouraged. Some free riding is therefore a welcome feature of these fairer use stories.

Folks from the software and pharmaceutical industries have a similar attitude. And both fields have grown exponentially in the internet age thanks to digital technology. They describe "under-commercializing" their IP (making enough money while also anticipating and tolerating unauthorized uses) in order to help others participate in the field. Howard, a veteran IP attorney who has advised high-tech clients in software development for over forty years, explained that copying is a norm among software innovators—a form of best practice (and free riding) to build better and faster programs:

> A software programmer . . . would consider [it] malpractice in their field to create a program from scratch if there's a perfectly good set of algorithms . . . laying around that they could use. You know, "It's tried, proven; we know this thing is bug-free, you know? Of course we want to use that one." Because if you create it from scratch, just like if we wrote a [legal] document [from scratch]—imagine! . . . What—are we going to have [legal] associates create documents in clean rooms?

According to Howard, failing to draw on useful inventions that are "laying around" is wasteful and contrary to computer science norms. In contrast, the pharmaceutical and medical device industries may appear to maintain a more exclusive and proprietary stance toward technological innovation. But even some professionals in these fields explained that it is wasteful and tragic to only develop or commercialize those medical treatments that would be market blockbusters. They described situations in which companies held out for higher royalties and failed to pursue welfare-enhancing projects as distressing and unethical. Dennis, the in-house pharmaceutical lawyer, recalled one instance in particular:

> So we killed this very promising therapeutic because we went to the companies [to license and] . . . no one would budge on their royalties. So we just killed the program. So I gave a talk . . . about that issue, and [said] that people in essence needed to be less aggressive, less greedy. And that went over like a lead balloon.

Michael, a pharmaceutical executive who worked as a consultant to dozens of drug companies over the past twenty years, lamented the same issue—which he said is in reality harming the companies themselves:

> Big Pharma in essence is almost, in a sense, creating [its] own demise [by relying on patented blockbuster drugs]. . . . That's what's backed Biogen into such a huge corner. . . . They have made—they are making almost $4 billion a year on one product. It's going to go off patent. And all these other compounds that they have looked at, "No, no, we're not interested. It's only going to earn 50 million. It's only going to earn 20 million," OK, isn't that better than zero once your number-one product goes off patent? They just don't get it.

He went on to describe the harm of such a singular focus on the market side:

> I've got to be honest with you: it frustrates the hell out of me, just the inefficiency and the waste, you know, on the innovator side, on the Big Pharma side. Because yeah, it's a for-profit industry, but if you were even just 10 percent more careful with your money and the way you behaved, there are a lot more drugs you could develop, and a lot more people you could help. I mean, the waste is staggering. It's absolutely staggering.

These condemnations may come as a surprise for two reasons. First, they come from actors *within* the industry, whose salaries and livelihoods depend on the success of the pharmaceutical companies. Second, these actors have devoted their careers to helping the industry thrive. The accounts of Dennis and Michael were both truthful and sincere. And they resemble those of many other interviewees from diverse fields who likewise describe resource sharing and under-commercialization as mutually beneficial for collaborators, competitors, and strangers.

These fairer use stories wrestle with the conflict between greed and generosity. At the center are hardworking creators and innovators who contend that their overarching goal is to continue creating and innovating. They aim to develop their—and others'—relevant domain expertise in terms of breadth, complexity, and reach. It is a picture of human flourishing grounded in an experience of interrelated and interdependent community practices of art and science. Enabling more and varied work across professional fields and experience levels fosters opportunity at all levels, develops skills across a broad range of actors, and may also justify a higher bar for exclusivity for higher-quality or scarcer work product. These fairer use stories feature a combination of interdependent creative and innovative practices with intellectual autonomy that prioritizes refinement and skill development over privileged access and financial gain. And the moral of the story is clear: collective enrichment comes from fulfilling work that is appreciated by others and sustains community welfare.

III. ADJACENT STORIES: ACCOUNTS IN THE NEWS

Like so much law that is relevant every day, intellectual property law on the ground appears distinct from its form on the books.[63] "Fairer uses" are workarounds or adaptations. They are normative adjustments (which may at times demonstrate obliviousness) to the formal legal rules defining exclusive entitlements to creative or inventive work. These everyday variations on intellectual property rules comprehend diverse and broad justifications for the lines drawn between the public domain and private, exclusive control. Beyond objective cost-benefit and revenue-seeking explanations, the fairer use stories detailed above demonstrate that creators and innovators expect *reasonableness* and *moral content* in rules governing exclusivity. Reasonableness and morality anchor negligence law, contract enforcement, and other legal fields.[64] But the strict-liability anti-copying framework of formal IP law is foreign to fairer use stories, which feature public-mindedness, forbearance, and pragmatism. The internet's viral copying and dissemination—an inexorable reality of the twenty-first century—render formal IP rules incidental and elevate the importance of everyday fairer uses.

Fairer use stories show that everyday creators and innovators are likely to be flattered and shrug off copying as an inconsequential or expected part of creativity or innovation. Transgressions that are legally actionable—borrowing, sharing, derivatives, improvements, copying as skill development or homage—are part of everyday practices of creativity and innovation. Artists and inventors may sometimes seek fair or proportionate remuneration, reasonable profit sharing, or a nominal dignitary fee; this too seems normal to them, something that is or would be reciprocated to support the community broadly imagined. By contrast, when stronger claims arise of professed wrongful copying—accounts of which the next chapter discusses in detail—they are personal trespasses, professional injuries, and deceits that corrupt relationships and institutions; these are topics that greatly agitate the interviewees. These strong claims concern a lack of respect that degrades creative and innovative ecosystems. Creative and innovative communities prioritize avoiding this degradation to sustain their work and its benefits.

How widespread are the fairer use accounts described in the interviews? As with the previous chapters, we could look to court disputes for fundamental values, such as distributive justice, that may explain rules interpreting copyright, trademark, or patent law. Beyond court cases, journalistic accounts from well-known creators and innovators also provide details of practices that prioritize fairer uses over exclusivity for the purposes of community sustainability and human flourishing. This chapter concludes as it began: with these more popular and public accounts.

Let's return to the NPPA representative who complained that lawful mass digitization (specifically the Google Books project) is as wrong as the racial segregation permitted by *Plessy v. Ferguson*. He identified at least two problems with mass digitization that, if we can look beyond the troubling analogy to racism, raise reasonable concerns for creators and innovators in the Digital Age. One was the degradation of authors by the undifferentiated massive aggregation of their works for the purpose of what he called "mass monetization." The other was his understanding of Google's failure (as well as the failure of other aggregators and search companies) to share the platform's rewards with those essential to its utility. Together, his complaints amplify the importance of dignity and respect (authors are not an undifferentiated mass) and also the importance of fair resource allocation when the colossal benefits truly derive from the work of so many.

There are several possible answers to these complaints. One could be: *It is impossible to credit or remunerate all contributors—that is the point of the "big pool" and the public domain.* Or: *This is exactly how intellectual property was intended to work—some uses are free by design to enable the progress of science and the useful arts.* But what do we say to the description of Google's dominating control and overwhelming resources (when compared to individual authors) as a deeply felt injury of exploitation? Spun in part as a story of having natural rights to the fruit of one's labor, the NPPA representative's story is also one that critiques the consolidation of power and resources by digital platforms that enrich themselves seemingly at the expense of others.

The error of *Plessy v. Ferguson* was eventually and broadly understood after half a century of social and political upheaval. Likewise, the NPPA spokesperson suggested that the harm of the digital era's vastly unequal power and resource distribution—accelerated by internet platforms that coast on collective, unremunerated labor—will also eventually be perceived as deeply unfair and wrong. Google offends the NPPA spokesperson with its platform's lack of mutuality or reciprocation by building from a big pool of resources that are not in the public domain but are treated as such. This is the perception of photographers who want to be paid reasonable license fees from Google's financial billions, billions earned in part from the redistribution of photographic work. Google is a generative platform; its existence facilitates businesses as well as science and art. But it also depresses the value and earning capacity of many creators and innovators, such as journalists and photographers (to name a few), leaving them with a foreboding feeling of professional precarity. This is only one way to frame the debate, of course. But understanding it this way highlights the various features of the fairer use stories discussed above that are grounded in distributive justice concerns over IP in our Digital Age.

Here are some others.

A. Reconceiving the Public Domain: Play and Self-Determination

In 2015, *The New York Times* reported on the influences that British composer Thomas Adès, "Britain's compositional messiah,"[65] had on many musicians and composers. The article described how other musicians in fact copied from Adès and bragged about it. Among others, the article profiled one such case—that of Christopher Cerrone, a well-known composer in his own right:

> Cerrone described the microscopic details he filched from Mr. Adès for his opera *Invisible Cities*, a finalist for the 2014 Pulitzer Prize in music. [Adès's *Asyla*] acted as a textbook for unconventional but effective instrumental writing, he said. "A huge percussion battery? It's in there. A quarter-tone piano? It's in there. Weird, bass oboe solo? It's in there." When Mr. Adès attended a performance of *Invisible Cities*, Mr. Cerrone said, "I walked up to him—there was a scene with almglocken and quarter-tone harp—and I was like, 'I stole this from you.'"[66]

Cerrone went on to say that the practice is as pervasive as it is acceptable. "I'm influenced by music by my peers all the time," he stated. "I try to steal from it as much as possible." In the same article, another composer, Andrew Norman, "voiced similar enthusiasm for Mr. Adès's oeuvre. 'There's something about his music that is particularly, so vividly imagined that people love stealing from it, myself included.'"[67] And another, Gabriel Kahane, describes the practice as part of "the history of all art [that] can be expressed as a conversation between members of a community who are all stealing from each other."[68] The musicians described their "stealing" in a friendly way. The newspaper article quoted musician after musician effusing praise for Adès's work and celebrating the trend of "borrowing" or "stealing" from it: "Teasing out [Adès's] place in American music reveals much about how today's composers absorb influence and forge a dialogue with one another."[69] Their descriptions sound a lot like the artists and scientists I interviewed whose accounts endorsing borrowing and copying fill this chapter.

What did Mr. Adès have to say about all this "stealing" or "borrowing" or "reimagining" of his work? "'It's completely news to me,' Mr. Adès said with a laugh when asked about his influence."[70] And in fact, he told the reporter that he does not think that anyone is really copying him:

He has a very different approach to musical influence. To truly imitate his path would mean rejecting his music. "I want to be shocked; I want to be outraged," he said. "If I felt, 'Oh, yeah, I'm familiar with this,' I would think, actually in that case—perhaps this isn't anything to do with me at all."[71]

Adès explained that in his musical practice, he seeks the truly new, not the imitative, and that he does not much care about derivative or familiar work. We could debate how much his deflection reflects an acceptance of the distributive justice principles espoused by everyday creators and innovators and how much of it is his own conception of himself as, in his words, "a great non-follower."[72] Either way, the net effect sounds a lot like the same breathing room that everyday creators and innovators view as essential to creative and innovative practices.

The musicians interviewed for the *New York Times* article, including Thomas Adès, rely on a rich public domain. Unlike the legal public domain, the musicians' reconceived public domain includes material and resources that they themselves add to "the big pool" and from which they and others draw to produce expressive work. That which is "stolen" or "borrowed" or reused may be signature features of others' work. But this "stealing" (in the musicians' words) or homage (in a more general sense) is both anticipated and celebrated. With less focus on an originating author, these musicians instead consider making music a process of ongoing and generative conversation among artists, which is made more possible (and possibly more transformative) in the internet age.

B. Expecting Respect: Dignity and Reciprocity

A widely reported story from 2014 accused the band Led Zeppelin of having unlawfully copied its famous song "Stairway to Heaven" from a song titled "Taurus" from the self-titled 1968 album of a lesser-known band, Spirit. Spirit never made it as big as Led Zeppelin, and "Stairway to Heaven" has been an iconic song since its release in 1971. Led Zeppelin defended the allegations of unlawful copying in two ways: the band argued that any material allegedly copied was unprotected musical cliché or otherwise standard musical expression, and it said that Spirit had waited too long to sue (forty-plus years) and that the delay precluded financial or other legal relief. In 1997, seventeen years prior to the lawsuit, the guitarist

for Spirit, Randy California, was blunt about what he considered to be unauthorized use:

> I'd say it was a rip-off. . . . And the guys made millions of bucks on it and
> never said "Thank you," never said "Can we pay you some money for it?"
> It's kind of a sore point with me. Maybe someday their conscience will make
> them do something about it.[73]

Despite his grudge, Randy California never sued; he drowned in 1997 at
the age of 45.

Michael Skidmore, a trustee of California's estate, brought a lawsuit
seventeen years after his death on the eve of Led Zeppelin's re-release of
the album containing "Stairway to Heaven." Some might complain that the
lawsuit's appearance on the eve of the re-release was grossly opportunistic.
Whatever the lawsuit's motivation, the quote above evidences Randy California's long-standing hurt feelings from what he considered uncredited
borrowing and windfall profits and also his wish that Led Zeppelin would
eventually make things right. Although he never sued during his lifetime,
Randy California clearly felt slighted, and he thought that musicianship
required more than saying and doing nothing about work that is influenced
by other work. No doubt the lack of credit among peers and the disparity
in revenues from the similarly styled songs released close in time aggrieved
him all the more. California expected respect, at least in the form of ac-
knowledgment, and he begrudged the lack of reciprocation by peers who
quickly surpassed him in fame and fortune.

On the eve of trial in 2016, lawyers for Skidmore said that the plaintiff
would accept a one-dollar settlement in exchange for writing credit for the
song, which under contract and copyright law would also generate future
profits from its use. "It's always been about credit where credit is due," one
of the plaintiff's attorneys said. The other attorney said that any recovery
under the lawsuit would support the Randy California Project, a charitable
organization established upon California's death that provides instruments
and music lessons to children in low-income families in California.[74] The
defendants rejected the settlement offer, and the lawsuit went to trial instead.
A jury returned a verdict for Led Zeppelin, but in 2018, an appeals court
overturned the verdict, ruling that the trial judge incorrectly instructed the
jury about applicable copyright law.

There will not be a retrial, and the appellate decision in Led Zeppelin's favor has had significant consequences for music copyright, liberating what the court called "generic or commonplace [musical] elements" from copyright protection.[75] Had there been a retrial, or in the next musical copying lawsuit, one wonders whether hurt feelings and failure to credit will remain out of the courtroom. Will discussion of how musicians normally borrow from each other be relevant? Professional norms are not a defense to infringement. Both Randy California and Led Zeppelin explicitly built on already existing music to write their own, sometimes with explicit recognition and sometimes as an unconscious call-and-response in musical conversation, but that is irrelevant to the application of copyright law in this case. We can doubt the plaintiff's articulated charitable motives or consider them irrelevant to the infringement determination. But we can also understand them as explaining what matters to musicians. The practice of making music is based in part on the mutuality among musicians of borrowing, iterating, acknowledging each other's contributions, and sharing in the benefits. By sidelining as irrelevant these fundamental values that anchor distributive justice concerns, we would be forgiven for thinking that copyright law fails the creators and innovators it aims to support. And by ignoring the accelerated opportunities in the Digital Age for borrowing, iterating, sharing, and crediting, we may justifiably wonder if copyright law is woefully out of sync with the twenty-first-century practices of everyday creators and innovators.

C. Enriching Work and Culture: Intellectual Autonomy and Developing Domain Knowledge

In 2012, Twitter made headlines for initiating a new patent pledge with its employees.[76] Previously, Twitter employees were required to assign whatever inventions they made at work to the company. But now, Twitter promised that the patents it filed based on employee work would not be used offensively against other companies or individuals without the employee-inventor's permission. Typically, when employees contribute to inventions, an agreement exists between employee and employer that the invention will belong to the employer to exploit (or not) as it chooses. Employees are named inventors, as required by patent law, but typically the employer owns the patent (through an assignment) and whatever profits or liabilities it generates. Twitter's new agreement did not alter this business practice default, but it gave employees something more in the bargain: the ability to prevent its employer from suing competitors or others based on the patent. Why would Twitter do this?

When the "Innovator Patent Agreement" was announced, Twitter explained its reasoning on its company website:

> One of the great things about Twitter is working with so many talented folks who dream up and build incredible products day in and day out. Like many companies, we apply for patents on a bunch of these inventions. However, we also think a lot about how those patents may be used in the future; we sometimes worry that they may be used to impede the innovation of others. For that reason, we are publishing a draft of the Innovator's Patent Agreement, which we informally call the "IPA."
>
> The IPA is a new way to do patent assignment that keeps control in the hands of engineers and designers. It is a commitment from Twitter to our employees that patents can only be used for defensive purposes. We will not use the patents from employees' inventions in offensive litigation without their permission. What's more, this control flows with the patents, so if we sold them to others, they could only use them as the inventor intended.
>
> . . . With the IPA, employees can be assured that their patents will be used only as a shield rather than as a weapon.[77]

One may be skeptical of Twitter's munificence. Was it to attract or retain engineers and stay competitive in a fast-growing sector? Was it a public relations stunt to convince Twitter's competitors and other high-tech giants to engage in a mutually beneficial patent détente? After all, the IPA does not forsake Twitter's patents entirely but instead enlarges the stakeholders who have a say in how the patents may be used. The difference between an offensive and defensive patent suit is not always clear. The first asserts the patent to retain exclusivity, preventing another from making or using the invention (or a close variation) without payment. The second asserts the patent as a shield to avoid interference by someone seeking to stop the making or using of the invention (or a close variation) without payment. Could Twitter take advantage of this ambiguity to minimize the effect of its promise to employees and maximize its company control over its patent portfolio?

If Twitter developed the IPA to attract excellent engineers—and it was successful—then the company has a reason to honor its pledge to use its patents as "shields," not swords. Optimistic about the IPA's benefits, the company called others to #jointheflock:

> [The IPA] will apply to all patents issued to our engineers, both past and present. We are still in early stages, and have just started to reach out to other companies to discuss the IPA and whether it might make sense for them too. In the meantime, we've posted the IPA on GitHub with the hope that you will take a look, share your feedback and discuss with your companies. And, of course, you can #jointheflock and have the IPA apply to you.[78]

But Twitter further explained the reason for its "hack" of the patent system: it sought to facilitate its employees' innovative successes and personal fulfillment by maximizing their autonomy, skill development, and domain expertise. This of course directly benefits Twitter, but it also benefits the broader community of inventors and startups and the social fabric in which they operate:

> Today is the second day of our quarterly Hack Week, which means employees—engineers, designers, and folks all across the company—are working on projects and tools outside their regular day-to-day work. The goal of this week is to give rise to the most audacious and creative ideas. These ideas will have the greatest impact in a world that fosters innovation, rather than dampening it, and we hope the IPA will play an important part in making that vision a reality.[79]

Twitter claimed that the IPA is a way of making patent-protected innovation work for as many people as possible and that it enriches the work environment by suppressing the worry that profit maximization and monopolization of resources will interfere with innovative practices. The explicit concern was that patents impede innovation, and that their accumulation and aggressive assertion choke experimentation. As patent scope expands over the decades and patent boundaries are drawn to be ambiguous and broad, companies like Twitter understandably develop tactics to rein in an IP system that seems to work against progress. Twitter's IPA experiment does not, however, denigrate the patent system. Instead, with its announcement and continued counseling to join the IPA, it injects substantive values into its call to consider signing onto the pledge and reshaping what patents are for:

> Whether the IPA may be right for your organization depends on a lot of factors, including whether your business model is based on generating revenue from patent licensing fees or whether it is based on competing by innovating and providing the best product or service.[80]

The IPA represents an attempt to democratize the patent system, making it work better for more people by attending to the values of its everyday innovators, such as intellectual autonomy and skill-building.

Twitter is right to worry about overbroad patents and patent thickets impeding innovation.[81] Increasingly, research and news reports explain that "companies are spending more on patent litigation than on in-house research," which is "a clear indicator that our patent system needs serious restructuring."[82] The headlines over the past decade complaining of "patent trolls" extorting good faith manufacturers and producers dominate conversations about patent law and IP law reform.[83] The growing enthusiasm for agreements like Twitter's IPA demonstrates their reasonableness and common sense.

And Twitter is not alone. In 2014, Tesla promised not to "initiate patent lawsuits against anyone who, in good faith, wants to use its technology."[84] Its Patent Pledge essentially made the portfolio of Tesla patents on electronic vehicle technology free for all to use under conditions intended to "accelerate the advent of sustainable transport" and "encourage the advancement of a common, rapidly-evolving platform for electric vehicles."[85] This surely benefits Tesla. But as Tesla rightly acknowledges, it also benefits "other companies making electronic vehicles and the world."[86]

Around the same time, a group of researchers and entrepreneurs launched the Defensive Patent License (DPL), which claims to be "troll proofed" and "innovation protected."[87] Like the IPA, the DPL is "designed to protect innovators by networking patents into . . . mutually beneficial legal shields that are 100% committed to defending innovation and reducing patent litigation abuse."[88] The power of pooling resources and committing only to defensive use also "helps prevent [trolls] from patenting open technologies and pulling them out of public use."[89] Like Tesla's pledge (and going further than Twitter's IPA), members of the DPL network place their patents under the DPL and agree to a defensive patent pledge. This makes them "eligible to receive royalty-free licenses from every other user's portfolio."[90] The DPL initiative aims to be "a way for patents to be used for good, and support innovators instead of threatening them."[91]

The trend continues. Google initiated a similar patent initiative called the LOT (License on Transfer) in 2014, which works to protect members from trolls through immunity agreements.[92] And IBM recently disclaimed rights over a patent for an automatic-reply email feature, which was given the distinction of winning the "stupid patent of the month" award.[93] Abandoning a patent dedicates it to the public domain, something IBM could have done without spending time and money pursuing patent protection at the Patent and Trademark Office. (Simply publishing an "enabling description" or drawing of the invention prevents patenting by the inventor and others because it defeats a necessary claim of novelty.) It is possible that IBM was shamed into filing a patent disclaimer with the PTO after negative public opinion about its patents grew. But being motivated by shame suggests strong norms of collectivism and cooperation. When leading companies espouse these values in the context of intellectual property, they echo deeply rooted debates concerning distributive justice.

These debates revolve around broader access to essential resources, the freedom to pursue creative and innovative work, mutual respect for creative and innovative practices that build professional community norms, and an ethical commitment to human flourishing in the context of abundant opportunity and rapid change in the Digital Age. These values are reflected in the fairer use stories that everyday creators and innovators tell of ideal conditions for art and science with implications for a flourishing social and political future.

5   Precarity and Institutional Failures

> [Today] the level of photographs [in news and general media]
> isn't as high. Bear in mind, they're reaching into a pool that
> everyone else is reaching into, so a lotta times you're seeing
> pictures you've already seen in other publications. Because
> they're not careful about having unique content. The death
> of every publication . . . has always been lack of original
> content. Original content always drives the wagon. . . .
> Even in commercial [photography] . . . I think one thing
> that's happened is that first off, resources are not as great,
> so they're relying on subscription services. . . . [And] that
> material . . . has often been regurgitated in the newspapers
> or websites. . . . Even worse than repetitive content is the
> distrust lax photographic standards generate.
>
> —Dan, a veteran sports and news photographer

INTELLECTUAL PROPERTY'S CONSTITUTIONAL aim is to achieve "progress of science and useful arts" by granting authors and inventors durationally limited property-like rights in their writings and inventions. But the foregoing chapters demonstrate that exclusivity and property-like rights in creative and innovative work may degrade, not develop, community sustainability. In the new century, intellectual property rights and the economic models that have sustained them are under critical scrutiny. Other fundamental rights deeply rooted in our constitutional system and new economic models of flourishing markets are also being reconfigured for our Digital Age. As intellectual property law develops from the new human and digital networks of the twenty-first century, everyday practices of creativity and innovation transpiring on these networks reform

266

twentieth-century social and political values for the internet era. These values of equality, privacy, and distributive justice, as discussed in previous chapters, are central to human flourishing but have been largely absent from IP policy. This chapter focuses on the inverse of these values: intellectual property harms newly transfigured in the new century.

IP injuries are typically conceived in individual terms and as economic injuries. An infringer is a thief.[1] A corporation overclaiming IP rights is greedy or engaged in immoral financial conquest.[2] Usual IP harms include substitutional rivalry, forgone licensing fees, and loss of exclusivity.[3] The individualized terms are unmistakable. Complainants suffer because of bad motives or bad acts, and volition and intent are critical components of the claims.[4] Often, injuries sound like comic book–style combat complete with underdogs, heroes, and villains, perhaps a result of the adversarial system that structures disputes as individualized parties facing off against each other.[5]

The IP harms that this chapter highlights are distinct. They are harms to communities, systems, and institutions, not to individuals. Though they obviously concern individual people, intellectual property complaints nonetheless encompass harm to social structures. Accounts from everyday creators and innovators explain that IP harms in the twenty-first-century digital ecosystem erode the essential connections that secure individuals in meaningful and functioning groups—communities, organizations, and institutions—on which we rely to live and work. These stories of distress shift perspective from a focus on the legal interests of individuals to the interrelatedness and structure of social life. With this shift, the shape and purposes of IP law also shift, demanding new explanations from those based in individual financial incentives to community and social welfare. This chapter explains the contours of this shift over the terrain of intellectual property for everyday creators and innovators in both theoretical and empirical terms. It features accounts of the connectivity and interdependence that are essential to sustained human flourishing but are threatened today in the internet age, exacerbating precarity and obscuring our shared fate.

As with the preceding chapters, the first part establishes a theoretical framework for the data analysis that follows. That framework reorients the focus from individual claimants to social systems and structures by drawing on contemporary sociopolitical literature describing precarity or "precaritization." The second part analyzes interview accounts from creators and innovators through this lens, explaining IP harms as degrading essential social structures and relations. In their accounts of precarity eroding social systems and communities, everyday creators and innovators champion the central role of law—and the systems, structures, and sociopolitical and economic organizations it makes possible—to promote the fundamental values highlighted in the previous chapters that bind us together in productive and sustainable communities.[6]

I. A STRUCTURAL ORIENTATION OF INTELLECTUAL PROPERTY HARMS

The shift from an individual analysis to a structural one makes sense when we think of intellectual property and its constituent elements as themselves products of systems and organizations. Intellectual property law tends to focus on the author, the inventor, the consumer, and the brand owner as the agents of copyright, patent, and trademark law. This chapter instead explains how the accounts of everyday creators and innovators elucidate the inevitable but often invisible connections between those individual agents, the common practices in which they engage, and the structures in which both are situated. These systemic connections produce authors, inventors, consumers, and brand owners while simultaneously enacting the structural mechanisms through which creativity and innovation are produced and regulated by law as well as by other institutions (professional organizations, for example). These connections constitute intellectual property as a system of interactive and interdependent relations forming larger and durable structures that are essential to intellectual property's "progress" mandate.

Understanding intellectual property as a set of systems in terms of their processes and contexts brings welcome clarity to the analysis of IP disputes and discourses. It helps diagnose deeply rooted problems of intellectual property in the Digital Age—and suggest possible solutions. For example, some of the intellectual property problems arising in the Digital Age concern the virality of copying and its opportunities and drawbacks, which include more sharing and productivity but perhaps also less equality, privacy, and revenue for those doing the lion's share of work.[7] Disputes among individual entities resemble zero-sum debates in which one person's win is the other person's loss. And individual remedies such as injunctions and payments do not prevent the problems from recurring.[8] As all who have chased a take-down request or unknowingly bought counterfeit goods know, the internet resembles a game of whack-a-mole: no one individual ever wins, and so many of us feel disempowered. But when we analyze individual injuries in terms of an emergent structure with particular, identifiable characteristics and patterns of actions, the mechanisms and relationships that explain the problem of digital connectivity become more readily identifiable, as do the benefits we seek from an IP system that may well be failing us. Instead of winners and losers, we think of system mechanisms, flaws, corrections, and adjustments in order to make the system as a whole work better.

To be sure, the IP system as a whole is constitutive of participants' be-liefs and behaviors, but those beliefs and behaviors change and adapt in character and effect when part of a larger structure. For example, when a person complains of a particular infringement by another, it may sound like a dispute between people about taking without asking. If viewed in the context of a structure that is instantiated by repeated practices and predict-able winners, however, the harm may be better understood as a system in which foreseeable users experience outsized benefits and others suffer reg-ular unjustified losses. This new perspective reconceives the analysis from a zero-sum calculation where one person loses because another wins to a system-level analysis in which the evaluation of its success include metrics of proportionality, fairness, accountability, and transparency.

Trenchant critiques of IP as a dysfunctional system lacking qualities such as proportionality and fairness appear in the accounts from everyday creators and innovators. They depict the current IP system as corrupted by incumbency bias; as profoundly out of balance in terms of contribu-tions, risks, and rewards; and as plagued by a breakdown in civility norms exhibiting dishonest, meanness, and cutthroat behavior. In contrast and by implication, the ideal system would celebrate shared interdependence, punish coercion and threats, disincentivize exclusivity and hierarchy lack-ing social and shared benefits, reward only truly new and original work to avoid wasted time and money, and enable more freedom to work. Contrary to the IP legal system they experience, the ideal IP regime would prioritize punishment of mendacity, misrepresentation, and denigrating practices over protecting exclusivity and control for market gains. Everyday creators and innovators expect reasonable disagreement and principled restraint among participants. But they also assume a baseline of truthfulness, transparency, and respect for others. Their accounts arrive at a moral consensus that demands cooperation and forbearance to produce quality work and minimizes destructive competition that produces mediocrity or stifles better work from being done.

This moral consensus about how an IP system should ideally function sounds like a reaction to precarity, or "precaritization," defined as the state or production of insecurity and vulnerability born of unevenly distributed cultural and economic resources.[9] Precarity produces the experience of disenfranchisement, displacement, and uncertainty regarding one's expectation for future betterment, both as an individual and as a member of a community.[10] It is a function of advanced capitalist society in which free market ideologies of possessive individualism dominate, capacity for collective action weakens, and feelings of belonging are about identity and difference rather than mutual interdependence and a shared fate.[11]

Some suggest that precarity is strongly experienced in the creative and innovative industries where "regimes of intellectual property operate as an architecture of division . . . produc[ing] a new class relation special to the information age."[12] Missing from the twenty-first-century digital ecosystem and exacerbating precarity are affective relations with invigorated political power built through new collaborative and interdependent work and class alliances. These affective relations fail to emerge (regularly or at all) and thus cannot resist the growing and diverse relations of domination by the consolidated wealth and power of networked digital capital.[13] The networked digital ecosystem, ironically, can breed isolation instead of mutuality. Thus, it seems that complaints about the IP system and its subversion of affective alliances may be expressions of resistance to the property relations that define the IP system and that claim to build connections when in fact they produce divisions.[14] The interview accounts conjure an ideal structure with moral narratives of collaboration, accountability, and quality standards that are antidotes to the Digital Age's exacerbation of IP's features of ownership, exclusivity, and skeptical relativism. Whereas the internet era may amplify rather than reduce precarity, the stories that everyday creators and innovators tell revive what in the past was called "the commons" and today is promoted as a "new public sphere,"[15] promoting accountable governance, expertise, and shared benefits.

These accounts defy the pull of the hegemonic capitalist narrative fueled by supply and demand as well as control and scarcity. That hegemonic story goes like this: we work hard to make something valuable, and law (of patents, copyrights, and so forth) gives us a way to prevent someone from taking it away without paying. In this story of law and capital, equality is achieved when law treats all alike who create and innovate according to the same standards, and freedom is realized by making and selling valuable things that enable us to move between socioeconomic classes. Notice how in this story of capitalism, law and the state's authority to enforce it assume a precarity of power and self-determination in the very activity of producing art and science.[16] We require the state to protect that which we make and value. This generates a discursive circularity and produces further insecurity in the person's relationship to the state by demanding more laws that facilitate more individual control and ownership and thus also division.

We avoid this circularity by telling a different but similarly available story, one the everyday creators and innovators tell, that goes like this: we work long and hard to do and make things whether or not they are valued by the capital marketplace because doing so gives us purpose. In this alternative account, the intrinsic pull of creativity and innovation is so strong that the art and science continues even when contrary market and ownership forces seem all-powerful.[17] This subversive story (as related to the hegemonic one above) forces a reckoning.[18] It becomes possible to think that doing creative and innovative work and protecting one's ability to continue are not primarily about the value of capital and remuneration but about the activity being worthy in and of itself: a progress separate from market progress, one based in the affective relations it produces and self-determination.[19] This story revolves around mutual respect and voluntarism.

This alternative account emerges from the stories of everyday creators and innovators and contradicts the story of capital accumulation as the primary end of creative and innovative work. As described more below in the interview accounts, a sociolegal system degrades people and the collective work they love when it refuses to recognize this alternative narrative of creativity and innovation that celebrates the equitable processes, collaborative systems, and communities that produce them. Further, ignoring these sustaining social practices produces anxieties about who will recognize and care for creators and innovators as people who want (and need) to work. These anxieties fuel protectionism, which amplifies worries about resource scarcity and leads to privatization and selfishness, feeding the hegemonic story described above as the most obvious story in our legal system for complainants. This returns us to the focus on capital accumulation at the expense of the everyday value of work and its motivating affective relations. It also signals a more basic problem in civil society in the Digital Age: the dissolution of trust and investment in the interdependence of human communities.[20]

What follows is an elaboration of these harms fueled by precarity. These harms implicate the environment in which creators and innovators reasonably expect their practices to flourish. And thus their critiques concern the environment's failures to knit together sustaining communities of creative and innovative practices to enable their work. Arising from within the contexts of creative and innovative production and dissemination, these accounts are transactional and dynamic rather than substantive or static. This is important for two reasons. First, the accounts reject preexisting and static notions of harm—for example, that loss (of money) is necessarily bad. Instead, a transactional account considers the situational context of the "loss" and understands its significance in terms of an ongoing set of discursive or material relations with a past and a future.[21] Second, and relatedly, transactional and dynamic accounts of harm conceive the field of intellectual property as a set of actions rather than attributes. There is no zero-sum game when the playing field is always in motion. This perspective allows us to examine possibilities for remodeling intellectual property as relational instead of as based on individual intent and motive and to realize the solution to IP-related harms as about reforming systems and institutions and the contexts in which they act. For example, instead of describing standard IP harms to individuals as uncompensated losses or unpaid-for benefits, creators and innovators described broken IP systems that produce short-term thinking in a largely private realm rather than long-term relationships benefiting the public sphere. This reformulation subordinates the privilege of current individual value to a future with shared benefits, challenging law to conceptualize structures and solutions for harm avoidance that embrace longer time frames, sustainable personal relations, and equitable social structures.[22]

In this Digital Age, where expression and inventions travel faster and farther than ever before, the harm of depleted income and stolen assets may accelerate claims for control, exploit precarity, and accentuate individual economic incentives, thus further pitting people against each other. But when taken seriously and on their own terms, these accounts of IP harms critique a capital system measured by individual attributes and motivations. These critiques redirect our attention to systems, practices, and communities with a dynamic structure and to connection and collaboration opportunities made more public and powerful by the Digital Age's capacity to raise all boats in a collective tide. Rather than individual pursuit of maximum private reward as a means of warding off fear and insecurity, these everyday creators and innovators aim to secure affective and respectful work and community relations to shore up a vital public sphere. In their critiques of existing IP laws surface hopes for structural change for a sustainable future, also made possible by the Digital Age. They champion a system in which trust and interdependence predominate and practices of sharing, collaboration, transparency, and reciprocity advance science and art.

II. THREE CATEGORIES OF INTELLECTUAL PROPERTY HARMS
A. Incumbency Bias and Civility Breakdown

Descriptions of intellectual property harms initially appear personal. And yet when read as a whole and analyzed in terms of emergent themes, the interview accounts narrate common justifications for law's coercive intervention grounded in collectivity: to prevent violence and unjust dominance, some of the most intolerable societal injuries that we form groups to avoid.[23] Accounts from everyday creators and innovators about their work are replete with examples of these basic and deeply experienced harms, often expressed in metaphors for real violence.

Here are some examples. Kevin, a software engineer and internet entrepreneur, described his experience:

> All the companies that I work for, we all file patents. And we are pretty cynical about it. . . . We don't think these patents are really necessarily going to ever be worth anything . . . except in this whole morass that is people wagging sticks at each other and saying, "I am going to sue you over your patents."

Michael, a pharmacologist and IP attorney who works in the medical delivery business, is more explicit about the systemic violence built into the system. He depicted violent threats in gendered terms that evoke patriarchal dominance in the context of asserting patents: "To be totally frank with you, I'd say about 95 percent of the time, it's men spraying testosterone. Which frustrates the crap out of me. It's so unethical." Scott, an e-commerce entrepreneur on his second successful company, used softer language with the same effect, describing aggressive patent assertion entities as having the capacity "to level this company" and "put us out of business." These are expressions of organized or system-facilitated violence formed within IP's structure.

This language of physical violence and threats of destruction in the context of IP assertions also depicts extortion—the criminal offense of obtaining money or property from an individual or institution through coercion. Like physical violence, extortion is a fundamental form of societal breakdown or disorder representing resistance to acceptable social norms of honesty and nonviolence. Jacqueline, the digital technology company general counsel who bemoaned patent trolls in chapter 4, described her experience with aggressive IP owners as "extraordinarily painful" because companies are asked "to pay extortion in order to basically just make the [IP] litigation go away." This language of "painful" "extortion" emphasizes the experience of wrongdoing that resembles assault on a person or property, the prevention and punishment of which in order to maintain peaceful social order is the law's basic purpose.

The interview accounts also emphasized an imbalance of power related to size and influence that is central to successful extortion schemes, an imbalance that relies on exploiting existing socioeconomic systems and structures. For example, company executives like Donald liken the threat of patent litigation to a "shakedown," beginning with "unsophisticated small companies that don't have a lot of patent experience." After developing a record of settlements, these patent plaintiffs pursue larger companies and are able to settle for higher financial sums. "The first one they'll settle for $100,000. Then they want $250,000, and then they want $500,000," Donald explained. "They really identify the weak links in the chain" and "go after them" as a strategy. Only those who have the bigger "stick" or can withstand the "squeezing" will survive the threats.[24] These accounts of hurt and fear portray a system without balance, plagued by incumbency bias, and whose civility norms have broken down.

A system "without balance" means disproportionate outcomes given the quality and quantity of inputs by different participants. And "incumbency bias" means the perpetuation of exclusion through past successes, whether justified or not. The latter has been analyzed in the sociolegal literature in terms of how "the 'haves' come out ahead."[25] The critical factor in the interview accounts, however, is that the repeat players succeed not because they have learned to play the game but because their relative wealth and influence from past successes accumulate to assure their dominance and future successes. Both a lack of proportionality and a rigged system that maintains existing power and privilege predominate in the accounts of everyday creativity and innovation. These are signs of institutional failure according to norms of equal justice in a democratic society.

That significant financial returns from intellectual property rights do not correspond to meaningfully inventive or creative work is also a common complaint from creators and innovators. That is, the amount of money is out of proportion to the qualitative assessment of the work's contribution to science and the arts. Moreover, the wealth generated does not adequately return to those doing the work. Kevin, the telecommunication entrepreneur, described invention in the software industry as follows:

> [It is] this giant body of knowledge. . . . Most of it was invented before there were computers, and now people are adding to it a little teeny bit . . . and are saying "Well, now that I have added a teeny bit, . . . you can't send e-mail to a mobile device because I was the one who thought about sending a text message to the device to tell it [that] it had e-mail!" Like, you must be kidding me! And yet, here we are: RIM [Research in Motion, Ltd.] is out $1 billion because [patent] trolls got them on that.

Samuel, a senior copyright licensing attorney, described public criticism he hears about these same inequities misaligning inputs and gains: "They say, 'We think everything should be free because it's obscene how much money these people are making over here. I am working hard and I'm earning $60,000, and Lindsay Lohan is earning $60 million and she can't find her way out of a paper bag.'" This is an exaggerated account of the critique of profit windfalls, but Samuel is not wrong about the system's critics. What rational explanation exists for such distorted and imbalanced returns?

Meredith, a music agent, explained how the system benefits repeat and highly capitalized players: "Every time technological changes happen, the [music] industry just made more money selling the same music again, right? It's still the same music five times to the same customer, in a different format." By this explanation, technological change—which certain industry players can exploit more easily than others—becomes a significant source of revenue inequity. Ann, an award-winning independent filmmaker and producer, supported this claim from the perspective of a different industry. She described her frustration with platforms and archives that accumulate troves of photographs through low-cost purchases and hold creators and filmmakers hostage for essential raw material:

> It is rare that the person that actually took the photograph still owns it and holds it and is selling you the rights. Extremely rare. . . . Most common it's collectors or historical societies often who have been given the material for free . . . who are insisting on getting paid for it to be used. I can understand paying for copying costs and paying for processing, but oftentimes the pay goes way beyond that as a moneymaking venue.

To these everyday creators and innovators, a colonialization of digital networks and the capture of technological changes explain the disproportionate distribution of rewards for creative and innovative work.[26] Commercialization through new technologies and networks benefits few of the manifold new participants or even the older, sustaining contributors. A system supposed to promote progress in fact generates gross disparities that cause economic and psychological harm.

These accounts critique the disproportionality relating input to output from a system ostensibly devoted to promoting progress of science and the useful arts. Everyday creators and innovators are caught in the snare: they pay high costs to participate in a system that relies on them as essential but nonetheless fails to provide them sufficient compensation to sustain their participation. In their view, small contributions should reap smaller rewards, and smaller contributors or intermediaries should not be able to exploit the system to crush competitors or other integral participants who are trying to earn a living in an iteratively innovative environment. Those who labor within the system express dismay at disproportionate earnings explained not by talent but by timing and short-lived market fads.[27] To them, the wrong people are making the money—not those who create the work but those whose luck or existing privilege enables them to cash in and exclude others. Meredith, the music agent, gave a specific example of the technological trends feeding off independent musicians:

> Bose suddenly has a section on their website to just sell their PA systems to independent musicians. You have got Sonicbids and OurStage and these companies—Nimbit . . . that have popped up . . . to help these independent artists reach everybody. But also, let's be honest: they know that 80 percent of the money that they are making [is] not from people who are going to have long-term music careers.

Ann, the filmmaker, told a similar story of the photo aggregators making all the money, while those actively making photos or films struggle to make ends meet. This disparity makes little sense to creators and innovators or to the agents whose businesses support them.

An extreme version of this critique of profit windfalls and disproportionality exists within the debate over "nonpracticing" patent entities—those who "[scoop] up a handful of patents and . . . [start] suing people," as Donald, the technology CEO, said in chapter 4. He related a situation in which such an entity, a single person in this case, "made millions of dollars, and it's deplorable. . . . He does not sell a single good or service. All he does is shake down companies." Donald contrasted this abusive practice with what he thinks the Constitution actually envisioned when assigning to Congress the power to grant patents: to define rights between inventive competitors so they may recoup investment in their work to develop and commercialize it for the public. In Donald's example, the nonpracticing entity "does not conduct any business at all. He is not the inventor—he went out and bought [the patents]." This story echoes the critiques above: those reaping the most rewards appear to have invested or contributed the least, and they hinder the multitude of other contributors from advancing science and art. Of course, we could debate whether a platform's aggregation of photographs to make them viewable and searchable is less a contribution than the making of the photographs themselves. And certainly, accessing millions of photographs in one place (or music across multiple devices) is not a small feat. Moreover, it is something music and photography fans desire. At the heart of many of these critiques is not only the bloated arbitrage in the innovative ecosystem but the notion that those producing the underlying creative and innovative work being resold or leveraged by others experience these practices as hostage-taking. The system exists because of the very work they do, and yet they reap few of the spoils.

Ann used the word "hostage" to describe her experience of what should be ordinary business dealings:

> [It's not] necessarily the rules [of copyright], although those are difficult. What's disappointing is that people control access to those images, so that even if they don't own the copyright, or they cannot legally restrict the copyright, if they own the image, they can restrict your making a copy of it [because they have physical control], . . . and hold you hostage for inordinate amounts of money.

Others characterized contracting situations as "coercive," with the more powerful party setting terms. They used words like "feudal" and "rapacious" to portray those exerting control to protect their incumbent positions and to minimize their own risks at the expense of others. Jack, a computer science professor and founder of several successful startups, described the system's evolution in stark terms:

> [What is] happening with software licenses, and then with music licenses and with other licenses, . . . [is] we were moving to a world where there's an infinite number of things for rent, and no market to determine what's the value of the thing that you're renting. Because if there are ever an infinite number of houses for rent the cost would be near zero to rent. So there has to be something that controls the number of copies that are available to rent. But instead we've moved, in the software model, to [an] infinite rental model, with sort of a feudal lord setting the price. And this really bothered me.

Those with diverse and broad experience in IP businesses—both individuals and big firms—confirmed the existence of cutthroat commercial dealings. Irene is an IP attorney representing both individual authors and large publishing houses. She explained that book publishing and movie production are less "rapacious" than the music business. "You want to talk about an industry that grinds its authors into the ground? You talk music," she said.

Creators and innovators often see little choice but to accede to the will of the intermediary and to a system that favors the scale commercializers. They lose faith and hope in the system that they experience as taking advantage of them. Leo, a painter with several successful gallery shows and a growing reputation, complained that "people who buy a lot of art just think they can walk in and get what they want." And because of the price instability of paintings, he said that he feels particularly insecure about how to engage buyers without being exploited. Camille, a renowned sculptor whose livelihood depends on public commissions, described the "gallery museum world" as "corrupt," as opposed to the public commission process, which she said is "based on honorable trust, it really is. The reality is that I say, I'm gonna provide a good-quality product, and they say they're gonna pay me, and I'm trusting them, they're trusting me." But Max, another sculptor with a busy, successful public practice, was less sanguine about the financial side of things and echoed the coercion others reported (including some the photographers wrangling with contract negotiations in chapter 1):

> Theoretically it's a contract negotiation; in practice the city attorneys already got it down and they're not about to change almost anything. I've had some battles over certain bits of language, and occasionally I got some accommodation, but usually it comes down to, take it or leave it. You want a job? Sign the contract.

The "take it or leave it" approach to selling one's creative or innovative work may be the price we pay in a competitive market economy, but the lack of faith that these artists described undermines the virtue of open and fair markets. It also suggests a hierarchy of access and privilege: those with significant wealth or economy of scale control the welfare and opportunities of others, even if new entrants or everyday artists and innovators provide essential fodder for those on the top. To many, this exemplifies unfair advantage, not fair competition. Even businesspeople and senior attorneys who described being overpowered by large or aggressive entities claim that the problem is not normal competition but an attitude and strategy of using scale to exert an advantage. Donald explained: "So because we're selling to so many large companies, those procurement people . . . [have the] job to just absolutely minimize the costs on everything. And so they will take advantage of you. . . . They're famous for just squeezing people until they scream, until they die." Thomas is a software entrepreneur with a strong service side to his business. He described clients who seek to license his software as "almost coercive" because they contractually limit service charges for ongoing maintenance, putting "us on the hook to do a lot of additional work for them" without any extra pay. One might say that unequal bargaining power leads to these inequities and that it is not the IP system's job to fix them. But when IP lawyers and companies with some commercial leverage describe systemic abuse and mistrust as part of intellectual property regimes, IP law is failing to adhere to basic rule of law principles such as transparency, reciprocity, and accountability. Frank, an IP lawyer in the book publishing and licensing business, described this systemic mistrust:

> [There is substantial] distrust in the trade side of the business. And that's largely a perception of inequities and royalties and royalty calculations and reporting, which I'm sure are probably true to some extent. Royalty processing and payment and financial systems and the trade side of the publishing business has not always been of the highest quality.

Frank described accounting mismanagement, a lack of transparency, and the likelihood that fees legitimately earned do not find their rightful earner. In doing so, he characterized a system built on broken promises and mislaid assumptions regarding open markets and fair competition that are supposed to promote progress of science and the useful arts. The experience of individualized subordination or domination accretes into the larger system sustained by these abuses.

A predominant effect of the distrust, coercion, and disproportionate rewards is a system that accumulates wealth and power for those already advantaged in the game. This in turn leads to a sense that the system is rigged against the newcomer or the everyday creator or innovator. Theo, an advertising executive hoping to become an independent filmmaker, described protecting his copyrighted content from misuse by established players, such as platforms and other major distributors, complaining that it "would take a lot of energy [to sue], and probably I wouldn't win, 'cause they have big film studio lawyers and I just have me." The overwhelming sense from the interview accounts is that there are "insiders" and "outsiders" in the system—those who have leverage or quickly accumulate it and those who do not and are unlikely to. The description of "haves" and "have nots," or exclusion and inclusion in a system of opportunity, is also a picture of polarization—of giants and nobodies.

There appear to be few companies or individuals who form a "middle class" of the creative or innovative enterprises, creating a specter of scarcity and fear. If true, or even to the extent that it is believed to be true, then the system reproduces its own polarization and precarity. Paradoxically, this generates claims for stronger legal protections in the form of ownership and exclusivity for those who seek the law's help, while also abandoning those most vulnerable to venal forces, accumulating even more leverage for the giants. Like the IP assets that are accumulated, the rights they protect are unevenly beneficial in a system that is ideally for all but is in fact unrepresentative and unequitable in its application.[28]

B. A Deleterious System Affects Quality and Process

To survive in a system that seems rigged against them, creators and innovators resort to manipulative and opportunistic tactics. These tactics further degrade the integrity of the system's processes and the quality of its output, though they can occasionally help in individual circumstances. For example, when a patent troll sued Donald's educational software company, he resorted to mutually destructive behavior to prove a point: "I want[ed] [the plaintiff] to remember that [our company] . . . was a royal f'in' pain in the ass. That we were cheap; that we wouldn't settle; that we gave him a million pages of toilet paper [in discovery], and that he wouldn't want to sue us again." Donald explained that "the worst thing he could do" was settle, which would only encourage such plaintiffs to continue pursuing abusive litigation strategies. But his vengeful tactics were expensive and burdensome to the parties and the legal system, taking time and money away from meritorious pursuits.

Some interviewees explained how breaking the rules or "gaming the system" generates more innovation, producing perverse incentives. Ted, an in-house counsel at a technology firm developing new forms of renewable energy, described how engineers and business developers who are leaders in innovation are "looking to get the edge. [They are] always looking to game the system" regarding patent filings, regulatory compliance, and contract negotiation. Ted spoke of his colleagues with admiration and said that sometimes breaking the rules (whatever those are) is more advisable than playing by them.

> I think the most successful inventors here are the people who are constantly looking . . . how to buck the system. They see it as a challenge, like, "OK, those guys are doing that. Well, what if we do this? Will that get us around that? And what if we do this? Or hey, I read this article where they said they were going to do this. What about if we do this? Or what if we cut them off, and we file on this? Because we're doing something similar." . . . [They are looking for] shortcuts or just trying to get around things. They were probably horrible juvenile delinquents in their youth.

It is an arbitrary and capricious system that requires flouting the rules to survive or thrive or that makes a person a fool for following the rules in good faith. Such arbitrariness and capriciousness is in fact no law at all. On the other hand, some flexibility in the law—or in any system—enables adaptation and accommodates diverse participants and contexts. IP law, however, is not described simply as a flexible system to achieve its overall goal of progress of science and the useful arts. According to many interviewees, creativity and innovation in this IP system may underperform without some manner of rule-breaking.

Creators and innovators like Robert, a chemist and entrepreneur, described the IP system as having "plaque in its arteries" because it is "stopping the circulation of good ideas." In other words, the system stifles rather than promotes progress. This complaint aims less at individual people or entities than at a system that enables and even encourages aberrant behavior such as holdouts, which hinder innovation and creativity, contrary to its underlying purpose. Daniel, a composer and theater producer, described the solution as avoiding asking copyright owners for licenses because the "downside is if I brought it to [their] attention, [they'd say,] 'You can't sing this ever,' [and] it means that all those kids next year won't get the chance to sing it." So instead, he chooses to fly under the radar, using the musical work without permission and hoping not to get caught. Kevin, the software engineer and entrepreneur, described a similar situation in the patent context in which widespread and unreasonable patent enforcement prevented interoperability and further innovation in the cell phone communication industry:

[It] dramatically shrank the market for CDMA [code division multiple access]. . . . I don't know if we got as much innovation and as much progress, because we pretty much had to let [the patent holder] do all of it.

Ann, the independent filmmaker, described frustrations with overreaching IP claims in the context of copyright licensing requirements, creating challenges for finishing her documentaries: "At some point we need to come up with a system that does not preclude future generations from telling about our own patrimony and history." These accounts of avoiding compliance or holdout behavior describe the stifling of progress, which is usually defined as circulating ideas and developing new ones in a competitive environment of goodwill. They are explained as unreasonable IP assertions that undermine the system's ostensible goals. As such, the interviewees characterize the system as diseased or infirm.

A system with these characteristics also risks producing lower-quality output. Interviewees described this happening in several ways. The first is a "race to the bottom," in the words of Dennis, a biotechnology lawyer, who described how grandiose goals or cutthroat behavior diminish the possibility of anyone achieving or benefiting. We might analogize this as shooting for the moon and therefore missing opportunities closer to home. Michael, an IP lawyer who is also a pharmacologist, described this problematic behavior on the part of his pharmaceutical clients:

[They tell me,] "We're only interested in drugs that'll generate a billion or more dollars of revenue." But the mistake they are making is, there are many ways to get to a billion. You can have ten drugs that'll make $100 million each, or you can have one drug that'll make a billion. It's very hard to always hit a home run. And so Big Pharma has backed themselves into a huge corner.

Technology entrepreneurs like Kevin related this same phenomenon in their relationships with venture capital funds:

VCs haven't figured out how to deal with a normal company, which is not Google, which is not gonna go public and [make a] gazillion dollars. . . . They want at least two companies to win big, versus everybody to do well. So you're sort of screwed, because you're forced to take huge chances. . . . They're cowboys, they, you know, they shoot from the hip, and they want big returns, and they wanna look cool. And they actually think they know something. Actually, in reality, they don't know shit.

This all-or-nothing behavior precludes or nullifies opportunities for iterative creative and innovative work, which is how most durable progress is made.

A sclerotic system that induces risk-averse behavior also produces mediocre instead of cutting-edge results. Speaking about juried art contests that aim to reward and highlight the best public art, Camille, the sculptor, described the disillusioning effect of compromises on mediocrity: "What happens is that . . . three members of the . . . [jury will] feel very strongly about one, and three . . . [members will] feel very strongly about another. They'll both agree on a third one, so it's kind of the person . . . for which . . . there's the least amount of objection. . . . Which I don't think . . . makes for the best art choice." Compromises in quality stem from battles over control, which may relate to ego, liability issues, financial risk aversion, or superficial metrics of salability. Matthew, an information architect who designs website interfaces, described similar counterproductive pressures concerning client retention issues and cost concerns from upper management. He recounted a disagreement in which he had to compromise on an inferior solution:

> [I told my manager,] "I don't approve of this. . . . We designed it one way, we tested this way. I can't get behind this." She was like, "I need you to get behind this." I said, "I mean, I will do it, but I can't tell you it's the best solution because we have already proven that it's not."

According to creators and innovators, what may seem like superficial disagreements about substance are in fact significant compromises to work quality. For example, Joan, a world-renowned sculptor, contended that commissioning entities regularly require artists to waive rights codified in the 1990 Visual Artists Rights Act (VARA) to continue with installation of their works in order to manage municipal liability and freedom to operate.[29] She described this relinquishment of rights as "awful," elaborating on the issue as follows: "It has been to my detriment because I have lost control over the lighting, which is very important to me." Landing the job required Joan to compromise the work's quality because the commissioning entity would not proceed without a full waiver. Such pressures may be motivated by finances or an aversion to vanguard creative and innovative work, which may be ahead of its time and have less obvious upsides. In either case, a system devoted to innovation and creativity should not diminish risk-taking; it should enhance it.

Everyday creators and innovators described difficulties extracting themselves from this system that produces such compromised results. When possible, some said that they prefer working alone (as a consultant or independent contractor) to minimize the compounded harms of multiple, integrated systems that compromise their high-quality goals. This self-imposed isolation unfortunately leads to reduced collaboration and weakened community ties. Some eschew IP or contract lawyers altogether, opting out of formal legal processes. For example, Lisa, a novelist and nonfiction writer, called hiring a lawyer "the silliest waste of my money." Others avoid the for-profit system altogether. Whatever coping mechanisms exist, for most everyday creators and innovators, the intellectual property regimes form a backdrop to their work that produces these unwelcome distortions of quality and process.

Undoubtedly, the Digital Age and the internet's connectivity have enabled much more creativity and innovation. Does this not smooth these rough problems or at least compensate for them in other ways? Many creators and innovators have accepted the positive and negative effects of Digital Age networks on their working practice and its output—much in the way that one accepts aging as preferable to the alternative. There is no real option to go backward, so people make do.[30] Nonetheless, their specific complaints relate to the quality of the work produced and the extra effort that good work requires to be noticed and valued. These sentiments can be explained in terms of the problem of scale, crowding out, or "pollution."

Theo, the advertising executive and aspiring independent filmmaker, described the sense of "pollution" when he says "I'm the biggest music fan, . . . but I like music less because it doesn't feel special anymore. It's so cheap." Moving from albums to individual tracks and from finite tangible products to limitless, intangible digital downloads or subscription services leaves many pondering whether the affordability of a larger volume of music produces homogenization of music quality and listening tastes. Photographers echo this dismay, emphasizing that it not only takes more labor and investment to be noticed and paid as a professional photographer, but it is also more time-consuming to share photographs for profit or just for fun. Sean is a photographer who retired mid-career from photojournalism to join a family business. He too referred to "pollution":

> The world is awash in crappy photographs. . . . When a relative or friend says, "Hey, check out [photos of] my kid's blah—," it's not just "Look at this picture." It's log on and wade through fifty [photographs]—I mean, it's my job, . . . [that's] the way I look at it. I'm working [to curate your photos]. Pay me. I'll tell which one you shoulda sent me, you know? This is the only one ever worth looking at. It's pollution.

These complaints concern diminished quality resulting from voluminous production and exhausting search costs. They describe the reduction in standards and the broadening spectrum of music, photographs, or other creative or innovative work that we have come to accept as "good enough." Recall Carl Tremblay, the commercial photographer from chapter 1 who said, "The digital, I think, . . . has brought in 'It's good enough. It's good enough.' And . . . I think it . . . steals better work from being done, because you have the ability to look in the back of the camera and say, 'We got it.'" Or as Dan, the veteran sports and news photographer, explained in the epigraph at the beginning of this chapter, the "regurgitation" of photographic material and the lack of "unique content" is lowering standards for journalism and generating "distrust" in the media. These are not complaints about the democratization of creative fields per se; generally, creators and innovators embrace their fields being open to newcomers. Instead, these complaints revolve around the distortion of standards for high-quality work because the system incentivizes scale and profit over excellence and distinction.

Rarely, however, do these problems cause the creator or innovator to quit working (although Sean did stop making photographs for a living). Instead, people resign themselves to a more precarious financial and professional situation to do the work they value. As Leo, the contemporary paint artist, explained: "Life is about survival. . . . The difference between being able to be a full-time [artist] and having to go work in a library . . . has to do with livelihood. . . . What's the number? That's tough. It depends on whether you have a family, a lot of things." Some creatives are able to earn a livable wage by balancing fees between projects and by hiding costs and salaries in contract budgets. Camille, the sculptor, explained her "clever" accounting this way:

> Some projects you make more money on than others. I make sure that I give my clients lots for their money. Sometimes I do it very cleverly, so I don't actually end up not making money. I make enough money on my projects, but I never make outrageous amounts of money. I give [my clients] a budget, but how much money I actually make, they'll never know. . . . And that's the way it should be. When I had actually asked for 25 percent profit on something [explicitly in a contract], the lawyer [for the client] said, "What? This is outrageous."

Why must Camille hide her income to make her contract more palatable to the commissioning entity instead of being forthright about her living wage needs? This uncomfortable situation arises from the fear of not being appreciated and paid for the work requested due to the misperception of the incommensurability and subjectivity of the value of creative labor.

Photographers describe a similar uncomfortable dynamic when convincing clients to pay both for a photo shoot and the subsequent skill to transform the taken photos into art. Most clients are willing to pay for the time to take the photographs but not for the time, materials, skill, and assistance to finish them or to pay for additional copies. Skilled labor, time, and equipment are the costs of a photographer's business; the fees for making the photographs and for their subsequent uses are the income that photographers rely on to sustain their work. As Dan the veteran photojournalist explained, "We don't like the word 'day rate' anymore . . . because it looks like your day is only worth a [few bucks]. So we call that the 'creative fee' because, I mean, you're hiring me for my creative ability." The need for this obfuscation—building in a lack of transparency out of fear that consumers and clients will undervalue the skill and time sufficient to pay a photographer's salary—feeds the critique of a tarnished and dilapidated system in need of an overhaul.

Financial insecurity is a regular source of stress for many creators and innovators, whose goal is usually to earn enough to sustain the work they do. Theo, the advertising executive/aspiring filmmaker, described "something dispiriting about . . . pour[ing] your heart into [work] and spen[ding] thousands of dollars . . . and getting a 0.3 percent reward." Most interviewees nonetheless said that they continue work at their profession because they are passionate about it and can make ends meet. Daniel, the composer and theater producer who quit his job as a chemical engineer decades ago, put it this way: "This is a lot less lucrative than being a senior chemical engineer. And if I were in it for the money, I would have made a very poor choice of career." The experience of everyday creators and innovators who participate in the system of investment and market competition for labor and expertise—which should result in owning and profiting from the fruits of labor (be it a film, an invention, or a piece of art)—does not resemble the hegemonic story of capital. Lack of surplus value and high costs of necessary resources, like distributional platforms, time, assistants, space, and materials, frustrate the establishment of sustainable and predictable livelihoods for those invested in doing creative or innovative work. Without aid from an institution or organization that pays them and that often reaps most of the rewards as owners or proprietors, everyday creators and innovators subsist in a system in which they play a main role but that barely supports them and their interests.

Indeed, the interview accounts describe a system that largely exacerbates a prevalent sense of financial and relational precarity. Everyday creators and innovators rarely have enough material resources and trusted professional affiliations to continue working predictably. As Kim, a musician who has other jobs on the side, explained, "People are working musicians, but, you know, that looks like many different things, and that's a hustle. . . . You could end up anywhere. But for some people, that's fine. . . . You are playing with anybody . . . who is paying you." This precarity does not seem to extend to the intermediaries: lawyers, distributors, licensors, and large employers, who may also be clients or purchasers. As Ann, the independent filmmaker and producer, put it, "Now there's also an entire industry that has grown around gathering, buying entire attic-fulls of footage that someone has turned into a business. They categorize it . . . and then they sell it." Interviewees described difficulty in productively managing investment in their work—what they put in and what comes out. They also described those who benefit from that investment as less often the creators and innovators themselves but those who use, purchase, and build off the work. These are the institutional actors and those running the institutions; they may also be anonymous consumers. This disenfranchisement begets an experience of exploitation. The lack of a sense of shared fate (or shared reward) among the many essential aspects and actors in the system—the individuals, the audience, and the institutional partners—drives those aspects and actors apart and forces them into defensive postures.

As described in more detail below, creators and innovators assail the system's disparity of input and output, distributive equity, and personal values and morals. They also complain of its failure to account for how each person or institutional partner may be integral to the vitality of creativity and innovation generally and thus should be individually sustained for the good of the whole. This should be done even at the cost of a net sacrifice of one part to feed another. They experience the system's deficiencies as cruelties for its failure to attend to that which is profoundly personal—one's sense of belonging, dignity, and opportunity in congested and capricious socioeconomic times. These critiques are therefore rooted in the misalignment of fundamental human values and the absence of shared moral purpose that degrades community trust and stability.

C. Interdependence Rooted in Moral Consensus

In addition to the problems just described, some of the most common and extreme complaints symptomatic of an ailing system relate to unpunished lying and "stealing." Interviewees complained that the system neither punishes these bad acts nor promotes truth or dignity.

For example, although writers regularly summarize, quote, and borrow from other writers and researchers as a matter of practice and craft, they fiercely criticize instances of plagiarism, defined as close copying without attribution. Attribution is not required by copyright law but is often considered an honest practice and a sign of integrity and the dignified treatment of others. Jennifer, a writer and journalist, explained it like this:

> If you look at cases of plagiarism in journalism where it's become a scandal . . . it usually involves stealing—never just stealing an idea . . . but actual . . . quotes from people. . . . I mean, that's really going over the top. . . . It's fraud, because you are pretending that you spoke to this person when you didn't, right?

In the science and engineering fields, this kind of lying or stealing occurs through misrepresentation. Scientists and businesspeople confirm

that copying without payment, which may be infringement, is not as troubling as substantive misrepresentations in business negotiations or false
statements about quality testing results. Some artists and scientists go
so far as to say that this kind of misrepresentative "stealing" borders on
criminal behavior, like theft or fraud. Dennis, the biotechnology lawyer,
complained of this practice in the context of using another's pre-clinical
research results without asking: "My simple analogy is, I think it's wrong
for other people to steal other people's homework."[31] Karen, a visual artist,
said that another artist's copying her conceptual idea for an art installation
would feel "kind of dirty, like 'Yeah, they must be stealing something.'"

Yet artists and scientists are quite tolerant of creative and inventive borrowing described as necessary or usual for developing new work or teaching,
as chapter 4 illuminated in the context of distributive justice norms. Many
even described the increased copying practices as inevitable features of
the internet age and its globalization of production. These are not inconsistent concepts. Jonathan Adler, an artist-craftsman and designer of home
goods, described the dynamism of copying practices and quality standards
this way:

> Rarely does somebody take something of mine, copy it, and do a better job.
> But that does not matter to the consumer that much. That's the challenge. You
> know, I'm a quality-obsessed person, I'm . . . craft-obsessed, and in the same
> way images have become cheap, products have become cheap to people. So
> I don't mean to whinge, it just means there's positive and negatives to this
> change. On the one hand, that sort of globalization, the access to images and
> many fashion resources, has opened up a world for me in which I've gone
> from just making pots myself to making anything and everything in any and
> all different fabrications. That is a miracle. And a very positive one. The other
> thing is, I—and this is germane to intellectual property—I've surrendered to
> the chaos of the world, and I've kind of decided not to be too precious about
> it, and to understand that if I make something, it's gonna be copied almost
> immediately, and I have two options. I can either get irate, try to hold onto it,
> and, you know, steam and stew about the copies, or I can just, like, you know,
> move on to the next thing and understand that's the pace of the world we live
> in. It makes it really hard from a business standpoint, because planning and
> inventory are challenging, but from a pure design standpoint it kinda made

me better, because I can't just rest on my laurels, I have to be like the next, next, next thing.

We heard this refrain in the previous chapter: copying is inevitable, especially today, and this creates a pressure that can raise quality standards for creative and innovative work. But many artists and scientists nonetheless distinguish the inevitable borrowing practices and internet age copying from personality theft or identity erasure accompanied by lying about the work's origin and benefiting from that lie. These are moral failures that infect communities' sustained well-being and common aims by denying the dignity of individual contributors.

Many of the examples in the interviews describe the personal affront of stealing or lying as pretending to be someone whom one is not or to have done something one did not do. Both degrade by erasing another's human dignity. To accomplish either type of theft, the thief gleans from another's work or personality, perhaps even alleging to be that person or personality on the basis of claiming another's work as their own.[32] Daniel, the composer, explained the importance of being recognized for originating his work as central compensation, attribution being as or more important than a fee: "There isn't enough money in this business to compensate me or anybody who is involved in it for the effort they put in it. And that's true everywhere in the field. You know? But the compensation for everything you've done is to say, 'They did it.'" To some, this may seem contradictory and a dubious distinction. But understanding the essential difference between a fair and an unfair situation is critical to explaining what everyday creators and innovators consider broken in a system aiming to promote the progress of the work that they are committed to pursuing. Far from dubious or contradictory, it is straightforward: they seek to be acknowledged for the work that they do. They want to be seen and recognized as participants in an increasingly complex system of production and distribution that they experience as erasing efforts at both individual and collective contribution and collaboration.

Are these complaints of lying and stealing about rogue bad actors in a culture of creativity and innovation that is otherwise reliable and trustworthy? Or are these complaints about a society and system that is flawed and degenerating? The above-described discursive patterns concerning systemic failures leans to the latter. And yet it is endemic to American culture to blame individuals and not institutions. The celebrated story of "authors" and "inventors" with the IP-enabled dreams of fame and fortune is a mythical tale with origins located in the individual, a dominant story that effaces the socioeconomic organization of action and power.[33] We rarely blame or reorganize institutions when we can blame "the bad man" for the injury or insult.[34] The legal system is arranged to hold responsible individually named defendants, and it rarely restructures or dismantles institutions and organizations for their underlying failures or flaws. Who was blamed amid the professional scandals of past decades concerning tobacco, accounting, and the investment banks? The lying tobacco executives, the greedy accounting executives, and the scheming bankers who exploited regulatory loopholes to repackage bad debt.[35] The various systems that enabled these institutions were only weakly condemned. A few people went to jail. Some others paid large fines. But the business organizations that fed the crises in the first place remain relatively unchanged. Occasionally, calls for new or increased regulation to the existing system do arise: the Consumer Finance Protection Bureau in 2010 arose in response to the 2007 banking crisis, and 2009 legislation finally put tobacco products under FDA oversight after a 2006 court judgment found that the tobacco industry had lied for decades about health issues and marketing to children.[36] The 2020 U.S. presidential election cycle demonstrated with the vital but failed candidacies of senators Bernie Sanders and Elizabeth Warren that deep structural, institutional change, needed though it may be, is unlikely as yet to gain widespread acceptance.

Our Digital Age connects people and communities and builds new platforms and organizations at unprecedented volume and speed. What prevents connecting the individual infractions of lying, stealing, and incivility with an indictment of the structural flaws of social systems in which people participate? Reform would require critically examining the methodological, political, and economic individualism suffusing American culture and scholarship that has so far obscured the supereminent role of deep social structure.[37] Neoliberal economic theory, dominant in the mid- and late twentieth century in the United States, draws its force from the belief that society is an association of self-interested individuals whose wills and desires accumulate and compete, justifying free market mechanisms to maximize those preferences.[38] Accounts from everyday creators and innovators critique this "possessive individualism" as mistakenly focusing on individual liberty and idealized freedom instead of on the mutual obligations of equality and dignity.[39] From this mistake develops the view that individuals "own" their personalities and take credit for their individual capacities and owe nothing to their communities—leaving no obligation, commitment, or responsibility toward one another.[40]

Intellectual property law is part of this problem. Its most orthodox form explains creativity and innovation as incentivized by private property rights produced by authors and inventors, seeing only individuals and choice instead of social organization and constraints. So deep is the hegemonic tale of individualism in U.S. IP law that even as it has evolved to account for new business organizations and practices, these changes remain rooted in stories about individuals and not about structures of institutional power. For example, the U.S. copyright "work for hire" doctrine, an anomaly in international IP law, designates employers as constructive "authors" for their strategic investment in the employees who create original works of expression for them.[41] Companies can be authors too, keeping alive the legal fiction that companies are like people in our legal system. Contractual assignments of patented inventions or other IP assets from individuals to companies are routine in both employment relations and independent contracting situations, which are ubiquitous in a society that celebrates freedom to contract as a baseline liberty in a free and open market. The new business practices of patent aggregators or IP holding companies (sometimes called trolls, as described in chapter 4) are celebrated by some as innovative market engines even if they are not themselves inventors, supporting inventors, or even distributors of useful or valuable work.[42] IP law's explanations for these corporate practices embed theories of self-interested hard work, market efficiency, and meritocracy in line with liberal and neoliberal theories that take the individual—person or firm—as the relevant object of focus.[43] Defaulting to paradigms of individual agency and idiosyncratic motives (such as individual bad faith or willfulness) ignores the socioeconomic structures that facilitate these practices and predictive paths of action. This leaves unexamined the critical features of structure and systemic activity, such as institutional power and disparate economic effects.

The detailed accounts from creators and innovators challenge this hegemonic tale of aggregated individualism fueling progress and explaining outcomes or expectations. Their accounts of everyday work describe social structures and contexts that predictably shape opportunities and reveal moral preferences misaligned with IP law. In contrast to a market-determined outcome based on aggregated, independently determined preferences lauded as "objective" or "neutral," everyday creators and innovators describe a system that predictably underperforms according to reasonable measures of fairness, proportionality, and quality. It provides benefits only for a select few, failing in its mandate to promote the progress of science and the useful arts for the public. And the selection bias happens repeatedly. What IP law's individualistic outlook considers an uncoordinated playing field for random winners and losers in a system that sets consistent standards for authors and inventors, everyday creators and innovators consider a gambling system in which the house always wins.

Contrary to IP law's individualistic justifications, everyday creators and innovators describe social organization and patterns of behaviors that cultivate *interdependence* among its actors and reveal reliance on implicit structures of interaction. This interdependence may be obscured in light of dominant theories celebrating individual agency, but it is nonetheless apparent to creators and innovators, who explained it as vital to sustained good work and opportunity within their communities. Invisible interdependence and hidden structures of action hide the basis of normative behavior, such as the practices of sharing and borrowing that form structures of implicit cooperation. Making interdependence more visible elevates norms into a reliable, shared moral consensus.

Empirical accounts from everyday practice surface these norms and ethical concerns. Misaligned values and disputes centered on basic moral principles—lying, greed, and disrespect, for example—corrode and render irrational or unfair the legal systems on which people depend. This is consistent with the complaint that the system fails to acknowledge what is important to most of its subjects and participants. From these complaints, criteria emerge for pursuing ethical action in the array of deep value preferences among creators and innovators; these criteria—namely, proportionality, accountability, nonviolence, wage equity, respect for professional relations and expertise, truthfulness, and transparency—anchor the structure of interdependences that are recognized as both inevitable and imperative for progress in their fields. These criteria establish the conditions of production and progress of art and science in the Digital Age. They also characterize central tenets of the rule of law.

Indictments of value misalignment between behavior norms and what the IP system allows permeate the interview accounts, especially when creators and innovators draw on examples of infringing behavior that IP law should but may not prohibit. Here, the legal system is indicted for failing its constituents. Examples range from failure to pay for copies made (a value of labor argument) to not caring for work in a way that is respectful (a dignity argument). For example, Samuel, a general counsel for a copyright licensing clearinghouse, explained his company's philosophy of copyright in terms of a pitch to possible customers:

> It's the right thing to do to respect the fact that people are creating things that you're using. You pay the electric company, you pay the landlord, and you pay your employees, you pay the paper company that delivers the paper you put in the photocopier—why aren't you paying for the stuff that goes on the paper in the photocopier? And people will get that because it's an input and the prices are not absurd.

This explanation resonates with the "if value, then right" argument, which is problematic for copyright (and other IP regimes) because it ignores crucial limitations and exceptions such as fair use and first sale, deemphasizing IP's public goods nature and overemphasizing its private property features.[44] But this explanation is nonetheless characteristic of many creators and innovators, like the photographers in chapter 1. They rely on revenue from usage fees and permissions to continue their work and, especially in precarious economic times when intermediaries or aggregators are living large, they reasonably worry about being unable to continue because of nonpayment.

Steve, a brand manager and creative director for a media company, explained that the company (which he co-owns) provides the compromise that most creators seek in the context of proliferating copies in the Digital Age. For Steve and his clients, it is the difference between exact copies (which are bad) and adaptive engagement with the work (which is good).

> If [a fan] did a carbon copy of the original show—I mean straight from a Xerox machine—[my clients would] . . . be angry. But there were more people who sat there and said, "look, [this fan] is respecting [the work], but yet change it in such a way that we all can enjoy it."

The notions of "respecting" the work or using it "for a good humane cause" (as a professional photographer put it) both avoid the work's denigration and preserve its ability to be appreciated by others. Steve further explained that his clients accept fan fiction based on their works as long as fans "adher[e] to the core values of the characters," which means preserving the characters' integrity in much the same way we might defend ourselves against reputational and dignitary injury.[45]

These are excusably vague behavioral norms, originating as they do from descriptions of personal, material, and existential transgressions that often justify protecting equality, privacy, and distributive justice through law. They return us to contestable but fundamental values of contemporary democracies with origins in "ordered liberty"—a liberty that necessitates constraints and structure (the rules of law) to offer meaningful opportunities to thrive for its members.[46] Bob, an in-house IP lawyer for a publishing company, explained that he counsels his company to refrain from suit except under very limited circumstances when it's "clear infringement, . . . a no-brainer," and "we need to take a principled stand. We just can't go in there and try to leverage our property rights in a way that's inappropriate." The animating idea behind "principled" restraint is that creators and innovators are invested in the same system and the same laws that apply equally to us all—or should.

Bob, like his clients who do the work rather than shepherding it, perceives forbearance and mutuality as central to the system of which they are a small part. The articulation of ethical engagement generates a common culture and sustains communities of creative and innovative practices that are defined by a sense of shared fate in the future of good work. Everyday creators and innovators describe an inevitable dynamism in their relationships with others working as they do. They see structure and relationality where IP law and its dominant explanation for incentives and productivity see isolated individuals and profit maximization. Precarity that weakens interdependence and common bonds occurs on many levels. A lack of moral consensus intensifies when the law and social systems are so misaligned. And communities fall apart when law and legal solutions see only individuals instead of the structures on which they rely. As a framework for moving forward through the twenty-first century, we would need a compelling reason to ignore accounts from everyday creators and innovators whose work aims to advance science and the arts through interdependence and shared values, however contested and debated, like equality, privacy, and distributive justice. The alternative is to rely on a theory of market individualism that undermines interdependence and the democratic principles of accountability, transparency, proportionality, and equal justice that undergird the rule of law.

III. REENVISIONING IP FOR THE DIGITAL AGE

We end this final chapter where the book began: with a Supreme Court case debating intellectual property in terms that highlight what is at stake in the internet age. At the turn of this century, the U.S. Supreme Court was asked to resolve a case concerning the ethics of the internet's inherent promiscuity. *Metro-Goldwyn-Mayer Studios v. Grokster* (2005) addressed the lawfulness of peer-to-peer file-sharing and was born of the disputes starting in the mid-1990s about the legality of user-generated services and platforms that distribute copyrighted works.[47] Platform users infrequently own the works distributed among them. Most users of Grokster, the platform at issue in the case (and of Morpheus, a similar platform created by the suit's co-defendant, Stream-Cast Networks), were visitors to the sites without rights in the music they shared. The same is true today of YouTube, Pinterest, Twitter, and Facebook users who share and distribute diverse forms of multimedia content. Users of these platforms read, listen to, view, share, and repost other people's work. But the question in *Grokster* was not whether the users were liable for their actions on the platforms (that is, whether platform users were committing intellectual property infringement). The question was whether these new thrumming platforms should be liable for their users' behavior.

The case turned on the principle of "secondary liability"—the legal wrong of the platforms and not the "direct liability" or legal wrong of the user. Metro-Goldwyn-Mayer (MGM) did not sue the platform users—which would have amounted to suing its own fans and consumers. Instead, MGM sued the platforms for facilitating and exacerbating the users' infringement. Secondary liability claims strategically avoid attacking essential stakeholders, such as consumers. They are efficient and cost-effective lawsuits for combating infringement because when successful, they secure the highways of distribution without having to chase all those who drive on them. Secondary liability is an essential tool in the Digital Age to combat the whack-a-mole problem that networked virality generates. It is used in patent law, trademark law, and copyright law.

The legal problem with secondary liability is assessing blame: not all platforms or device manufacturers know or can know what occurs with their products or on their vast networks through the acts of millions of users. Is it appropriate to hold a platform liable if it is unaware of IP infringements? In other areas of law, we consider this problem in terms of premise liability and vicarious or contributory liability. When should the owner of a building be responsible for what occurs inside? When is a pharmaceutical company liable for the misuse of its drug by a doctor or patient? When should an employer be responsible for its employees' actions? When, in other words, should affiliated parties be responsible for each other's behavior as collaborators or co-conspirators? These challenging questions often turn on a balance of knowledge, responsibility for acquiring that knowledge, and capacity to avoid harm that is specifically calibrated for a particular context. Landlords may be less responsible than product manufacturers for whom it is less expensive and invasive to stem the harm for the most people involved. Employers may be more responsible given their supervisory authority than are loosely affiliated partners or landlords. What is the appropriate calibration in the context of internet platforms, and should they all be treated the same? Related to this complex, normative, and empirical question is whether too much liability for platforms—making them responsible for everything that occurs on their networks—will be cost-prohibitive and shutter too many of them, crushing the diverse creative and innovative opportunities that the internet affords. Requirements of perfect control might close the digital highways altogether, bringing the twenty-first-century productive ecosystem to a grinding halt or at least leaving us with few options for internet vitality.

The Supreme Court in *Grokster* held that the platforms could be liable for infringement, but it avoided these hard questions by defaulting to a paradigm of the individual bad actor. This solved absolutely nothing. And it was a surprising outcome because the court at first seemed to appreciate the nature of the problem as based on interdependence, the characteristics of system functions, and the new institutional structures born of the internet. According to the court, peer-to-peer systems provide the benefits of connectedness, sharing, improving public service, efficiency, and increased and dehierarchized access to information and culture:

> Defendants . . . distribute free software products that allow computer users to share electronic files through peer-to-peer networks. . . . The advantage of peer-to-peer networks . . . shows up in their substantial and growing popularity. Because they need no central computer server to mediate the exchange of information or files among users, the high-bandwidth communications capacity for a server may be dispensed with, and the need for costly server storage space is eliminated. . . . Given these benefits in security, cost and efficiency, peer-to-peer networks are employed to store and distribute electronic files by universities, government agencies, corporations, and libraries among others.[48]

The court understood that peer-to-peer systems enhance the capabilities of all users of the system and are based on values such as resource sharing, reciprocity, autonomy, and iterative improvement through uncoordinated, collective action. This is a nuanced understanding of Digital Age technology as the product of complex structures and social relations that serve the public good.

Some had hope that the Supreme Court would wrestle with the new problems of digital technology and clarify rules developed in the 1980s about copy and play devices like the VCR. Those rules evolved alongside transformative Digital Age technology, absolving device manufacturers such as the makers of photocopy machines, VCRs, and MP3 players of copyright infringement when these devices were capable of "commercially significant non-infringing uses" (a phrase borrowed from patent law). The *Grokster* decision cited the court's 1984 "Betamax case" (*Sony Corp. of America v. Universal City Studios*),[49] which effectively freed VCR technology from infringement liability, launching the movie rental (and later streaming) business. The court explained its reasons for that earlier celebrated decision, which boded well for *Grokster*—or seemed to:

> The doctrine [of commercially significant non-infringing uses] absolves the equivocal conduct of selling an item with substantial lawful as well as unlawful uses, and limits liability to instances of more acute fault than the mere understanding that some of one's products will be misused. It leaves breathing room for innovation and a vigorous commerce.[50]

Preserving breathing room and entrenching tolerated uses among key actors were central principles in the 1984 *Sony* decision and the technological developments that followed from that era. But the 2005 *Grokster* decision did not clarify or extend this reasoning from older VCR devices to the new peer-to-peer platforms. The court pivoted and avoided answering the hard question as to whether these new platforms are a systemic paradigm shift in need of a new analysis. Instead, it held Grokster and StreamCast liable on the basis of a well-established common-law principle rooted in bad motive and intent—the individual actor theory—prohibiting the intentional inducement of illegal activity. The court failed to apply a system-based analysis and defaulted to twentieth-century (and earlier) theories of individualism and market-based incentives.

The court said that Grokster and StreamCast engaged in "purposeful, culpable expression and conduct" that "foster[ed] infringement."[51] It explained that "where evidence goes beyond a product's characteristics or the knowledge that it may be put to infringing uses, and shows statements or actions directed to promoting infringement" (what the court later described as "clear expression or other affirmative steps taken to foster infringement"), the party or platform is liable for resulting acts of infringement by third parties[52]—whether or not those third parties (the users) are also held accountable. The court recast the dispute over platform liability from a system-level analysis of distributive networks to an individual-level analysis punishing bad motive or purpose, ascribing individual, human features to the digital platform to avoid addressing what is essentially a system failure.

This recasting of the question was particularly disappointing given how well the court explained how new Digital Age technologies generate structural complexities that IP law still appears unprepared to address. The court assured readers that an important balance must be maintained in IP law "between the respective values of supporting creative pursuits through copyright protection and promoting innovation in new communication technologies by limiting the incidence of liability for copyright infringement."[53] And the court even explained the system's interconnected nature: "The more artistic protection is favored, the more technological innovation may be discouraged; the administration of copyright law is an exercise in managing the trade-off."[54] The *Grokster* ruling's shortcomings notwithstanding, these are promising overtures for digging into the twenty-first-century context of digital technology to adapt legal rules for new, diverse stakeholders in terms of a reevaluation of system-wide values in our unprecedented networked society:

> The tension between the two values is the subject of this case, with its claim that digital distribution of copyrighted material threatens copyright holders as never before, because every copy is identical to the original, copying is easy, and many people (especially the young) use file-sharing software to download copyrighted works. This very breadth of the software's use may well draw the public directly into the debate over copyright policy . . . and the indications are that the ease of copying songs or movies using software like Grokster's and Napster's is fostering disdain for copyright protection. As the case has been presented to us, these fears are said to be offset by the different concern that imposing liability, not only on infringers but on distributors of software based on its potential for unlawful use, could limit further development of beneficial technologies.[55]

The court's explanation highlighted the risks and rewards of the Digital Age. It raised the specter of disdain for the rule of law—a scary prospect that the internet's anonymity and chaotic power makes even more relevant. The court's language also championed the social, economic, and political opportunities arising from the "beneficial technologies" that the internet enables. It signaled an understanding that some balance is required and that this is an issue both of public concern and of private investment. And yet by resorting to theories of moral culpability and "impos[ing] greater responsibility upon a defendant whose conduct was intended to do harm" to resolve the case, the court punted. It did not stem the tide of copying that initiated MGM's complaint, and it left open the hardest questions that have only grown more complex: about platform control and dominance, user participation and responsibility, and our mutual obligations to sustaining diverse and accessible creative and innovative environments in a manner equitable for all.

Scholars and industry actors have watched and studied how *Grokster* utterly failed to halt the peer-to-peer file-sharing of copyrighted works.[56] Whether the ruling has also discouraged innovation is contested.[57] Some say that *Grokster* set too high a bar for infringement by inducement. Proving "purposeful, culpable expression and conduct" is difficult. Given this high standard, it is unsurprising that there have been few findings of liability citing *Grokster*. More critically, however, we all rely on and celebrate the myriad benefits of peer-to-peer file-sharing; these platforms are irresistible. Everyone shares photographs, poems, news articles, videos, and songs with friends over the internet, through email, cloud storage services, and social media platforms. Another possible explanation for *Grokster*'s weak legacy, therefore, is its failure to address the vital nature of Digital Age terrain and its profound transformation of human behaviors and relationships in the twenty-first century.

Addressing system-level liability and structural mechanisms of responsibility and power may seem more abstract and complicated than analyzing individual motive and intent. But are they really? We understand how to identify and describe practices and norms that coalesce into predictable systems with durable structure.[58] We lack neither appreciation nor evidence for prescribed ethics within creative and innovative communities, which include sharing, collaborations, credit, truthfulness, and transparency.[59] We can study and explain these practices and expectations, as this book and others have sought to do.[60] Sometimes the systemic values anchoring the practices are amplified by their breach or absence, as accounts from this chapter reveal. But because these values are predictable and desirable within creative and innovative communities, they form the deep structure that everyday creators and innovators rely on and perpetuate with their own actions to do good work. These are knowable, identifiable features of everyday creativity and innovation. They are part of practices infused with intellectual property and should be part of IP law.

For IP law to avoid engaging these values or structural characteristics and to instead revolve around individual motives and narrowly drawn economic incentives reproduces the very problem that *Grokster* was brought to solve: it decides the rules of community engagement by resting the decision on a single actor or action. It sees only individuals when today more than ever we are inextricably connected in interdependent communities and institutions. This myopia exacerbates the social, economic, and political precarity that we experience in a Digital Age generated by networks and fueled by dynamic connectivity but that still celebrates the independence and self-possession of individual authors and inventors.

We can avoid this tension by accepting the alternative accounts from everyday creators and innovators who demand an end to precarity-fueled rationales justifying control and exclusivity over creative and innovative work. We can address the new problems of Digital Age technology for creators and innovators by affirming the centrality of those fundamental values in the systems that sustain their work and by dismantling features that fail to foster mutuality and interdependence among its members. By rendering interdependence visible and at the forefront, we can come to understand that the normative behavior that fosters mutuality is a condition of sustainability and betterment, not a series of exchanges, transactions, or competition. This revives or reimagines a public sphere richer and more collaborative than our intellectual property system currently protects. And it links the public sphere's centrality to the interdependence that creators and innovators deem essential to promote the progress of science and useful arts.

Conclusion

EVERY YEAR, THE UNITED STATES Supreme Court decides cases that reshape constitutional concepts like equality, dignity, and the fair opportunity to flourish. Recently, the Supreme Court heard arguments about how the city of Philadelphia denied Catholic Social Services a role in the city's foster care service because the organization refused to place children with same-sex couples.[1] It also heard arguments about whether the decade-old Affordable Care Act is constitutional (yet again!) because its tax penalty was reduced to zero by the most recent Republican administration.[2] Cases on the recent and current Supreme Court dockets concern civil rights of transgender people, freedom for immigrants who arrived as children to continue living in the United States, and whether non-citizens count for the purpose of the U.S. census.[3] Lawyers argue these cases wielding complex and tangled legal doctrinal tools that most people do not understand. But these cases raise issues that are fundamental to the lives of ordinary people, who therefore pay attention to the cases' developments and outcomes.

The intellectual property cases on the Supreme Court docket are different. They do not obviously raise issues of fundamental rights to health care, to be counted, to dignity or equality. It is understandable that most people are not focusing on currently pending or recently decided intellectual property cases at the Supreme Court to the same extent. They include a case about whether the state of Georgia's laws will be covered by copyright (and thus accessible only with permission and for a fee) or whether state laws will be open to all.[4] The recent case of *Google v. Oracle*, or "Googacle" as some media pundits have called it, concerns copyright protection for computer software (application user interfaces, known as "APIs") and whether Google's transformation of Oracle's APIs is fair use.[5] The Court also recently decided whether administrative judges of the U.S. Patent and Trademark Office are constitutionally defined "officers of the United States" who must be appointed by the president with the Senate's advice and consent.[6] For perhaps obvious reasons, ordinary people do not know about these cases; typically, only intellectual property lawyers and scholars follow them and consider their outcomes consequential.

If recent decades are a measure of our near future, however, these Supreme Court intellectual property cases and the media descriptions of them will resonate with constitutional values deeply rooted in our nation's history. And that is because intellectual property's evolution incorporates diverse and broad-reaching legal and cultural concepts that concern more than financial assets and investment vehicles. In the internet age, intellectual property is a feature of everyday life. It plays a role in how we share personal expressions and images of ourselves online, whether there is fair competition for quality consumer goods, and whether we own what we buy.[7] It played a role in the misinformation and content moderation of internet platforms during the historic and consequential 2016 and 2020 presidential elections.[8] It will play a role in ending the COVID-19 global pandemic.[9] In terms of the recent Supreme Court IP cases mentioned above, intellectual property is a framework that enables people, as an example, to debate access to law and justice when a state seeks to control who can read and copy the legislation to which its citizens are held accountable.[10] It is the terrain over which competing views of "progress of science and useful arts" are debated within the most consequential industry of the twenty-first century: the computer industry.[11] And the debate over administrative judges at the U.S. Patent and Trademark Office, the case arguably the fewest people will pay attention to, is a fight about best practices under our Constitution for democratic accountability and transparency in an increasingly complex governmental system devoted to the rule of law.[12]

The "why" of intellectual property's mainstreaming in everyday culture is easy to understand. The internet's primary affordances of viral copying and distribution, behaviors that IP law controls, pit essential mechanisms for everyday life against antiquated twentieth-century rules for copyright, patent, and trademark law. Something has got to give in this standoff between networked connectivity and privatized exclusivity. Policymakers and scholars may be working to craft reasonable, evidence-based accommodations to shape limitations on the freewheeling internet highways and to liberate IP rules from outdated industry structures and marketplace assumptions. But everyday people who appreciate and fear the power of the Digital Age are also part of the conversations today, claiming for themselves the benefits of and protections from previously obscure IP regulations.

It is harder to understand the effect of IP's mainstreaming into everyday life on the policy proposals, scholarly studies, and popular conceptions of IP. This book suggests several hypotheses.

The first is that intellectual property law is no longer about "promoting progress of science and the useful arts" by simply granting to authors and inventors a limited property right. The qualities of "progress" and the characteristics of the "property" are both under reconsideration in the Digital Age. From this follows that the incentive story—if property, then progress—is also up for revision. The causal calculation is either much more complicated or built on faulty assumptions.

The second is that intellectual property law disputes, which are today more common and diverse (according to characteristics of party identity and theory of injury), revolve around fundamental values and less around financial costs or benefits concerning exclusive rights to creative and innovative output. Values of equality, privacy, distributive justice, and institutional resiliency are central to human flourishing and human dignity and are all currently under siege despite widespread and swift technological progress. This book shows how intellectual property disputes, which traditionally assess the costs and benefits of exclusivity over innovation in terms of their trickle-down effects on general welfare, are contests about fundamental values whose contours are shifting in the internet age.

A third hypothesis explaining the effect of IP's mainstreaming in everyday culture is that intellectual property law is a new terrain over which to fight about old problems in service of an updated form of "progress" focused on shared resources, resources that are not limited to clean air and water but also include information and privacy.[13] This new terrain reframes old debates. I do not mean to imply it is a return to an idyllic past or that this evolution "against progress" reflects the cyclical rise and fall of dominant industries, a push and pull of history.[14] My point is simpler but also time-sensitive. Interrogating emerging fundamental values deeply rooted in our system of constitutional democracy within the new contexts of intellectual property reminds us that we have not achieved equality, protected privacy, fortified our democratic institutions, or provided a fair opportunity to thrive for all in this age of rapid technological innovation, and these failures are spreading and becoming potentially cataclysmic. The contemporary intellectual property stories in this book undermine the optimism of Information Age capitalism, born of individualism and market freedom, and urge us to shift gears. The stories emphasize instead a kind of egalitarianism, structured around a revitalization of public interests and human interconnectedness that the Digital Age makes more urgent and possible. These new intellectual property stories re-center and extend the public domain's importance and situate our shared fate within it as a measure of hopeful progress for the twenty-first century.

This is another way of saying that intellectual property has become a legal and cultural touchstone for contemporary problems. Intellectual property originally provided opportunity for economic and social mobility as an antidote within a market system of entrenched class hierarchies. It was both a lottery ticket and evidence of creator and inventor status. When the lottery ticket hit, the winners felt justified in their efforts and embraced the system that helped them. But the massive accumulation of intellectual property over the twentieth century has not helped the majority of everyday creators and innovators. Conceived in consequentialist and utilitarian terms—collect IP to enable financial freedom and admirable social status for the most people possible—IP's failure to produce those consequences has led to its transfiguration in moral, value-based terms that cannot be measured in numbers or with cost-benefit calculations. Some IP owners still assert control to bring about financial rewards or prevent financial ruin. But as this book shows, many IP owners and the arguments wielded on their behalf ground IP assertions in non-negotiable moral imperatives—equality, self-determination, privacy, and community-based human flourishing.

We can sustain simultaneous commitments to both consequentialist and absolutist moral reasoning in law and society by allocating them to separate jurisdictions or social categories (for instance, by distinguishing rules among strangers from those within families). But in the twenty-first century, intellectual property debates are a site of clashing jurisdictions and social categories, challenging boundaries and proposing reform. When intellectual property looks like a consequentialist system and partners with the view of technological progress driven by accumulation, it denies or obscures the material and moral risks of "progress as more." When harms and risks are inevitably exposed, IP claimants then depart the consequentialist and utilitarian script and look elsewhere for justification. Courage is required to experiment with ethical justifications and new forms of governance (new rules or jurisdictions) that limit private acquisition and instead promote public-mindedness, especially given rising levels of precarity.[15] But it turns out that pursuing technological innovation and accumulation without ethical constraints, as IP law has over the twentieth century, produces identifiable human devolution and devastation.

Intellectual property law and culture has pursued a manifest destiny approach to capitalist acquisition in the twenty-first century. It homogenized cultural tastes and polarized politics and journalism, all the while paying lip service to diversity, democratic self-governance, and individualized identities. The new IP stories in this book reject the malevolence that characterizes manifest destiny's "aggressive land acquisition and imperialism"[16] by inflecting intellectual property law with the constitutional ideals of equality, privacy, distributive justice, and inclusive democratic institutions. These IP stories are against progress insofar as it means more, and they pursue a better future by rejecting as wasteful, excessive, and unfair the outsized and imbalanced wealth our nation's current system produces. These new IP stories help reimagine and reshape debates about the role of fundamental values in a pluralistic society in support of creativity and innovation in the internet age.

We may all be photographers with our cell phones making and sharing millions of photographs over email and internet platforms. But accounts from everyday working photographers—as well as from the other creators and innovators in this book—describe how professional standards are essential to doing good work. Photographers explain that preserving their community norms of individual dignity, equality, fairer uses, and free speech will promote trust among individuals and organizations and will elevate truthful communication in the internet age. This may be an optimistic story, but it is also novel in its account of intellectual property's aim of progress of science and the useful arts. The story says that intellectual property law and the public domain—consisting not only of that which is free but also that which is shared—have central roles to play in the future revitalization of these fundamental values. It is a story worth telling.

Appendix A:
Research Method and Data Collection

This book employs a mixed method to approach the question of intellectual property's changing role in contemporary legal and popular culture.

Chapter 1 is a case study of digital photographers. It analyzes a data set of thirty long-form interviews using on a qualitative empirical method described more fully below. Chapters 4 and 5 rely on qualitative empirical methods to analyze data drawn from a combination of three interview-based data sets described herein and in Appendix B.

Chapters 1, 4, and 5 are based on interview data I collected using a semi-structured interview method. I followed a method of non-representative stratified sampling utilizing variables relevant to the questions under investigation.[1] This qualitative empirical analysis complements the digital humanities and narrative analysis in Chapter 2 and the legal doctrinal analysis in Chapter 3. My aim was to broadly investigate the legal and popular meaning of intellectual property from within and outside "the law," e.g., other than through court decisions and statutes. Reading and interpreting cases and statutes as both legal and cultural texts explains them as features of both law and culture. In Chapters 1, 4 and 5, I investigate the everyday life of creativity and innovation from within relevant communities (and also the place of intellectual property law that may regulate them) to situate the legal texts and their interpretations in lived experience.

Chapter 2 is textual analysis of a data set containing all the United States Supreme Court cases about federal intellectual property law since

1984. I analyzed the cases in two ways. I read them closely attending to
their language and structure as one might with literary texts, genres, and
canons. I also analyzed them using the digital humanities method of topic
modeling (Latent Dirichlet Allocation, or (LDA)), a kind of automated text
analysis that determines word patterns and infers topics within unstruc-
tured or untrained data.[2] I worked with a graduate student at Northeastern
University within the NULab for Texts, Maps, and Networks to develop
the topic modeling program (using Python). And after several rounds of
cleaning the case data and running the program, "topics" emerged within
the million-plus word data set suggesting relationships between the language of intellectual property and other words such as *national, American,
dignity, fair, uniform, similar, harmony,* and *equity.* From these iterative
topic modeling outputs, I began exploring more deeply the stories of and
variations on equality and constitutional law in both individual cases and
groups of cases about intellectual property, as described in chapter 2. Topic
modeling is an exploratory method for hidden or latent semantic topics in
data and, as chapter 2 shows, only the starting point for a more complex
narrative and historical analysis.

Chapter 3 is a textual and legal analysis of court cases using more traditional methods of legal interpretation and doctrinal analysis.

QUALITATIVE METHODS

Lawyers, legislators, and scholars are more familiar with textual and doctrinal analyses and close readings of cases and statutes. Qualitative empirical research is less familiar, and so I explain it further here. I chose
a qualitative empirical method for several reasons. Qualitative empirical
work remains rare in legal studies. Collecting the data is time-consuming
and costly. Nonetheless, qualitative research is vital for understanding the
significance and variation of lived experience that law affects. It complements and enriches (and can be especially useful when combined with)
quantitative research, which remains the dominant empirical research
method in legal scholarship today. Qualitative methods develop insights
about the underlying forms and dynamics of the phenomenon under
study. Unlike quantitative research, in which researchers seek to generate precise estimates based on a sample that can be generalized with estimated degrees of error to a larger population, qualitative researchers seek

"analytic generalizations" that attach meaning, rather than measurement, to the phenomena observed.[3]

Qualitative research is useful to identify and explain situated knowledge (i.e., actors' experiences and interpretations) about a particular object, practice, or field, e.g., "What is "copyright law" for?" and "How is innovation achieved in this community?" Qualitative studies identify variations in these interpretations, events, and behaviors through data that is "densely textured, locally grounded, meaningful to the subjects themselves."[4] A hallmark of qualitative research is developing the categories and their explanations from within the narrative structures that interviewees provide in ways that can be further analyzed in other studies, both qualitative and quantitative.

Another reason I use a qualitative research method is that narratives and popular concepts are explanatory and justificatory tools in the constitution of law and culture. Qualitative field research collects actors' accounts of their lived experiences, which in this study reveal how interviewees develop and make sense of their professional lives in art and science. A systematic analysis of the data offers explanations of how interviewees achieve "progress" in their fields. If we are interested in understanding or more precisely defining the creative and innovative practices as they relate to intellectual property law, these interviews provide direct evidence from the individuals who actually create and innovate in IP-rich fields.

The qualitative researcher aims to identify a comprehensive set of relevant variations in the studied experience or practice.[5] To get there, the researcher identifies the population to be studied and the key dimensions that are hypothesized to generate distinctions in the experience under analysis. This "stratifies" the population into relevant sub-groups within those dimensions. Talking with people across many sub-groups increases the chances of identifying relevant variations and achieving comprehensiveness in the explanation of the phenomena. Having a complete set of variations may be impossible, but the goal is to discern as full a set as possible. The signal that a researcher has identified as full a set as possible is known as "saturation"—the point when the most recent interviewees are providing accounts that align with previous accounts.[6] Qualitative work will not lead to a statistical measure of correlations among variables or a mathematical test of causal inference. But a core benefit of qualitative interview-based research—and the key reason qualitative methods are superior for the questions I explore in this book—is the ability to generate multifaceted and nuanced explanations for complex social phenomena.

1. Interview Data

Since 2008, I have conducted over 100 interviews with a range of creators and innovators, their lawyers and business partners. The first fifty interviews were collected between 2008 and 2013, and I wrote about them in my previous book, *The Eureka Myth: Creators, Innovators, and Everyday Intellectual Property* (2015). But I didn't stop collecting data after finishing *The Eureka Myth*. From the hypotheses I generated therein, I was propelled to ask further questions of more people and focus my inquiry in several ways.

First, I sought to better understand the effects of the internet and digital technology on the practices of creativity and innovation, especially as they relate to earning a living and developing productive partnerships in one's field. How does the generativity of our internet age facilitate and frustrate working creators and innovators? How do creators and innovators manage the opportunities and drawbacks of the internet's virality and essential copying technology? I returned to the interview data to look closer at answers that might shed light on these questions. To do this, I recoded and reanalyzed the original data with new codes and concepts in light of new hypotheses about the relationship of the internet and the Digital Age to contemporary and evolving practices of creativity and innovation. And in some cases, I followed up with interviewees to clarify or ask additional and more specific questions.

Second, the initial set of interviews produced an array of motivations for and ways of doing creative and innovative work in IP-rich fields. That initial set of interviews was with a wide range of professionals—e.g., writers, visual artists, filmmakers, software developers, chemical engineers, and biologists as well as business partners and lawyers tasked with commercializing their work. Most of the accounts were diverse and contextualized, but patterns emerged, as I described in *The Eureka Myth*. Anti-copying protection and making a living in creative and innovative IP-rich fields are complexly related, but in *The Eureka Myth*, I identified commonalities across fields and professional identities. Nonetheless, photographers stood out as more uniform in their answers and more extreme in their views. I had only a small sample of photographers in the initial set, and qualitative work at its best generates hypotheses to test. It provides evidence of the existence of the variables themselves but does not enable conclusions about distributions of the identified relevant variables over a larger population. So I sought a larger sample of photographers to test their conspicuousness within the original interview data set.

This produced the photographer case study. With research collaborators Peter DiCola and Eva Subotnik, I interviewed thirty photographers between 2016 and 2018. We stratified the sample between, on the one hand, newly emerging photographers with a practice that began with digital photography, and, on the other hand, established photographers who began their practice with film photography. This roughly correlated to pre-2004 photographers and those who began their work in 2004 or after. We also stratified our sample among five categories of photographers: photojournalists, commercial photographers, fine art photographers, portrait photographers, and event photographers. These categories are based on the organization of the photography business into different genres, which we derived from the literature on the history and business of photography.[7] Chapter 1 describes and analyzes the data from the photographer interviews as a case study, explaining how fundamental values of equality, privacy, distributive justice, and institutional resiliency play important roles in photographic practice in the internet age. Our research team published additional articles analyzing other aspects of the data set.[8] The data analyses are based on interview data as well as observational research from gallery visits, trade shows, conference attendances, and professional photographic materials (trade journals, websites, and social media).

For me, the initial set of interviews in *The Eureka Myth* generated yet another line of inquiry: the role of "design" in the twenty-first-century creative and innovative ecosystems. With collaborator Mark McKenna, I began studying designers and design practice with the hypothesis that the ascendency of "design" as both a business and aesthetic endeavor can be explained as one response to the internet's novel affordances of viral copying and dissemination. Most of the creators and innovators in my first data set identified in traditional ways—as "writers," "artists," "scientists," or "engineers." But some also called themselves "information architects" or "graphic artists" focusing on web design and information flows. New forms of creativity and innovation developed with the Digital Age. And I became interested in how old and new professional identities within creative and innovative fields—e.g., between "graphic artist" and "web designer" —were interacting with intellectual property laws.

Design practice may uniquely combine form and function as both its purpose and standard of excellence—at least this was our working hypothesis when we embarked on the qualitative research.[9] This coherence puts pressure on traditional categories of intellectual property that keep separate characteristics of form and function. How can we understand this tension in light of the ascendance of design's dominance and intellectual property's mainstreaming in everyday legal and popular culture? Design encompasses features of traditional aesthetic practice (textual and visual artistry) and innovative technology (digital device engineering and manufacturing). It is a hugely popular twenty-first-century blend of creativity and innovation. We thought designers and their everyday practice would provide insight into the role or relevance of intellectual property regulation in the twenty-first century.

For the design case study, we interviewed twenty-four designers between 2018 and 2020. We targeted seven groups of designers based on the history of design practice: automotive, household goods, user interface, fashion, graphic art, medical and technological devices, and services. Within those categories, we interviewed designers in consultancies and in-house designers as well as established legacy designers and younger, emerging design professionals. Some designers work across these sub-groups or have developed expertise in more than one area. As it turned out, many designers consider interdisciplinarity and boundary blurring essential to excellence in design and thus, despite expertise in a particular sub-field (in medical devices, for example, or user interface design), many reject disciplinary categories, although not all do. (Automotive and graphic designers described sticking to their specialization as both a preference and a field characteristic.) Research and data analysis with this set of interviews with designers is ongoing, but they form part of the interview corpus I draw from for this book.

2. Interview Process and Data Analysis

Most interviews lasted about one hour. Each followed an interview protocol (an outline and list of questions) that was approved by the relevant Institutional Review Board (IRB). The semi-structured interview allowed us standardization across all the interviews within each data set and across the data sets. But the protocol also allowed deviation and follow-up when necessary to clarify potential contradictions or to dig deeper into apparent idiosyncrasies or parallels. Interviewees could elect to be on or off the record. I use pseudonyms when quoting off-record interviews, and the biographical details for the confidential interviews in Appendix B have been generalized in order to protect anonymity. All of the interviews were recorded and transcribed by a professional transcriber.

As we conducted the interviews and read the transcripts and then reread and analyzed them, we revised our understandings and interpretations of the phenomena under study. Interview analysis follows several steps. First, after each interview, we wrote a memo summarizing it in two to three pages. This would include any notes made during the interview, a description of notable stories or quotations from the interviewee, and a list of overarching themes from the interview. The memos were often co-drafted and shared to produce a common framework of the ongoing analysis.

Second, we read the interview transcripts closely. We studied the interviews at the level of language (word choice, narrative structure, and content) and conceptual themes, which were drawn from reading across the transcripts and from the literature in the relevant fields (photography or design practice, for example). We then generated a list of code words developed deductively from preliminary findings and inductively from the emergent language, repetitions, narrative structure, and conceptual themes contained in the interviews.

Third, we read the transcripts again to code them, first by hand and then using a system developed as a team using Atlas.ti (for the photographers and the initial data set) and Excel (for the designers). The coding allowed us to search and sort the data by code or any other category we had established. Coding together and interpreting the interviews as a research group enhanced intercoder reliability, which was critical to the descriptive and interpretive validity of qualitative empirical analysis.[10] Where there were differences in interpretation, we discussed and resolved them. By its very nature, working with qualitative data is an interpretive process. Nonetheless, strong consensus can be achieved by regularly sharing coding on a common text and thus collectively developing common parameters for interpretation.

Chapter One draws only on the photographer case study. Chapters Four and Five combine the data from the photographer case study, the designer study, and the earlier interview data set. (All three data sets are described in more detail in Appendix B.) The qualitative software programs allow for the combining, segregating, and sorting of all three data sets according to chosen categories.

This book is a study of cultural scripts and beliefs embodied in legal texts and interview accounts of lived experiences. It respects the language used in both as sources of meaning and signs of purpose. The validity of the interpretation of the legal texts in Chapters 2 and 3 will depend on my narrative methods, legal and historic arguments, and analytic persuasion. The validity of the interview data depends on whether the interview responses reliably describe recognizable practices, whether the descriptions are sufficiently thick to be credible, and whether the theoretical interpretations are sufficiently grounded in these and comparative data.[11] For this reason, quoting the interviews at length is necessary so that readers can assess the interpretation of the accounts for themselves.

We did our best to emulate the methods of well-regarded and robust qualitative interview studies to assure optimal validity. Quality of interviewing matters a lot. The first set of interviews I did myself, and I employed a graduate student to work with me to read, code, and interpret them.[12] For the photographer and designer interviews, we conducted all but a few of the interviews in teams to facilitate careful listening and questioning in a conversational style building from a trustworthy context. This is because:

> The more discursive, conversational style of the interview affords opportunities to prompt respondents to explain seeming oversights and inconsistencies, which serve as consistency or reliability checks of sorts. These same in-depth techniques are also well suited for getting underneath the superficial, socially desirable, or conventional responses people give when accounting for their behavior because the depth of information generated allows the researcher to detect deeper levels of meaning that the respondent herself may not be aware of, but which reveal underlying motivations that conventional or initial accounts belie.[13]

Despite my confidence that the interviews are robust and probing, our interpretations are necessarily suggestive rather than exhaustive. Qualitative work by its nature generates hypotheses about social phenomena. In the spirit of "progress of science and the useful arts," I encourage further research building from the data analysis in this book.

Appendix B:
Interviews

As Appendix A describes, this book draws from three interview data sets. The first is a stratified set of creators, innovators, business partners, and attorneys in IP-rich fields, which interviews I conducted between 2008 and 2013 according to an interview protocol (outline and questions) approved by the Institutional Review Board (IRB) of Suffolk University, where I was then a faculty member.[1] The second is a stratified set of photographers I interviewed with collaborators Peter DiCola and Eva Subotnik between 2016 and 2018 according to IRB protocols approved by our respective employers: Northwestern University, St. John's University, and Northeastern University. Chapter 1 primarily draws from this second set of interviews. The third is a stratified set of designers I interviewed with collaborator Mark McKenna between 2018 and 2020 according to IRB protocols approved by Northeastern University and the University of Notre Dame. The varying conditions of the interviews are described below for each set.

I. CREATORS, INNOVATORS, BUSINESS PARTNERS, AND ATTORNEYS IN IP-RICH FIELDS: 2008–2013

These interviewees were promised anonymity according to consent forms that each signed to participate in this study. The following biographies lack additional detail to honor that promise of anonymity. I have tried to give enough information for readers to evaluate the stratification of the sample but not so much that anonymity is compromised. Unless otherwise noted, interviewees work full-time at their described profession. Where noted with an asterisk (*), the interviewee is an attorney/businessperson as well as a creator/innovator. Interviewees are listed in alphabetical order by their pseudonym to facilitate search while reading the book. All information is current up to 2017 and does not reflect changed circumstances after that time.

*Alex.** A computer scientist and entrepreneur running a company (one of many he started, some of which he sold) that develops and sells access to a web-based product for online use. He is a named inventor on several software patents.

*Andrew.** A scientist and high-technology entrepreneur with a graduate degree in physics who is currently running his third company. A previous company was sold for $30 million, and another failed to get off the ground. He is a named co-inventor on several patents.

Ann. An award-winning documentary filmmaker who has her own film production company and recently won several national awards for her films. She is a former staff producer for public television.

Barbara. An author of books for children and teens. She has written over 120 books in various series and began her writing career writing novelizations of successful films. Her first job in publishing was as a contract manager and editor in a national publishing company. She left that work after many years to support herself with her own writing.

Bob. An in-house attorney who is also a vice president of a large privately held publishing company that has educational and trade divisions with offices around the world. He has been working in publishing for nearly his entire career with early stints as a litigator.

Camille. A sculptor with an international reputation whose focus is public art. She employs a studio assistant and has worked on her art full-time for nearly her entire career. She taught for some years before working full-time on her public installations.

*Carol.** A former academic biologist who achieved tenured status at a nationally regarded university and who then changed careers and went to law school. She is now a partner in a boutique law firm counseling diverse clients on intellectual property issues, with a particular focus on patent-related issues, including patent prosecution.

Cary. An in-house intellectual property counsel for an alternative-energy company that was recently acquired by an international conglomerate. He previously worked as chief patent counsel in various companies with diverse focuses: consumer goods (longest tenure of over a decade), semiconductors, and electronic test equipment. He began his career as a chemical engineer.

Dan. A chemical engineer who worked at global companies on product development, earning awards for his work. He is a co-inventor on several patents. Later he worked as a chemical engineer in several civil engineering firms that were smaller in scale. He retired early to become a music composer. He runs a nonprofit community opera company that performs his operas as well as those by others.

David. A photographer who shows and sells his work but also works part-time in retail. Earlier in his career, he worked full-time as fashion and as an advertising photographer.

Dennis. An in-house patent attorney at a publicly traded, global pharmaceutical company. In his earlier career, he worked in similar positions as in-house patent counsel for other large pharmaceutical companies.

Donald. An in-house attorney who is also vice-president for an e-commerce company that provides e-commerce platforms to clients, is in its third decade, and was recently acquired for $1 billion. In his earlier career, he worked for a publicly traded, multinational toy and entertainment company.

Elizabeth. A writer and formerly a copyeditor at various national magazines. She earned an MFA in writing. She is currently writing a novel and is financially supported by her husband.

Frank. A copyright attorney who is general counsel for global educational publishing company with particular focus on scientific and medical publications.

Gary. An intellectual property lawyer in a large law firm with a focus on copyright and trademark issues. Before law school, he worked in a national publishing company advising on the selection and cultivation of authors and markets.

Helen. A sculptor who focuses on public installations. She has worked full-time as a sculptor for nearly her entire career. She employs a studio assistant.

Howard. An intellectual property lawyer since the 1980s, for a long time as a partner in a large law firm and now as a partner in his own small boutique law firm that specializes in advising companies about their intellectual property strategies. He works with all sorts of intellectual property (patents, copyright, trademark, and trade secrets).

*Ilene.** A genetic biologist who recently graduated law school and became a patent attorney with a small law firm. Before law school, she worked for several years in academia and in the pharmaceutical industry.

Irene. A solo practitioner specializing in copyright and trademark issues, serving companies and individual clients with specialties in publishing and media issues, both for profit and nonprofit firms. In her earlier career, she worked at a large law firm specializing in copyright and trademark law and worked in-house as general counsel at several large publishing companies.

Jack. An award-winning computer scientist at a major research university. He is the inventor on several patents, some of which were sold or were the foundation of companies in which he had a financial stake.

Jacqueline. An in-house general counsel of a privately held internet company that sells online content and space and whose IPO was recently stalled. In her earlier career, she was in-house counsel for leading technology companies.

Jennifer. A journalist who was formerly bureau chief in Europe for an international news organization and is on staff at a nationally syndicated radio station. She is also the coauthor of a well-regarded book.

Joan. A sculptor with an international reputation and her own studio that employs several assistants. She began as a painter but became a sculptor after several years. She works on her art full-time.

John. A senior licensing officer in the technology transfer office at a top-tier university known for its research in science and engineering.

Joseph. A publishing executive working on development and marketing in a niche press with an international reputation. He previously worked as a buyer in bookstores.

Karen. An artist in her mid-forties with a growing international reputation whose sculptures, paintings, drawings, and installations have earned her international accolades, awards, and grants. She works on her art full-time.

*Kevin.** A software and hardware engineer who no longer designs programs or products but is a consultant and entrepreneur, investing in high tech companies with a focus on telecommunications. He worked in some of the early, founding computer companies as a software engineer when the companies were still small and helped them grow. He has since been involved in both startups and public companies in the industry.

Kim. A musician with her own band and several albums who is also an aspiring actress. She works in the healing arts and as a freelance writer in addition to performing.

*Leo.** A painter (and a retired lawyer) in the later stages of life who is developing a reputation as an artist in the contemporary art scene. He spends most of his time painting and is represented by a gallery, which has hosted several of his art shows.

*Leora.** An in-house counsel at international medical device company with a focus on intellectual property, compliance, and contracts. She began her career as an engineer and is a named inventor on several patents involving consumer goods.

Lisa. An author of adult fiction and non-fiction with several writing awards and bestsellers. She began her career as a teacher and a journalist but now writes full-time.

Mary. A singer-songwriter with several solo albums and a busy performing schedule. For a time, she was represented by a music agent and a well-regarded music label. She began her music career supplementing her income with a flexible part-time job.

*Matt.** An information architect with a background in software development and architecture who previously had his own company developing websites and internet commerce and marketing strategies for a wide variety of companies. Later he became a senior account developer at an internet commercial and marketing company.

Max. An internationally known artist with a focus on architectural works. He employs a studio assistant and has worked on his art and architecture his entire career.

Melanie. An award-winning documentary filmmaker who has her own film production company. She regularly works in public television and earlier in her career was a photographer, a photographic journalist, and an assistant producer to an acclaimed filmmaker.

Meredith. A music agent with her own marketing firm that specializes in promoting singer-songwriters but also represents other kinds of artists and small businesses. Previously, she worked as a marketing executive at a large advertising agency.

Michael. A pharmacologist with his own consulting company that advises scientists, startups, and small and large businesses on how to manufacture their products for large-scale production and distribution. He also earned a law degree after his company was established in order to provide his clients with a more thorough consulting service.

Peter. An in-house patent attorney at a publicly traded, global pharmaceutical company. He began his career at a large law firm as a patent prosecutor.

Paul. An intellectual property attorney and partner at a mid-size law firm serving individual and corporate clients.

Richard. A business executive whose focus is on building companies around products in the medical and health fields. He currently works at an international nonprofit building their research and development ventures. He is an experienced venture capital investor and has been a partner and founder of several funds focusing on bioengineering and the life sciences.

Robert. An award-winning chemist at a major research university who has also started a company (with outside investment and expertise) based on a patented invention that combines his expertise in computer software, math, and chemistry.

Sudie. An artist who focuses on sculpture who supports herself with a combination of her own work and salaried employment curating public art projects. She lives in subsidized housing for artists.

Samuel. A copyright attorney who is the general counsel of a nonprofit licensing organization. In an earlier career, he was a senior in-house attorney for a national retail chain and a senior attorney at a large law firm with specialty in intellectual property and antitrust.

Scott. A marketing executive running his own company that develops web-based marketing platforms and strategies. He began his career as an investment banker but left in order to start his first company (also an online advertising and direct marketing company), which he sold after several years.

Sean. An award-winning photographic journalist who worked with national and international newspapers. He left professional photography within a decade to work in a family business.

Seth. An in-house attorney for a small and profitable print and online publishing company. In his earlier career, he was a litigator working for the government and in-house at a university.

Steve. A marketing and business executive who co-owns a small, prosperous company that focuses on developing brands and merchandise lines through brand extension for entertainment companies (film, television, and toys). Previously, he worked as an executive in marketing and development in Fortune 500 companies.

Susan. A director of the technology transfer office and its operations at a top-tier university known for its research in science and engineering.

Ted. An in-house attorney who is also vice president of a small startup energy company that is in its second decade. He was an IP attorney at a law firm prior to working in-house.

*Theo.** An advertising executive with an expertise in film and video working in an internationally acclaimed advertising agency. He also makes his own films. His first feature film won awards at national and international film festivals.

*Thomas.** A software engineer who founded his own company before graduating college. He has worked as co-owner and partner since then, growing and diversifying his company's products and services, which revolve around data management. His company remains private.

II. PHOTOGRAPHERS: 2016–2018

Photographers were given the option of anonymity on the consent forms that they signed to participate in this study. Where indicated, pseudonyms have been provided for those photographers who elected to remain anonymous. The biographies of confidential interviews lack additional detail to honor that promise of anonymity. As with Set 1 above, I aim to provide enough information for readers to evaluate the stratification of the sample but not so much that anonymity is compromised. Where full names are provided, photographers consented to their name being used. Interviewees are listed in alphabetical order by their first name or pseudonym.

Where possible, I provide links to the photographers' websites so that readers may appreciate the photographers' photographs. All information is current at the time of the interview and does not reflect changed circumstances since 2018.

Abigail (pseudonym). A New York–based photographer with a distinguished fine art and portrait practice whose works are held in numerous private and museum collections. She is also the author of many books of photography.

Above Summit. A Boston-based photography company begun in 2013 with two principles, Emilie Pickering and Jovan Tanasijevic, who also run Lovely Valentine, an event photography company with a focus on weddings. Above Summit is a drone photography company with clients ranging from commercial real estate to university clients.

Alejandro (pseudonym). A New York–based photographer whose first career was in corporate advertising. He became a full-time photographer in 2007, and his focus is on architecture, interiors, and landscapes for commercial and media clients. He is also developing a fine art practice.

Alison (Ali) Campbell. A Boston-educated photographer who focuses on portraiture, documentary photography, and visual storytelling. She is also a designer who combines her photography practice with branding strategies for clients. www.alicampbell.co

Andy Levine. A Boston-based photographer who began his career as a television producer for the Boston Celtics, for which he won several Emmys. He recently switched to photography full-time and is developing a commercial practice. www.andylevinecreative.com

Andrew (Drew) Epstein. A Boston-based attorney and partner at Barker, Epstein & Loscocco. He has been representing photographers, illustrators, design firms, and museums for over forty years. He is the former president and board member of the Photographic Resource Center at Boston University and trustee of the Griffin Museum. He is also a collector of photography. www.photolaw.net

Bob Carey. A New York–based photographer for over twenty years, making photographs for a wide range of commercial and media clients. His photographs are in many permanent collections and museums, and his Tutu Project raising breast cancer awareness through photography garnered international fame. www.bobcarey.com/#/genre/portfolio

Carl Tremblay. A Boston-based commercial and lifestyle photographer since the 1980s with a developed practice in food photography. www.carltremblay.com

Craig Dale. A New Jersey–based photographer with a previously active portrait, commercial, and editorial practice and a specialty in medical photography. He now runs a photography education program called "Beyond the Photo" for all ages, teaching classes for adult hobbyists, for teenagers about visual literacy, and for young elementary school children. www.beyondthephoto.com/about/craig-dale/ and www.beyondthephoto.com/about/craig-dale/.

Dan (pseudonym). A Boston-based photojournalist who splits his career between freelance and staff with an expertise in sports photography. He worked for *Sports Illustrated* for a large portion of his career and currently has a busy advertising and commercial practice.

Danielle Guenther. A New York/Pennsylvania–based photographer and visual artist with a focus on lifestyle photography. Previously a musician, she recently transitioned to photography and began her company making photographs of families and children and also working for editorial and commercial clients. She has become known for her series art photography. www.danielleguentherphotography.com

Emily (pseudonym). A New York–based fine art and documentary photographer. She recently graduated from art school and is already winning awards. She is also developing an editorial and commercial practice.

Esther (pseudonym). A New York–based photographer with a growing business focusing on animal portraits, people portraits, food and fashion for editorial and advertising clients.

Felice Frankel. A Boston-based science and fine art photographer, with awards and grants from the National Science Foundation, the Guggenheim Foundation, National Endowment for the Arts, and the Alfred P. Sloan Foundation. She is also a research scientist at MIT, where her photography practice plays a central role. She is the author of several books on picturing science and nature. www.felicefrankel.com

James (pseudonym). A Boston-based photojournalist with an active editorial and commercial practice. He is also a filmmaker and a photo essayist.

Kim Gerlach. A New York/New Jersey–based photographer who recently transitioned from a full-time practice as an in-house lawyer to starting her own family portrait photography business. www.kimlorraine. com/

Lee Crosson. A Maine-based photographer who specializes in landscape photography. He works full-time as a respiratory specialist with a developing and award-winning passion for photography. www.flickr. com/photos/135350269@N03/

Linda (pseudonym). A New York–based photographer with an active editorial practice who now focuses on fine art and documentary photography, supported by national and international grants and awards.

Lou Jones. A Boston-based photographer with decades of experience in commercial, editorial, travel, and documentary practice. He served on the boards of the ASMP, the Photographic Resource Center, and the Griffin Museum of Photography. He helped found the Center for Digital Imaging Arts of Boston University and has written many books about photography practice. www.fotojones.com

Mark Ostow. A Boston-based portrait, editorial, and street photographer. He began professionally full-time in 1990 after selling his typesetting business. He also co-owns two cafés and runs a photography workshop for teenagers called Teen Photo Workshop. www.ostow.com/ and www.teenphotoworkshops.com

Martha (pseudonym). A Boston-based photojournalist with a long career at the *Boston Globe* dating to the mid-1980s.

Michael Grecco. A New York/Los Angeles–based photographer since the 1980s, with a focus on celebrity, fashion, and editorial photographs. He also is starting a business helping photographers enforce the copyrights in their photographs on the internet. www.grecco.com

Noreen (pseudonym). A New York–based photojournalist, documentary photographer and filmmaker, and author. She is a member of a photography and film collective and teaches at a university.

Patti Schumann. A Chicago-based agent for photographers and filmmakers with over twenty years of experience representing clients and enhancing their practice. She is founder and principal at Schumann & Co. www.schumannco.com

Rick Friedman. A Boston-based photojournalist with three decades of experience, known for his political and celebrity photographs. He also works for commercial clients, and for the past two decades he teaches popular lighting workshops all over North America as well as in the Middle East. www.rickfriedman.com

Sarah Newman. A Boston-based photographer and installation artist with worldwide exhibits. She works as the Director of Art and Education at metaLAB at Harvard. Her photography and art installations have won numerous awards and informs her current projects exploring the social and philosophical dimensions of artificial intelligence. www.sarahwnewman.com

Shane (pseudonym). A New York–based photojournalist with an active portrait practice for more than a decade. He also works for commercial clients. His portraits are commissioned on behalf of authors for their publications.

Silk Studios. A New York–based photographer, Josh Silk has been a photographer since the 1990s specializing in weddings, events, and portraits. www.silkstudioweddings.com/about

Stan Rowin. A Boston-based commercial and editorial photographer since the 1980s, active in professional organizations through the 2000s and president and chairman of the board of the American Society of Media Photographers. He is the coauthor of "Universal Photographic Digital Imaging Guidelines and Professional Business Practices in Photography." www.stanstudio.com

Stephanie Gomez. A New York–based photographer focusing on portraits and street photography who just started a fine arts program at SUNY Purchase. She developed significant photography experience from an after-school photography program called SALT. www.nycsalt.org

Steve Giralt. A New York–based photographer since the early 2000s with an active commercial, advertising, and editorial practice. www.stevegiralt.com

Yunghi Kim. A New York–based freelance photojournalist with decades of experience, both internationally and nationally. She spent a decade as a staff photojournalist before working full-time as a freelance

photographer since the mid-1990s. She was a member of Contact
Press Images since 1995. www.yunghikim.com

III. DESIGNERS: 2018–2020

Designers were given the option of anonymity on the consent forms that
each signed to participate in this study. Where indicated, pseudonyms
have been provided for those designers who elected to remain anonymous.
The biographies for confidential interviews lack additional detail to honor
that promise of anonymity. As with Sets I and II above, I aim to provide
enough information for readers to evaluate the stratification of the sample but not so much that anonymity is compromised. Graduation dates
are provided for the younger designers. Where full names are provided,
designers consented to their name being used. Interviewees are listed in
alphabetical order by their first name or pseudonym. All information is
current at the time of the interview and does not reflect changed circumstances since 2020.

> *Alissa Rantanen.* A Chicago-based designer working as a design manager
> at Insight Product Development, where she conducts ethnographic
> research to create design-based solutions largely for medical and
> health care devices. She previously worked as a freelance graphic de-
> signer. She graduated in 2013 with a BFA in industrial design.
>
> *Allen (pseudonym).* A Cambridge-based designer at IDEO. Before joining
> IDEO, he worked as a mechanical engineer and project leader.
>
> *Ann-Marie Conrado.* Professor of industrial design at the University of
> Notre Dame and a consultant for Fortune 500 companies. Since 1993,
> she has been an active designer with extensive experience in indus-
> trial design.
>
> *Denise Burchell.* A San Francisco-based designer at Salesforce with over
> twenty years of experience in the design industry with a specialty in
> user experience design. Previous work experience includes *Mother
> Jones,* CNET, *Inc.,* AKQA, and IDEO.
>
> *Felicia Ferrone.* A Chicago-based industrial and furniture designer. She
> began work in 1994 as an architect in Milan before returning to the
> United States to found *fferrone,* her international namesake brand, in
> 2010. She also serves as the Director of Graduate Studies in industrial

design at the University of Illinois at Chicago School of Design, where she is also a clinical associate professor.

Frank (pseudonym). A San Francisco–based designer currently working for Intuitive as an industrial designer. His previous experience in industrial design includes four years with Smart Design. He graduated with a master's degree in cross-cultural design in 2012.

George Aye. Co-Founder and Director of Innovation at Greater Good Studio with several decades of design experience. He is an adjunct professor at the School of the Art Institute of Chicago. He worked for seven years at the global innovation firm IDEO before joining the Chicago Transit Authority as its first "human-centered" designer.

Jennifer (pseudonym). A Bay Area–based designer working at Facebook on user interface and product design for internal and external products. Prior to working at Facebook, she worked at Yahoo! on similar design projects. She graduated with a degree in human factors design and ergonomics in 2009.

Jay Newman. A Bay Area–based designer who works as a director at Jump Associates. He prototypes new tools for modeling businesses through financial forecasting, discovery driven planning, and human-centered design. Before joining Jump Associates, he worked at First Annapolis Consulting, where he helped financial institutions and retailers evaluate markets, launch products, adopt technologies, and enter strategic partnerships.

John Traub. A Brooklyn-based designer with multinational brand clients. Prior to establishing his own design firm, he worked at PepsiCo, Smart Design, and Evo Design as an industrial designer. He is also a member of the Design Faculty at the New School. He graduated in 2011 with a BFA in industrial design.

Jonathan Adler. Potter, designer, and author with retail stores in New York City, Miami, Dallas, Los Angeles, San Francisco, and London. In addition to the household goods for which he and his brand are famous, he has also designed hotels, public art installations, and a life-size version of Barbie's Malibu Dream House for Mattel to celebrate the doll's 50th anniversary.

Kathleen Low. User-design strategist based in California, currently at Impossible as a Senior Design Manager. She also helped launch the educational startup company EdgeMakers, Inc. as the Head of Design and Media. She has degrees in human-centered healthcare design and visual communication from 2010.

Kate (pseudonym). A New York–based marketing and design professional currently working at OXO. Prior to OXO, she worked in various strategy positions at marketing firms.

Kevin Lam. A California-based motion designer employed at BCG Digital Ventures. He previously worked as a motion graphics designer at Masimo Corporation. He graduated with a BFA in graphic design in 2011.

Laura Forlano. A Chicago-based associate professor of design at the Institute of Design at the Illinois Institute of Technology and Director of the Critical Futures Lab. Her research interests focus on the socio-technical systems and infrastructures at the intersection of emerging technologies, material practices, and the future of cities.

Lee Moreau. A Boston-based founder of Other Tomorrows, a design and strategy consultancy. He has extensive experience as a designer in cutting-edge design firms, such as Continuum (Boston), 2x4 (New York), and IDEO (San Francisco). He is also an architect and has been a lecturer in MIT's design program.

Maggie Waller. A New York–based designer and former global design manager at HypeBeast. She has also worked as a graphic designer at Levi Strauss & Co. and PONY. She graduated with a BA in industrial design in 2011.

Michael Kahwaji. Senior design manager responsible for brand implementation and product development in the global refrigeration category at Whirlpool, where he was previously the design lead. Prior to his position at Whirlpool, he worked as an industrial designer at Zircon Corporation in California developing DIY and commercial-grade tools.

Michael Rock. Founding partner and creative director at the graphic design studio 2x4 and adjunct professor of graphic design at Yale School of Art since 1991 and a professor at the Columbia University Graduate School of Architecture. At 2x4, he leads both cultural and commercial projects for a variety of international and national clients.

Michelle Crowley. Partner and landscape architect at Crowley and Cottrell, a Massachusetts landscape architecture firm. She has twenty years of experience in landscape design, and her projects range from private residences to land reclamation projects.

Mike Smith. A San Francisco–based designer and director at Jump Associates. For the past twenty years, he has focused on strategy consulting from a design perspective. Prior to joining Jump Associates, he worked as an industrial designer at Flextronics and Design GmbH and RnR Products. He also co-founded both Good Stuff Labs and Spark Factor Design.

Naomi Cottrell. Partner at Crowley and Cottrell with an extensive design practice. With fifteen years of experience, she previously worked at Reed Hilderbrand and LeBlanc Jones.

Patrick Schiavone. A Detroit-based designer currently serving as the Chair for Product Design at the College for Creative Studies. For more than twenty years, he worked for the Ford Motor Company, where he led the design of three generations of the Ford F-150. Thereafter, he worked as vice president of Whirlpool Corporation Global Design, where he led seven international design studios and helped update the look and expand the usability of Whirlpool's global brands.

Richard Gresens. A Michigan-based designer who runs his own design, strategy, and innovation consultancy. Previously, he was the vice president of industrial design at Newell Brands, a senior director for global laundry design at Whirlpool, and chief designer of North American trucks at Ford Motors. He was also chief designer at William M. Schmidt Associates.

Notes

Introduction

1. Naruto v. Slater, 888 F.3d. 418 (2018). There is some debate as to whether Naruto is male or female and about Naruto's age. See, e.g., Sarah Jeong, "Did PETA Name the Right Macaque in Its 'Monkey Selfie' Lawsuit?," *Vice*, Sept. 25, 2015, www.vice.com/en/article/ae353a/did-peta-name-the-right-macaque-in-its-monkey-selfie-lawsuit. David Slater, the photographer, describes Naruto as female. In most other relevant respects, I refer to facts in the court decision, although that is not to concede that courts always get the facts right.

2. For Slater's own account of how he lured the monkeys to the camera, see his professional website, www.djsphotography.co.uk/original_story.html. See also "Ape-rture Priority Photographer Plays Down Monkey Reports," *Amateur Photographer*, July 5, 2011, www.amateurphotographer.co.uk/latest/photo-news/ape-rture-priority-photographer-plays-down-monkey-reports-16224. Slater's description of how he set up the camera to encourage the monkeys to play with it has been repeated in many such media accounts. Some have described Slater's descriptions as self-serving, however.

3. "Photographer Goes Ape over Monkey Selfie: Who Owns the Copyright?," *Amateur Photographer*, Aug. 7, 2014, www.amateurphotographer.co.uk/latest/photo-news/photographer-goes-ape-over-monkey-selfie-who-owns-the-copyright-5054.

4. See, e.g., Stephen Morris, "Shutter Happy Monkey Turns Photographer," *The Guardian*, July 4, 2011, www.theguardian.com/world/2011/jul/04/shutter-happy-monkey-photographer.

5. Macaca nigra self-portrait.jpg, Wikipedia Commons, https://commons.wikimedia.org/wiki/File:Macaca_nigra_self-portrait.jpg#filehistory.

6. Julia Carrie Wong, "Monkey Selfie Photographer Says He's Broke: 'I'm Thinking of Dog Walking,'" *The Guardian*, July 12, 2017, www.theguardian.com/environment/2017/jul/12/monkey-selfie-macaque-copyright-court-david-slater.

7. "Every photographer dreams of a photograph like this," Slater said of the image of a primate grinning toothily into the lens. "If everybody gave me a pound for every time they used [the photograph], I'd probably have £40m in my pocket. The proceeds from these photographs should have me comfortable now, and I'm not." Wong, "Monkey Selfie Photographer."

8. David J. Slater, *Wildlife Personalities* (San Francisco: Blurb Inc., 2014), 11.

9. Compendium of U.S. Copyright Office Practices, § 313.2, U.S. Copyright Office, Dec. 22, 2014, 22. ("To qualify as a work of 'authorship' a work must be created by a human being. . . . Works that do not satisfy this requirement are not copyrightable. The Office will not register works produced by nature, animals, or plants.")

10. Compendium of U.S. Copyright Office Practices, § 313.2, 22.

11. Compendium of U.S. Copyright Office Practices, § 313.2, 22. There appears to be no record at the U.S. Copyright Office of Slater attempting to register copyright in his name for the photo of Naruto.

12. At present writing, Wikimedia Commons has over sixty-four million files.

13. See PETA's website and mission statement at www.peta.org/about-peta.

14. For an analysis of how David Slater may be an author even if Naruto pushed the camera button, see Jane C. Ginsburg and Luke A. Budiardjo, "Authors and Machines," *Berkeley Technology Law Journal* 34 (2019): 343–456.

15. U.S. Constitution, Article I, § 8, cl. 8.

16. Austin Clemens, "Eight Graphs That Tell the Story of U.S. Economic Inequality," Washington Center for Equitable Growth, Dec. 9, 2019, https://equitablegrowth.org/eight-graphs-that-tell-the-story-of-u-s-economic-inequality. The titles of the graphs are:

- The Top 10%'s Share of All Income Has Risen by 6 Points Since 1963
- The Majority of All Wealth in the U.S. Is Controlled by the Top 10%
- Inequality Has Increased More Rapidly in the U.S. than Europe
- At Similar Levels of Education, Women, and Especially Women of Color, Earn Less
- Growth Alone Isn't Enough: When Inequality Is High, Mobility Suffers
- The Great Gatsby Curve: High Inequality Tends to Mean Low Mobility
- College Completion Gaps by Income Persist and Grow
- The Life Expectancy Gap in the U.S. Is Rising.

On political polarization, see, e.g., Kevin M. Kruse and Julian E. Zelizer, *Fault Lines: A History of the United States Since 1974* (New York: W. W. Norton & Co., 2019); Julie E. Cohen, *Between Truth and Power: The Legal Constructions of Information Capitalism* (New York: Oxford University Press, 2019), 86–89; Yochai Benkler, Robert Faris, and Hal Roberts, *Network Propaganda: Manipulation, Disinformation, and Radicalization in American Politics* (New York: Oxford University Press, 2018).

17. See Walter Benjamin, "The Work of Art in the Age of Mechanical Reproduction" in *Illuminations: Essays and Reflections*. (New York: Harcourt, Brace, Jovanovich, 1968): 217–62.

18. In my previous book, *The Eureka Myth*, I show empirically through qualitative interview research with authors and inventors in diverse fields how the grand incentive narrative is today overstated and incomplete to the point of being false. See Jessica Silbey, *The Eureka Myth: Creators, Innovators, and Everyday Intellectual Property* (Stanford, CA: Stanford University Press, 2015). On the phrase "grand incentive narrative," see Simone A. Rose, "The Supreme Court and Patents: Moving Toward a Postmodern Vision of 'Progress'?," *Fordham Intellectual Property Media and Entertainment Law Journal* 23 (2013): 1197–1219. See also Margaret Chon, "Postmodern 'Progress': Reconsidering the Copyright and Patent Power," *DePaul Law Review* 43 (1993): 97–146, at 104, 124, discussing "grant narratives such as 'Progress'" and "delusionary grand narratives of the Enlightenment."

19. See note Benjamin, "Work of Art in the Age of Mechanical Reproduction." See also Tony Judt, "What Is Living and What Is Dead in Social Democracy?"

20. For early work on this topic to which I am indebted, see Margaret Chon, "Intellectual Property and the Development Divide," *Cardozo Law Review* 27 (2006): 2821–2912; Margaret Chon, "Intellectual Property Equality," *Seattle Journal for Social Justice* 9 (2010): 259–73; and Chon, "Postmodern 'Progress.'" See also Jessica Silbey, "Progress Evaluated: A Qualitative Analysis of 'Promoting Progress' through IP," in *The SAGE Handbook of Intellectual Property*, ed. Debora Halbert and Matthew David (London: SAGE, 2014). On the promotion of progress as a structural limitation on Congress's power, see Jeanne C. Fromer, "The Intellectual Property Clause's External Limitations," *Duke Law Journal* 61, no. 7 (2012): 1329–1414; and Dotan Oliar, "Making Sense of the Intellectual Property Clause: Promotion of Progress as a Limitation on Congress's Intellectual Property Power," *Georgetown Law Journal* 95 (2006): 1771–1842. See also Thomas B. Nachbar, "Intellectual Property and Constitutional Norms," *Columbia Law Review* 104 (2004): 272–362, which argued that the "promote the progress" language is merely preambulatory; and Edward C. Walterscheid, "To Promote the Progress of Science and Useful Arts: The Anatomy of a Congressional Power," *IDEA* 43, no. 1 (2002): 1–56, which argued that the clause limits Congress's power to the "promotion of progress" (but fails to define the term). On the sparse history and contemporary manifestations of the progress clause, see Ned Snow, "The Meaning of Science in the Copyright Clause," *Brigham Young University Law Review* 2 (2013): 259–318; Malla Pollack, "What Is Congress Supposed to Promote? Defining 'Progress' in Article 1, Section 8, Clause 8 of the United States Constitution, or Introducing the Progress Clause," *Nebraska Law Review* 80, no. 4 (2001): 754–815; Paul Heald and Suzanna Sherry, "Implied Limits on the Legislative Power: The Intellectual Property Clause as an Absolute Constraint on Congress," *University Illinois Law Review* 4 (2000): 1119–60; Bruce W. Bugbee, *Genesis of American Patent and Copyright Law* (Washington, D.C.: Public Affairs Press, 1967).

21. Barton Beebe, "Bleistein, the Problem of Aesthetic Progress, and the Making of America Copyright Law," *Columbia Law Review* 117, no. 2 (2017): 319–97; Alfred Yen, "Copyright Opinions and Aesthetic Theory," *Southern California Law Review* 71 (1998): 247–302.

22. Snow, "Meaning of Science in the Copyright Clause," quoting James Madison and various contemporary writings. See also Malia Pollack, "Dealing with Old Father William, or Moving from Constitutional Text to Constitutional Doctrine: Progress Clause Review of the Copyright Term Extension Act," *Loyola Los Angeles Law Review* 36 (2002): 376. "'Science' means 'knowledge' in an anachronistically broad sense."

23. Edward C. Walterscheid, *The Nature of the Intellectual Property Clause: A Study in Historical Perspective* (New York: W. S. Hein & Company, 2002), 126. See also Beebe, "Bleistein."

24. Beebe, "Bleistein."

25. Beebe, "Bleistein."

26. Colleen V. Chien, "Of Trolls, Davids, Goliaths, and Kings: Narratives and Evidence in the Litigation of High-Tech Patents," *North Carolina Law Review* 87 (2009): 1571–1615; Colleen V. Chien, "From Arms Race to Marketplace: The Complex Patent Ecosystem and Its Implications for the Patent System," *Hastings Law Journal* 62 (2010): 297; Colleen V. Chien, "Startups and Patent Trolls," https://papers.ssrn.com/sol3/papers.cfm?abstract_id=2146251; Mark Lemley and Douglas Melamed, "Missing the Forest for the Trolls," *Columbia Law Review* 113, no. 8 (2013): 2117–89.

27. On problems of increasing scope in IP, see Jeanne C. Fromer and Mark P. McKenna, "Claiming Design," *University of Pennsylvania Law Review* 167 (2018): 123–210; Mark A. Lemley and Mark P. McKenna, "Scope," *William and Mary Law Review* 57, no. 6 (2016): 2197–285; Jessica Litman, "Billowing White Goo," *Columbia Journal of Law and the Arts* 31, no. 4 (2008): 587–601. The "right of publicity" and trade secrets have also experienced expansion over the twentieth century. See also generally Jennifer E. Rothman, *The Right of Publicity: Privacy Reimagined for a Public World* (Cambridge, Mass.: Harvard University Press, 2018), which traces the evolution of the right of publicity as an expanded right of privacy through the twentieth century; and Sharon K. Sandeen, "The Evolution of Trade Secret Law and Why Courts Commit Error When They Do Not Follow the Uniform Trade Secrets Act," *Hamline Law Review* 33 (2010): 493–543, which discusses the evolution of trade secret law from common law to the enactment of Uniform Trade Secret Act.

28. The Copyright Act of 1790, "An Act for the encouragement of learning by securing the copying of maps, charts, and books, to the authors and proprietors of such copies, during the times therein mentioned." See section 1, ". . . shall have the sole right and liberty of printing, reprinting, publishing and vending such map, chart, book or books, for the term of fourteen years from the recording the title."

29. See Bleistein v. Donaldson Lithographing Co., 188 U.S. 239, 251 (1903).

30. Christopher Beauchamp, *Invented by Law: Alexander Graham Bell and the Patent that Changed America* (Cambridge, Mass.: Harvard University Press, 2015), 13–32.

31. Diamond v. Chakrabarty, 447 U.S. 303, 309 (1980) (citing House reports from the passage of the new Patent Act in 1952).

32. State Street Bank and Trust Company v. Signature Financial Group, Inc., 149 F.3d 1368 (Fed. Cir. 1998) (extending patents to business methods); Association for Molecular Pathology v. Myriad Genetics, Inc., 569 U.S. 576 (2013) (upholding as valid patentable subject matter purified human gene). See also Sarah Burstein, "How Design Patent Law Lost Its Shape," *Cardozo Law Review* 41 (2019): 555–637, describing the trend of patenting of parts of articles of manufacture instead of the whole article.

33. "U.S. Patent Activity Calendar Years 1790 to the Present: Table of Annual U.S. Patent Activity Since 1790," U.S. Patent and Trademark Office, www.uspto.gov/web/offices/ac/ido/oeip/taf/h_counts.htm.

34. According to the director of the U.S. Patent and Trademark Office, Andrei Iancu, August 2020 was a record-breaking month for the number of trademark filings. See "Remarks by Director Iancu at the Intellectual Property Owners Association's 2020 Virtual Annual Meeting," Sept. 21, 2020, www.uspto.gov/about-us/news-up-dates/remarks-director-iancu-intellectual-property-owners-associations-2020-an-nual. ("Through the end of August 2020, trademark filings are 3.2% above filings for the same period last year and are slightly higher than we expected. In fact, August 2020 is our biggest filing month yet, with 76,400 classes. We should see more than 700,000 classes for the year.")

35. The Trade-Mark Cases, 100 U.S. 82 (1879). See Trademark Act of 1905, U.S.C. Title 15, "An Act to authorize the registration of trademarks used in commerce with foreign nations or among the several States or with Indian tribes, and to protect the same."

36. Qualitex Co. v. Jacobson Products Co., Inc., 514 U.S. 159 (1995), which extended trademark protection to single colors. The first trademarked smell in the United States was a plumeria blossom–scented embroidery thread issued in 1990. For a discussion of an increasing trend, see Jacob Gershman, "Eau de Fracking? Companies Try to Trademark Scents," *Wall Street Journal*, Apr. 14, 2015.

37. See 15 U.S.C. sec. 1052. ("No trademark by which the goods of the applicant may be distinguished from the goods of others shall be refused registration on the principal register on account of its nature. . .")

38. Two Pesos, Inc. v. Taco Cabana, Inc., 505 U.S. 763 (1995).

39. The midcentury substantial revision of intellectual property statutes included the Trademark Act in 1946, the Patent Act in 1952, and the Copyright Act in 1976.

40. Barton Beebe, "Intellectual Property Law and the Sumptuary Code," *Harvard Law Review* 123, no. 4 (2010): 809–89, esp. 814–15. "For the past two centuries, our system of consumption-based social distinction has performed an important social function: it has facilitated the construction of individual and group identity. But for two reasons, one primarily social, the other primarily technological, our modern sumptuary code is breaking down. . . . The power of our mimetic technology has thus forced a difficult question: how can a 'culture of the copy' dedicated to and increasingly capable of the reproduction and near-production of nearly everything

also produce distinctions, rarities, *uncopies*, and how can it protect these distinctions from the very forces of dilution that characterize the culture? More essentially, how can a powerfully mimetic culture maintain a sumptuary code?"

41. The causal account of economic growth and accumulation and expanding breadth of intellectual property is highly contestable. The point is not its factual accuracy but the perception of its accuracy, which is essential for the IP incentive story to persist.

42. James Boyle, *The Public Domain: Enclosing the Commons of the Mind* (New Haven, Conn.: Yale University Press, 2008).

43. See Margaret Chon, "Intellectual Property and the Development Divide" and "Postmodern 'Progress.'"

44. See Mark P. McKenna, "The Rehnquist Court and the Groundwork for Greater First Amendment Scrutiny of Intellectual Property," *Washington University Journal of Law and Policy* 21 (2006): 11–29, which counted cases from 1972 to 2006. From 2006 to 2020, the Supreme Court's IP case load has continued apace, with approximately twenty-eight patent cases, fourteen copyright cases, and twelve trademark cases.

45. See John Villasenor, "Intellectual Property: Valuable to Every Discipline," *Chronicle of Higher Education* (Commentary), Aug. 4, 2014.

46. See *Silicon Valley*, seasons 1–6 (2013–19), HBO.

47. See Sonia Katyal and Eduardo Penalver, *Property Outlaws: How Squatters, Pirates, and Protesters Improve the Law of Ownership* (New Haven: Yale University Press, 2010), which makes a related argument but within property law itself, arguing how resistance to "old" forms of private property in the form of outlaw behavior such as piracy and squatting can lead to legal change that is more socially responsive and functional for more people. See also Robert Merges, *Justifying Intellectual Property* (Cambridge, Mass.: Harvard University Press, 2011), which from within a philosophical tradition derives justification for intellectual property as property, that is also justified by the importance of protecting the public domain, human dignity, and proportionality. For a critique of Merges's argument, see Gordon Hull, review essay: "Robert Merges, Justifying Intellectual Property," *Ethics and Information Technology* 14, no. 2 (2012): 169–77.

48. Debating the role and form of self-governance and equality as a founding principle of U.S. constitutionalism, see J. Harvey Wilkinson, *Cosmic Constitutional Theory: Why Americans Are Losing Their Inalienable Right to Self-Governance* (New York: Oxford University Press, 2012); and Erwin Chemerinsky, "The Inescapable Constitutional Theory," *University of Chicago Law Review* 80 (2013): 935–52.

49. Eldred v. Ashcroft, 537 U.S. 186 (2003).

50. Golan v. Holder, 565 U.S. 302 (2012).

51. Bowman v. Monsanto, 569 U.S. 278 (2013).

52. For a critique of *Eldred*, see Pamela Samuelson, "The Constitutional Law of Intellectual Property after *Eldred v. Ashcroft*," *Journal of Copyright Society of the U.S.A.* 50 (2003): 547–80n7. For a critique of *Golan*, see Howard B. Abrams, "*Eldred*,

Golan, and Their Aftermath," *Journal of the Copyright Society of the U.S.A.* 60, no. 4 (2013): 491–527.

53. During his lifetime, J. D. Salinger successfully sued a biographer, Ian Hamilton, and his publisher, Random House, to enjoin a biography that incorporated his unpublished letters. Salinger v. Random House, Inc., 811 F.2d 90 (2nd Cir. 1987) held that an author's control over unpublished letters supersedes the rights of third parties to publish extracts under fair use. See also Salinger v. Colting, 607 F.3d 68 (2nd Cir. 2010); "Salinger Sues over 'Catcher in the Rye' Sequel," Reuters, June 1, 2009; and Andrew Albanese, "J.D. Salinger Estate, Swedish Author Settle Copyright Suit," *Publishers Weekly*, Jan. 11, 2011.

54. Garcia v. Google, Inc., 743 F.3d 1258 (9th Cir. 2014), *amended by* 766 F.3d 929 (9th Cir. 2014); *rev'd en banc*, 786 F.3d 733 (9th Cir. 2015).

55. Hill v. Public Advocate, 35 F. Supp. 3d 1347, 1351–52 (D. Colo. 2014).

56. Eric Goldman and Jessica Silbey, "Copyright's Memory Hole," *Brigham Young University Law Review* (2019): 929–96.

57. Jessica Litman, "Lawful Personal Use," *Texas Law Review* 85 (2007): 1871–1922; Tim Wu, "Tolerated Use," *Columbia Journal of Law and the Arts* 31 (2008): 617.

58. Tony Judt, "What Is Living and What Is Dead in Social Democracy?," *New York Review of Books*, Dec. 17, 2009.

59. Chon, "Postmodern 'Progress,'" 125, critiques the intellectual progress narrative as "insufficiently emancipatory and inattentive to everyday acts and calling for a 'bottom-up' approach . . . that recognizes that 'progress' ive acts may be backward as well as forward . . . This more readily accommodates limits to growth, such as calls for sustainable development. It is one that operates 'self-consciously' within a global context of information technology, and thus pays heed to differences in access to information and to the consequences of knowledge distribution."

60. Ray Kurzweil, *The Singularity Is Near: When Humans Transcend Biology* (New York: Penguin, 2005). See also Chon, "Postmodern 'Progress,'" 126, describing optimism of the late twentieth century and the "hubris of Enlightenment faith [as] its premise of the idea of limitless growth, a premise whose falseness is now attracting widespread attention. . . . A spectacular increase in growth has not resulted in a minimally acceptable standard of living for even a quarter of the world's population."

61. Paul Starr, "A Different Road to a Fair Society" (reviewing *A Society of Equals* by Pierre Rosanvallon), *New York Review of Books*, May 22, 2014. For a "real-world" critique of this view, see Ursula M. Franklin, *The Real World of Technology* (Toronto: House of Anansi Press, 2004).

62. These statements are not hard to verify. See, e.g., Camilo Maldonado, "Price of College Increasing Almost 8 Times Faster Than Wages," *Forbes*, July 24, 2018; John Cassidy, "Ten Years After the State of the Great Recession, Middle-Class Incomes Are Only Just Catching Up," *New Yorker*, Sept. 13, 2018; and Louis Menand, "Karl Marx, Yesterday and Today," *New Yorker*, Oct. 3, 2016. "After 1945, wages rose as national incomes rose, but the income of the lowest earners peaked in 1969, when the minimum hourly wage in the United States was $1.60. That is the equivalent of $10.49

today, when the national minimum wage is $7.25. And, as wages for service-sector jobs decline in earning power, the hours in the workweek increase, because people are forced to take more than one job." On the rising costs of health care, see, e.g., "Trends in Health Care Spending," American Medical Association, www.ama-assn.org/about/ research/trends-health-care-spending. On March 12, 2010, Amnesty International issued a report titled "Deadly Delivery: The Maternal Health Care Crisis in the USA," which according to Amnesty's website "documented that although the United States spends more on health care than any other country, it ranked forty-first (at the time of publication) in terms of maternal death." Available online at www.amnestyusa.org/ reports/deadly-delivery-the-maternal-health-care-crisis-in-the-usa. See also Khiara M. Bridges, *Reproducing Race: An Ethnography of Pregnancy as a Site of Racialization* (Berkeley: University of California Press, 2011), 107–11, discussing racial disparities in maternal mortality rates and racial disparities in maternal mortality rates. See also Marian F. MacDorman et al., "Is the United States Maternal Mortality Rate Increasing?," *Obstetrics and Gynecology* 128, no. 3 (2016): 447–55. "Despite the United Nations Millennium Development Goal for a 75% reduction in maternal mortality by 2015, the estimated maternal mortality rate for 48 states and Washington, D.C., increased from 2000–2014, while the international trend was in the opposite direction. There is a need to redouble efforts to prevent maternal deaths and improve maternity care for the 4 million U.S. women giving birth each year."

63. Judt, "What Is Living and What Is Dead?"

64. Judt, "What Is Living and What Is Dead?"

65. Judt, "What Is Living and What Is Dead?"

66. George Lakoff, "The 'New Centrism' and Its Discontents," Jan. 25, 2011, https:// georgelakoff.com/2011/01/25/the-new-centrism-and-its-discontents.

67. For canonical discussions investigating the constitutive language of law, see, e.g., James Boyd White, *When Words Lose Their Meaning* (Chicago: University of Chicago Press, 1985); James Boyd White, "Law, Economics, and Torture," in *Law and Democracy in the Empire of Force*, ed. H. Jefferson Powell and James Boyd White (Ann Arbor: University of Michigan Press, 2009), 265–84.

68. Joshua Rothman, "Are Things Getting Better or Worse?," *New Yorker*, July 23, 2018.

Chapter 1

1. "The Coming World of Photography," *Popular Photography*, February 1944, https://perma.cc/AA7R-TKJG.

2. Ai Weiwei, *Ai Weiwei's Blog: Writings, Interviews, and Digital Rants, 2006–2009*, edited and translated by Lee Ambrozy (Cambridge, Mass.: MIT Press, 2011), 9.

3. For a survey of these debates, see Alan Trachtenberg, ed., *Classic Essays on Photography* (New Haven, Conn.: Leete's Island Books, 1980). See also François Brunet, *The Birth of the Idea of Photography*, translated by Shane B. Lillis (Cambridge, Mass.: MIT Press, 2019).

4. Trachtenberg, *Classic Essays on Photography*, 294.

5. Trachtenberg, *Classic Essays on Photography*, 74. Holmes was talking specifically about stereoscopes that depended on photographic technology. Today we call them "viewfinders"—devices projecting two photographs of the same object taken at slightly different angles producing an impression of dimensionality.

6. Woodrow Hartzog and Jessica Silbey, "The Upside of Deep Fakes," *Maryland Law Review* 78, no. 4 (2019): 960–66; Robert Chesney and Danielle Citron, "Deep Fakes: A Looming Challenge for Privacy, Democracy, and National Security," *California Law Review* 107 (2019): 1753–1820; Mary Ann Franks and Ari Ezra Waldman, "Sex, Lies, and Videotape: Deep Fakes and Free Speech Delusions," *Maryland Law Review* 78, no. 4 (2019): 892–98.

7. Gerry Badger, *The Genius of Photography: How Photography Has Changed Our Lives* (London: Quadrille Publishing, 2001), 8.

8. For a full description of the research methodology and empirical data collection process, see Appendix A (Research Methodology).

9. As of this writing (2021), it is estimated that Google processes 3.5 billion searches per day and has approximately 92 percent of the search engine market share worldwide.

10. Rachel Gillett, "Why We're More Likely to Remember Content with Images and Video," *Fast Company*, Sept. 18, 2014, www.fastcompany.com/3035856/why-were-more-likely-to-remember-content-with-images-and-video-infogr, cited a study by online marketing company HubSpot that found that "tweets with images are 94% more likely to be retweeted than tweets without"; Noah Kagan, "Why Content Goes Viral: What Analyzing 100 Million Articles Taught Us," *Huffington Post*, June 13, 2014, www.huffpost.com/entry/why-content-goes-viral-wh_b_5492767, found that "twice as many people, on average[,] share posts with at least one image in the post."

11. I learned during my field work that one of the milestones that accelerated the transition from film to digital photography was the events of September 11, 2001. The desire for immediate imagery of the terrorist attacks that could be satiated by digital cameras and phone cameras shaped the photojournalism industry thereafter. By 2005, most newspapers and media outlets demanded digital files, faster turnaround on assignments, and more images.

12. Lou Jones, *Final Exposure: Portraits from Death Row* (Boston: Northeastern University Press, 1996).

13. Jessica Litman, "What We Don't See When We See Copyright as Property," *Cambridge Law Journal* 77, no. 3 (2018): 536–58.

14. Mark Rose, *Authors and Owners: The Invention of Copyright* (Cambridge, Mass.: Harvard University Press, 1993).

15. Burrow-Giles Lithographic Co. v. Sarony, 111 U.S. 53, 61 (1884).

16. *Burrow-Giles*, 111 U.S. at 61 defined the author as "the person who effectively is as near as he can be the cause of the picture which is produced—that is, the person who has superintended the arrangement, who has actually formed the picture by putting the persons in position, and arranging the place where the people are to be—the man who is the effective cause of that."

17. Fair use is outlined in the Copyright Act, 17 U.S.C. § 107. In full it states:

Notwithstanding the provisions of sections 106 and 106A, the fair use of a copyrighted work, including such use by reproduction in copies or phonorecords or by any other means specified by that section, for purposes such as criticism, comment, news reporting, teaching (including multiple copies for classroom use), scholarship, or research, is not an infringement of copyright. In determining whether the use made of a work in any particular case is a fair use the factors to be considered shall include—

(1) the purpose and character of the use, including whether such use is of a commercial nature or is for nonprofit educational purposes;
(2) the nature of the copyrighted work;
(3) the amount and substantiality of the portion used in relation to the copyrighted work as a whole; and
(4) the effect of the use upon the potential market for or value of the copyrighted work.

The fact that a work is unpublished shall not itself bar a finding of fair use if such finding is made upon consideration of all the above factors.

18. See Andrew Gilden, "Raw Materials and the Creative Process," *Georgetown Law Journal* 104 (2016): 368–69, discussing how transformative standard will allow a "preexisting image" to be considered a "component" when "used as raw material, transformed in the creation of new" art.

19. Pamela Samuelson, "Justifications for Copyright Limitation and Exceptions," in *Copyright Law in the Age of Limitations and Exceptions*, ed. Ruth L. Okediji (New York: Cambridge University Press, 2017), 12, 25–26.

20. See 17 U.S.C. § 106(2) for the derivative work right; see also H.R. Rep. no. 94-1476, at 1049 (1976). A derivative work is defined in the statute at 17 U.S.C § 101 as "a work based upon one or more preexisting works, such as a translation, musical arrangement, dramatization, fictionalization, motion picture version, sound recording, art reproduction, abridgment, condensation, or any other form in which a work may be recast, transformed, or adapted. A work consisting of editorial revisions, annotations, elaborations, or other modifications which, as a whole, represent an original work of authorship, is a 'derivative work.'"

21. This poses significant First Amendment challenges that are familiar in constitutional doctrine. When does more speech of a certain kind threaten the ability of others to speak freely and should therefore be limited? And is limiting the speech of others viewpoint discrimination, which is categorically prohibited except under the most stringent of circumstances? The ongoing debate in constitutional law about appropriate line drawing in this context reflects some of the everyday challenges photographers wrestle with to limit or allow use of their photographs as part of others' critical or political speech. See, e.g., Rebecca Tushnet, "Copyright as a Model for

Free Speech Law: What Copyright Has in Common with Anti-Pornography Laws, Campaign Finance Reform, and Telecommunications Regulation," *Boston College Law Review* 42, no. 1 (2000): 1–79; and Rebecca Tushnet, "Copy This Essay: How Fair Use Doctrine Harms Free Speech and How Copying Serves It," *Yale Law Journal* 114, no. 3 (2004): 535–91.

22. Jack M. Balkin, "Information Fiduciaries and the First Amendment," *UC Davis Law Review* 49, no. 4 (2016): 1183–1234; Lina M. Khan and David E. Pozen, "A Skeptical View of Information Fiduciaries," *Harvard Law Review* 133 (2019): 497–541; Claudia Haupt, "Platform as Trustees: Information Fiduciaries and the Value of Analogy," *Harvard Law Review Forum* 134, no. 2 (2020): 34–41.

23. Originality is a concept deeply embedded in copyright law, and here the photographers' beliefs and attitudes align with copyright doctrine. See *Burrow-Giles*, 111 U.S. at 61, describing photographic authors as "superintend[ing] the arrangement . . . form[ing] the picture" and the author in a constitutional sense, to mean "he to whom anything owes its origin; originator; maker." See also *Feist Publications v. Rural Telephone Service Co.*, 499 U.S. 340, 345 (1991). "The *sine qua non* of copyright is originality. To qualify for copyright protection, a work must be original to the author. Original, as the term is used in copyright, means only that the work was independently created by the author (as opposed to copied from other works), and that it possesses at least some minimal degree of creativity." On photographic authors in particular, see Robert Hirsch, *Seizing the Light: A Social and Aesthetic History of Photography*, 3rd ed. (New York: Routledge, 2017), 87–88, describing Napoleon Sarony as a "modern-day director." Eva Subotnik addresses copyright interests of photographic subjects in the case law as a "legally relevant hierarchy" in which the photographer is the only author either by law or contract. Eva E. Subotnik, "The Author Was Not an Author: The Copyright Interests of Photograph Subjects from Wilde to Garcia," *Columbia Journal of Law and the Arts* 39, no. 3 (2016): 449–63.

24. Jessica Silbey, Eva E. Subotnik, and Peter DiCola, "Existential Copyright and Professional Photographers," *Notre Dame Law Review* 95, no. 1 (2019): 263–326. Even though photographers claim copyright's centrality to their identities as professionals, copyright registration and legal enforcement are rare among photographers. After-the-fact enforcement of copyright is infrequent among professional photographers, who are busy and spend most of their time generating new business rather than enforcing prior agreements.

25. See, e.g., 17 U.S.C. §§ 102(b), which excludes from copyright protection "any idea, procedure, process, system, method of operation, concept, principle, or discovery, regardless of the form in which it is described, explained, illustrated, or embodied in such work." See also *Feist Publications*, 499 U.S. 340, 345 (excluding facts from copyright protection because they lack human authorship or "originality" under Copyright Law); *Eldred v. Ashcroft*, 537 U.S. 186, 219 (2003) ("The Copyright Clause and the First Amendment seek related objectives—the creation and dissemination of information. When working in tandem, these provisions mutually reinforce each other, the first (the Copyright Clause) serving as an "engine of free expression,"

Harper & Row, Publishers, Inc. v. Nation Enterprises, 471 U.S. 539, 558 (1985), the second (the First Amendment) assures that government throws up no obstacle to its dissemination. At the same time, a particular statute that exceeds proper Copyright Clause bounds may set Clause and Amendment at cross-purposes, thereby depriving the public of the speech-related benefits that the Founders, through both, have promised.); and *Campbell v. Acuff-Rose Music, Inc.*, 510 U.S. 569, 579 (1994), describing fair use as the "guarantee of breathing space within the confines of copyright."

26. Some photographers described having a release form long ago drafted by a friend or lawyer that exists on their phone or laptop for quick signature by the subject. One typical explanation from a professional event photographer, Josh Silk, went: "I forget how we got our initial contract. I think we might have used a form or something that we got, or we borrowed from other photographers' contracts. We were part of an initial . . . wedding photography group for many years, in which we all kinda shared information freely. So I'm sure some of it came out of that."

27. Holly Stuart Hughes, "Photographers and Casting Directors on the Pros and Cons of Using "Real People" for Advertising Shoots," *Photo District News*, Sept. 12, 2018. "The push to cast non-professionals in the lifestyle and portrait-driven campaigns . . . is part of a trend to be more 'authentic.' That's become a buzzword. . . . [A] younger group of art directors and creative directors [who] come from a world of social media want their advertising to blend with the images people share daily. . . . They can see through the 'stocky' lifestyle photography that features models.

28. See *Burrow-Giles*, 111 U.S. at 61.

29. Eva E. Subotnik, "Artistic Control After Death," *Washington Law Review* 92, no. 1 (2017): 253–313. Professor Subotnik describes successors in interest as kinds of copyright stewards, but this concept applies equally well to photographers in terms of their subjects.

30. This is not true of commercial photographers making photographs for advertisers and other brand clients. Photographers describe these kinds of photographs as being subject to tighter reuse control because of their primary commercial nature and because these clients have stronger and more explicit contract provisions delineating exclusivity. Some fine art and portrait photographers did describe returning to the subject to tell them about the photograph's reuse in a book, but this return to the subject was rare in the interviews.

31. See, e.g., Silbey, *Eureka Myth*, describing artists' and inventors' relationship to their work in terms of family relations and their children.

32. See Tushnet, "Copyright as a Model for Free Speech Law"; and Tushnet, "Copy This Essay."

33. *Campbell*, 510 U.S. 569. Compare *Katz v. Google Inc.*, 802 F.3d 1178 (11th Cir. 2015), which held that use was fair and no privacy violation occurred because subject is a public figure, with *Hill v. Public Advocate of the U.S.*, 35 F. Supp. 3d 1347 (D. Colo. 2014), which determined that a question of fact regarding fair use existed but there was no privacy violation because of the public interest in the subject matter.

34. Andrew Abbott, *The System of Professions: An Essay on the Division of Expert Labor* (Chicago: University of Chicago Press, 1988), 2–3, 8–9, conceives of professions as having an ecology and turfs in need of cultural mapping with boundary conflicts. See also Andrew Abbott, "Things of Boundaries," *Social Research* 62, no. 4 (1995): 857, 882, which asserts that boundary building and connecting is the proper starting place for investigating stable and shifting social entities, such as professions.

35. See 17 U.S.C. § 102(b). See also *Feist Publications*, 499 U.S. 340, 345 (excluding facts from copyright protection because they lack human authorship or "originality" under Copyright Law).

36. For a short discussion of the tensions between copying and control in intellectual property in view of technological development, see Jessica Silbey, "Photocopier," in *A History of Intellectual Property in 50 Objects*, ed. Dan Hunter and Claudy Op den Kamp (New York: Cambridge University Press, 2019), 233–40; and Jessica Silbey, "How Xerox's Intellectual Property Prevented Anyone from Copying Its Copiers," *Smithsonian Magazine*, July 2, 2019.

37. Jennifer E. Rothman, *The Right of Publicity: Privacy Reimagined for a Public World* (Cambridge, Mass.: Harvard University Press, 2018), 37.

38. Chapter 3 discusses, among other cases with overlapping privacy and copyright claims, Garcia v. Google, Inc., 786 F.3d 733 (9th Cir. 2015), in which the plaintiff failed to prove copyright ownership in order to proceed with lawsuit seeking to take down film she had been defrauded to make; Balsley v. LFP, Inc., 691 F.3d 747 (6th Cir. 2012), in which the subject of the photo received assignment of the photographer's copyright in order to sue to enjoin further distribution of photo of her in a wet T-shirt contest; Monge v. Maya Mags., Inc., 688 F.3d 1164 (9th Cir. 2012), in which subjects of wedding photos registered copyright in their name in order to sue to prevent their publication; and *Hill*, 35 F. Supp. 3d 1347, in which the photographer joined with photographic subjects to sue to control the use of an engagement photo.

39. François Brunet, *The Birth of the Idea of Photography*, trans. Shane B. Lillis (Cambridge, Mass.: MIT Press, 2019), xiii.

40. Gillett, "Why We're More Likely to Remember Content with Images and Video"; Kagan, "Why Content Goes Viral."

41. W. J. T. Mitchell, *What Do Pictures Want? The Lives and Loves of Images* (Chicago: University of Chicago Press, 2004), 9.

42. John Dewey, *Art as Experience* (New York: Minton, Balch & Company, 1934).

43. This is because the Digital Millennium Copyright Act provides a safe harbor from infringement for platforms or websites that host content, such as photographs. As long as the platforms agree to take down the infringing content uploaded by users when notified, the platforms are not responsible for infringement damages. 17 U.S.C. § 512 (a)–(d), describing standards for immunity from copyright infringement for various internet providers and websites. See also Annemarie Bridy, "Copyright's Digital Deputies: DMCA-Plus Enforcement by Internet Intermediaries," in *Research Handbook on Electronic Commerce Law*, ed. John A. Rothchild (Northampton, Mass.: Edward Elgar Publishing, 2016), 185–208; Timothy Armstrong, "Digital Rights

Management and the Process of Fair Use," *Harvard Journal of Law and Technology* 20, no. 1 (2006): 49–121.

44. See, e.g., Jaqueline Tobin, "Photographer Wins Landmark Lawsuit Against Buzzfeed," *Rangefinder*, August 19, 2020, www.rangefinderonline.com/news-features/industry-news/photographer-wins-landmark-lawsuit-against-buzzfeed.

45. Porter Wells, "Court Orders 'Copyright Troll' into Firm Management Course," Bloomberg Law, May 8, 2020, news.bloomberglaw.com/ip-law/court-orders-copyright-troll-into-firm-management-course; "Attorney Richard Liebowitz Not Slowing Down, Sues Midwest Communications in Latest Copyright-Infringement Action," *Inside Radio*, May 22, 2020, www.insideradio.com/free/attorney-richard-liebowitz-not-slowing-down-sues-midwest-communications-in-latest-copyright-infringement-action/article_f8c24aba-9bf8-11ea-9af4-dbc6a0ea6a87.html; Bill Donahue, "During Pandemic, Prolific Copyright Lawyer Keeps Suing," *Law360*, Mar. 27, 2020, www.law360.com/articles/1257593/during-pandemic-prolific-copyright-lawyer-keeps-suing.

46. Mike Masnik, "Judge Benchslaps Richard Liebowitz Again over His Request to Not Have to Tell Everyone about Previous Sanctions, *Techdirt*, July 23, 2020, www.techdirt.com/articles/20200723/12333544963/judge-benchslaps-richard-liebowitz-again-over-his-request-to-not-have-to-tell-everyone-about-previous-sanctions.shtml.

47. Ashley Cullins, "Has This Man Sued You? A 'Copyright Troll' Takes on Hollywood," *Hollywood Reporter*, Apr. 6, 2018, www.hollywoodreporter.com/amp/thr-esq/has-man-sued-you-a-copyright-troll-takes-hollywood-1099156.

48. 17 U.S.C. §§ 504(c)(1) statutory damages range from $750 to $30,000 per infringing work, and (2) statutory damages for willful infringement up to $150,000 per infringing work. See also Alicia Calzada and Mickey Osterreicher, "Suing for Copyright Infringement? 10 Things to Consider," National Press Photographers Association, March–April 2018, https://nppa.org/magazine/copyright-infringement-10-things-consider.

Chapter 2

1. Eldred v. Ashcroft, 537 U.S. 186 (2003).

2. Golan v. Holder, 565 U.S. 302 (2012).

3. U.S. Constitution, Amendment XIV, Cl. 1. "All persons born or naturalized in the United States, and subject to the jurisdiction thereof, are citizens of the United States and of the state wherein they reside. No state shall make or enforce any law which shall abridge the privileges or immunities of citizens of the United States; nor shall any state deprive any person of life, liberty, or property, without due process of law; *nor deny to any person within its jurisdiction the equal protection of the laws*" (emphasis added).

4. I am particularly indebted to Professor Wendy Gordon for helping me think through this articulation of this chapter's focus.

5. Amartya Sen, "Equality of What? The Tanner Lecture on Human Values," lecture, Stanford University, Stanford, California, May 22, 1979. On the variability

of equality's dimensions, see T. M. Scanlon, *Why Does Inequality Matter?* (Oxford: Oxford University Press, 2018); Ronald Dworkin, *Sovereign Virtue: The Theory and Practice of Equality* (Cambridge, Mass.: Harvard University Press, 2002); Elizabeth Anderson, "What Is the Point of Equality?," *Ethics* 109, no. 2 (1999): 287–337; Thomas Nagel, *Equality and Partiality* (New York: Oxford University Press, 1991); Peter Westen, *Speaking of Equality: An Analysis of the Rhetorical Force of "Equality" in Moral and Legal Discourse* (Princeton, N.J.: Princeton University Press, 1990); and Harry Frankfurt, "Equality as a Moral Ideal," *Ethics* 98, no. 1 (1987): 21–43.

6. Treating each person the same may exacerbate differences that generate social, economic, and political hierarchies, which by their nature make equality (whatever that may mean in a given context) harder to sustain. For example, giving everyone, even the rich, $1,000 a month treats everyone the same without assuring equality of opportunity. And yet providing "each according to their needs" may mean that some people get nothing, which does not affect human flourishing but may produce resentment and thus social strife.

7. See especially Anderson, "What Is the Point of Equality?"

8. Anderson, "What Is the Point of Equality?"

9. On the relationship between intellectual property and American identity, see Anjali Vats, *The Color of Creatorship: Intellectual Property, Race, and the Making of Americans* (Stanford, Calif.: Stanford University Press, 2020).

10. Jill Lepore, *These Truths: A History of the United States* (New York: W. W. Norton & Co., 2018), 98.

11. Lepore, *These Truths*, 99. For a paradigm-shifting analysis of U.S. Constitutional law that reaches "beyond the black/white binary [to] . . . highlight the centrality of federal Indian law and this Nation's tragic history with colonials to public law," see Maggie Blackhawk, "Federal Indian Law as Paradigm Within Public Law," *Harvard Law Review* 132, no. 7 (2019): 1787–1877.

12. The U.S. Civil War started in 1861 with the secession from the United States by South Carolina. See Lepore, *These Truths*, 292–307.

13. For the phrase "domestic dependent nation," see Cherokee Nation v. Georgia, 30 U.S. 1 (1831). The U.S. Constitution is largely silent on the status of the people and nations that populated the continent prior to the European colonials, except U.S. Constitution, Art. I, § 2 ("Representatives and direct Taxes shall be apportioned among the several states which may be included within this Union, according to their respective Numbers, which shall be determined by adding to the whole Number of free Persons, including those bound to Service for a Term of Years, and excluding Indians not taxed, three fifths of all other persons"); and U.S. Constitution, Article I, § 8, Cl. 3 ("Congress shall have the power to regulate Commerce with foreign nations and among the several states, and with the Indian tribes." Together with U.S. Constitution, Article IV, § 2 ("No Person held to Service of Labour in one State, under the Laws thereof, escaping into another, shall, in Consequence of any Law or Regulation therein, be discharged from such Service of Labour, but shall be delivered up on Claim of the Part to whom such Service or Labour may be due.") these clauses imply hierarchy of people based on national origin and race. These are commonly

referred to as the "three-fifths clause," the "commerce clause," and "fugitive slave clause," respectively.

14. Confederate states that refused to ratify the Fourteenth Amendment were not allowed back into the union of the United States, and their elected officials were forbidden from taking part in the 39th Congress; the Republican-controlled Reconstruction Congress refused to seat congresspersons who would not accept the Fourteenth Amendment under the constitutional authority to "judge the qualification of its members." See U.S. Constitution, Article I, § 5 ("Each House shall be the Judge of the Elections, Returns and Qualifications of its own Members, and a Majority of each shall constitute a Quorum to do Business."). Because the Civil War's premises were union, freedom, and equality for all persons under law, and because these principles prevailed with the North's victory, Republican congresspersons considered the acceptance of these principles necessary to participate in and benefit from government. On this procedural history of the Fourteenth Amendment's passage, see Akhil Reed Amar, *America's Constitution: A Biography* (New York: Random House, 2005), 365–80. See also Bruce Ackerman, "Constitutional Politics/Constitutional Law," *Yale Law Journal* 99, no. 3 (1989): 453–547; and Paul Brest et al., *Processes of Constitutional Decisionmaking*, 6th ed. (New York: Wolters Kluwer, 2015), 364–67.

15. See U.S. Constitution, Article I, § 9 ("No Title of Nobility shall be granted by the United States: And no Person holding any Office of Profit or Trust under them, shall, without the Consent of the Congress, accept of any present, Emolument, Office, or Title, of any kind whatever, from any King, Prince, or foreign State."); and U.S. Constitution, Article IV, § 2 ("The Citizens of each State shall be entitled to all Privileges and Immunities of Citizens in the several States.").

16. See U.S. Constitution, Art. I, § 2 and Art. IV, § 2. See also U.S. Constitution, Article I, § 9 ("The Migration or Importation of such Persons as any of the States now existing shall think proper to admit, shall not be prohibited by the Congress prior to the Year one thousand eight hundred and eight, but a Tax or duty may be imposed on such Importation, not exceeding ten dollars for each Person."). This clause is understood to allow importation into the United States of enslaved people until 1808, and that Congress could after that date, if it so chose, ban such practice. This did not ban the institution of domestic slavery in the United States, however; it simply made human reproduction and rape the source of more enslaved people for plantation labor.

17. Abraham Lincoln said of slavery that "the thing is hid away, in the constitution just as an afflicted man hides away a wen or a cancer, which he dares not cut out at once, lest he bleed to death; with the promise, nevertheless, that the cutting may begin at the end of a given time." James M. McPherson, *The Illustrated Battle Cry of Freedom: The Civil War Era* (New York: Oxford University Press, 2003), 127.

18. Adam H. Domby, *The False Cause: Fraud, Fabrication, and White Supremacy in Confederate Memory* (Charlottesville: University of Virginia Press, 2020); Gary W. Gallagher and Alan T. Nolan, eds., *The Myth of the Lost Cause and Civil War History* (Bloomington: Indiana University Press, 2000). The "lost cause" is a discredited

Confederate account of what was lost and what was gained by the Civil War. It requires either a wholesale forgetting of the horrors of slavery or an abhorrent explanation of the institution based in violent paternalism and beliefs of racial inferiority.

19. The persistent isolation of Native Americans would continue, however. See Elk v. Wilkins, 112 U.S. 94 (1884), which held that the Citizenship Clause of the Fourteenth Amendment did not grant Native Americans birthright citizenship because as members of sovereign tribes—albeit "domestic dependent nations" —they were not "subject to the jurisdiction" of the United States. This decision has been ably discussed and criticized; see, e.g., Maggie Blackhawk, "Federal Indian Law as Paradigm Within Public Law," at 1842–44; Bethany R. Berger, "Birthright Citizenship on Trial: Elk v. Wilkins an United States v. Wong Kim Ark," *Cardozo Law Review* 37: 1185–1258. Not until The Indian Citizenship Act of 1924 did Congress (not the Court through constitutional interpretation) grant citizenship on all Native Americans born within the territorial limits of the country.

20. Dred Scott v. Sandford, 60 U.S. 393 (1857).

21. This citizenship clause was interpreted to exclude Native Americans; see Elk v. Wilkins, 112 U.S. 94 (1884).

22. Slaughterhouse Cases, 83 U.S. 36 (1873).

23. Amar, *America's Constitution*, 388–92.

24. Strauder v. West Virginia, 100 U.S. 303 (1880).

25. Plessy v. Ferguson, 163 U.S. 537 (1896) blessed racial segregation under the doctrine of "separate but equal" and will be discussed later in this chapter. On the issue of sex equality, an early equal protection case concerned the state of Illinois's refusal to grant Myra Bradwell a law license because she was female. In *Bradwell v. Illinois* 83 U.S. 130 (1873), the Supreme Court heard arguments about how the Declaration of Independence and the Civil War Amendments' promises of equal rights included women such that women, like men, should have the right to independently labor and own the fruits thereof irrespective of social status. And yet the Court (over a single dissent) held that the Fourteenth Amendment did not promise equality on the basis of sex, denying a woman's right to enter any profession she sought, including law. The Court said that a "woman [in Illinois] ha[s] no legal existence separate from her husband," and therefore cannot make contracts—an incapacity precluding the practice of law. In other words, per *Bradwell*, the Fourteenth Amendment does not protect against distinctions on the basis of sex. It would take the civil rights era of the 1960s and the growing feminist movement in the 1970s for the Supreme Court to change its view of the Constitution's promise of equality applying to women as well as men.

26. Civil Rights Cases, 109 U.S. 3 (1883).

27. State and federal prohibitions of discrimination in employment, housing, or public accommodations are numerous. States pass these laws and expand or contract them pursuant to their police powers. Congressional laws limiting discrimination in these contexts are predominantly passed pursuant to the interstate commerce power as a matter of regulating interstate commerce, not pursuant to congressional power

to prohibit states' denial of equal protection of the laws. See Heart of Atlanta v. U.S. 379 U.S. 241 (1964) and Katzenbach v. McClung, 379 U.S. 294 (1964).

28. U.S. v. Carolene Products, 304 U.S. 144 (1838).

29. U.S. v. Carolene Products, 304 U.S. 144 (1838).

30. *Carolene Products*, 304 U.S. 144. "The existence of facts supporting the legislative judgment is to be presumed, for regulatory legislation affecting ordinary commercial transactions is not to be pronounced unconstitutional unless in the light of the facts made known or generally assumed it is of such a character as to preclude the assumption that it rests upon some rational basis within the knowledge and experience of the legislators." The Court established a caveat to this broad deference by the judicial branch to the legislative branch in the famous footnote 4, the full text of which reads:

> There may be narrower scope for operation of the presumption of constitutionality when legislation appears on its face to be within a specific prohibition of the Constitution, such as those of the first ten Amendments, which are deemed equally specific when held to be embraced within the Fourteenth. . . . [citations omitted]
>
> It is unnecessary to consider now whether legislation which restricts those political processes which can ordinarily be expected to bring about repeal of undesirable legislation, is to be subjected to more exacting judicial scrutiny under the general prohibitions of the Fourteenth Amendment than are most other types of legislation. On restrictions upon the right to vote, see Nixon v. Herndon . . .; on restraints upon the dissemination of information, see Near v. Minnesota, . . .; on interferences with political organizations, see Stromberg v. California, . . .; as to prohibition of peaceable assembly, see De Jonge v. Oregon, . . .
>
> Nor need we enquire whether similar considerations enter into the review of statutes directed at particular religious, Pierce v. Society of Sisters, . . . or national, Meyer v. Nebraska, . . . or racial minorities . . .; whether prejudice against discrete and insular minorities may be a special condition, which tends seriously to curtail the operation of those political processes ordinarily to be relied upon to protect minorities, and which may call for a correspondingly more searching judicial inquiry.

31. *Plessy*, 163 U.S. 537.

32. The condition of the railcars were not the same, but equality of accommodation was assumed for the purposes of the litigation. See C. Vann Woodward, "The Case of the Louisiana Traveler," in *Quarrels That Have Shaped the Constitution*, ed. John A. Garrity (New York: Harper & Row, 1987), 157–74, esp. 165.

33. See Sen, "Equality of What?"; and Anderson, "What Is the Point of Equality?"

34. One result of this doctrine of economic due process was to presume all men (but not women and children) free to pursue their economic goals—a libertarian vision of the American Dream—even when in reality very few were so free. The case of Lochner v. New York, 198 U.S. 45 (1905) epitomizes this philosophy. In it, the Court struck down New York's wage and hour laws on the basis of fundamental freedom to

contract and due process, insisting that bakers and bakery owners should be able to negotiate independently, man-to-man, as equals, without the paternalistic guidance of state regulation limiting the terms of those contracts for anyone's benefit, even the public health.

35. Anupam Chander, "The New, New Property," *Texas Law Review* 81 (2003): 715–96, in which Chander evaluates the "new, new world of cyberspace" in terms of its fit with older property regimes of the eighteenth and nineteenth centuries.

36. One notable exception to this is Sony Corp. of America v. Universal City Studios, Inc., 464 U.S. 417 (1984), which was decided 5–4. This important case decided the legality of home video recorders under copyright law. I discuss this case in chapter 5.

37. Since the 1990s, predictable conversations among justices have developed around common concerns. Justices Ruth Bader Ginsburg and Stephen Breyer often sparred about the proper scope of copyright and patent law, although two recent and contentious copyright decisions found them writing together: Allen v. Cooper, 589 U.S. ___, 140 S. Ct. 994 (2020) and Georgia v. Public.Resource.Org, Inc. 590 U.S. ___, 140 S. Ct. 1498 (2020). Justice Ginsburg typically erred on the side of longer-lasting rights with more substantive scope, whereas Justice Breyer has tended to be more skeptical of intellectual property's ability to promote progress of science and the useful arts and a fair marketplace, preferring to embrace more limitations and exceptions to intellectual property ownership. Justices Breyer and Ginsburg often agreed on cases concerning racial and sex equality. Their disagreements concerning intellectual property discussed in this chapter therefore may be surprising when seen as grounded in principles that form the bases of other forms of equality on which they agree. This is evidence of the latency of the terms of the debate on which these intellectual property cases are disputed. Identifying the trenchant equality concerns in these cases about intellectual property remains an important challenge for clarifying the disagreements and identifying the stakes in IP regulation today.

38. Masterpiece Cakeshop v. Colorado Civil Rights Commission, 584 U.S. ___, 138 S. Ct. 1719 (2018). See also Stormans, Inc., v. Wiesman, 794 F.3d 1064 (9th Cir. 2015), cert. denied 579 U.S. ___ (2016), over dissents by Justices Alito and Thomas.

39. See, e.g., Sarah J. Jackson, Moya Bailey, and Brooke Foucault Welles, *#HashtagActivism: Networks of Race and Gender Justice* (Cambridge, Mass.: MIT Press, 2020); Deborah L. Rhode, "#MeToo: Why Now? What Next?," *Duke Law Journal* 69, no. 2 (2019): 377–428; and F. Hollis Griffin, *Feeling Normal: Sexuality and Media Criticism in the Digital Age* (Bloomington: Indiana University Press, 2016).

40. Some may argue that economic efficiency is an optimal form of justice. But "concepts such as justice, fairness, equity, reasonableness, and equality are not the subject of mathematical calculus; they are values formed from the human experience of living in a community with others. If such concepts . . . are simply translated into economic equivalent of efficiency and wealth maximization, they lose much of their

social and cultural meaning." Robin Paul Malloy and David Driesen, "Critiques of Law and Economics," in *The Oxford Handbook on Law and Economics*, vol. 1, *Methodology and Concepts*, ed. Francesco Parisi (Oxford: Oxford University Press, 2017), 312.

41. Alvin Toffler, *The Third Wave* (New York: William Morrow & Co., 1980). "Prosumer" is a portmanteau of the words *provider* and *consumer*, and it defines a consumer who also produces. Typical prosumers are those using commons-based peer production—do-it-yourselfers—based in the Web 2.0 technologies and the so-called sharing economy. See George Ritzer and Nathan Jurgenson, "Production, Consumption, Prosumption: The Nature of Capitalism in the Age of the Digital 'Prosumer,'" *Journal of Consumer Culture* 10, no. 1 (2010): 13–36.

42. The saying is "Equal rights for others does not mean less rights for you. It's not pie."

43. "Caste systems and other social arrangements that involve stigmatizing differences in status are leading historical examples of objectionable inequality. In these systems, members of some groups are regarded as inferior. They are excluded from social roles and occupations that are seen as most desirable, or even relegated to occupations that are regarded as demeaning and beneath the dignity of members of other groups. The evil involved in such arrangements has a comparative character: what is objectionable is being treated as *inferior to others* in a demeaning way." Scanlon, *Why Does Inequality Matter?*, 4–5 (emphasis in original). "The evil involved in such arrangements is a comparative one. It is not the tasks themselves that are demeaning—they may be necessary tasks that someone has to perform in any society. What is objectionable is being marked as inferior to others in a demeaning way. The remedy is to abolish the social system that defines and upholds these distinctions between superior and inferior." T. M. Scanlon, "When Does Equality Matter?," paper presented at a conference on equality at the John F. Kennedy School of Government at Harvard University, Cambridge, Massachusetts, April 2004, 7, https://web.law.columbia.edu/sites/default/files/microsites/law-theory-workshop/files/scanlonpaper.pdf.

44. Anderson, "What Is the Point of Equality?," 320.

45. See *Eldred*, 537 U.S. at 193–94, upholding the Copyright Term Extension Act (CTEA) of 1998, which amended the durational provisions of the Copyright Act at 17 U.S.C. §§ 302, 304 (1998).

46. *Eldred*, 537 U.S. 186.

47. *Eldred*, 537 U.S. at 204, 231.

48. *Eldred*, 537 U.S. at 194.

49. Feist Publications, Inc. v. Rural Telephone Service Co., 499 U.S. 340, 349 (1991) stated that "the primary objective of copyright" is "'to promote the Progress of Science and useful Arts'" [alteration in original], quoting U.S. Constitution, Article I, § 8, Cl. 8. See also Mazer v. Stein, 347 U.S. 201, 219 (1954) ("The economic philosophy behind the [Copyright] clause . . . is the conviction that encouragement of individual effort by personal gain is the best way to advance public welfare through the talents of authors and inventors.").

50. *Eldred*, 537 U.S. at 212.

51. *Eldred*, 537 U.S. at 255–57 (Breyer, J., dissenting).

52. *Eldred*, 537 U.S. at 207n15.

53. *Eldred*, 537 U.S. at 207, quoting Copyright Term Extension Act of 1998, H.R. Rep. No. 105–452, at 4 (1998).

54. *Eldred*, 537 U.S. at 207n14. See also "Brief for Motion Picture Association of America as Amici Curiae Supporting Respondents," at 14–20 in the *Eldred* docket at the Supreme Court, which argued that films are fragile and restoration is expensive such that longer terms will incentivize more restoration by facilitating recuperation of investment in that restoration process.

55. In these exceptional cases of prejudice or irrationality, targeting of a suspect class, or burdening a fundamental right, the Court abandons deference and engages in strict scrutiny of the legislative purpose and effect. See U.S. R.R. Ret. Bd. v. Fritz, 449 U.S. 166, 174–75 (1980). Notably, Justice Breyer suggested that the level of scrutiny should be more than rational basis because the copyright extension intrudes on speech and raises First Amendment concerns. See *U.S. R.R. Ret. Bd.*, 449 U.S. at 244. Were this position to have prevailed, the lack of evidentiary support that both existing and future copyright holders are incentivized by the twenty-year extension might have doomed the term extension.

56. *Eldred*, 537 U.S. at 192–93, quoting U.S. Constitution, Article I, § 8, cl. 8 (emphasis added).

57. See James J. Guinan Jr., "Study No. 30: Duration of Copyright," prepared for the Subcommittee on Patents, Trademarks, and Copyrights of the U.S. Senate Committee on the Judiciary, 86th Cong., 2nd Sess., Jan. 1957 (Washington, D.C.: Government Printing Office, 1961), detailing extension of copyright term from fourteen years for the first Copyright Act in 1790 to fifty-six years as of 1957 (twenty-eight years plus a renewal term of twenty-eight years), www.copyright. gov/history/studies/study30.pdf. The 1976 Copyright Act changed copyright term to life of the author plus fifty years; the CTEA extended it to life of the author plus seventy years.

58. *Eldred*, 537 U.S. at 200, 208.

59. *Eldred*, 537 U.S. at 194.

60. *Eldred*, 537 U.S. at 266 (Breyer, J., dissenting) (emphasis added).

61. See Bleistein v. Donaldson Lithographing Co., 188 U.S. 239, 251 (1903). "It would be a dangerous undertaking for persons trained only to the law to constitute themselves final judges of the worth of pictorial illustrations, outside of the narrowest and most obvious limits."

62. *Eldred*, 537 U.S. at 193 (emphasis added).

63. *Eldred*, 537 U.S. at 194 (emphasis added).

64. *Eldred*, 537 U.S. at 200.

65. *Eldred*, 537 U.S. at 205–6. "Congress sought to ensure that American authors would receive the same copyright protection in Europe as their European counterparts."

66. Jessica Litman, *Digital Copyright* (Amherst, N.Y.: Prometheus Books, 2001) provides a history of the 1998 copyright legislation. For a history of the DMCA, the CTEA, and SOPA and PIPA (the PROTECT IP Act) in particular, see Bill D. Herman, *The Fight over Digital Rights: The Politics of Copyright and Technology* (New York: Cambridge University Press, 2013).

67. Litman, *Digital Copyright*. See also Aram Sinnreich, *The Piracy Crusade: How the Music Industry's War on Sharing Destroys Markets and Erodes Civil Liberties* (Amherst: University of Massachusetts Press, 2013).

68. *Eldred*, 537 U.S. at 233.

69. *Eldred*, 537 U.S. at 248.

70. *Eldred*, 537 U.S. at 248.

71. Herman, *Fight over Digital Rights*, 35.

72. Herman, *Fight over Digital Rights*, 48–52.

73. *Eldred*, 537 U.S. at 227 (emphasis in original).

74. *Eldred*, 537 U.S. at 240 (Stevens, J., dissenting). Breyer reiterated this point: "Copyright statutes must serve public, not private, ends; . . . they must seek 'to promote the Progress' of knowledge and learning; and . . . they must do so both by creating incentives for authors to produce and by removing the related restrictions on dissemination after expiration." *Eldred*, 537 U.S. at 247–48 (Breyer, J., dissenting).

75. *Eldred*, 537 U.S. at 250 (Breyer, J., dissenting).

76. See Amy Goodman, "The SOPA Blackout Protest Makes History," *The Guardian*, Jan. 18, 2012, www.theguardian.com/commentisfree/cifamerica/2012/jan/18/sopa-blackout-protest-makes-history ("An unprecedented wave of online opposition to the SOPA and PIPA bills before Congress shows the power of a free internet."); and Herman, *Fight over Digital Rights*.

77. Toffler, *Third Wave*, 27. See also Don Tapscott, *The Digital Economy: Promise and Peril in the Age of Networked Intelligence* (New York: McGraw-Hill, 1995), 62; and Ritzer and Jurgenson, "Production, Consumption, Prosumption," 17.

78. For a description of how law and society subordinate women to men by defining women as different and thus justifying their unequal treatment, or by measuring women by male standards and thus justifying women's subordination when they do not match up, see Catharine A. MacKinnon, *Toward a Feminist Theory of the State* (Cambridge, Mass.: Harvard University Press, 1989), 219. See also Catharine A. MacKinnon, *Feminism Unmodified: Discourses on Life and Law* (Cambridge, Mass.: Harvard University Press, 1987), 123.

79. The shortsightedness of the "separate but equal" doctrine recurs in complaints of religious free exercise claims that prioritize equality of religious belief over rights of equal public accommodation and access to birth control or wedding cakes. See "State v. Arlene Flowers, Inc.," *Harvard Law Review* 133, no. 2 (2019): 731–38; and Elizabeth Sepper, "Gays in the Moralized Marketplace," *Alabama Civil Right and Civil Liberties Law Review* 7, no. 1 (2015): 129–71.

80. Metro-Goldwyn-Mayer Studios, Inc. v. Grokster, Ltd., 545 U.S. 913 (2005).

81. Wal-Mart Stores, Inc. v. Samara Brothers, Inc., 529 U.S. 205 (2000).

82. *Wal-Mart*, 529 U.S. at 213.

83. *Brown v. Board of Education* overruled *Plessy v. Ferguson* on the basis that "separate but equal" in the context of racially segregated education created inherently unequal citizenship, which is forbidden by the U.S. Constitution. Brown v. Board of Education of Topeka, 347 U.S. 483 (1954).

84. Matal v. Tam, 137 S. Ct. 1744 (2017).

85. *Matal*, 137 S. Ct. at 1750.

86. *Matal*, 137 S. Ct. at 1768.

87. *Matal*, 137 S. Ct. 1744.

88. *Matal*, 137 S. Ct. at 1764.

89. *Matal*, 137 S. Ct.

90. *Matal*, 137 S. Ct. at 1763.

91. For examples of purportedly sexist, homophobic, and obscene marks—such as WHORE, COCK BLOCKER, PHAG, among others—and the USPTO's treatment of them, see Megan Carpenter and Mary Garner, "NSFW: An Empirical Study of Scandalous Trademarks," *Cardozo Arts and Entertainment Law Journal* 33 (2016): 321–65. For examples of racist marks debated as "disparaging" by the USPTO, such as HEEB and REDSKINS, see Megan Carpenter and Kathryn Murphy, "Calling Bulls**t on the Lanham Act: The 2(a) Bar for Immoral, Scandalous, and Disparaging Marks," *University of Louisville Law Review* 49 (2010): 465–83.

92. Iancu v. Brunetti, 139 S. Ct. 2294 (2019).

93. *Iancu*, 139 S. Ct. at 2303.

94. American Broadcasting Company v. Aereo, Inc., 573 U.S. 431 (2014); Bowman v. Monsanto Co., 569 U.S. 278 (2013).

95. Limitations on Exclusive Rights: Secondary Transmissions of Broadcast Programming by Cable, 17 U.S.C. § 111.

96. American Broadcasting Company v. Aereo, Inc., 573 U.S. 431, 450 (2014).

97. *Aereo*, 573 U.S. at 459 (Scalia, J., dissenting).

98. *Aereo*, 573 U.S. at 462. The "Betamax case" refers to Sony Corp. of America v. Universal City Studios, Inc., 464 U.S. 417 (1984). Sony manufactured and sold the Betamax home video tape recorder. Universal City Studios, as the copyright owner of some television programs, sued Sony for copyright infringement, alleging that because consumers used the Betamax to record and play back its copyrighted works, Sony was liable for copyright infringement. The Supreme Court ruled that VCR manufacturers are not liable for copyright infringement.

99. This patent law doctrine has historical common-law roots. See, e.g., Aro Mfg. Co. v. Convertible Top Replacement Co., 377 U.S. 476 (1964); and Morgan Envelope Co. v. Albany Perforated Wrapping Paper Co., 152 U.S. 425 (1894). See also Wilber-Ellis Co. v. Kuther, 377 U.S. 422 (1964), which held that the purchaser may modify an article to improve or alter functionality. Compare Quanta Computer, Inc. v. LG Electronics, Inc., 553 U.S. 617 (2008) regarding patent exhaustion with Kirtsaeng v. John Wiley & Sons, Inc., 568 U.S. 519 (2013) regarding copyright. For copyright, this is a statutory protection (17 U.S.C. § 109), whereas in patent law, it is a common-law doctrine.

100. J. E. M. Ag Supply, Inc. v. Pioneer Hi-Bred International, Inc., 534 U.S. 124 (2001).

101. *Bowman*, 569 U.S. at 287.

102. *Plessy*, 163 U.S. at 543.

103. "Our holding today is limited—addressing the situation before us, rather than every one involving a self-replicating product. We recognize that such inventions are becoming ever more prevalent, complex, and diverse. In another case, the article's self-replication might occur outside the purchaser's control. Or it might be a necessary but incidental step in using the item for another purpose. . . . We need not address here whether or how the doctrine of patent exhaustion would apply in such circumstances." *Bowman*, 569 U.S. at 289.

104. *Plessy*, 163 U.S. at 550.

105. *Plessy*, 163 U.S. at 550.

106. There is a small but growing scholarship and advocacy community focused on civil rights and human rights and IP. Examples of seminal articles include Margaret Chon, "Intellectual Property and the Development Divide," *Cardozo Law Review* 27, no. 6 (2006): 2821–2912; and Keith Aoki, "Distributive and Syncretic Motives in Intellectual Property Law (with Special Reference to Coercion, Agency, and Development)," *UC Davis Law Review* 40, no. 3 (2007): 717–801. See also Madhavi Sunder, *From Goods to the Good Life: Intellectual Property and Global Justice* (New Haven, Conn.: Yale University Press, 2012).

107. On *Myriad Genetics* and the history of the ACLU's historic involvement in bringing and winning the case, see Jorge Contreras, *The Genome Defense: Inside the Epic Legal Battle to Determine Who Owns Your DNA* (New York: Workman Press, 2021). See also Association for Molecular Pathology v. Myriad Genetics, 569 U.S. 576 (2013) and www.aclu.org/issues/privacy-technology/medical-and-genetic-privacy/fight-take-back-our-genes.

108. Green v. County School Board of New Kent County, 391 U.S. 430 (1968) held that freedom of choice plans were insufficient to desegregate schools and approved affirmative desegregation methods. Swann v. Charlotte-Mecklenburg Board of Education, 402 U.S. 1 (1971) approved mandatory busing of students on the basis of race to desegregate previously segregated schools.

109. Parents Involved in Community Schools v. Seattle School District No. 1, 551 U.S. 701 (2007) struck down voluntary desegregation efforts on the basis that Seattle School District had never been segregated as a matter of law, only as a matter of fact.

110. Adam Liptak, "Brown v. Board of Education: Second Round," *New York Times*, Dec. 10, 2006 (explaining the debate as to whether *Brown v. Board of Education* struck down laws racially segregating schools or required integrated schools); Louis Menand, "Brown v. Board of Education and the Limits of Law," *New Yorker*, Feb. 12, 2001, 91–96. See also Jack M. Balkin, ed., *What* Brown v. Board of Education *Should Have Said: The Nation's Top Legal Experts Rewrite the Landmark Civil Rights Decision* (New York: New York University Press, 2001).

111. *Golan*, 565 U.S. 302.

112. *Golan*, 565 U.S. at 318–19 (internal quotation marks omitted).

113. *Eldred*, 537 U.S. at 221.

114. *Golan*, 565 U.S. at 308.

115. *Golan*, 565 U.S. at 312.

116. *Golan*, 565 U.S. at 315.

117. The anti-subordination principle is sometimes understood as competing with anti-classification or equal treatment. See Reva B. Siegel, "Equality Talk: Antisubordination and Anticlassification Values in Constitutional Struggles over Brown," *Harvard Law Review* 117, no. 5 (2004): 1470–1547.

118. Jack M. Balkin and Reva B. Siegel, "The American Civil Rights Tradition: Anticlassification or Antisubordination?," *University of Miami Law Review* 58, no. 1 (2003): 9–33.

119. The Freedmen's Bureau, the name for the U.S. Bureau of Refugees, Freedmen, and Abandoned Lands, only lasted from 1865 to 1872 before it was dismantled. But while in operation, provided material support in terms of land and funds to formerly enslaved persons. It also established hospitals and schools for freedmen and was instrumental in founding Fisk University. Howard University, founded in 1867, was named after Major General Oliver Howard, the first head of the Freedmen's Bureau and the third president of Howard University.

120. Grutter v. Bollinger, 539 U.S. 306, 327 (2003). "As we have explained, whenever the government treats any person unequally because of his or her race, that person has suffered an injury that falls squarely within the language and spirit of the Constitution's guarantee of equal protection. But that observation says nothing about the ultimate validity of any particular law; that determination is the job of the court applying strict scrutiny. When race-based action is necessary to further a compelling governmental interest, such action does not violate the constitutional guarantee of equal protection so long as the narrow-tailoring requirement is also satisfied. Context matters when reviewing race-based governmental action under the Equal Protection Clause." (internal citations and quotation omitted).

121. MacKinnon, *Feminism Unmodified*, 33; see also MacKinnon, *Toward a Feminist Theory*, 219.

122. MacKinnon, *Feminism Unmodified*; MacKinnon, *Toward a Feminist Theory*.

123. MacKinnon, *Feminism Unmodified*, 34–39.

124. Catharine A. MacKinnon, *Sexual Harassment of Working Women: A Case of Sex Discrimination* (New Haven, Conn.: Yale University Press, 1979), 102, 117–18. "The only question [for equality] . . . is whether the policy or practice in question integrally contributes to the maintenance of an underclass or a deprived position because of gender status. . . . The social problem addressed is not the failure to ignore woman's essential sameness with man, but the recognition of womanhood to women's comparative disadvantage" (117).

125. Robert Spoo, *Without Copyrights: Piracy, Publishing, and the Public Domain* (New York: Oxford University Press, 2013), 2, 70; Mark Rose, *Authors and Owners: The Invention of Copyright* (Cambridge, Mass.: Harvard University Press, 1993), 17.

126. On the "manufacturing clause," which required printing in the United States for works to be protected by U.S. copyright law, see Spoo, *Without Copyrights*, 67–68.

127. Supreme Court affirmative action jurisprudence in the context of race began in 1976, with Regents of the Univ. of California v. Bakke, 438 U.S. 265 (1978), and with gender arguably not until 1996, with the decision of U.S. v. Virginia, 518 U.S. 515 (1996). There has never been a Supreme Court decision evaluating a gender-based affirmative action plan. *U.S. v. Virginia* concerned the level of judicial scrutiny for equality violations on the basis of gender (Virginia Military Institute did not allow women to enroll), which would also apply to programs that afforded affirmative action to women. See *U.S. v. Virginia*, 518 U.S. at 530–31.

128. *Golan*, 565 U.S. at 334.

129. *Golan*, 565 U.S. at 334.

130. *Golan*, 565 U.S. at 327n28.

131. *Golan*, 565 U.S. at 333.

132. Spoo, *Without Copyrights*, 158–59. Spoo wrote about how obscenity law at this time severely hampered the publishing industry, especially when the modernists were writing novels and poems and short stories with "dirty" words and erotic content. See Spoo, *Without Copyrights*, 182–83. Some obscenity laws were enforced through the postal service by means of declaring manuscripts "nonmailable." Spoo suggested that the "absence of copyright registration records for issues of *The Little Review* [which contained many of the early works of Joyce] . . . may be the direct result of the post office's obscenity suppressions. Nonmailable issues could not readily have been deposited in the Copyright Office. Once the magazine had acquired the stigma of obscenity, moreover, the register of copyrights has a plausible ground for effusing to register claims of copyright in the issues." Spoo, *Without Copyrights*, 159.

133. *Golan*, 565 U.S. at 354.

134. *Golan*, 565 U.S. at 345.

135. On copyright expiration promoting works' availability, see Imke Reimers, "Copyright and Generic Entry in Book Publishing," *American Economics Journal* 11, no. 3 (2019): 257–84; see also Paul J. Heald, "How Copyright Keeps Works Disappeared," *Journal of Empirical Legal Studies* 11, no. 4 (2014): 829–66, esp. 830.

136. *Golan*, 565 U.S. at 333. However, Robert Spoo questioned whether American authors were held back by European competition; see Spoo, *Without Copyrights*, 143, 303n148.

137. Spoo, *Without Copyrights*, 2.

138. Robert Spoo, "Ezra Pound's Copyright Statute: Perpetual Rights and the Problem of Heirs," *UCLA Law Review* 56, no. 6 (2009): 1775–1833.

139. See *Golan*, 565 U.S. at 325n26, 331.

140. Heald, "How Copyright Keeps Works Disappeared," 855.

141. Wendy J. Gordon, "Dissemination Must Serve Authors: How the U.S. Supreme Court Erred," *Review of Economic Research on Copyright Issues* 10, no. 1 (2013): 1–19.

142. Spoo, *Without Copyrights*, 74, 280n10.

143. Spoo, *Without Copyrights*.

144. On Ezra Pound's legal battles against U.S. copyright law, see Spoo, *Without Copyrights*, 116–53.

145. Spoo, *Without Copyrights*, 168, 186.

146. Where the opposite is true and doctors are predominantly women, as in Russia, being a physician is not as prestigious or as well-paying a job. See, e.g., Aditi Ramakrishnan, Dana Sambuco, and Reshma Jagsi, "Women's Participation in the Medical Profession: Insights from Experiences in Japan, Scandinavia, Russia, and Eastern Europe," *Journal Women's Health* 23, no. 11 (2014): 927–34, which described how women comprised a majority of physicians in the Soviet Union, and that the prestige of the profession declined; it became "one of the poorest-paid professional occupations. Simultaneously, women were encouraged to work as physicians in this new landscape, resulting in the feminization of the profession."

147. Scanlon, "When Does Equality Matter?," 7.

148. On copyright having a bilateral structure mirroring the correlativity of a private law action, refuting the possibility that copyright's public domain is not essential to its internal structure, see Abraham Drassinower, "Copyright Is Not About Copying," *Harvard Law Review* 125, no. 7 (2012): 108–19.

149. Grutter v. Bollinger, 539 U.S. 306, 326 (2003). "Absent searching judicial inquiry into the justification for such race-based measures, we have no way to determine what classifications are 'benign' or 'remedial' and what classifications are in fact motivated by illegitimate notions of racial inferiority or simple racial politics. We apply strict scrutiny to all racial classifications to 'smoke out' illegitimate uses of race by assuring that [government] is pursuing a goal important enough to warrant use of a highly suspect tool." (internal citations and quotation omitted).

150. New York Times v. Tasini, 533 U.S. 483 (2001).

151. *Tasini*, 533 U.S. at 493.

152. *Tasini*, 533 U.S. at 495n3.

153. *Tasini*, 533 U.S. at 497.

154. *Tasini*, 533 U.S. at 497.

155. *Tasini*, 533 U.S. at 497.

156. Ronan Deazley, Martin Kretschmer, and Lionel Bently, eds., *Privilege and Property: Essays on the History of Copyright* (Cambridge, U.K.: Open Book Publishers, 2010); Ronan Deazley, *On the Origin of the Right to Copy: Charting the Movement of Copyright Law in Eighteenth-Century Britain (1695–1775)* (Portland, Ore.: Hart Publishing, 2004), 15–16, 38, 87.

157. *Tasini*, 533 U.S. at 497.

158. *Tasini*, 533 U.S. at 498n6.

159. *Tasini*, 533 U.S. at 519–20.

160. *Tasini*, 533 U.S. at 520.

161. *Tasini*, 533 U.S. at 520n17.

162. *Tasini*, 533 U.S. at 498n6.

163. Martha Woodmansee and Peter Jaszi, eds., *The Construction of Authorship: Textual Appropriation in Law and Literature* (Durham, N.C.: Duke University Press, 1994).

164. *Tasini*, 533 U.S. at 502n11.

165. *Tasini*, 533 U.S. at 523n20.

166. *Tasini*, 533 U.S. at 523n20.

167. Abraham Drassinower, *What's Wrong With Copying?* (Cambridge, Mass.: Harvard University Press, 2015), 119.

168. Anderson, "What Is the Point of Equality?," 320.

169. A 2020 Supreme Court case, Georgia v. Public.Resource.Org, 590 U.S. ___, 140 S. Ct. 1498, described the problem of copyright inequality as a matter of "economy class" versus "first class" access to alleged copyrighted works that were annotated statutes. Intriguingly, this case expanded the copyright public domain on the theory of authorship, but only because the "author" in the case was the state of Georgia. When the state in its governing capacity creates expressive works that must be read and followed, the "author" is the people and full access to the works must be made available. It remains to be seen whether the case's holding will expand access to other state legal materials that are not government edicts.

170. Stanford University v. Roche Molecular Systems, Inc., 563 U.S. 776 (2011).

171. *Roche*, 563 U.S. at 786–87.

172. *Roche*, 563 U.S. at 792.

173. *Roche*, 563 U.S. at 796.

174. *Roche*, 563 U.S. at 793.

175. *Roche*, 563 U.S. at 798 (citing to restrictions under the Bayh-Dole Act at 35 U.S.C §§ 202–3).

176. *Kirtsaeng*, 568 U.S. 519 (2013).

177. *Kirtsaeng*, 568 U.S. at 536.

178. *Kirtsaeng*, 568 U.S. at 536.

179. *Kirtsaeng*, 568 U.S. at 552.

180. Impressions Products, Inc. v. Lexmark International, Inc., 137 S. Ct. 1523 (2017).

181. *Lexmark*, 137 S. Ct. at 1536.

182. *Lexmark*, 137 S. Ct. at 1538.

183. *Lexmark*, 137 S. Ct. at 1536.

184. *Lexmark*, 137 S. Ct. at 1536.

185. *Lexmark*, 137 S. Ct. at 1536.

186. Georgia v. Public.Resource.Org, 590 U.S. ___, 140 S. Ct. 1498 (Roberts wrote the majority opinion, holding that the state of Georgia cannot copyright its official annotations of its statutes).

187. See the Civil Rights Act of 1866, 14 Stat. 27–30 (1866), passed just after the Civil War; the law was intended to help newly freed enslaved people and all other Black people experience civil, social, and political equality. "All persons within the jurisdiction of the United States shall have the same right in every State and Territory to make and

enforce contracts, to sue, be parties, give evidence, and to the full and equal benefit of all laws and proceedings for the security of persons and property as is enjoyed by white citizens, and shall be subject to like punishment, pains, penalties, taxes, licenses, and exactions of every kind, and to no other." For a discussion of the Civil Rights Act of 1866, see Brest et al., *Processes of Constitutional Decisionmaking*, 348–52.

188. Lepore, *These Truths*, 119–28.

Chapter 3

1. Julie E. Cohen, *Configuring the Networked Self: Law, Code, and the Play of Everyday Practice* (New Haven, Conn.: Yale University Press, 2012); Neil Richards, *Intellectual Privacy: Rethinking Civil Liberties in the Digital Age* (New York: Oxford University Press, 2016); Helen Nissenbaum, *Privacy in Context: Technology, Policy, and the Integrity of Social Life* (Stanford, Calif.: Stanford University Press, 2010); Marc Rotenberg, Julia Horwitz, and Jeramie Scott, eds., *Privacy in the Modern Age: The Search for Solutions* (New Press, 2016); Kenneth A. Bamberger and Deirdre K. Mulligan, *Privacy on the Ground: Driving Corporate Behavior in the United States and Europe* (Cambridge, Mass.: MIT Press, 2016); Meg Leta Jones, *Control + Z: The Right to Be Forgotten* (New York: New York University Press, 2016); Daniel J. Solove, *Understanding Privacy* (Cambridge, Mass.: Harvard University Press, 2008); Samantha Barbas, *Laws of Image: Privacy and Publicity in America* (Stanford, Calif.: Stanford University Press, 2016); Woodrow Hartzog, *Privacy's Blueprint: The Battle to Control the Design of New Technologies* (Cambridge, Mass.: Harvard University Press, 2018). See also Danielle Keats Citron, "Sexual Privacy," *Yale Law Journal* 128, no. 7 (2019): 1870–1960.

2. Solove, *Understanding Privacy*, 1. In 1975, Judith Jarvis Thomson wrote that "perhaps the most striking thing about the right to privacy is that nobody seems to have any very clear idea what it is." Judith Jarvis Thomson, "The Right to Privacy," *Philosophy and Public Affairs* 4, no. 4 (Summer 1975): 295–314. For his part, Daniel J. Solove wrote that "privacy is a concept in disarray. Nobody can articulate what it means. As one commentator has observed, 'privacy suffers from an embarrassment of meanings.' Privacy is far too vague a concept to guide adjudication and lawmaking, as abstract incantations of the importance of 'privacy' do not fare well when pitted against more concretely stated countervailing interests." Solove, "A Taxonomy of Privacy," *University of Pennsylvania Law Review* 154, no. 3 (2006): 477–560, esp. 478.

3. As Julie Cohen has written in work developing new tools for theorizing privacy, turning it "inside out" as it were, "the quest for theoretical consistency is itself an artifact of privacy's framing within particular philosophical and political traditions." Julie Cohen, "Turning Privacy Inside Out," *Theoretical Inquiries in Law* 20, no. 1 (2019): 1–22, esp. 4.

4. Stuart P. Green, *Thirteen Ways to Steal a Bicycle: Theft Law in the Information Age* (Cambridge, Mass.: Harvard University Press, 2012). On Google Ngram Viewer, a search of "IP theft" will show a dramatic rise of the term "IP theft" between 1993 and 2018, where previously it was a rare term.

5. William L. Prosser, "Privacy," *California Law Review* 48, no. 3 (1960): 383–423.

6. For contested accounts of the birth of privacy law, see Jessica Lake, *The Face That Launched a Thousand Lawsuits: The American Women Who Forged a Right to Privacy* (New Haven, Conn.: Yale University Press, 2016), 3–7; Charles E. Colman, "About Ned," *Harvard Law Review Forum* 129, no. 3 (2016): 128–52; Daniel J. Solove and Neil M. Richards, "Privacy's Other Path: Recovering the Law of Confidentiality," *Georgetown Law Journal* 96 (2007): 123–82.

7. On the structure and function of origin stories generally and in intellectual property law specifically, see Jessica Silbey, "The Mythical Beginnings of Intellectual Property," *George Mason Law Review* 15, no. 2 (Winter 2008): 319–79.

8. Samuel D. Warren and Louis D. Brandeis, "The Right to Privacy," *Harvard Law Review* 4, no. 5 (1890): 193–220.

9. See also Daniel J. Solove, "A Brief History of Information Privacy Law," section 1.3.3, in *Proskauer on Privacy: A Guide to Privacy and Data Security Law in the Information Age*, ed. Christopher Wolf (New York: PLI Press, 2006).

10. Benjamin C. Zipursky and John C. P. Goldberg, "Tort as Wrongs," *Texas Law Review* 88, no. 5 (2010): 917–86; see also Wendy Jane Gordon, "Copyright as Tort Law's Mirror Image: 'Harms,' 'Benefits,' and the Uses and Limits of Analogy," *McGeorge Law Review* 34, no. 3 (Spring 2003): 533–40.

11. Warren and Brandeis, "Right to Privacy," 193.

12. Warren and Brandeis, "Right to Privacy," 193.

13. Warren and Brandeis, "Right to Privacy," 193.

14. Warren and Brandeis, "Right to Privacy," 198. Arguably, this "right to be let alone" comes from Thomas Cooley's 1888 *Law of Torts* as an extension of physical torts to assaults without physical contact. Thomas M. Cooley, *A Treatise on the Law of Torts*, 2nd ed. (Chicago: Callaghan & Co., 1888), 29, cited in Warren and Brandeis, "Right to Privacy," 195n4.

15. On photography as an amateur pastime arising in the 1880s, see Lake, *Face That Launched a Thousand Lawsuits*, 7. See also Jennifer E. Rothman, *The Right of Publicity: Privacy Reimagined for a Public World* (Cambridge, Mass.: Harvard University Press, 2018), 12–13, describing how these amateur photographers were sometimes called "kodakers."

16. Warren and Brandeis, "Right to Privacy," 198–99.

17. Millar v Taylor, 4 Burr. 2303, 98 ER 201 (1769).

18. Prince Albert v. Strange, 64 Eng. Rep. 293, 295 (Ch.) (1849).

19. *Strange*, 64 Eng. Rep., at 312 (Bruce, V.C.).

20. Abraham Drassinower, *What's Wrong with Copying?* (Cambridge, Mass.: Harvard University Press, 2015), 114–20. "While privacy and copyright could each come to bear on the fact of unauthorized publication of unpublished work, the distinction between 'personal information' and 'work of authorship' would ensure that each regime would construe that fact from its own distinct juridical standpoint" (117).

21. Warren and Brandeis, "Right to Privacy," 207. Warren and Brandeis wrote that the right to be let alone "is entirely independent of copyright laws, and their extension into the domain of art" (200).

22. Warren and Brandeis, "Right to Privacy," 205.

23. Warren and Brandeis, "Right to Privacy," 207–11.

24. Warren and Brandeis, "Right to Privacy," 211.

25. Warren and Brandeis, "Right to Privacy," 213.

26. Griswold v. Connecticut, 381 U.S. 479, 484 (1965) ("zones of privacy" determined with reference to the penumbra of the Bill of Rights); Roe v. Wade, 410 U.S. 113 (1973) ("right of privacy" determined with reference to the Fourteenth Amendment due process clause).

27. Katz v. United States, 389 U.S. 347 (1967); Carpenter v. United States, 585 U.S. ___, 138 S. Ct. 2206 (2018) extended the right of privacy to a cell phone user's cell phone tower data.

28. Warren and Brandeis, "Right to Privacy," 207.

29. Warren and Brandeis, "Right to Privacy," 207.

30. On how a privacy invasion "both belittles and perverts," destroying the "robustness of thought and delicacy of feeling," see Warren and Brandeis, "Right to Privacy," 196 ("No enthusiasm can flourish, no generous impulse can survive . . .").

31. Cohen, *Configuring the Networked Self*; Richards, *Intellectual Privacy*; Nissenbaum, *Privacy in Context*; Rotenberg, Horwitz, and Scott, eds., *Privacy in the Modern Age*; Bamberger and Mulligan, *Privacy on the Ground*; Jones, *Control + Z*; Solove, *Understanding Privacy*; Barbas, *Laws of Image*; Hartzog, *Privacy's Blueprint*; Citron, "Sexual Privacy."

32. Khiara Bridges presents the critique that the moral construction of poverty demands that poor mothers have no privacy and cannot be trusted with privacy. See Khiara M. Bridges, *The Poverty of Privacy Rights* (Stanford, Calif.: Stanford University Press, 2017).

33. See Erwin Chemerinsky, "Rediscovering Brandeis's Right to Privacy," *Brandeis Law Journal* 45, no. 4 (2007): 643–58.

34. Laura K. Donohue, "The Fourth Amendment in a Digital World," *New York University Annual Survey of American Law* 71, no. 6 (2017): 533–685.

35. U.S. Constitution, Amendment III (prohibition of quartering soldiers except during times of war); U.S. Constitution, Amendment IV (prohibition against unreasonable searches and seizures of persons, houses, papers, and effects).

36. United States v. Jones, 565 U.S. 400 (2012) (search of car violated Fourth Amendment); Riley v. California, 573 U.S. 373 (2014) (search of cell phone requires warrant); *Carpenter*, 585 U.S. ___, 138 S. Ct. 2206 (2018) (extended the right of privacy to a cell phone user's cell phone tower data).

37. Notably, state and federal government might have immunity from monetary copyright liability (although not injunctive relief) under the doctrine of sovereign immunity, whereas private individuals and organizations do not. *Allen v. Cooper*, 140 S. Ct. 994 (U.S. 2020). In this way, copyright (and intellectual property more generally) is protective of privacy as against private actors not the government.

38. Warren and Brandeis, "Right to Privacy," 193.

39. Union Pacific Railway Co. v. Botsford, 141 U.S. 250, 251 (1891). "No right is held more sacred, or is more carefully guarded by the common law, than the right of every

individual to the possession and control of his own person, free from all restraint or interference of others, unless by clear and unquestionably authority of law." See also Solove, "Brief History of Information Privacy Law." Bodily autonomy claims brought under the Constitution usually resonate with the Fourth Amendment (unreasonable searches of a person) and the Fifth Amendment (prohibiting the deprivation of "life [and] liberty . . . without due process of law").

40. Wendy E. Parmet, "Informed Consent and Public Health: Are They Compatible When It Comes to Vaccines?," *Journal of Health Care Law and Policy* 8, no. 1 (2005): 71–110, esp. 82–83.

41. Jamal Greene traced the right to privacy from *Griswold v. Connecticut* (1965) to *Lawrence v. Texas* (2003) in terms of privacy's controversial embodiment in abortion jurisprudence and sexual liberty rights. See Jamal Greene, "The So-Called Right to Privacy," *UC Davis Law Review* 43, no. 3 (2010): 715–47; Griswold v. Connecticut, 381 U.S. 479 (1965); Lawrence v. Texas, 539 U.S. 558 (2003).

42. In addition to injunctive relief, copyright law has statutory penalties ranging from $750 to $150,000 per infringing work (17 USC § 504). See esp. § 412, requiring work to be registered prior to infringement or within three months of publication. Trademark damages are more often injunctive relief (15 USC § 1117) but may sometimes also include monetary damages to recover defendant's profits and damages sustained by plaintiff. The Supreme Court recently decided Romag Fasteners, Inc. v. Fossil, Inc., 590 U.S. ___ (2020), making trademark damages determination more uncertain than previous decades. Damages for patent infringement is usually a reasonable royalty for use of the infringing product plus fees and costs, with some complicating factors. See Timothy R. Holbrook, "Boundaries, Extraterritoriality, and Patent Infringement Damages," *Notre Dame Law Review* 92, no. 4 (17): 1745–94; Dmitry Karshtedt, "Enhancing Patent Damages," *UC Davis Law Review* 51, no. 4 (2018): 1427–1541.

43. See generally Chemerinsky, "Rediscovering Brandeis's Right to Privacy."

44. Anita Allen, "Coercing Privacy," *William and Mary Law Review* 40, no. 3 (1999): 723–57; Anita L. Allen, *Unpopular Privacy: What Must We Hide?* (New York: Oxford University Press, 2011). For a critique of decisional and intellectual privacy—privacy as essential to autonomous moral agency of individuals—see Julie E. Cohen, "What Privacy Is For," *Harvard Law Review* 126, no. 7 (2013): 1904–33.

45. Anita Allen, *Unpopular Privacy*, 18 ("If there are not limits to state power to control of the details of individuals lives, there can be no meaningful political freedom at all, hence Jed Rubenfeld's notion that decisional privacy critically checks totalitarianism. Some philosophers have maintained that extremes of state control over the details of individual lives interferes with the formation of autonomous personality and therefore with meaningful citizenship and democracy.") See also Jeb Rubenfeld, "The Right to Privacy," *Harvard Law Review* 102, no. 4 (1989): 737–807. On spiritual and intellectual privacy, see also Laurence H. Tribe, *American Constitutional Law*, 2nd ed. (Mineola, N.Y.: Foundation Press, 1988), 1160–61 ("the free exercise clause was at the very least designated to guarantee freedom of conscience by preventing any degree of compulsion in matters of belief"); and Richards, *Intellectual Privacy*.

46. Obergefell v. Hodges, 576 U.S. 644 (2015), quoting *Lawrence*, 539 U.S. 558. One root of these privacy cases is *Griswold v. Connecticut* (1965), one of the foundational reproductive freedom cases. As Chief Justice Roberts stated in his *Obergefell* dissent, "The majority suggests that 'there are other, more instructive precedents' informing the right to marry. Although not entirely clear, this reference seems to correspond to a line of cases discussing an implied fundamental 'right of privacy.' *Griswold*, 381 U.S. 479, 486 (1965). In the first of those cases, the Court invalidated a criminal law that banned the use of contraceptives. Id., at 485–86. The Court stressed the invasive nature of the ban, which threatened the intrusion of 'the police to search the sacred precincts of marital bedrooms.' Id. at 485. In the Court's view, such laws infringed the right to privacy in its most basic sense: the 'right to be let alone.'" *Eisenstadt v. Baird*, 405 U.S. 438, 453–54, n. 10 (1972) (internal quotation marks omitted); see Olmstead v. United States, 277 U.S. 438, 478 (1928) (Brandeis, J., dissenting)." Roberts, J. dissent, slip op., at 17 (some citations omitted).

47. *Obergefell*, 576 U.S. 644, Roberts, J. dissent, slip op., at 6 (quoting William Blackstone's commentaries).

48. *Obergefell*, 576 U.S. at 17.

49. See *Lawrence*, 539 U.S. 558, tying privacy in sexual intimacy with consenting adults to homes; and *Griswold*, 381 U.S. at 484, tying reproductive privacy to the marital bedroom. For a critique of privacy in fact residing in the home, see, e.g., Bridges, *Poverty of Privacy Rights*, which demonstrated how poor mothers lack privacy; and Jeannie Suk, *At Home in the Law: How Domestic Violence Revolution Is Transforming Privacy* (New Haven, Conn.: Yale University Press, 2009), which demonstrated how deterring and prosecuting domestic violence has reshaped the privacy of the home.

50. *Obergefell*, 576 U.S. 644 ruled that marriage privacy and freedom is fundamental to dignity.

51. Warren and Brandeis, "Right to Privacy," 214–16. See also Rothman, *Right of Publicity*, 35–38, 48–50, 138–59, 181–85.

52. On the priority of priority—the "origin myth"—in intellectual property law, see Silbey, "Mythical Beginnings of Intellectual Property."

53. See 17 USC § 102(b).

54. See 15 U.S.C. § 1125(c)(1)(C) ("dilution by tarnishment" described as an "association arising from the similarity between a mark or trade name and a famous mark that harms the reputation of the famous mark). Cases alleging dilution by tarnishment include Louis Vuitton Malletier S.A. v. Haute Diggity Dog, LLC, 507 F.3d 252 (4th Cir. 2007) (alleging tarnishment of Louis Vuitton by dog toys called "Chewy Vuitton"); Starbucks Corporation v. Wolfe's Borough Coffee, Inc., 588 F.3d 97 (2009) (alleging tarnishment of Starbucks Coffee by Wolfe's Borough Coffee blend called "Charbucks Blend").

55. Trademark law does not protect generic words or images that are used descriptively. For trademark protection to attach, the trademark owner must prove the mark is "distinctive" of the mark owner's goods and services and is not merely descriptive of them. See 15 USC § 2(f). Trademark law also provides for defense to

infringement when the use of "term or device . . . is descriptive of and used fairly and in good faith only to describe the goods or services of" the defendant. See 15 U.S.C. § 33(b)(5). And there are several defenses to trademark dilution rooted in the First Amendment freedoms of speech, including "non-commercial use of the mark," "all forms of news reporting and commentary," and parodying, criticizing, or commenting on the famous mark. See 15 U.S.C. § 43(c)(3).

56. See, e.g., Abraham Drassinower, "The Art of Selling Chocolate: Remarks on Copyright's Domain," in *From "Radical Extremism" to "Balanced Copyright": Canadian Copyright and the Digital Agenda*, ed. Michael Geist (Toronto: Irwin Law, 2010), 121–50, esp. 132–33, which argued that copyright cannot be "balanced" or weighed as if on a scale to determine its proper scope or standards of protection.

57. For a unique and eloquent elaboration of the conflict between authorship and free speech as a reexamination of meaning of copying and the right to control copies, see Drassinower, *What's Wrong with Copying?*

58. Warren and Brandeis, "Right to Privacy," 193.

59. These torts are public disclosure of private facts, misappropriation of private facts, false light (or 'publicity") claims, intrusion upon seclusion, and breach of confidence. Solove, "Brief History of Information Privacy Law."

60. Cohen, "Turning Privacy Inside Out." See also Virginia Eubanks, *Automating Inequality: How High-Tech Tools Profile, Police, and Punish the Poor* (New York: St. Martin's Press, 2017); Safiya Umoja Noble, *Algorithms of Oppression: How Search Engines Reinforce Racism* (New York: New York University Press, 2018); Frank Pasquale, *The Black Box Society: The Secret Algorithms That Control Money and Information* (Cambridge, Mass.: Harvard University Press, 2015).

61. Warren and Brandeis, *Right of Privacy*, 196.

62. Warren and Brandeis, *Right of Privacy*, 196.

63. Omer Tene and Jules Polonetsky, "A Theory of Creepy: Technology, Privacy, and Shifting Social Norms," *Yale Journal of Law and Technology* 16, no. 1 (2013): 59–101.

64. Cohen, "Turning Privacy Inside Out," 14.

65. Cohen, "Turning Privacy Inside Out," 9.

66. Cohen, "Turning Privacy Inside Out." Cohen is right to critique the idealization of autonomy and self-determination given the inevitable fact of socially constructed subjects. Her sophisticated theory of privacy as boundary management in *Configuring the Networked Self* explains the tensions inherent in demand for self-determination and the fact of social construction.

67. Cohen, *Configuring the Networked Self*, 239–41.

68. Paul Ohm and Jonathan Frankle, "Desirable Inefficiency," *Florida Law Review* 70, no. 4 (2018): 777–838.

69. Facts and ideas are uncopyrightable whether private or previously undisclosed. See 17 U.S.C § 102(b). Trademark law has similar (though more flexible) restrictions on protectability and exclusive use by requiring trademark owners to make burdensome evidentiary showings in order claim marks that are descriptive of their goods (e.g., using truthful facts about goods or services as trademarks, such

as "Softsoap" or "SweetTarts"). See 15 USC § 2(f). Trademark law also provides for defense to infringement when the use of "term or device . . . is descriptive of and used fairly and in good faith only to describe the goods or services of" defendant. See 15 U.S.C. § 33(b)(5). To obtain patent protection, patents must teach and enable a person having ordinary skill in the art to make and use the invention; disclosure of the invention is essential. See 35 U.S.C. § 112. The information about the patent is not "free" insofar as use of the invention as described in the patent is exclusive to the patent holder, but reading about the patented invention and the information about it is open to the public. Trade secrets are the only intellectual property regime—albeit an often overlooked one—that demands confidentiality for protection.

70. Nissenbaum, *Privacy in Context*, 77.

71. Richards, *Intellectual Privacy.*

72. Charles Fried, "Privacy," *Yale Law Journal* 77, no. 3 (1968): 475–93, esp. 477.

73. Nissenbaum, *Privacy in Context*, 86–88, citing Priscilla M. Regan, *Legislating Privacy: Technology, Social Values, and Public Policy* (Chapel Hill: University of North Carolina Press, 1995).

74. "Property Rights in Letters," *Yale Law Journal* 46, no. 3 (1937): 493–504; Ned Snow, "A Copyright Conundrum: Protecting Email Privacy," *Kansas Law Review* 55, no. 3 (2007): 501–73; Shyamkrishna Balganesh, "Privative Copyright," *Vanderbilt Law Review* 73, no. 1 (2020): 1–71 (collecting early cases).

75. Julie E. Cohen, "Copyright as Property in the Post-Industrial Economy: A Research Agenda," *Wisconsin Law Review* (2011): 141–65.

76. Pope v. Curll, 2 Atk. 342, 26 Eng. Rep. 608 (Ch. 1741). See also Mark Rose, "The Author in Court: Pope v. Curll, (1741)," *Cardozo Arts and Entertainment Law Journal* 10, no. 2 (1991–92): 475–93; Balganesh, "Privative Copyright," describing how early cases relied on copyright to protect authorial privacy in what Balganesh conceives of in dignitary terms.

77. A most alarming example of this are "deep fakes" and "non-consensual pornography." See, e.g., Amanda Levendowski, "Using Copyright to Combat Revenge Porn," *New York University Journal of Intellectual Property and Entertainment Law* 3, no. 2 (Spring 2014): 422–46; and Danielle K. Citron and Robert Chesney, "Deep Fakes: A Looming Challenge for Privacy, Democracy, and National Security," *California Law Review* 107, no. 6 (2019): 1753–1830.

78. Eva E. Subotnik, "Artistic Control After Death," *Washington Law Review* 92, no. 1 (2017): 253–313 (discussing cases). See also Robert Spoo, "'Ah, You Publishing Scoundrel!': A Hauntological Reading of Privacy, Moral Rights, and the Fair Use of Unpublished Works," *Law and Literature* 25, no. 1 (Spring 2013): 85–102. Spoo reports that the "estate's opposition [to the publication of James Joyce's letters] was grounded in its oft-averred commitment to protecting Joyce's privacy and that of members of his family, living and dead. As Stephen Joyce bluntly told a *New Yorker* interviewer, Joyce's private life was "'no one's fucking business.'" Spoo, "'Ah, You Publishing Scoundrel!,'" 94. See also Robert Spoo, "Archival Foreclosure: A Scholar's Lawsuit Against the Estate of James Joyce," *American Archivist* 71, no. 2 (Fall/Winter 2008):

544–51; Shloss v. Sweeney, 515 F. Supp. 2d. 1068 (2007); Salinger v. Random House, Inc. 811 F.2d 90 (2nd Cir. 1987); Colting v. Salinger, 607 F.3d 68 (2nd Cir. 2010).

79. "Intellectual Property: The Willa Cather Trust," Willa Cather Foundation website, n.d., www.willacather.org/about/permissions/intellectual-property.

80. Subotnik, "Artistic Control After Death," 269.

81. Ron Rosenbaum, "Dmitri's Choice: Nabokov Wanted His Final, Unfinished Work Destroyed. Should His Son Get Out the Matches?," *Slate*, Jan. 16, 2008, www.slate.com/articles/life/the_spectator/2008/01/dmitris_choice.html.

82. Mark Rose, "The Author in Court: Pope v. Curll (1741)," *Cultural Critique* 21 (Spring 1992): 197–217, esp. 197.

83. Mark Rose, *Authors in Court: Scenes from the Theater of Copyright* (Cambridge, Mass.: Harvard University Press, 2016), 16.

84. Rose, *Authors in Court*.

85. Rose, *Authors in Court*, 15.

86. Balganesh, "Privative Copyright" (collecting early cases).

87. U.S. Constitution, Amendments I, IV. See also Chemerinsky, "Rediscovering Brandeis's Right to Privacy."

88. Subotnik, "Artistic Control After Death," 265–66, citing Joseph L. Sax, *Playing Darts with a Rembrandt: Public and Private Rights in Cultural Treasures* (Ann Arbor: University of Michigan Press, 1999), 46, 135–38; and Nili Cohen, "The Betrayed(?) Wills of Kafka and Brod," *Law and Literature* 27, no. 1 (2015): 1, 13.

89. "Nabokov's Novel to Be Published, Against His Dying Wish," *All Things Considered*, NPR, Apr. 30, 2008, www.npr.org/templates/story/story.php?storyId=90073521. See also the introduction in Andrew Jewell and Janis Stout, eds., *The Selected Letters of Willa Cather* (New York: Alfred A. Knopf, 2013), viii. Jewell and Stout suggest that "Cather's testamentary restriction on the publication of her letters . . . was an act consistent with her long-held desire to shape her own public identity."

90. On the fun of creating and the pleasure of flow that sustains creativity, see Mihaly Csikszentmihalyi, *Creativity: Flow and the Psychology of Discovery and Invention* (New York: Harper Perennial Books, 1996), 107–26.

91. Csikszentmihalyi, *Creativity*, 113–15, describing creators' goals centered on challenges, building skills, and intrinsic problem-solving about the world as they find it. See also Jessica Silbey, *The Eureka Myth: Creators, Innovators, and Everyday Intellectual Property* (Stanford, Calif.: Stanford University Press, 2015), 39, describing an author's experience of writing as her "filter on the world" and how she "recycle[s] an experience . . . to [make] order out of all this stuff that's so hard to navigate."

92. Silbey, *Eureka Myth*, 87–88, describing a scientist comparing the shuttering of his project to his child's death.

93. On the risk that authors might destroy works rather than rely on untrustworthy heirs or an inconsistent legal system, see Subotnik, "Artistic Control After Death," 56. Subotnik argues that allowing authors to preserve privacy through trusts may be a way to promote creativity and when destruction of the work is likely, trusts should be explored.

94. Right of publicity can endure beyond the person in some states. Compare California law that (like copyright) endures seventy years beyond death (Cal. Civ. Code § 3344) with New York law, which ends with death (NY CLS Civ. R. § 51).

95. In Harper & Row Publishers, Inc. v. Nation Enterprises, 471 U.S. 539 (1985), the Supreme Court held the magazine liable for copyright infringement for its scooping of the as-of-yet unpublished memoirs of former president Gerald Ford relating to Richard Nixon's resignation. In doing so, it described the right of first publication and the right of privacy as related but distinct interests that copyright law can protect. The court said: "We also find unpersuasive respondents' argument that fair use may be made of a soon-to-be-published manuscript on the ground that the author has demonstrated he has no interest in nonpublication. This argument assumes that the unpublished nature of copyrighted material is only relevant to letters or other confidential writings not intended for dissemination. It is true that common-law copyright was often enlisted in the service of personal privacy. See Warren and Brandeis, "Right to Privacy" 198–99 (1890). In its commercial guise, however, an author's right to choose when he will publish is no less deserving of protection." *Harper & Row*, 471 U.S. at 554–55.

96. 17 U.S.C § 107 provides:

Notwithstanding the provisions of sections 106 and 106A, the fair use of a copyrighted work, including such use by reproduction in copies or phonorecords or by any other means specified by that section, for purposes such as criticism, comment, news reporting, teaching (including multiple copies for classroom use), scholarship, or research, is not an infringement of copyright. In determining whether the use made of a work in any particular case is a fair use the factors to be considered shall include—

(1) the purpose and character of the use, including whether such use is of a commercial nature or is for nonprofit educational purposes;
(2) the nature of the copyrighted work;
(3) the amount and substantiality of the portion used in relation to the copyrighted work as a whole; and
(4) the effect of the use upon the potential market for or value of the copyrighted work.

The fact that a work is unpublished shall not itself bar a finding of fair use if such finding is made upon consideration of all the above factors.

97. 17 U.S.C § 107. "The fact that a work is unpublished shall not itself bar a finding of fair use if such finding is made upon a consideration of all the above [fair use] factors."

98. Despite the statutory admonition, courts appear to remain highly influenced by the unpublished nature of the work when determining whether a use is fair. See Barton Beebe, "An Empirical Study of U.S. Copyright Fair Use Opinions, 1978–2005," *University of Pennsylvania Law Review* 156, no. 3 (2008): 549–624, esp. 612–15 (finding

that twenty-nine out of thirty-seven cases concerning unpublished works asserted that this fact disfavored a finding of fair use, while the fact that the work is published has become a stronger positive factor favoring fair use); and Pamela Samuelson, "Unbundling Fair Uses," *Fordham Law Review* 77, no. 5 (2009): 2537–2621, esp. 2579. ("drawing expression from unpublished or unfinished works is likely to cut against fair use"); but cf. Matthew Sag, "Predicting Fair Use," *Ohio State Law Journal* 73, no. 1 (2012): 47–77 (finding no significant effect of unpublished nature of the work on fair use analysis).

99. Spoo, "'Ah, You Publishing Scoundrel!,'" 88.

100. Drassinower, *What's Wrong with Copying?*, 115.

101. Drassinower, *What's Wrong with Copying?*, 115.

102. Drassinower, *What's Wrong with Copying?*, 115.

103. Drassinower, *What's Wrong with Copying?*, 117.

104. Drassinower, *What's Wrong with Copying?*, 117.

105. See 17 USC § 102(b).

106. Drassinower explained that "privacy and copyright may overlap over identical facts, especially in the case of unpublished works of authorship, [but this] need not obscure the fundamental distinction between the causes of action." Drassinower, *What's Wrong with Copying?*, 118. Fair enough, but the distinction between copyright and privacy is collapsing in the Digital Age, as works of authorship (and not only the facts they contain) are launched into the public sphere without authorization over the internet.

107. A counterpart to the protection of the author's "deliberate choice" to make a work unavailable (see *Harper & Row*, 471 U.S. at 553) is the choice to publish, which is also the prerogative of the copyright owner. Jake Linford, "A Second Look at the Right of First Publication," *Journal of the Copyright Society of the U.S.A.* 58, no. 3 (2011): 585–664, esp. 585, 589–90. The "right of divulgation" or disclosure is a moral right in Europe, and it is described as the choice whether or not to publish. It is related to the common-law right of first publication of a literary work. See R. Anthony Reese, "The Public Display Right: The Copyright Act's Neglected Solution to the Controversy over RAM 'Copies,'" *University of Illinois Law Review* 2001, no. 1 (2000): 83–101, esp. 95nn43–44. When copyright law is used to conceal or hide work from the public that authors eventually wanted to disseminate, copyright's progress goal is thwarted. See Guy Pessach and Michal Shur-Ofry, "Copyright and the Holocaust," *Yale Journal of Law and the Humanities* 30, no. 2 (2018): 121–72: "Applying ordinary copyright doctrine, therefore, results . . . in clear irony: victims' works were concealed deliberately in order to enable their future dissemination; yet viewed through the copyright lens, this very fact renders them unpublished works, thereby hindering a finding of fair use and undermining their chances of being disseminated." Pessach and Shur-Ofry, "Copyright and the Holocaust," 151.

108. Hartzog, *Privacy's Blueprint*; Woodrow Hartzog, "The Case Against Idealizing Control," *European Data Protection Law Review* 4, no. 4 (2018): 423–32.

109. See Nancy K. Baym, *Playing to the Crowd: Musicians, Audiences, and the Intimate Work of Connection* (New York: New York University Press, 2018).

110. Estate of Martin Luther King, Jr., Inc. v. CBS, Inc., 194 F.3d 1211 (11th Cir. 1999) held that Martin Luther King's nationally televised "I Have a Dream" speech was a limited publication of that work and retained its copyright despite lacking registration and notice; as such, the estate could continue to demand payment for reproduction of the speech and his performance of it under copyright law.

111. Baker v. Libbie, 210 Mass. 599 (1912) held that an executor may enjoin the publication of private letters of his testator. See also Grigsby v. Breckinridge, 65 Ky. 480, 2 Bush 480, 489 (1867) ("The only right to be enforced against the holder [of the letter] is a right to prevent publication.").

112. On the protection of letters via laws of "confidential communications," see Richards and Solove, "Privacy's Other Path."

113. On the problem of limited publication doctrine and the significance of publication (and first publication) in copyright legislation, see Deborah R. Gerhardt, "Copyright Publication: An Empirical Study," *Notre Dame Law Review* 87, no. 1 (2011): 135–204, esp. 140–42.

114. *Baker*, 210 Mass. 599; *Grigsby*, 65 Ky. 480.

115. Levendowski, "Using Copyright to Combat Revenge Porn," discussed incidents of revenge porn and the potential reach of copyright law to effect takedowns and damages. See also Balsley v. LFP, Inc., 691 F.3d 747 (6th Cir. 2012) (upholding copyright infringement determination for posting online of photograph from a wet T-shirt contest without permission from photograph subject); Swatch Group Management Services Ltd. v. Bloomberg L.P., 756 F.3d 73 (2nd Cir. 2014) (no copyright infringement for unauthorized publication of sound recording and transcript of investor conference call); Online Policy Group v. Diebold, Inc., 337 F. Supp. 2d 1195 (N.D. Cal. 2004) (no copyright infringement for publication of internal company emails revealing flaw in voting machines); Monge v. Maya Magazines, Inc., 688 F.3d 1164 (9th Cir. 2012) (unauthorized use of purloined photographs of private but newsworthy wedding held to infringe their copyright).

116. See Woodrow Hartzog and Frederic Stutzman, "The Case for Online Obscurity," *California Law Review* 101, no. 1 (2013): 1–50, esp. 26, criticizing but acknowledging the line of cases that finds unreasonable expectation of privacy for posted content on internet, even if password-protected, citing United States v. Gines-Perez, 214 F. Supp. 2d 205, 225 (D.P.R. 2002).

117. See, e.g., Katz v. Google, Inc., 802 F.3d 1178 (11th Cir. 2015), which held that a tenant fairly republished a photograph of a landlord to criticize his business practices; Dhillon v. Does 1–10, No. C 13-01465 SI, 2014 WL 722592 (N.D. Cal. Feb. 25, 2014), which held that the defendant fairly reused the plaintiff's headshot to criticize the plaintiff's political views; Caner v. Autry, 16 F. Supp. 3d 689 (W.D. Va. 2014), in which a university president sought to suppress further dissemination of videos of which he was not the author because they supported others' claims that he lied.

118. Richards and Solove, "Privacy's Other Path"; Ari Ezra Waldman, "A Breach of Trust: Fighting Nonconsensual Pornography," *Iowa Law Review* 102, no. 2 (2017): 709–33. These cases also protect the exploitation of or injury to one's persona (as represented by their image or other manifestation of identity). One can trace the origins of privacy and the right of publicity at the turn of the twentieth century at the onslaught of "easy-to-use and portable cameras, and an associated explosion in amateur photography." Rothman, *Right of Publicity*, 12. Rothman demonstrated how the right to privacy can be found in the roots of the right of publicity and is a response to the changes in news media and image and printing technology at the turn of the twentieth century. The right of publicity "provides the basis to control the unwanted dissemination of one's name and likeness, and other indicia of identity for another's advantage," which is usually commercial (but does not have to be). Rothman, *Right of Publicity*, 3. This historical understanding of the shared origins of publicity and privacy rights does not by itself help us untangle the copyright interests from the privacy ones, however. Even more puzzling is whether disentanglement is possible today. But documenting the entanglement is one further step toward understanding the phenomenon of privacy's intellectual property sidekick in the Digital Age.

119. *Swatch*, 756 F.3d 73, found no copyright infringement for unauthorized publication of sound recording and transcript of investor conference call; *Diebold*, 337 F. Supp. 2d 1195, found no copyright infringement for publication of internal company emails revealing flaw in voting machines.

120. *Swatch*, 756 F.3d at 85.

121. *Swatch*, 756 F.3d at 84.

122. *Diebold*, 337 F. Supp. 2d 1195.

123. Feist Publications Inc. v. Rural Telephone Service Co., 499 U.S. 340, 349 (1991), describing "thin" copyright as containing low originality and a high quantity of facts or other excludable copyright subject matter.

124. *Diebold*, 337 F. Supp. 2d at 1203.

125. *Riley*, 573 US 373.

126. *Carpenter*, 585 US __, 138 S. Ct. 2206.

127. Waldman, "Breach of Trust," 722.

128. See Malla Pollack, "What Is Congress Supposed to Promote? Defining 'Progress' in Article I, Section 8, Clause 8 of the United States Constitution, or Introducing the Progress Clause," *Nebraska Law Review* 80, no. 4 (2001): 754–815.

129. Jessica Silbey, "Evidence Verité and the Law of Film," *Cardozo Law Review* 31, no. 4 (2010): 1257–99 (iconic public images generate multiple social and legal meanings beyond their initial contextual existence and origins); Jessica Silbey, "Images in/of Law," *New York Law School Law Review* 57, no. 1 (2012–13): 171–83 (describing how images are intuitively understood and yet collectively inscrutable, posing unique problems for resolving legal conflicts that demand common and shared language).

130. See, e.g., Rachel Gillett, "Why We're More Likely to Remember Content with Images and Video," *Fast Company*, Sept. 18, 2014, www.fastcompany.com/3035856/why-were-more-likely-to-remember-content-with-images-and-video-infogr (citing

a study by online marketing company HubSpot that found "tweets with images are 94% more likely to be retweeted than tweets without"); Noah Kagan, "Why Content Goes Viral: What Analyzing 100 Million Articles Taught Us," *Huffington Post*, June 13, 2014, www.huffpost.com/entry/why-content-goes-viral-wh_b_5492767 ("twice as many people, on average[,] share posts with at least one image in the post."); and An Xiao Mina, "That Merkel Photo Is More Like a Meme than a Renaissance Painting," *Atlantic*, June 11, 2018, www.theatlantic.com/technology/archive/2018/06/that-merkel-photo-is-more-like-a-meme-than-a-renaissance-painting/562505.

131. Rothman, *Right of Publicity*, 13, quoting Judge John Clinton Gray of the New York Court of Appeals in Roberson v. Rochester Folding Box Co., 64 N.E. 442, 450 (N.Y. 1902).

132. Warren and Brandeis, "Right to Privacy," 196.

133. Waldman, "Breach of Trust," 722.

134. Levendowski, "Using Copyright to Combat Revenge Porn"; Waldman, "Breach of Trust."

135. On copyright law's content neutrality and content-based discrimination under a First Amendment analysis, see Alfred C. Yen, "Rethinking Copyright's Relationship to the First Amendment," *Boston University Law Review* 100, no. 4 (2020): 1215–69.

136. See Rebecca Tushnet, "Fair Use's Unfinished Business," *Chicago-Kent Journal of Intellectual Property* 15, no. 2 (2016): 399–411, which described overbroad and abusive copyright claims under the Digital Millennium Copyright Act that, antithetical to the First Amendment, removed millions of works from the internet as a form of prior restraint.

137. See Bleistein v. Donaldson Lithographing Co., 188 U.S. 239, 251 (1903) prohibited "aesthetic discrimination" in copyright law.

138. *Monge*, 688 F.3d 1164.

139. See Pamela Samuelson, "Protecting Privacy Through Copyright Law?," in *Privacy in the Modern Age*, 191–99, esp. 194–95, speculating that Monge purchased the copyrights from the photographer.

140. *Monge*, 688 F.3d at 1176.

141. *Monge*, 688 F.3d at 1177–78. For critiques of this reasoning, see Andrew Gilden, "Copyright's Market Gibberish," *Washington Law Review* 94, no. 3 (2020): 1019–84.

142. *Harper & Row*, 471 U.S. at 561.

143. *Monge*, 688 F.3d at 1177–78.

144. *Balsley*, 691 F.3d 747.

145. Eldred v. Ashcroft, 537 U.S. 186, 219 (2003). "As *Harper & Row* observed: 'The Framers intended copyright itself to be the engine of free expression. By establishing a marketable right to the use of one's expression, copyright supplies the economic incentive to create and disseminate ideas.'"

146. But see Rebecca Tushnet, "My Fair Ladies: Sex, Gender, and Fair Use in Copyright," *American University Journal of Gender, Social Policy, and the Law* 15, no. 2 (2007): 273–304, which showed how sexualization of copyrighted work is often considered fair use. "By favoring sexualization over other types of critique, fair use

doctrine systematically treats sex as especially oppositional and liberating, when in fact it has no monopoly on critique and no necessarily disruptive effect on a copyright owner's message." Tushnet, "My Fair Ladies," 275.

147. Paul Ohm, "Sensitive Information," *Southern California Law Review* 88, no. 5 (2015): 1125–95, esp. 1161.

148. Danielle Keats Citron and Mary Anne Franks, "Criminalizing Revenge Porn," *Wake Forest Law Review* 49, no. 2 (2014): 345–91.

149. On the harms of revenge porn, see Citron and Franks, "Criminalizing Revenge Porn."

150. For an overview of the literature and a critique of its inevitable strengthening of intellectual property rights, see Michael A. Carrier, "Cabining Intellectual Property through a Property Paradigm," *Duke Law Journal* 54, no. 1 (2004): 1–145.

151. *Eldred*, 537 U.S. at 219.

152. Zenith Laboratories, Inc. v. Bristol-Myers Squibb Co., 19 F.3d 1418 (Fed. Cir. 1994). I am grateful to Erika Lietzan for this example.

153. *Zenith Laboratories*, 19 F.3d 1418.

154. *Zenith Laboratories*, 19 F.3d at 1420, 1421.

155. Moore v. Regents of the University of California, 51 Cal. 3d 120, 271 Cal. Rptr. 146, 793 P.2d 479 (1990).

156. *Moore*, 51 Cal. 3d at 138.

157. *Moore*, 51 Cal. 3d at 139.

158. *Moore*, 51 Cal. 3d at 139.

159. *Moore*, 51 Cal. 3d at 139.

160. *Moore*, 51 Cal. 3d at 139.

161. *Moore*, 51 Cal. 3d at 140.

162. Priscilla Wald, "What's in a Cell? John Moore's Spleen and the Language of Bioslavery," *New Literary History* 36, no. 2 (2005): 205–25; James Boyle, *Shamans, Software, and Spleens: Law and the Construction of the Information Society* (Cambridge, Mass.: Harvard University Press, 1996).

163. Raynor v. State, 440 Md. 71, 96, 99 A.3d 753, 768 (2014); Maryland v. King 569 U.S. 435 (2013). For a history of intellectual property in blood, milk, and semen, see Kara W. Swanson, *Banking on the Body: The Market in Blood, Milk, and Sperm in Modern America* (Cambridge, Mass.: Harvard University Press, 2014).

164. See Evan Selinger and Woodrow Hartzog, "The Inconsentability of Facial Surveillance," *Loyola Law Review* 66, no. 101 (2019): 101–22.

165. Jim Salter, "North Face Settles Lawsuit against South Butt," NBCNews.com, Apr. 11, 2010, www.nbcnews.com/id/36334733/ns/business-consumer_news/t/north-face-settles-lawsuit-against-south-butt/#.XP_J1NNKgW8. As reported, "the [defendant] company sells products with the tag line, 'Never Stop Relaxing,' a parody of The North Face line, 'Never Stop Exploring.' A wavelike pattern and the company name appear near the upper right or left shoulder on jackets and shirts, similar to the logo and placement used by The North Face." The issue in the case as reported by news outlets was between parody and piracy.

166. Solove, "Brief History of Information Privacy Law."

167. Intellectual property scholarship analyzing its intersection with reputational interests is vast. See, e.g., Laura Heymann, "The Law of Reputation and the Interest of the Audience," *Boston College Law Review* 51, no. 2 (2011): 1341–1439; Eric Goldman, "The Regulation of Reputational Information" in *The Next Digital Decade: Essays on the Future of the Internet*, ed. Szoka and Marcus (Washington, DC: TechFreedom, 2010): 293–304; Amy Adler and Jeanne Fromer, "Taking Intellectual Property Into Their Own Hands," *California Law Review* 107, no. 5 (2019): 1455–1530. See also Silbey, *Eureka Myth*, 149–83.

168. See 15 U.S.C § 1125(c).

169. Federal Trademark Dilution Revision Act, Pub. L. No. 109-312, 120 Stat. 1730 (2006), codified at 15 U.S.C § 1125(c) (2006), amending Federal Trademark Dilution Act, Pub L. No. 104-98, 109 Stat. 985 (1996).

170. Louis Vuitton Malletier S.A. v. Haute Diggity Dog, LLC, 507 F.3d 252 (4th Cir. 2007) alleged tarnishment of Louis Vuitton by dog toys called "Chewy Vuitton" and Tiffany by "Sniffany" dog toy.

171. Starbucks Corporation v. Wolf's Borough Coffee, Inc., 588 F.3d 97 (2009) alleged tarnishment of Starbucks Coffee by Wolf Borough Coffee blend called "Charbucks Blend."

172. For a range of criticisms of trademark dilution, see, e.g., Sandra L. Rierson, "The Myth and Reality of Dilution," *Duke Law and Technology Review* 11, no. 2 (2012): 212–312; Britt Lovejoy, "Tarnishing the Dilution by Tarnishment Cause of Action: Starbucks Corp v. Wolfe's Borough Coffee, Inc. and V. Secret Catalogue, Inc. v. Mosely, Compared," *Berkeley Technology Law Journal* 26, no. 1 (2011): 623–54; Rebecca Tushnet, "Gone in 60 Milliseconds: Trademark Law and Cognitive Science," *Texas Law Review* 86, no. 3 (2008): 507–68; and Barton Beebe, "The Continuing Debacle of U.S. Antidilution Law: Evidence from the First Year of Trademark Dilution Revision Act Case Law," *Santa Clara Computer and High Technology Journal* 24, no. 3 (2008): 449–67.

173. Moseley v. V Secret Catalogue, Inc., 537 U.S. 418 (2003); Toys "R" Us, Inc. v. Feinberg, 98 Civ. 2780 (AGS), 1998 WL 760219 (S.D.N.Y.).

174. Kent Greenfield, *Corporations Are People Too (And They Should Act Like It)* (New Haven, Conn.: Yale University Press, 2018). See also Burwell v. Hobby Lobby Stores, Inc., 573 U.S. 682 (2014), which allowed closely held corporations to be exempt from regulations to which owners object on the basis of religious belief; and Citizens United v. Federal Election Commission, 558 U.S. 310 (2010), which held that corporate political spending is protected speech.

175. See v. City of Seattle, 387 U.S. 541 (1967) (companies are protected by unreasonable search and seizure under Fourth Amendment); Ross v. Bernhard, 396 U.S. 531 (1970) (the Seventh Amendment guarantees the right to a jury trial in stockholders' derivative actions in which the corporation would be entitled to a jury trial).

176. Grosjean v. American Press Co., 297 U.S. 233 (1936) (corporations are persons for the purpose of the equal protection clause).

177. Martin Kihn, "Taylor Swift and the Future of Brand Marketing," *Gartner for Marketers* (blog), June 5, 2018, https://blogs.gartner.com/martin-kihn/taylor-swift-delivers-a-master-class-in-marketing; Cliff Dumas, "Brand Like Taylor Swift," *Cliff Dumas Media* (blog), https://cliffdumas.com/brand-like-taylor-swift; see also Nancy K. Baym, *Playing to the Crowd: Musicians, Audiences, and the Intimate Work of Connection* (New York: New York University Press, 2018), 162.

178. Ashley Rodriguez, "Citizens Bank Marks Retail Rebrand with Customer Loyalty Push," *Ad Age*, Apr. 27, 2015, www.adage.com/article/cmo-strategy/citizens-bank-marks-retail-rebrand-customer-loyalty-push/298253; Jason Lynch, "State Farm's New This Is Us Campaign Includes Three Ad Shots in the Style of NBC's Hit Drama," *Adweek*, Jan. 9, 2018, www.adweek.com/tv-video/state-farms-new-this-is-us-campaign-includes-3-ads-shot-in-the-style-of-nbcs-hit-drama.

179. Scholz v. Goudreau, 132 F. Supp. 3d 239 (D. Mass. 2015).

180. See 15 U.S.C § 1125(a) (unregistered trademark infringement provision).

181. *Scholz*, 132 F. Supp. 3d 239.

182. Janie Campbell, "Street Artists Sues American Eagle for Using His Work in . . . Just About Everything," July 29, 2014, *Huffington Post*, www.huffingtonpost.com/2014/07/29/aholsniffsglue-american-eagle-artist-lawsuit-copyright_n_5627862.html.

183. Campbell, "Street Artists Sues American Eagle."

184. Marta Iljadica, *Copyright Beyond Law: Regulating Creativity in the Graffiti Subculture* (New York: Bloomsbury Publishing, 2016)

185. Castillo v. G&M Realty LP, 950 F.3d 155 (2nd Cir. 2020).

186. Alan Feuer, "GM Used Graffiti in a Car Ad. Should the Artist be Paid?," *New York Times*, July 17 2018, www.nytimes.com/2018/07/17/arts/design/general-motors-graffiti-artist-copyright.html; Jonathan Bailey, "Graffiti: At the Edge of Copyright," Plagiarism Today, Mar. 15, 2018, www.plagiarismtoday.com/2018/03/15/graffiti-at-the-edge-of-copyright.

187. See 35 U.S.C. § 256.

188. Shukh v. Seagate Tech., LLC, 803 F.3d 659, 662–63 (Fed. Cir. 2015).

189. Czarnik v. Illumina, Inc., 437 F. Supp. 2d. 252, 256 (D. Del. 2006) (standing satisfied where plaintiff alleged that his omission from patents harmed his reputation in the scientific community, deprived him of prestige, and impacted his ability to secure a lucrative position at a start-up company); Barnette v. Dicello, 616 F. Supp. 2d. 709, 714 (N.D. Ohio 2007) (standing not satisfied where plaintiff failed to show how patent designation would constitute a mark of success in his field); Krauser v. Evolution IP Holdings, Inc., 975 F. Supp. 2d. 1247 (S.D. Fla.2013) (upholding correction of inventorship claim for plaintiff because "an erroneous patent application is *itself* an injury to his reputation sufficient to confer Article III standing" even without any concrete financial or economic injury).

190. Pedersen v. Geschwind, 141 F. Supp. 3d 405 (2015).

191. *Pedersen*, 141 F. Supp. 3d at. 413, 416.

192. *Pedersen*, 141 F. Supp. 3d at 413.

193. *Pedersen*, 141 F. Supp. 3d 405. The argument that federal courts must have limited jurisdiction—which is true as a matter of U.S. constitutional structure and is the cornerstone of the state-federal balance—is sometimes criticized as a "too much justice" argument. Open the doors of the courthouse too wide, and too many aggrieved will seek its solace. The response is that state courts are not so limited.

194. *Pedersen*, 141 F. Supp. 3d at 416.

195. *Pedersen*, 141 F. Supp. 3d at 417.

196. *Pedersen*, 141 F. Supp. 3d at 416.

197. Obergefell v. Hodges, 576 U.S. 644 (2015); Lawrence v. Texas, 539 U.S. 558 (2003).

198. *Pedersen*, 141 F. Supp. 3d at 416.

199. *Pedersen*, 141 F. Supp. 3d at 408.

200. Louis Vuitton Malletier, S.A. v. My Other Bag, Inc., 18-293-cv (2nd Cir., Mar. 15, 2019). See also "Louis Vuitton Wins Last Round in Fight Over 'My Other Bag,'" *The Fashion Law*, Mar. 18, 2019, www.thefashionlaw.com/louis-vuitton-wins-the-last-round-in-fight-over-my-other-bag.

201. Nadia Plesner, "Simple Living & Darfurnica," www.nadiaplesner.com/simple-living--darfurnica1.

202. Mattel, Inc. v. Pitt, 229 F. Supp. 2d 315 (SDNY 2002) ("Dungeon Barbie"); Mattel v. MCA, 296 F. 3d 894 (9th Cir. 2002), affirming 28 F. Supp. 2d 1120 (C.D. Cal. 1998) (Barbie in the Aqua song "Barbie Girl"); Mattel Inc. v. Walking Mountain Prods., 353 F.3d 792 (9th Cir. 2003) ("Food Chain" Barbie). For a discussion of all these cases, see Rebecca Tushnet, "Make Me Walk, Make Me Talk, Do Whatever You Please: Barbie and Exceptions," in *Intellectual Property at the Edge: The Contested Contours of IP*, ed. Rochelle Cooper Dreyfuss and Jane C. Ginsburg (Cambridge, U.K.: Cambridge University Press, 2014), 405–26.

203. Mike Masnick, "NY Times Files Ridiculous Copyright Lawsuit over Book that Mocks NYT for Glamorizing War," *TechDirt*, Jan. 26, 2015, www.techdirt.com/articles/20160125/22005433418/ny-times-files-ridiculous-copyright-lawsuit-over-book-that-mocks-nyt-glamorizing-war.shtml.

204. Whitney v. People of the State of California, 274 U.S. 357, 377 (1927) (Brandeis, J., concurring) ("If there be time to expose through discussion the falsehood and fallacies, to avert the evil by the processes of education, the remedy to be applied is more speech, not enforced silence.").

205. Kristina Hill et al. v. Public Advocate of the United States, 35 F. Supp. 3d 1347, 1351–52 (D. Colo. 2014).

206. *Hill*, 35 F. Supp. 3d at 1355.

207. See 17 USC § 107. The factor that supported the Plaintiff was factor 3, "the amount and substantiality of the portion used." The entire photograph work was used in this case.

208. David Walker, "Photographer Wins $2501 for Infringement in Anti-Gay Attack Ad Case," *PDNPulse*, June 23, 2014, https://pdnpulse.pdnonline.com/2014/06/photographer-wins-2501-infringement-anti-gay-attack-ad-case.html.

209. *Katz v. Google*, 802 F.3d 1178; Katz v. Chevaldina, 111 U.S.P.Q. 2d 1281 (S.D. Fla. 2014).

210. *Katz v. Google*, 802 F.3d at 1180.

211. *Katz v. Google*, 802 F.3d at 1184.

212. See Restatement (Second) of Torts, § 652E (1979). See also Gary T. Schwartz, "Explaining and Justifying a Limited Tort of False Light Invasion of Privacy," *Case Western Reserve Law Review* 41, no. 3 (1991): 885–919. Defamation requires proof of reputational harm, false light does not.

213. See Dhillon v. Does 1–10, in which the defendant reused the plaintiff's headshot fairly to criticize plaintiff's political views.

214. Scott v. WorldStarHipHop, Inc., 10-CV-9538 (PKC)(RLE), 2012 WL 5835232 (S.D.N.Y. Nov. 14, 2012).

215. Scott v. WorldStarHipHop, 10-CV-9538 (PKC/RLE) (S.D.N.Y May 2, 2012).

216. *Caner*, 16 F. Supp 3d 689.

217. Eric Goldman and Jessica Silbey, "Copyright's Memory Hole," *Brigham Young University Law Review* 2019, no. 4 (2019): 929–96.

218. Garcia v. Google, Inc., 743 F.3d 1258 (9th Cir. 2014), amended, 766 F.3d 929 (9th Cir. 2014); reversed en banc, 786 F.3d 733 (9th Cir. 2015).

219. *Garcia v. Google*, 766 F.3d 929 (9th Cir. 2014).

220. *Garcia v. Google*, 786 F.3d at 744 (9th Cir. 2015).

221. *Garcia v. Google*, 786 F.3d at 746.

222. *Garcia v. Google*, 786 F.3d at 745.

223. *Garcia v. Google*, 786 F.3d at 747.

224. Rothman, *Right of Publicity*. See also Stacey L. Dogan, "Haelan Laboratories v. Topps Chewing Gum: Publicity as a Legal Right," in Dreyfuss and Ginsburg, *Intellectual Property at the Edge*, 17–38; and Stacey Dogan, "Bullying and Opportunism in Trademark and Right-of-Publicity Law," *Boston University Law Review* 96, no. 3 (2016): 1293–1324.

225. Quinn Norton, "The International Fight Over Marcel Duchamp's Chess Set," *Atlantic*, Sept. 8, 2015, www.theatlantic.com/technology/archive/2015/09/the-international-fight-over-marcel-duchamps-chess-set/404248; Johnathan Band, "Can You Copyright a Dream?," *Politico*, Jan. 12, 2015, www.politico.com/magazine/story/2015/01/selma-martin-luther-king-can-you-copyright-a-dream-114187; Brittany Spanos, "Marvin Gaye's Children: What Our Father Would Say about Lawsuit," *Rolling Stone*, Mar. 18, 2015, www.rollingstone.com/music/news/marvin-gayes-children-what-our-father-would-say-about-lawsuit-20150318; Colting v. Salinger, 607 F.3d 68 (2nd Cir. 2010).

226. Stuart Dredge, "GoldieBlox Agreed to Pay $1 Million to Charity in Beastie Boys Settlement," May 13, 2014, *The Guardian*, www.theguardian.com/technology/2014/may/13/goldieblox-beastie-boys-girls-settlement. See also Jon Blistein, "Beastie Boys Settle Lawsuit Over 'Girls' Toy Commercial," *Rolling Stone*, www.rollingstone.com/music/music-news/beastie-boys-settle-lawsuit-over-girls-toy-commercial-184719.

227. Dredge, "GoldieBlox Agreed to Pay $1 Million." See also Subotnik, "Artistic Control After Death," 255.

228. Pharrell Williams, et al. v. Bridgeport Music et al., 895 F.3d 1106 (9th Cir. 2018).

229. Spanos, "Marvin Gaye's Children."

230. Spanos, "Marvin Gaye's Children."

231. On reinforcing "family ties" as a basis for "dead hand control," see Subotnik, "Artistic Control After Death," 276.

232. See 17 U.S.C. § 106(A). ("Visual Artists' Rights Act" granting limited moral rights to specific category of visual art only).

233. Andrew Gilden, "Sex, Death, and Intellectual Property," *Harvard Journal of Law and Technology* 32, no. 1 (Fall 2018): 67–114; Subotnik, "Artistic Control After Death."

234. Pierce v. Society of Sisters, 268 U.S. 510 (1925) (parental autonomy over educational choices for children); *Lawrence*, 539 U.S. 558 (privacy rights related to sexual intimacy between consenting adults of the same sex); *Obergefell*, 576 U.S. 644 (privacy related to marriage).

235. Ray D. Madoff, *Immortality and the Law: The Rising Power of the American Dead* (New Haven, Conn.: Yale University Press, 2010), 125–26.

236. Madoff, *Immortality and the Law*. But see National Archives and Records Administration v. Favish, 541 U.S. 157, 166–67 (2004) (allowing relatives of deceased to enjoin publication of photos of deceased's body "to secure their own refuge from a sensation-seeking culture for their own peace of mind and tranquility, not for the sake of the deceased . . .. [I]t is proper to conclude from Congress' use of the term "personal privacy" that it intended to permit family members to assert their own privacy rights against public intrusions long deemed impermissible under common law and cultural traditions. This does not mean that the family is in the same position as the individual who is the disclosure's subject. We have little difficulty, however, in finding in our case law and traditions the right of family members to direct and control disposition of the body of the deceased and to limit attempts to exploit pictures of the deceased family member's remains for public purposes.")

237. Abraham Drassinower, "Copyright Is Not About Copying," *Harvard Law Review* 125, no. 1 (2012): 108–19, describing how copyright has a bilateral structure mirroring the correlativity of a private law action and refuting that copyright's public domain is inessential to its internal structure.

238. United States v. Virginia, 518 U.S. 515 (1996), a landmark case in which the U.S. Supreme Court held unconstitutional the male-only admission policy of the public Virginia Military Institute and required the admission of women.

239. Drassinower, "Copyright Is Not About Copying"; see also Drassinower, *What's Wrong with Copying?*, 9–10, describing and criticizing the balancing approach to assessing copyright infringement and value.

240. See Carrier, "Cabining Intellectual Property through a Property Paradigm"; Cohen, "Copyright as Property in the Post-Industrial Economy."

Chapter 4

1. Failure to provide copyright notice and registration between 1976 and 1989 could be "cured" under certain conditions laid out in the statute. See 17 U.S.C. §§ 401–6. For registration, see §§ 17 USC 408–12. Although registration remains required to file a lawsuit and be eligible for statutory damages, only a small fraction of copyright authors register their work today.

2. Before 1976, only works that were published, registered, and marked with notice of copyright authorship were protected by federal copyright law.

3. David R. Hansen et al., "Solving the Orphan Works Problem for the United States," *Columbia Journal of Law and the Arts* 37, no. 1 (2013): 1–55, esp. 7–8.

4. Authors Guild v. Google, Inc., 804 F. 3d 202 (2015). See also Authors Guild v. HathiTrust, 755 F.3d 87 (2d Cir. 2014).

5. On how copyright expiration promoted the works availability, see Imke Reimers, "Copyright and Generic Entry in Book Publishing," *American Economics Journal* 11, no. 3 (2019): 257–84; see also Paul J. Heald, "How Copyright Keeps Works Disappeared," *Journal of Empirical Legal Studies* 11, no. 4 (2014): 829–66.

6. *Authors Guild v. Google*, 804 F. 3d 202.

7. "Remedies and Procedures Regarding Orphan Works" roundtable, Copyright Office of the United States, Mar. 11, 2014, Library of Congress, Washington, D.C., 117–18, transcript available at www.copyright.gov/orphan/transcript/0311LOC.pdf. See also www.copyright.gov/orphan/2014roundtable.html.

8. Plessy v. Ferguson, 163 U.S. 537 (1896).

9. It should be obvious that all that is free is not necessarily worthless. Take love, friendship, and gifts, for starters. See also Lewis Hyde, *The Gift: How the Creative Spirit Transforms the World* (New York: Random House, 1983). In copyright specifically, ideas and facts are "free" because they are uniquely valuable and thus unprotectable. See 17 U.S.C. § 102(b). There is a public domain—or "free" zone—in every intellectual property regime. The assertion that what is free is worthless is a category error. To be sure, Garrett Hardin's theory of tragedy of the commons feeds the overapplication of the equivalence of free or "commons" with cheap or "uncared for." Garrett Hardin, "The Tragedy of the Commons," *Science*, Dec. 13, 1968, 1243–48. The response in theDigital Age has been the tragedy of the "anticommons." Michael Heller, "The Tragedy of the Anticommons: A Concise Introduction and Lexicon," *Modern Law Review*, 76, no. 1 (2013): 6–25. For canonical anticommons literature in IP, see Michael A. Heller and Rebecca S. Eisenberg, "Can Patents Deter Innovation? The Anticommons in Biomedical Research," *Science*, May 1, 1998, 698–701; and Michael A. Heller, "The Tragedy of the Anticommons: Property in the Transition from Marx to Markets," *Harvard Law Review* 111, no. 3 (1998): 621–88. The NPPA representative seemed to think that all uses of copyrighted works require payment, but that is not how copyright law works.

10. "Remedies and Procedures Regarding Orphan Works" roundtable transcript, 118.

11. Pamela Samuelson, "Enriching Discourse on Public Domains," *Duke Law Journal* 55, no. 4 (2006): 783–834.

12. Jessica Litman, *Digital Copyright* (New York: Prometheus Books, 2001), describing the intense partisan lobbying that shaped the 1976 Copyright Act.

13. Historically speaking, the absence of intellectual property persisted much longer than its presence. For studies on the creativity or innovation that persists in the absence of IP, see for example Elizabeth L. Rosenblatt, "Intellectual Property's Negative Space: Beyond the Utilitarian," *Florida State University Law Review* 40, no. 3 (2013): 441–86; Kate Darling and Aaron Perzanowski, *Creativity Without Law: Challenging the Assumptions of Intellectual Property* (New York: New York University Press, 2017); and Petra Mosher and Michela Giorcelli, "Copyrights and Creativity: Evidence from Italian Opera in the Napoleonic Age," *Journal of Political Economy* 128, no. 11 (2020).

14. See Darling and Perzanowski, *Creativity Without Law*. This does not mean that intellectual property has no effect on productivity or quality. But that effect is complex and contingent. See for example Mosher and Giorcelli, "Copyrights and Creativity." See also Jessica Silbey, *The Eureka Myth: Creators, Innovators, and Everyday Intellectual Property* (Stanford, Calif.: Stanford University Press, 2015).

15. Silbey, *Eureka Myth*.

16. John Locke, *Second Treatise of Government* (Indianapolis, Ind.: Hackett Publishing, 1980), chap. 5, para. 27.

17. Samuel Fleischacker, *A Short History of Distributive Justice* (Cambridge, Mass.: Harvard University Press, 2004), 4–7, describing this as Robert Nozick's position.

18. Fleischacker, *Short History of Distributive Justice*. See also John Rawls, *A Theory of Justice* (Cambridge, Mass.: Belknap Press, 1971).

19. Fleischacker, *Short History of Distributive Justice*. See also Rawls, *Theory of Justice*.

20. William W. Fisher, "The Implications for Law of User Innovation," *Minnesota Law Review* 94, no. 5 (2010): 1417–77; Heller, "Tragedy of the Anticommons"; James Boyle, *The Public Domain: Enclosing the Commons of the Mind* (New Haven, Conn.: Yale University Press, 2008).

21. See, e.g., Campbell v. Acuff-Rose Music, Inc., 510 U.S. 569, 579 (1994). "Although such transformative use is not absolutely necessary for a finding of fair use, . . . the goal of copyright, to promote science and the arts, is generally furthered by the creation of transformative works. Such works thus lie at the heart of the fair use doctrine's guarantee of breathing space within the confines of copyright, . . . and the more transformative the new work, the less will be the significance of other factors, like commercialism, that may weigh against a finding of fair use."

22. Mark A. Lemley, "IP in a World without Scarcity," *New York Law University Law Review* 90, no. 2 (2015): 460–515, argued that the internet puts pressure on intellectual property's justification for creating scarcity in intangible goods for the purpose of generating productive markets.

23. Peter Drahos, *A Philosophy of Intellectual Property* (New York: Ashgate Publishing, 1996); Robert P. Merges, *Justifying Intellectual Property* (Cambridge, Mass.:

Harvard University Press, 2011), 102. See also Madhavi Sunder, *From Goods to a Good Life: Intellectual Property and Global Justice* (New Haven, Conn.: Yale University Press, 2012), 7, 29–32.

24. Fleischacker, *Short History of Distributive Justice*, 5–10.

25. For recent studies on the apparent inverse relationship of IP's broadening scope to abundance and diversity of resources, see, e.g., Glynn S. Lunney Jr., "Copyright and the 1%," *Stanford Technology Law Review* 23, no. 1 (2020): 1–70, which described evidence in the video game industry. See also Gregory R. Day and W. Michael Schuster, "Patent Inequality," *Alabama Law Review* 71, no. 1 (2019): 115–63, describing evidence from patent portfolios and innovation.

26. Silbey, *Eureka Myth*, 274–85.

27. Barton Beebe, "Bleistein, The Problem of Aesthetic Progress, and the Making of American Copyright Law," *Columbia Law Review* 117, no. 2 (2007): 331–98, esp. 345–46. As for trademark law, federal trademark law is authorized under the commerce clause of the Constitution, not its IP clause. But it is also a form of intellectual property. And with trademarks, we behave as if more is also better: more differentiation, more source identification, more branding. But see Barton Beebe and Jeanne C. Fromer, "Are We Running Out of Trademarks: An Empirical Study of Trademark Depletion and Congestion," *Harvard Law Review* 131, no. 4 (2018): 945–1045.

28. Howard Gilman, *The Constitution Besieged: The Rise and Demise of Lochner Era Police Powers Jurisprudence* (Durham, N.C.: Duke University Press, 1993); Sidney Fine, *Laissez Faire and the General Welfare State* (Oxford: Oxford University Press, 1956).

29. Lochner v. New York, 198 U.S. 45 (1905).

30. *Lochner*, 198 U.S. 45. See also Gilman, *Constitution Besieged*.

31. See, e.g., Bleistein v. Donaldson Lithographic Co., 188 U.S. 239, 251 (1903) (holding that the market decides the aesthetic value of copyright).

32. *Bleistein*, 188 U.S. at 244 (defendant's argument preceding the opinion in the U.S. Reports, vol. 188, 1902, www.loc.gov/item/usrep188239).

33. *Bleistein*, 188 U.S. at 251.

34. *Bleistein*, 188 U.S. at 251.

35. Diamond v. Chakrabarty, 447 U.S. 303, 309 (1980).

36. See 15 U.S.C § 1052.

37. Fleischacker, *Short History of Distributive Justice*.

38. Peter Lee, "Toward a Distributive Agenda for U.S. Patent Law," *Houston Law Review* 55, no. 2 (2017): 321–77; Molly Van Houweling, "Distributive Values in Copyright," *Texas Law Review* 83, no. 6 (2004): 1535–79; Oren Bracha and Tahla Syed, "Beyond Efficiency: Consequence-Sensitive Theories of Copyright," *Berkeley Technology Law Journal* 29, no 1 (2014): 229–316, esp. 291.

39. Lee, "Toward a Distributive Agenda for U.S. Patent Law"; Van Houweling, "Distributive Values in Copyright"; Bracha and Syed, "Beyond Efficiency."

40. It is not at all clear whether exclusive rights or exemptions to exclusive rights promote diversity of means and output. See Carys J. Craig, "Technological Neutrality:

Recalibrating Copyright in the Information Age," *Theoretical Inquiries in Law* 17, no. 2 (2016): 601–32; Brad A. Greenberg, "Rethinking Technology Neutrality," *Minnesota Law Review* 100, no. 4 (2016): 1495–1562.

41. Balance is a problematic concept in intellectual property because it involves a public good that is scarce only artificially. Imagining IP rights on a scale conjures images of a finite amount of creativity and innovation that is or can be produced. That distorts the reality that everyday creators and innovators describe and justifies further scarcity or exclusivity, as I describe in chapter 5. For a critique of the idea of balance in IP, see Abraham Drassinower, *What's Wrong with Copying?* (Cambridge, Mass.: Harvard University Press, 2015), 47–50. To be sure, court cases and dominant treatises nonetheless embrace the idea of balance as a framework for optimizing IP regulation.

42. Primavera De Filippi and Samer Hassan, "Blockchain Technology as Regulatory Technology: From Code Is Law to Law Is Code," *First Monday* 21, no. 12 (2016), www.firstmonday.org/ojs/index.php/fm/article/view/7113/5657.

43. Jennifer M. Urban, Joe Karaganis, and Brianna L. Schofield, *Notice and Takedown in Everyday Practice*, Takedown Project report (Berkeley, Calif.: TakedownProject.org, 2016), www.illusionofmore.com/wp-content/uploads/2016/04/Berkeley_Columbia-on-512-takedown.pdf. See also Jennifer Urban, Joe Karaganis, and Brianna L. Schofield, "Notice and Takedown: Online Service Provider and Rightsholder Accounts of Everyday Practice," *Journal of the Copyright Society of the U.S.A.* 64 (Summer 2017): 371–411; Annemarie Bridy, "Copyright's Digital Deputies: DMCA-Plus Enforcement by Internet Intermediaries," in *Research Handbook on Electric Commerce Law*, ed. John A. Rothchild (Cheltenham, U.K.: Edward Elgar Publishing), 185–208; and Annemarie Bridy, "Notice and Takedown in the Domain Name System: ICANN's Ambivalent Drive into Online Content Regulation," *Washington and Lee Law Review* 74, no. 3 (2017): 1345–86.

44. On walled gardens and their pros and cons, see Greg Lastowka, "Walled Gardens and the Stationers' Company 2.0," working paper, *Revista de Internet, Derecho y Política*, Jan. 21, 2013; Salil Mehra, "Paradise Is a Walled Garden? Trust, Antitrust, and User Dynamism," *George Mason Law Review* 18, no. 4 (2011): 889–952; and Rob Frieden, "The Internet of Platforms and Two-Sided Markets: Implications for Competition and Consumers," *Villanova Law Review* 63, no. 2 (2018): 269–320.

45. For a detailed description of interviews and methodology, see Appendix A (Research Methods).

46. On the importance of preserving "play" as a matter of creativity, privacy, and self-determination, see Julie E. Cohen, *Configuring the Networked Self: Law, Code, and the Play of Everyday Practice* (New Haven, Conn.: Yale University Press, 2011).

47. Bracha and Syed, *Beyond Efficiency*, 251, defined autonomy as a state of having "reflectively adopted, chosen, and refined by [oneself], determining [one's] projects and preferences free from both coercion and manipulation."

48. Tim Wu, "Tolerated Use," *Columbia Journal of Law and the Arts* 31 (2007): 617–35.

49. Mark Lemley, "The Myth of the Sole Inventor," *Michigan Law Review* 110, no. 5 (2012): 709–60.

50. Independent creation is a defense in copyright infringement lawsuits but is hard to prove, leaving the second creator in a risky position. For a discussion of independent creation defense, Julie E. Cohen et al., *Copyright in the Global Information Economy*, 5th ed. (New York: Wolters Kluwer, 2020), 265–72. Simultaneous invention is no defense in patent law and is nonetheless quite common and creates lamentable inefficiencies. Mark Lemley, "The Myth of the Sole Inventor," *Michigan Law Review* 110, no. 5 (2012): 709–60.

51. Bracha and Syed, *Beyond Efficiency*, 256. ("A just and attractive society, in turn, is one that fosters the social conditions conducive to flourishing lives, and equitably provides opportunities for all its members to realize their human capacities.")

52. Trademark law allows for non-confusing use of another's trademark when co-branding or engaging in comparative advertising. For a discussion of the range of trademark law concerns in light of brand extension, see Mark McKenna, "Testing Modern Trademark Law's Theory of Harm," *Iowa Law Review* 95 (2009–2010): 63–117.

53. Peter Decherney, "Not Too Late for a Lawsuit against Led Zeppelin's 'Stairway to Heaven,'" *Forbes*, May 21, 2014.

54. Decherney, "Not Too Late."

55. Copyright law in particular permits unauthorized copying when the secondary use is "transformative," implying a new message, a new meaning, and a new audience for the work. *Campbell v. Acuff-Rose Music*, 510 U.S. 569, 579. See also Pamela Samuelson, "Justifications for Copyright Limitation and Exceptions," in *Copyright Laws in the Age of Limitations and Exceptions*, ed. Ruth L. Okediji (New York: Cambridge University Press, 2017), 12–59, esp. 25–26. Trademark law also permits unauthorized copying when the use is expressive or descriptive and does not confuse consumers. See William McGeveran, "Four Free Speech Goals for Trademark Law," 18 *Fordham Intellectual Property Media and Entertainment Law Journal* 18, no. 5 (2008): 1205–27.

56. For examples of such complaints, see Walt Hickey, "The Long History of Musicians Telling Republicans to Stop Playing Their Music," *FiveThirtyEight*, June 17, 2015; Bill Chappell, "Neil Young Is Displeased That Donald Trump Was "Rockin' in the Free World," NPR, June 17, 2015; Ryan Gajewski, "R.E.M. Slams Donald Trump for Using Their Song in 'Moronic Charade of a Campaign,'" *Hollywood Reporter*, Sept. 9, 2015; and David Robb, "BMI Warns Donald Trump Campaign to Stop Playing Rolling Stones' 'You Can't Always Get What You Want' at Rallies—Update," Deadline.com, June 27, 2020. For legal analysis of these complaints, see Cathay Smith, "Political Fair Use," *William and Mary Law Review* 62, no. 6 (2021): 2003–74.

57. Brett M. Frischmann, Michael J. Madison, and Katherine J. Strandburg, eds., *Governing Knowledge Commons* (New York: Oxford University Press, 2014).

58. For a discussion of the intersection of First Amendment prohibitions of regulation of speech with professional self-regulation of speech, see, e.g., Claudia Haupt, "Professional Speech," *Yale Law Journal* 125, no. 5 (2016): 1238–1303.

59. Mark A. Lemley and A. Douglas Melamed, "Missing the Forest for the Trolls," *Columbia Law Review* 113, no. 8 (2013): 2117–89.

60. Joe Mullin, "It's Finally Over: Mastermind behind Prenda Law Porn Trolls Pleads Guilty," *Ars Technica*, Mar. 6, 2017; Joe Mullin, "Prenda Law 'Copyright Trolls' Steel and Hansmeier Arrested: Lawyers Who Turned Porn Lawsuits into Big Business Now Face Criminal Charges," *Ars Technica*, Dec. 16, 2016.

61. Colleen V. Chien, "Of Trolls, Davids, Goliaths, and Kings: Narratives and Evidence in the Litigation of High-Tech Patents," *University of North Carolina Law Review* 87, no. 5 (2009): 1571–1615.

62. See Silbey, *Eureka Myth*, 81–147, describing how everyday creators and innovators make do with misaligned intellectual property rules.

63. Stewart Macaulay, Lawrence M. Friedman, and Elizabeth Mertz. eds., *Law in Action: A Socio-Legal Reader* (Mineola, N.Y.: Foundation Press, 2007), 1–6. See also Jean-Louis Halperin, "Law in Books and Law in Action: The Problem of Legal Change," *Maine Law Review* 64, no. 1 (2011): 45–76, describing a theory of legal change through the history of the sociolegal movement from Roscoe Pound in 1910 to the present.

64. See Alan Miller and Ronen Perry, "The Reasonable Person," *New York University Law Review* 87, no. 2 (2012): 323–92, esp. 304–5. Strict liability and the possibility of excessive damages in both copyright and patent law belie any possibility of reasonableness inquiries. Good faith or attribution counts for very little. This is not as true with trademark law, where intent in infringement analysis is one factor among many. See, e.g., 17 U.S.C. § 504(c) (2012), which provided for a range of damages between $200 and $150,000 per infringing copyrighted work.

65. William Robin, "They're Always Borrowing His Stuff," *New York Times*, Feb. 6, 2015.

66. Robin, "They're Always Borrowing His Stuff."

67. Robin, "They're Always Borrowing His Stuff."

68. Robin, "They're Always Borrowing His Stuff."

69. Robin, "They're Always Borrowing His Stuff."

70. Robin, "They're Always Borrowing His Stuff."

71. Robin, "They're Always Borrowing His Stuff."

72. Robin, "They're Always Borrowing His Stuff."

73. "Randy California: Five Fast Facts You Need to Know," *Heavy*, May 20, 2014, www.heavy.com/news/2014/05/randy-california-led-zeplin-spirit-taurus-lawsuit.

74. "Led Zeppelin Told They Can Settle Stairway Lawsuit for $1—and Writing Credit," *The Guardian*, Apr. 27, 2016, www.theguardian.com/music/2016/apr/27/led-zeppelin-told-settle-stairway-heaven-lawsuit-1-dollar-writing-credit.

75. Ben Sisario, "Led Zeppelin Wins Long 'Stairway to Heaven' Copyright Case," *New York Times*, Oct. 5, 2020.

76. Adam Messinger, "Introducing the Innovator's Patent Agreement," Apr. 17, 2012, https://blog.twitter.com/official/en_us/a/2012/introducing-the-innovator-s-patent-agreement.html.

77. Messinger, "Introducing the Innovator's Patent Agreement."

78. Messinger, "Introducing the Innovator's Patent Agreement."

79. Messinger, "Introducing the Innovator's Patent Agreement."

80. Twitter, Innovators Patent Agreement FAQ, undated, accessed Dec. 15, 2020, www.xscode.com/twitter/innovators-patent-agreement.

81. James Bessen and Michael J. Meurer, *Patent Failure: How Judges, Bureaucrats, and Lawyers Put Innovators at Risk* (Princeton, N.J.: Princeton University Press, 2009); Carl Shapiro, "Navigating the Patent Thicket: Cross Licenses, Patent Pools, and Standard Setting," in *Innovation Policy and the Economy*, vol. 1, ed. Adam B. Jaffe, Josh Lerner, and Scott Stern (Cambridge, Mass.: MIT Press, 2001): 119–50; Dan L. Burk and Mark A. Lemley, "Policy Levers in Patent Law," *Virginia Law Review* 89 (2003): 1575–1696.

82. Tolulope Edionwe, "Tech Companies Are Hoarding Patents But They Should Be Donating Them," *The Outline*, Mar. 7, 2017, www.theoutline.com/post/1198/tech-companies-are-hoarding-patents-but-they-should-be-donating-them?zd=2&z-i=nklest4z.

83. Eduardo Porter, "Patent Trolls Recede as Threat to Innovation: Will Justices Change That?," *New York Times*, Nov. 21, 2017; Robert Gebelhoff, "Patent Trolls: A Primer," *Washington Post*, Nov. 16, 2015; "A Question of Utility," *The Economist*, Aug. 8, 2015; Adam Liptak, "Supreme Court Ruling Could Hinder 'Patent Trolls,'" *New York Times*, May 22, 2017; Robin Feldman, "Slowing the Patent Trolls," *New York Times*, Mar. 28, 2014.

84. Tesla, "Patent Pledge," June 12, 2014, www.tesla.com/about/legal#patent-pledge.

85. Tesla, "Patent Pledge."

86. Tesla, "Patent Pledge."

87. Defensive Patent License (DPL) website, www.defensivepatentlicense.org.

88. DPL website.

89. DPL website.

90. DPL website.

91. DPL website.

92. LOT Network website, 2020, www.lotnet.com.

93. Daniel Nazer, "Stupid Patent of the Month: IBM Patents Out-of-Office Email," Electronic Freedom Foundation (EFF), Feb. 28, 2017, www.eff.org/deeplinks/2017/02/stupid-patent-month-ibm-patents-out-office-email; Iain Thomson, "Congratulations IBM for 'Invention' Out-of-Office Email. You Win Stupid Patent of the Month," *The Register* (UK), Mar. 1, 2017, www.theregister.co.uk/2017/03/01/ibm_out_of_office_email/; Jeff John Roberts, "IBM Gives Up 'Stupid' Patent for Out-of-Office Email," *Fortune*, Mar. 3, 2017.

Chapter 5

1. See Grand Upright Music Ltd. v. Warner Bros. Records, Inc., 780 F. Supp. 182, 183 (S.D.N.Y. 1991). The first sentence of this decision about music copyright and music sampling is "Thou shalt not steal."

2. See Colleen V. Chien, "Of Trolls, Davids, Goliaths, and Kings: Narratives and Evidence in the Litigation of High-Tech Patents," *North Carolina Law Review* 87, no. 5 (2009): 1571–1615, esp. 1576. "This Article puts these concerns into context by identifying the major stories of patent litigation and then matching actual suits, based on party profile, to these stories."

3. See Wendy J. Gordon, "The Concept of 'Harm' in Copyright," in *Intellectual Property and the Common Law*, ed. Shyamkrishna Balganesh (New York: Cambridge University Press, 2013), 452–83, esp. 462–63 (describing these injuries).

4. For a well-cited example of evading infringement liability because of lack of volition, see Cartoon Network, LP v. CSC Holdings, Inc., 536 F.3d 121, 131–33 (2nd Cir. 2008), which rejected liability for a cable company's direct infringement because the copying was done at the direction of users, who were not sued. See also Mala Chatterjee and Jeanne C. Fromer, "Minds, Machines, and the Law: The Case of Volition in Copyright Law," *Columbia Law Review* 119, no. 7 (2019): 1887–1916.

5. See Rochelle Cooper Dreyfuss, "Expressive Genericity: Trademarks as Language in the Pepsi Generation," *Notre Dame Law Review* 65, no. 3 (1990): 397–424, esp. 407, which explained how courts are so busy thinking about parties that they do not consider the public interest that parties—usually defendants—represent. For patterned stories in IP litigation, see Chien, "Of Trolls, Davids, Goliaths, and Kings," 1577. "While each patent dispute is unique, most fit the profile of one of a limited number of patent litigation stories."

6. The previous three chapters described the fundamental values grounding intellectual property discourse as values rooted in the person, although they are by necessity also relational and structural. Equality is by its nature comparative. Privacy requires accepting societal trade-offs of nondisclosure and isolation for self-determination and autonomy. And distributive justice requires attention to dispersal and management of community resources.

7. For an early discussion of the Digital Age problems of networked communications and intellectual property law, see Alfred C. Yen, "Internet Service Provider Liability for Subscriber Copyright Infringement, Enterprise Liability, and the First Amendment," *Georgetown Law Journal* 88 (2000): 1–56. For a more recent article, see Annemarie Bridy, "Is Online Copyright Enforcement Scalable?," *Vanderbilt Journal of Entertainment and Technology Law* 13, no. 4 (2011): 695–737.

8. For discussions of complexities of injunctive relief after the Supreme Court's decision in eBay Inc. v. MercExchange, L.L.C., 547 U.S. 388, 394 (2006), in which the court held that injunction does not necessarily follow from a finding of infringement, see Peter J. Karol, "Trademark's eBay Problem," *Fordham Intellectual Property Media and Entertainment Law Journal* 26, no. 3 (2016): 627–88, esp. 636–37; and Christopher B. Seaman, "Permanent Injunctions in Patent Litigation after eBay: An Empirical Study," *Iowa Law Review* 101, no. 5 (2008): 1949–2019, esp. 1968–74. See also Annemarie Bridy, "Why Pirates (Still) Won't Behave: Regulating P2P in the Decade after Napster," *Rutgers Law Journal* 40, no. 3 (2009): 565–611, esp. 583, which discussed usage of preliminary injunctions to regulate peer-to-peer networks.

9. Sharryn Kasmir, "Precarity," in *The Cambridge Encyclopedia of Anthropology*, 2018, www.anthroencyclopedia.com/entry/precarity. "Precarity is a multi-stranded concept, associated with a set of terms, including precarious, precariousness, precaritization, and 'the precariat', that make an historical argument about capitalism, pronounce a shift in class relations, and predict novel social movements and political struggles." See also Isabell Lorey, *State of Insecurity: Government of the Precarious*, trans. Aileen Derieg (London: Verso, 2015), 10–12, which described precarity as a condition of human existence; Brett Neilson and Ned Rossiter, "Precarity as a Political Concept, or, Fordism as Exception," *Theory, Culture, and Society* 25, nos. 7–8 (2008): 51–72, esp. 54 ("To understand precarity as a political concept we must revisit the whole Fordist episode, its modes of labour organization, welfare support, technological innovation and political contestation."); and Guy Standing, "The Precariat: From Denizens to Citizens?," *Polity* 44, no. 4 (2012): 588–608, esp. 591 ("In sum, those in the precariat have precarious jobs, without a sense of occupational identity or career in front of them, they have no social memory on which to draw, no shadow of the future hanging over their relationships, and have a limited and precarious range of right.").

10. Charles Masquelier, "Bourdieu, Foucault, and the Politics of Precarity," *Distinktion: Journal of Social Theory* 20, no. 2 (2018): 135–55.

11. See Masquelier, "Bourdieu," 138, 140, quoting Lorey, *State of Insecurity*, discussing precarity in Foucauldian terms.

12. Neilson and Rossiter, "Precarity as a Political Concept," 59 (citation omitted), noting the internet's extension of intellectual property regimes, such as copyright in cultural industries, patents in technological industries, and trademarks in advertising, despite the internet playing an especially large role in the new levels of precarity.

13. Julie E. Cohen, *Between Truth and Power: The Legal Constructions of Informational Capitalism* (Oxford: Oxford University Press, 2019).

14. Neilson and Rossiter, "Precarity as a Political Concept," 59, explaining how "antagonism" between creators and controllers of intellectual property "moves around a property relation."

15. Compare Mark Rose, "The Public Sphere and the Emergence of Copyright: *Areopagitica*, the Stationers' Company, and the Statute of Anne," *Tulane Journal of Technology and Intellectual Property* 12, no. 1 (2009): 123–44, esp. 132 (which explored the emergence of copyright law within the Habermasian public sphere in the 1600s and 1700s) with Lewis Hyde, *Common as Air: Revolution, Art, and Ownership* (New York: Farrar, Straus and Giroux, 2010), 13–14 (describing cultural commons of the twentieth and twenty-first centuries and rendering the common assets visible for appropriate public stewardship).

16. See Lorey, *State of Insecurity*, 64–65, which explored how the state can utilize precarity as a "normalized mode of governing."

17. Hyde, *Common as Air*, 12. "The West [has] entered a period of unabashed market triumphalism, during which many things long assumed to be public or common . . . were removed from the public sphere and made subject to the exclusive rights of private ownership."

18. See Patricia Ewick and Susan S. Silbey, "Subversive Stories and Hegemonic Tales: Toward a Sociology of Narrative," *Law and Society Review* 29, no. 2 (1995): 197–226, esp. 217–19, which explored how subversive narratives undermine hegemonic narratives, producing opportunities for resistance to social and political structures.

19. See Barton Beebe, "Bleistein, The Problem of Aesthetic Progress, and the Making of American Copyright Law," *Columbia Law Review* 117, no. 2 (2017): 319–98, esp. 331–30, which critiqued copyright doctrine originating from *Bleistein v. Donaldson* (1903) and its measurement of "aesthetic progress" as commercial success. See also Jessica Silbey, *The Eureka Myth: Creators, Innovators, and Everyday Intellectual Property* (Stanford, Calif.: Stanford University Press, 2015), 68–69. "Although the law grants creators and innovators the rights to *intangibles* (i.e., intellectual property), in the context of my interviews, the overwhelming focus of pleasure and drive concerns *tangible* work output, physical skills, and personal connection to the work (and to appreciative audiences)."

20. Shoshana Zuboff, *The Age of Surveillance Capitalism: The Fight for a Human Future at the New Frontier of Power* (New York: Hachette, 2019), 7. "[Many older] visionary projects imagined a digital future that empowers individuals to lead more-effective lives. Today [the] rights to privacy, knowledge, and application have been usurped by a bold market venture powered by unilateral claims to others' experience and the knowledge that flows from it."

21. See Wendy J. Gordon, "Of Harms and Benefits: Torts, Restitution, and Intellectual Property," *Journal of Legal Studies* 21, no. 2 (1992): 449–82 (exploring four ways creators suffer harm in market context).

22. See Gordon, "Of Harms and Benefits," 468, which investigated the nature of interdependence of copyrighted goods and the problem of requirement payment for all benefits reaped as destroying "the synergy on which culture and commerce both rest." See also Wendy J. Gordon, "Harmless Use: Gleaning from Fields of Copyrighted Works," *Fordham Law Review* 77, no. 5 (2009): 2411–35, which explored the reciprocity inherent in the authorial role as a basis for discerning harmless uses from those for which there should be compensation.

23. See generally Max Weber, "Politics as a Vocation (Address at Munich University 1918)," in *From Max Weber: Essays in Sociology*, ed. and trans. H. Gerth and C. Wright Mills (New York: Routledge, 1998), 77–128, arguing that the state has the exclusive right to legitimate uses of force to prevent further violence.

24. The full context of the statement is: "And you know, [large, unnamed new business partner is] famous for just squeezing people until they scream, until they die."

25. Marc Galanter, "Why the 'Haves' Come Out Ahead: Speculations on the Limits of Legal Change," *Law and Society Review* 9, no. 1 (1974): 95–160.

26. These complaints resemble those from the NPPA representative whose account began Chapter 4 criticizing the "monetization of content" by companies like Google.

27. Studies of IP within particular industries suggest that the benefits of IP are not rationally distributed among innovators and creators. See Glynn S. Lunney Jr., "Copyright and the 1%," *Stanford Technology Law Review* 23, no. 1 (2020): 1–70, which

described evidence in the video game industry. See also Gregory Day and W. Michael Schuster, "Patent Inequality," *Alabama Law Review* 71 (2019): 115–63, which described evidence from patent portfolios and innovation.

28. Some recent quantitative empirical work confirms the sense of outsized winners in the IP industry. See Barton Beebe and Jeanne C. Fromer, "Are We Running Out of Trademarks? An Empirical Study of Trademark Depletion and Congestion," *Harvard Law Review* 131, no. 4 (2018): 945–1045, which described advantages to incumbent trademark applications where "incumbents have already established their rights in increasingly depleted spaces." See also Lunney Jr., "Copyright and the 1%"; Day and Schuster, "Patent Inequality."

29. If municipalities want to move sculptures in the future or make other changes that might affect the art's presentation, the artist's permission might be required under the VARA. Having artists waive VARA rights gives municipalities maximum freedom over the public space they manage. For disputes over these issues, see, e.g., Kelly v. Chicago Park District, 635 F.3d 290 (7th Cir. 2011) and Phillips v. Pembroke Real Estate, Inc., 459 F.3d 128 (1st Cir. 2006).

30. Silbey, *Eureka Myth*, chapter 3, "Making Do with a Misfit," esp. 81.

31. He was talking about the Supreme Court case *Merck KGaA v. Integra Lifesciences I, Ltd.*, 545 U.S. 193 (2005), which held that the use of patented compounds in preclinical studies is insulated from infringement liability under 35 U.S.C. §271(e) (1) as long as there is a reasonable basis to believe that the compound tested could be the subject of an FDA submission and the experiments will produce the types of information relevant to an IND or an NDA. Dan filed a brief in the case for the contrary result, objecting to the use of such patented compounds without authorization as "stealing."

32. Gordon, "Harmless Use"; Gordon, "Concept of 'Harm' in Copyright," 462–63; Gordon, "Of Harms and Benefits."

33. Jessica Silbey, "Mythical Beginnings of Intellectual Property," *George Mason Law Review* 15, no. 2 (2008): 319–79.

34. Oliver Wendell Holmes Jr., "The Path of Law," *Harvard Law Review* 10 (1897): 457–78.

35. Carrick Mollenkamp et al., *The People vs. Big Tobacco: How the States Took on the Cigarette Giants* (Princeton, N.J.: Bloomberg Press, 1998); Michael Lewis, *The Big Short: Inside the Doomsday Machines* (New York: W. W. Norton, 2010); Bethany McLean and Peter Elkind, *The Smartest Guys in the Room: The Amazing Rise and Scandalous Fall of Enron* (New York: Penguin, 2003). See also Tanina Rostain and Milton Regan, *Confident Games: Lawyers, Accountants, and the Tax Shelter Industry* (Cambridge, Mass.: MIT Press, 2014).

36. The Consumer Finance Protection Bureau (CFPB) is a U.S. government agency authorized by the Dodd-Frank Wall Street Reform and Consumer Protection Act in 2010 in response to the financial crisis of 2007. Dodd-Frank Wall Street Reform and Consumer Protection Act, 12 U.S.C. § 5514 (defining the scope of the CFPB's supervisory and enforcement powers). The Family Smoking Prevention and Tobacco Control

Act (TCA), passed in 2009, gave the FDA authority to regulate the manufacturing, distribution, and marketing of tobacco products to protect the public health. See 21 U.S.C. § 387(a) (2009) (federal authority over tobacco products).

37. Of course, entire academic disciplines are devoted to studying social, economic, and political structures that are less obvious or visible than individual people and institutions, like companies or government. This would be true of sociology, anthropology, and certain fields of political science and economics, to name a few disciplines that interrogate structures and social organization as sources for explanation of collective human behavior and variable phenomena.

38. Russell Hardin, "The Utilitarian Logic of Liberalism," *Ethics* 97, no. 1 (1986): 47–74; Michael Weiler, "The Rhetoric of Neo-Liberalism," *Quarterly Journal of Speech* 70, no. 4 (1984): 362–78. See also Zuboff, *Age of Surveillance Capitalism*, 18.

39. See C. B. MacPherson, *The Political Theory of Possessive Individualism: From Hobbes to Locke* (Oxford: Clarendon Press, 1962).

40. Despite the beneficent spread of pluralism and moral heterogeneity, both may in fact fuel isolation and righteous individualism by undermining cultural solidarity and social interdependence often based on a moral consensus.

41. Under U.S. copyright law, an employer is the author of a work made by an employee within the scope of their employment. See 17 U.S.C. § 201(b) (2018) ("In the case of a work made for hire, the employer or other person for whom the work was prepared is considered the author for purposes of this title . . .").

42. See Chien, "Of Trolls, Davids, Goliaths, and Kings," 1596, which defined nonpracticing entity or "patent assertion entity" as entities that use patents primarily to obtain license fees rather than to support the development or transfer of technology.

43. See generally C. B. MacPherson, *The Political Theory of Possessive Individualism: From Hobbes to Locke* (Oxford: Clarendon Press, 1962), which explored ideas about ownership in terms of the concept of "possessive individualism"; and Silbey, "Mythical Beginnings of Intellectual Property," which described intellectual property doctrine's mythology of the individual and the ideology of individualism as the central beneficiary of and justification for rights.

44. 17 U.S.C. § 107 (2018) ("The fair use of a copyrighted work . . . for purposes such as criticism, comment, news reporting, teaching (including multiple copies for classroom use), scholarship, or research, is not an infringement of copyright."); 17 U.S.C. § 109(a) ("The owner of a particular copy or phonorecord lawfully made under this title, or any person authorized by such owner, is entitled, without the authority of the copyright owner, to sell or otherwise dispose of the possession of that copy or phonorecord.").

45. See discussion of First Amendment contradictions in Chapter 4.

46. The notion of "ordered liberty" originates in Palko v. Connecticut, 302 U.S. 319, 324–25 (1937) and concerns limitations on freedom by the need for order in society. The concept of "ordered liberty" was one of the first standards by which provisions of the Bill of Rights were applied against the states through the Due Process Clause of the Fourteenth Amendment.

47. Metro-Goldwyn-Mayer Studios, Inc., v. Grokster, Ltd., 545 U.S. 913 (2005).
48. *Grokster*, 545 U.S. at 920.
49. Sony Corp. of America v. Universal City Studios, Inc., 464 U.S. 417 (1984).
50. *Grokster*, 545 U.S. at 933.
51. *Grokster*, 545 U.S. at 937.
52. *Grokster*, 545 U.S. at 937.
53. *Grokster*, 545 U.S. at 928.
54. *Grokster*, 545 U.S. at 928.
55. *Grokster*, 545 U.S. at 928.
56. Rebecca Giblin, "Physical World Assumptions and Software World Realities (and Why There are More P2P Software Providers than Ever Before)," *Columbia Journal of Law and the Arts* 35, no. 1 (2012): 57–118; Bridy, "Why Pirates (Still) Won't Behave."
57. See, e.g., Peter S. Menell, "Indirect Copyright Liability and Technological Innovation," *Columbia Journal of Law and the Arts* 32 (2009): 375–99.
58. This is what social scientists do as a matter of their discipline and professional research practices. For canonical case studies, see, e.g., Robert C. Ellickson, *Order Without Law: How Neighbors Settle Disputes* (Cambridge, Mass.: Harvard University Press, 1991); and Elinor Ostrom, *Governing the Commons: The Evolution of Institutions for Collective Action* (Cambridge: Cambridge University Press, 1990).
59. The norm literature in IP is rich and growing. A few examples include Emmanuelle Fauchart and Eric von Hippel, "Norms-Based Intellectual Property Systems: The Case of French Chefs," *Organizational Science*, 19, no. 2 (2008): 187–201; David Fagundes, "Talk Derby To Me: Intellectual Property Norms Governing Roller Derby Pseudonyms," *Texas Law Review* 90, no. 5 (2011): 1093–1152; Aaron Perzanowski, "Tattoos and IP Norms," *Minnesota Law Review* 98, no. 2 (2013): 511–90; and Stephanie Plamondon Bair and Laura G. Pedraza-Farina, *Anti-Innovation Norms*, Northwestern University Law Review 112, no. 5 (2018): 1069–1136. See also Silbey, *Eureka Myth*.
60. See Silbey, *Eureka Myth*; Kate Darling and Aaron Perzanowski, *Creativity Without Law: Challenging the Assumptions of Intellectual Property* (New York: New York University Press, 2017); Kembrew McLeod and Peter DiCola, *Creative Licenses: The Law and Culture of Digital Sampling* (Chapel Hill, North Carolina: Duke University Press, 2011).

Conclusion

1. Fulton v. City of Philadelphia, No. 19-123, 593 U.S. __ (2021), decided June 17, 2021.
2. Texas v. California, No. 19-1019 and California v. Texas, No. 19-840, 593 U.S. __ (2021), decided June 17, 2021.
3. Bostock v. Clayton County, 140 S. Ct. 173 (2020) (extending the federal ban on discrimination "based on sex" to gay, lesbian and transgender employees); Department of Homeland Security v. Regents of the University of California, 140 S. Ct. 1891 (2020) (holding that Trump administration's rescission of Deferred Action

for Childhood Arrivals (DACA) was "arbitrary and capricious" and reversing the order); Trump v. New York, No. 20-366, argued November 30, 2020 (considering the constitutionality of Trump administration's order to the secretary of commerce to exclude noncitizens from the base population number for purposes of apportioning seats in the House of Representatives as part of the 2020 Census).

4. Georgia v. Public.Resources.Org, 140 S. Ct. 1498 (2020).

5. Google v. Oracle, No. 18-956, 141 S.Ct. 1183, decided April 5, 2021. mLex, a news division of Lexis Nexis, reported on the Google v. Oracle litigation using the title "Googacle" starting in June 2016; see https://mlexmarketinsight.com/insights-center/reports/Googacle. This follows from reporting and conversations on Twitter linked by the #Googacle hashtag, which was made popular by journalist Sarah Jeong. Jeong covered the Google v. Oracle district court trial tried by Judge William Alsup in the Northern District of California in May 2016 for Motherboard Vice. Jeong now writes for *The New York Times*. See @sarahjeong on Twitter.

6. U.S. v. Arthrex, No. 19-1434 (2020), 594 U.S. __ (2021), decided on June 21, 2021.

7. Aaron Perzanowski and Jason Schultz, *The End of Ownership: Personal Property in the Digital Economy* (Cambridge, Mass.: MIT Press, 2016).

8. See, e.g., Tarleton Gillespie, *Custodians of the Internet: Platforms, Content Moderation, and the Hidden Decisions that Shape Social Media* (Yale University Press 2018). See also Michael Goodyear, "Is There No Way to the Truth? Copyright Liability as a Model for Restricting Fake News," *Harvard Journal of Law and Technology* 34 (2020); Ben Wagner, "Digital Election Observation: Regulatory Challenges around Legal Online Content," *The Political Quarterly*, October 16, 2020; Joan Donovan et al., "A Blueprint for Documenting and Debunking Misinformation Campaigns," *Neiman Reports*, October 20, 2020; Matthew Ingram, "Facebook's belated, vague, unhelpful election idea," *Columbia Journalism Review*, September 4, 2020; Claire Wardle, "What Role Should Newsrooms Play in Debunking COVID-19 Misinformation," *Neiman Reports*, April 8, 2020.

9. See, e.g., Marianna Mazzucato, "Capitalism Is Broken. The Fix Begins with a Free Covid-19 Vaccine," *New York Times*, October 8, 2020; Ana Santos Rutschman, "The Covid-19 Vaccine Race: Intellectual Property, Collaboration(s), Nationalism, and Misinformation," *Washington University Journal of Law and Policy* 64 (2020).

10. "The animating principle behind this rule [that judges or legislators cannot be copyright authors of the law] is that no one can own the law. Every citizen is presumed to know the law and it needs no argument to show . . . that all should." Georgia v. Public.Resource.Org, Inc., Slip Opinion at pp. 7–8.

11. Describing the "rapidly changing technological, economic, and business-related circumstances" of the computer industry as factors in its decision. Google v. Oracle, Slip. Opinion at 15.

12. Explaining the background of the decision as a theory of executive power and democracy and as based on the circumstances that "Today, thousands of officers wield executive power on behalf of the President in the name of the United States. That power acquires its legitimacy and accountability to the public through 'a clear

and effective chain of command' down from the President, on whom all the people vote." US. v. Arthrex, Slip Opinion at 7.

13. We can think of shared resources in terms of the importance of infrastructure and a protected or managed commons, as many have in the law and technology field (see, e.g., Brett Frischmann, *Infrastructure: The Social Value of Shared Resources* (New York: Oxford University Press, 2012), and also about nature and definition of those resources, be it information, equality, or privacy that must be communally maintained and mutually respected for all to enjoy their benefits.

14. I am grateful to anonymous reviewers for developing my thoughts in this paragraph and throughout this conclusion.

15. I am grateful to Evan Selinger for this insight as he describes it in terms of privacy law and technology. See Evan Selinger, "Why Technologies Fail to Think of Moderation as a Virtue and Other Stories about AI," *Los Angeles Review of Books*, October 14, 2019.

16. Kinley Brauer, "Manifest Destiny Revisited," *Diplomatic History* 23 (1999): 379–84.

Appendix A

1. See Jan E. Trost, "Statistically Nonrepresentative Stratified Sampling: A Sampling Technique for Qualitative Studies," *Qualitative Sociology* 9 (1986): 54–57.

2. I am grateful for help I received in 2018–2019 with the topic modeling from Northeastern University graduate student Jeffrey Sternberg. For a description of LDA and digital humanities approaches generally, see David Blei, "Topic Modeling and Digital Humanities," *Journal of Digital Humanities* 2 (2012), available at http://journalof-digitalhumanities.org/2-1/topic-modeling-and-digital-humanities-by-david-m-blei/.

3. Pamela Stone, *Opting Out: Why Women Really Quit Careers and Head Home* (Berkeley, Calif.: University of California Press, 2007), 243, 248.

4. Jack Katz, "Ethnography's Warrants," *Sociological Methods and Research* 25 (1997): 391–423, 392.

5. Mario Luis Small, "How Many Cases Do I Need?" *Ethnography* 10 (2009): 5–38. In contrast to quantitative methods, interview research does not use a random sample, nor does it provide a measure of the frequency that variations appear.

6. See Small, "How Many Cases Do I Need?" 25–28 (explaining the concept of saturation).

7. See, e.g., Grant Scott, *The Essential Student Guide to Professional Photography* (Burlington, Mass.: Focal Press, 2016), 90–126.

8. Jessica Silbey, Eva Subotnik, and Peter DiCola, "Existential Copyright and Professional Photography," *Notre Dame Law Review* 95 (2019): 263–326; Jessica Silbey, "Justifying Copyright in the Age of Digital Reproduction: The Case of Photographers," *University of California Irvine Law Review* 9 (2019): 405–54; Jessica Silbey, "Control Over Contemporary Photography: A Tangle of Copyright, Right of Publicity, and the First Amendment," *Columbia Journal of Law and the Arts* 42 (2019): 351–64.

9. Our first paper reporting on the designer interviews is forthcoming. See Mark McKenna and Jessica Silbey, "Investigating Design" (forthcoming 2022) (draft on file with author).

10. For a discussion of intercoder reliability, see Joseph A. Maxwell, "Understanding and Validity in Qualitative Research," *Harvard Educational Review* 62 (1992): 279–300, 287–91.

11. Matthew Miles and A. Michael Huberman, *Qualitative Data Analysis* (Thousand Oaks, Calif.: SAGE, 1994), 245–85.

12. See Jessica Silbey, *The Eureka Myth: Creators Innovators and Everyday Intellectual Property* (Stanford, Calif.: Stanford University Press: 2015), 287–95. My deepest gratitude to Todd Thurhemier for his dedication to the research project and for his skills as a computer scientist, musician, and lawyer.

13. Stone, *Opting Out,* 254n3.

Appendix B

1. For more information about this data set and its collection, stratification, and coding methods, see Jessica Silbey, *The Eureka Myth: Creators, Innovators, and Everyday Intellectual Property* (Stanford, Calif.: Stanford University Press: 2015), 287–95.

Bibliography

Abbott, Andrew. *The System of Professions: An Essay on the Division of Expert Labor*. Chicago: University of Chicago Press, 1988.

Adler, Amy. "Fair Use and the Future of Art." *New York University Law Review* 91 (2016): 559–98.

Adler, Amy, and Jeanne Fromer. "Taking Intellectual Property into Their Own Hands." *California Law Review* 107 (2019): 1455–1530.

Allen, Anita. *Unpopular Privacy: What Must We Hide?* New York: Oxford University Press, 2011.

Amar, Akhil Reed. *America's Constitution: A Biography*. New York: Random House, 2005.

Anderson, Elizabeth. "What is the Point of Equality?" *Ethics* 109 (1999): 287–337.

Andrews, Lori B. "The 'Progress Clause': An Empirical Analysis Based on The Constitutional Foundation of Patent Law." *North Carolina Journal of Law and Technology* 15 (2014): 537–96.

Ang, Tom. *Photography: The Definitive Visual History*. London: DK Publishing, 2014.

Arthurs, John. "Acquisition and Harm." *Canadian Journal of Philosophy* 17 (1989): 337–47.

Azoulay, Ariella. *The Civil Contract of Photography*. Translated by Rela Mazali and Ruvik Danieli. New York: Zone Books, 2008.

Badger, Gerry. *The Genius of Photography: How Photography Has Changed Our Lives*. London: Quadrille Publishing, 2007.

Bair, Stephanie Plamondon. "Rational Faith: The Utility of Fairness in Copyright." *Boston University Law Review* 97 (2017): 1487–1531.

Balganesh, Shyamkrishna. "The Uneasy Case Against Copyright Trolls." *Southern California Law Review* 86 (2013): 723–82.

Bamberger, Kenneth A., and Deirdre E. Mulligan. *Privacy on the Ground: Driving Corporate Behavior in the United States and Europe.* Cambridge, Mass.: MIT Press, 2015.

Barbas, Samantha. *Laws of Image: Privacy and Publicity in America.* Stanford, Calif.: Stanford University Press, 2015.

Beauchamp, Christopher. "The First Patent Litigation Explosion." *Yale Law Journal* 125 (2016): 848–934.

Beckerman-Rodau, Andrew. "The Aftermath of eBay v. MercExchange." *Journal of the Patent and Trademark Office Society* 89 (2007): 607–92.

Beebe, Barton. "*Bleistein,* the Problem of Aesthetic Progress, and the Making of American Copyright Law." *Columbia Law Review* 117 (2017): 319–98.

———. "An Empirical Study of US Copyright Fair Use Opinions, 1978–2005." *University of Pennsylvania Law Review* 156 (2008): 549–624.

———. "Fair Use and Legal Futurism." *Law and Literature* 24 (2012): 1–15.

———. "Intellectual Property Law and the Sumptuary Code." *Harvard Law Review* 123 (2010): 809–89.

Beebe, Barton, and Jeanne Fromer. "Are We Running Out of Trademarks? An Empirical Study of Trademark Depletion and Congestion." *Harvard Law Review* 131 (2018): 945–1046.

Benjamin, Ruha. *Race After Technology.* Medford, Mass.: Polity Press, 2019.

Benjamin, Walter. *Illuminations: Essays and Reflections.* Translated by Harry Zohn. New York: Harcourt Brace, 1968.

Benkler, Yochai. *Wealth of Networks: How Social Production Transforms Markets and Freedom.* New Haven, Conn.: Yale University Press, 2006.

Bentley, Lionel, and Jane Ginsberg. "The Sole Right. . . Shall Return to Authors": Anglo-American Authors' Reversion Rights from the Statute of Anne to Contemporary U.S. Copyright." *Berkeley Technology Law Journal* 25 (2011): 1475–1600.

Bessen, James, and Michael Meurer. *Patent Failure: How Judges, Bureaucrats, and Lawyers Put Innovators at Risk.* Princeton, N.J.: Princeton University Press, 2009.

Billig, Mick, Susan Condor, Derek Edwards, Mike J. Gane, David Middleton, and Alan Radley. *Ideological Dilemmas: A Social Psychology of Everyday Thinking.* London: Sage, 1988.

Blackhawk, Maggie. "Federal Indian Law as Paradigm Within Public Law." *Harvard Law Review* 132, no. 7 (2019): 1787–1877.

Bodó, Balázs. "The Common Pathways of Samizdat and Piracy." In *Samizdat: Between Practices and Representations: Lecture Series at Open Society Archives, Budapest, February–June 2013,* ed. Valentina Parisi, 19–34. Budapest: CEU Institute for Advanced Study, 2015.

Bowrey, Kathy. "The World Daguerreotyped—What a Spectacle! Copyright Law, Photography and the Commodification Project of Empire." Conference paper presented at Third International Society for the History and Theory of Intellectual Property (ISHTIP), Griffith University, Australia, 5–6 July 2011.

Boyd, Danah. *It's Complicated: The Social Lives of Networked Teens*. New Haven, Conn.: Yale University Press, 2014.

Bracha, Oren. *Owning Ideas: The Intellectual Origins of American Intellectual Property, 1790–1909*. New York: Cambridge University Press, 2017.

Bracha, Oren, and Tahla Syed. "Beyond Efficiency: Consequence-Sensitive Theories of Copyright." *Berkeley Technology Law Journal* 29 (2014): 229–316.

Brauneis, Robert, and Dotan Oliar. "An Empirical Study of Race, Ethnicity, Gender, and Age of Copyright Registrations." *George Washington Law Review* 86 (2018): 101–52.

Bridges, Khiara M. *The Poverty of Privacy Rights*. Stanford, Calif.: Stanford University Press, 2017.

Bridy, Annemarie. "Why Pirates (Still) Won't Behave: Regulating P2P in the Decade After Napster." *Rutgers Law Journal* 40 (2009): 565–611.

Brunet, Francois. *The Birth of the Idea of Photography*. Translated by Shane B. Lillis. Toronto: RIC Books, 2019.

Burk, Dan. "Copyright and Feminism in Digital Media." *Journal of Gender, Society, Policy, and Law* 14 (2006): 519–49.

———. "The Curious Incident of the Supreme Court in Myriad Genetics." *Notre Dame Law Review* 90 (2014): 505–42.

———. "Diversity Levers." *Duke Journal of Gender, Law, and Policy* 23 (2015): 25–43.

———. "Feminism and Dualism in Intellectual Property." *Journal of Gender, Society, Policy, and Law* 15 (2007): 183–206.

Burk, Dan L., and Mark A. Lemley. *The Patent Crisis and the Courts Can Solve It*. Chicago: University of Chicago Press, 2009.

———. "Policy Levers in Patent Law." *Virginia Law Review* 89 (2003): 1575–1696.

Butterfield, Toby. "Moving Beyond Transformativenes: How Courts Evaluate the Purpose and Character of Secondary Uses." *Journal of the Copyright Society* 65 (2018): 147–67.

Carpenter, Megan, and Mary Garner. "NSFW: An Empirical Study of Scandalous Trademarks." *Cardozo Arts and Entertainment Law Journal* 33 (2016): 321–65.

Carpenter, Megan, and Kathryn Murphy. "Calling Bulls**t on the Lanham Act: The 2(a) Bar for Immoral, Scandalous, and Disparaging Marks." *University of Louisville Law Review* 49 (2010): 465–83.

Chander, Anupam. "The New, New Property." *Texas Law Review* 81 (2003): 715–796.

Chander, Anupam, and Madhavi Sunder. "Copyright's Cultural Turn." *Texas Law Review* 91 (2013): 1397–1412.

———. "'Is Nozick Kicking Rawls's Ass? Intellectual Property and Social Justice." *University of California, Davis Law Review* 40 (2007): 563–78.

Chander, Anupam, Madhavi Sunder, and Uyen Le. "Golan v. Holder." *American Journal of International Law* 106 (2012): 637–42.

Chemerinsky, Erwin. "Rediscovering Brandeis' Right to Privacy." *Brandeis Law Journal* 45 (2006–2007): 643–57.

Chien, Colleen V. "Of Trolls, Davids, Goliaths, and Kings: Narratives and Evidence in the Litigation of High-Tech Patents." *University of North Carolina Law Review* 87 (2009): 1571–1615.

Chon, Margaret. "Copyright's Other Function." *Chicago-Kent Journal of Intellectual Property* 15 (2016): 364–78.

———. "Intellectual Property and the Development Divide." *Cardozo Law Review* 27 (2006): 2821–2912.

———. "Intellectual Property Equality." *Seattle Journal for Social Justice* 9 (2010): 259–73.

———. "Intellectual Property 'from Below': Copyright and Capability for Education." *University of California, Davis Law Review* 40 (2007): 803–47.

———. "Postmodern 'Progress' Reconsidering the Copyright and Patent Power." *DePaul Law Review* 43 (1993): 97–146.

———. "Transforming Talks: Public Dialogue About Social Justice in a Post-9-11 Age." *Seattle Journal of Social Justice* 1 (2002): 13–28.

Citron, Danielle Keats. *Hate Crimes in Cyberspace.* Cambridge, Mass.: Harvard University Press, 2014.

Cofone, Ignacio, and Adriana Robertson. "Privacy Harms." *Hastings Law Journal* 69 (2018): 102–59.

Cohen, Julie. "Affording Fundamental Rights: A Provocation Inspired by Mireille Hildebrandt." *Critical Analysis of Law* 4 (2017): 78–90.

———. *Between Truth and Power: The Legal Constructions of Informational Capitalism.* Oxford: Oxford University Press, 2019.

———. *Configuring the Networked Self: Law, Code, and the Play of Everyday Practice.* New Haven, Conn.: Yale University Press, 2012.

———. "Copyright as Property in the Post-Industrial Economy: A Research Agenda." *Wisconsin Law Review* (2011): 141–65.

———. "Turning Privacy Inside Out." *Theoretical Inquiries in Law* 20 (2019): 1–31.

———. "What Is Privacy For?" *Harvard Law Review* 126 (2013): 1904–33.

Colman, Charles. "About Ned." *Harvard Law Review Forum* 129 (2016): 128–52.

Contreras, Jorge. *The Genome Defense: Inside the Epic Legal Battle to Determine Who Owns Your DNA.* New York: Workman Press, 2021.

Cooper, Elena. *Art and Modern Copyright: The Contested Image.* Cambridge: Cambridge University Press, 2018.

Craig, Carys. "Feminist Aesthetics and Copyright Law: Genius, Value, and Gendered Visions of Creative Self." In *Protecting and Promoting Diversity in IP Law*, ed. Irene Calboli and Sri Ragavan, 253–73. Cambridge: Cambridge University Press, 2015.

———. "Technological Neutrality: (Pre)serving the Purpose of Copyright Law." In *The Copyright Pentology: How the Supreme Court of Canada Shook the Foundation of Canadian Copyright*, ed. Michael Geist. Ottowa: University of Ottawa Press, 2013.

Crews, Kenneth. "Fair Use of Unpublished Works: Burdens of Proof and the Integrity of Copyright." *Arizona State Law Journal* 31 (1999): 1–90.

D'Agostino, Guiseppina. *Copyright, Contracts, Creators: New Media, New Rules.* Cheltenham, U.K.: Edward Elgar Publishing Ltd., 2010.

Darling, Kate, and Aaron Perzanowski. *Creativity Without Law: Challenging the Assumptions of Intellectual Property.* New York: New York University Press, 2017.

Day, Gregory, and W. Michael Schuster. "Patent Inequality." *Alabama Law Review* 71 (2019): 115–63.

Deazley, Ronan. *On the Origin of the Right to Copy: Charting the Movement of Copyright Law in Eighteen-Century Britain (1695–1775).* London: Hart Publishing, 2004.

Deazley, Ronan, Martin Kretschmer, and Lionel Bently. *Privilege and Property: Essays on the History of Copyright.* Cambridge: Open Book Publishers, 2010.

Desai, Deven. "The Life and Death of Copyright." *Wisconsin Law Review* (2011): 219–72.

———. "Property, Persona, and Preservation." *Temple Law Review* 81 (2008): 67–121.

DiCola, Peter. "Copyright Equality: Free Speech, Efficiency, and Regulatory Parity in Distribution." *Boston University Law Review* 93 (2013): 1837–1903.

Dogan, Stacey. "Bullying and Opportunism in Trademark and Right of Publicity Law." *Boston University Law Review* 96 (2016): 1293–1324.

Donohue, Laura. "Fourth Amendment in a Digital World." *New York University Annual Survey of American Law* 71 (2017): 553–686.

Drahos, Peter. *A Philosophy of Intellectual Property.* London: Dartmouth Publishing Company, 1996.

Drassinower, Abraham. "Copyright is Not About Copying." *Harvard Law Review* 125 (2012): 108–19.

———. *What's Wrong with Copying?* Cambridge, Mass.: Harvard University Press, 2015.

Dratler, Jay, Jr. "Common-Sense (Federal) Common Law Adrift in a Statutory Sea, or Why Grokster Was a Unanimous Decision." *Santa Clara Computer and High Technology Law Journal* 22 (2006): 413–54.

Dreyfuss, Rochelle Cooper. "Does IP Need IP? Accommodating Intellectual Production Outside the Intellectual Property Paradigm." *Cardozo Law Review* 31 (2010): 1437–73.

———. "Evaluating the Public Impact of Open Innovation." *Australian Economic Review* 44 (2011): 66–72.

———. "Expressive Genericity: Trademarks as Language in the Pepsi Generation." *Notre Dame Law Review* 65 (1990): 397–424.

———. "Reconsidering Experimental Use." *Akron Law Review* 50 (2017): 699–723.

Dreyfuss, Rochelle Cooper, and Elizabeth Siew-Kuan Ng, eds. *Framing Intellectual Property Law in the 21st Century: Integrating Incentives, Trade, Development, Culture, and Human Rights.* Cambridge: Cambridge University Press, 2018.

Dworkin, Ronald. *Sovereign Virtue: The Theory and Practice of Equality.* Cambridge, Mass.: Harvard University Press, 2002.

Edelman, Bernard. *Ownership of the Image: Elements for a Marxist Theory of Law.* Translated by Elizabeth Kingdom. London: Routledge, 1979.

Ellickson, Robert C. *Order Without Law: How Neighbors Settle Disputes.* Cambridge, Mass.: Harvard University Press, 1991.

Elmahjub, Ezieddin, and Nicholas Suzor. "Fair Use and Fairness in Copyright: A Distributive Justice Perspective on Users' Rights." *Monash University Law Review* 43 (2017): 274–98.

Embirbayer, Mustafa. "Manifesto for a Relational Sociology." *American Journal of Sociology* 103 (1997): 281–317.

Ewick, Patricia, and Susan S. Silbey. *The Common Place of Law: Stories from Everyday Life.* Chicago: University of Chicago Press, 1998.

———. "Subversive Stories and Hegemonic Tales: Toward a Sociology of Narrative." *Law and Society Review* 29 (1995): 197–226.

Fairfield, Joshua. *Owned: Property, Privacy, and the New Digital Serfdom.* New York: Cambridge University Press, 2017.

Farivar, Cyrus. *Habeas Data Privacy v. the Rise of Surveillance Tech.* Brooklyn: Melville House Publishing, 2018.

Farley, Christine Haight. "The Lingering Effects of Copyright's Response to the Invention of Photography." *University of Pittsburgh Law Review* 65 (2004): 385–434.

Fineman, Martha Albertson. "Evolving Images of Gender and Equality: A Feminist Journey." *New England Law Review* 43 (2009): 101–23.

Fisher, William. "The Implications for Law of User Innovation." *University of Minnesota Law Review* 94 (2010): 1417–77.

———. "Reconstructing Fair Use Doctrine." *Harvard Law Review* 101 (1988): 1659–1795.

Fleischacker, Samuel. *A Short History of Distributive Justice.* Cambridge, Mass.: Harvard University Press, 2004.

Flynn, Sean, Aidan Hollis, and Mike Palmedo. "An Economic Justification for Open Access to Essential Medicine Patents in Developing Countries." *Journal of Law, Medicine, and Ethics* 37 (2009): 184–208.

Frankfurt, Harry. "Equality as a Moral Ideal." *Ethics* 98 (1987): 21–43.

Franklin, Ursula. *The Real World of Technology.* Ontario: House of Anansi Press, 1990.

Franks, Mary Ann. *The Cult of Constitution: Our Deadly Devotion to Guns and Free Speech.* Stanford, Calif.: Stanford University Press, 2020.

———. "Justice Beyond Dispute." Book review of *Digital Justice: Technology and The Internet of Disputes* by Ethan Katsh and Orna Rabinovich-Einy. *Harvard Law Review* 131 (2018): 1374–97.

Frischmann, Brett. "Capabilities, Spillovers, and Intellectual Property: Towards a Human Flourishing Theory for Intellectual Property." *Review of Economic Research on Copyright Issues* 14 (2017): 1–38.

———. *Infrastructure: The Social Value of Shared Resources.* New York: Oxford University, 2012.

Frischmann, Brett M., Michael J. Madison, and Katherine J. Strandburg, eds. *Governing Knowledge Commons*. New York: Oxford University Press, 2014.

Fromer, Jeanne C. "Expressive Incentives in Intellectual Property." *Virginia Law Review* 98 (2012): 1745–1824.

———. "Should the Law Care Why Intellectual Property Rights Have Been Asserted?" *Houston Law Review* 53 (2015): 549–92.

Gaid, Melissa. "Data after Death: An Examination into Heirs' Access to a Decedent's Private Online Account." *Suffolk University Law Review* 49 (2016): 281–300.

Galanter, Marc. Why the "Haves" Come Out Ahead: Speculations on the Limits of Legal Change." *Law and Society Review* 9 (1974): 95–160.

Garcia, Kristelia. "Copyright Arbitrage." *California Law Review* 107 (2019): 199–266.

Giblin, Rebecca. "Physical World Assumptions and Software World Realities (And Why There are More P2P Software Providers Than Ever Before)." *Columbia Journal of Law and the Arts* 35 (2012): 57–118.

Gilden, Andrew. "Sex, Death, and Intellectual Property." *Harvard Journal of Law and Technology* 32 (2018): 67–114.

Gilman, Howard. *The Constitution Besieged: The Rise and Demise of Lochner Era Police Powers Jurisprudence*. Chapel Hill, N.C.: Duke University Press, 1993.

Ginsburg, Jane. "The Author's Place in the Future of Copyright." *Proceedings of the American Philosophical Society* 153 (2009): 147–59.

Goldberg, John, and Benjamin Zipursky. "Torts as Wrongs." *Texas Law Review* 88 (2010): 916–86.

Goldman, Eric. "An Overview of the United States' Section 230 Internet Immunity." In *Oxford Handbook of Online Intermediary Liability*, ed. Giancarlo Frosio. New York: Oxford University Press, 2020.

———. "The Regulation of Reputational Information." In *The Next Digital Decade: Essays on the Future of the Internet*, ED. BERIN Szoka and Adam Marcus, 293–304. Washington, D.C., TechFreedom, 2010.

Goold, Patrick R. "Unbundling the 'Tort' of Copyright Infringement." *Virginia Law Review* 102 (2016): 1833–99.

Gordon, Wendy. "Copyright as Tort Law's Mirror Image: 'Harms,' 'Benefits,' and the Uses and Limits of Analogy." *McGeorge Law Review* 34 (2003): 533–40.

———. "Copyright Owners' Putative Interests in Privacy, Reputation, and Control: A Reply to Goold." *Virginia Law Review Online* 103 (2017): 36–53.

———. "The Core of Copyright: Authors, Not Publishers." *Houston Law Review* 52 (2015): 613–78.

———. "Fair Use Markets: On Weighing Potential License Fees." *George Washington University Law Review* 79 (2011): 1814–56.

———. "Harmless Use: Gleaning from Fields of Copyrighted Works." *Fordham Law Review* 77 (2009): 2411–35.

———. "Of Harms and Benefits: Torts, Restitution and IP." *Journal of Legal Studies* 21 (1992): 449–68.

———. "A Property Right in Self-Expression: Equality and Individualism in the Natural Law of Intellectual Property." *Yale Law Journal* 102 (1993): 1533–1609.

———. "Render Copyright unto Caesar: On Taking Incentives Seriously." *Chicago Law Review* 71 (2004): 75–92.

———. "Toward a Jurisprudence of Benefits: The Norms of Copyright and the Problem of Private Censorship." *University of Chicago Law Review* 57 (1990): 1009–49.

Griffin, F. Hollis. *Feeling Normal: Sexuality and Media Criticism in the Digital Age.* Bloomington: Indiana University Press, 2016.

Grinvald, Leah Chan, and Sonia Katyal. "Platform Law and the Brand Enterprise." *Berkeley Technology Law Journal* 32 (2017): 1135–82.

Grinvald, Leah Chan, and Ofer Tur-Sinai. "Intellectual Property and the Right to Repair." *Fordham Law Review* 88 (2019): 1291–1332.

Gugliuzza, Paul. "The Supreme Court Bar at the Bar of Patents." *Notre Dame Law Review* 95 (2020): 1233–80.

Hartzog, Woodrow. *Privacy's Blueprint: The Battle to Control the Design of New Technologies.* Cambridge, Mass.: Harvard University Press, 2018.

Hartzog, Woodrow, and Daniel Solove. "The FTC and the New Common Law of Privacy." *Columbia Law Review* 114 (2014): 583–676.

Hasday, Jill. "The Principles and Practices of Women's Full Citizenship." *Michigan Law Review* 101 (2002): 755–810.

Haupt, Claudia. "Professional Speech." *Yale Law Journal* 125, no. 5 (2016): 1238–1303.

Heald, Paul. "Copyright Reversion to Authors (and the Rosetta Effect): An Empirical Study of Reappearing Books." *Journal of Copyright Society of the USA* 66 (2019): 59–114.

———. "How Copyright Keeps Works Disappeared." *Journal of Empirical Legal Studies* 11 (2014): 829–66.

Heller, Michael. "The Tragedy of the Anticommons." *Harvard Law Review* 111 (1998): 621–88.

———. "The Tragedy of the Anticommons: A Concise Introduction and Lexicon." *The Modern Law Review* 76 (2013): 6–25.

Heller, Michael, and Rebecca Eisenberg. "Can Patents Deter Innovation? The Anticommons in Biomedical Research." *Science* 280 (1998): 698–701.

Hellman, Deborah. "Two Concepts of Discrimination." *Virginia Law Review* 102 (2016): 895–952.

Henry, Leslie Meltzer. "The Jurisprudence of Dignity." *University of Pennsylvania Law Review* 160 (2011): 169–233.

Heymann, Laura A. "The Law of Reputation and the Interest of the Audience." *Boston Law Review* 52 (2011): 1341–1439.

———. "Reasonable Appropriation and Reader Response." *University of California, Irvine Law Review* 9 (2019): 343–66.

Hughes, Justin. "The Photographer's Copyright—Photograph as Art, Photograph as Database." *Harvard Journal of Law and Technology* 25 (2012): 339–413.

Hughes, Justin, and Robert P. Merges. "Copyright and Distributive Justice." *Notre Dame Law Review* 92 (2017): 513–78.

Hull, Gordon. *Biopolitics of Intellectual Property: Regulating Information and Personhood in the Information Age.* New York: Cambridge University Press, 2019.

———. "Robert Merges, Justifying Intellectual Property." *Ethics and Information Technology* 14, no. 2 (2012): 169–77.

Hyde, Lewis. *Common as Air: Revolution, Art, and Ownership.* New York: Farrar, Straus, and Giroux, 2010.

———. *The Gift: Creativity and the Artist in the Modern World.* New York: Vintage Books, 1979.

Igo, Sarah. *A History of Privacy in Modern America.* Cambridge, Mass.: Harvard University Press, 2018.

Iljadica, Marta. *Copyright Beyond Law: Regulating Creativity in the Graffiti Subculture,* London: Hart Publishing, 2016.

Jackson, Sarah, Moya Bailey, and Brooke Foucault Welles. *#Hashtag Activism: Networks of Race and Gender Justice.* Cambridge, Mass.: MIT Press, 2020.

Jamar, Steven. "Copyright and the Public Interest from the Perspective of Brown v. Board of Education." *Howard Law Journal* 48 (2005): 629–57.

Jones, Meg Leta. *Ctrl+Z: The Right to be Forgotten.* New York: New York University Press, 2016.

Kaminski, Margot. "Privacy and the Right to Record." *Boston University Law Review* 97 (2017): 167–242.

Kapczynski, Amy. "Cost of Price: Why and How to Get Beyond Intellectual Property Internalism." *University of California Los Angeles Law Review* 59 (2012): 970–1021.

———. "Order without Intellectual Property Law: Open Science in Influenza." *Cornell Law Review* 102 (2017): 1539–1648.

Kasmir, Sharryn. "Precarity." In *The Cambridge Encyclopedia of Anthropology,* ed. F. Stein et al. Cambridge: Cambridge University Press, 2018.

Katyal, Sonia. "Stealth Marketing and Antibranding: The Love That Dare Not Speak Its Name." *Buffalo Law Review* 58 (2010): 795–849.

———. "Trademark Intersectionality." *University of California Los Angeles Law Review* 57 (2010): 1601–99.

Katyal, Sonia, and Eduardo Penalver. *Property Outlaws: How Squatters, Pirates, and Protesters Improve the Law of Ownership.* New Haven, Conn.: Yale University Press, 2010.

Keller, Deidre A. "Copyright to the Rescue: Should Copyright Protect Privacy?" *University of California Los Angeles Journal of Law and Technology* 20 (2016): 1–40.

Khan, B. Zorina. "Accounting for Creativity: Lessons from the Economic History of Intellectual Property and Innovation." *Review of Economic Research on Copyright Issues* 17 (2020): 1–37.

Klonick, Kate. "The New Governors: The People, Rules, and Processes Governing Online Speech." *Harvard Law Review* 131 (2018): 1599–1669.

Lake, Jessica. *The Face That Launched a Thousand Lawsuits: The American Women Who Forged a Right to Privacy.* New Haven, Conn.: Yale University Press, 2016.

Landes, William M., and Richard A. Posner. *The Economic Structure of Intellectual Property Law.* Cambridge, Mass.: Harvard University Press, 2003.

Lee, Edward. "Suspect Assertions of Copyright." *Chicago-Kent Journal of Intellectual Property* 15 (2016): 379–98.

Lee, Peter. "Reconceptualizing the Role of Intellectual Property Rights in Shaping Industry Structure." *Vanderbilt Law Review* 72 (2019): 1197–1283.

———. "The Supreme Court's Myriad Effects on Scientific Research: Definitional Fluidity and the Legal Construction of Nature." *University of California, Irvine Law Review* 5 (2015): 1077–1114.

———. "Toward a Distributive Agenda for U.S. Patent Law." *Houston Law Review* 55 (2017): 321–75.

Lemley, Mark. "Did eBay Irreparably Injure Trademark Law?" *Notre Dame Law Review* 92 (2017): 1795–1814.

———. "Expecting the Unexpected." *Notre Dame Law Review* 92 (2017): 1369–94.

———. "IP in a World Without Scarcity." *New York Law University Law Review* 90 (2015): 460–515.

Lemley, Mark, and Mark McKenna. "Scope." *William and Mary Law Review* 57 (2016): 2197–2285.

Lemley, Mark, and A. Douglas Melamed. "Missing the Forest for the Trolls." *Columbia Law Review* 113 (2013): 2117–90.

Lepore, Jill. *These Truths: A History of the United States.* New York: Norton, 2018.

Lessig, Lawrence. *Code and Other Laws of Cyberspace.* New York: Basic Books, 1999.

Levendowski, Amanda. "Using Copyright to Combat Revenge Porn." *New York University Journal of Intellectual Property and Entertainment Law* 3 (2014): 422–46.

Lim, Daryl. "Living with Monsanto." *Michigan State Law Review* (2015): 559–663.

Linford, Jake. "A Second Look at the Right of First Publication." *Journal of the Copyright Society of USA* 58 (2011): 585–664.

Lipton, Jacqueline. "Mapping Online Privacy." *Northwestern University Law Review* 104 (2010): 477–516.

———. "A Taxonomy of Borrowing." *Fordham Intellectual Property, Media, and Entertainment Law Journal* 24 (2014): 952–96.

Litman, Jessica. "Billowing White Goo." *Columbia Journal of Law and the Arts* 31 (2008): 587–601.

———. "Campbell at 21/Sony at 31." *Washington Law Review* 90 (2015): 651–84.

———. *Digital Copyright.* Amherst, N.Y.: Prometheus Books, 2001.

———. "Imaginary Bottles." *Duke Law and Technology Review* 18 (2019): 127–36.

———. "Lawful Personal Use." *Texas Law Review* 85 (2007): 1871–1920.

———. "The Public Domain." *Emory Law Journal* 39 (1990): 965–1023.

Loren, Lydia Pallas. "Renegotiating the Copyright Deal in the Shadow of the 'Inalienable' Right to Terminate." *Florida Law Review* 26 (2010): 1329–71.

Lorey, Isabell. *State of Insecurity: Government of the Precarious.* London: Verso, 2015.

Lovejoy, Britt. "Tarnishing the Dilution by Tarnishment Cause of Action: Starbucks Corp v. Wolfe's Borough Coffee, Inc. and V. Secret Catalogue, inc. v. Mosely, Compared." *Berkeley Technology Law Journal* 26 (2011): 623–54.

Lunney, Glynn, Jr. "Copyright and the 1%." *Stanford Technology Law Review* 23 (2020): 1–70.

MacPherson, C. B. *The Political Theory of Possessive Individualism: From Hobbes to Locke.* Oxford: Clarendon Press, 1962.

Madison, Michael. "A Pattern-Oriented Approach to Fair Use." *William and Mary Law Review* 45 (2004): 1525–1690.

Malloy, Robin Paul, and David M. Driesen. "Critiques of Law and Economics." In *The Oxford Handbook of Law and Economics*, vol. 1, ed. Francesco Parisi. New York: Oxford University Press, 2017.

Mandel, Gregory. "The Public Perception of Intellectual Property." *Florida Law Review* 66 (2014): 261–312.

Masquelier, Charles. "Bourdieu, Foucault, and the Politics of Precarity." *Distinktion, Journal of Social Theory* 20 (2018): 135–55.

McCutcheon, Jani. "The Honour of the Dead: The Moral Right of Integrity Post-Mortem." *Federal Law Review* (Australia) 42 (2014): 485–518.

McGeveran, William. "Four Free Speech Goals for Trademark Law." *Fordham Intellectual Property Media and Entertainment Law Journal* 18 (2008): 1205–27.

———. "The Imaginary Trademark Parody Crisis (and the Real One)." *Washington Law Review* 90 (2015): 713–54.

McKenna, Mark. "The Rehnquist Court and the Groundwork for Greater First Amendment Scrutiny of Intellectual Property." *Washington University Journal of Law and Policy* 21 (2006): 11–29.

McKeown, M. Margaret. "Keynote Address: Censorship in the Guise of Authorship: Harmonizing Copyright and the First Amendment." *Chicago-Kent Journal of Intellectual Property* 15 (2016): 1–17.

Merges, Robert. *Justifying Intellectual Property.* Cambridge, Mass.: Harvard University Press, 2011.

Mosher, Petra, and Michela Giorcelli. "Copyrights and Creativity: Evidence from Italian Opera in the Napoleonic Age." *Journal of Political Economy* 128 (2020): 4163–4210.

Murray, Laura J., S. Tina Piper, and Kirsty Robertson. *Putting Intellectual Property in Its Place: Rights Discourses, Creative Labor, and the Everyday.* New York: Oxford University Press, 2014.

Nagel, Thomas. *Equality and Partiality.* New York: Oxford University Press, 1991.

Neilson, Brett, and Ned Rossiter. "Precarity as a Political Concept, or Fordism as Exception." *Theory, Culture, and Society* 25 (2008): 51–72.

Nissenbaum, Helen. *Privacy in Context: Technology, Policy, and the Integrity of Social Life.* Stanford, Calif.: Stanford University Press, 2010.

Nozick, Robert. *Anarchy, State, and Utopia.* New York: Basic Books, 1974.

O'Neill, Kate. "The Content of Their Characters: J. D. Salinger, Holden Caulfield, Fredrik Colting." *Journal for Copyright Society of the USA* 59 (2012): 291–345.

———. "Copyright Law and the Management of J. D. Salinger's Literary Estate." *Cardozo Arts and Entertainment Law Journal* 31 (2012): 19–42.

O'Rourke, Maureen. "Bargaining in the Shadow of Copyright Law." *Case Western Reserve Law Review* 53 (2003): 605–38.

Osei-Tutu, J. Janewa. "Agricultural Biotechnology: Drawing on International Law to Promote Progress." *Michigan State Law Review* (2015): 531–50.

Ostrom, Elinor. *Governing the Commons: The Evolution of Institutions for Collective Action.* Cambridge: Cambridge University Press, 1990.

Perry, Stephen. "Harm, History, and Counterfactuals." *San Diego Law Review* 40 (2003): 1283–1314.

Perzanowski, Aaron, and Jason Schultz. *The End of Ownership: Personal Property in the Digital Economy.* Cambridge, Mass.: MIT Press, 2017

Pessach, Guy, and Michal Shur-Ofry. "Copyright and the Holocaust." *Yale Journal of Law and Humanities* 30 (2018): 121–72.

Piketty, Thomas. *Capital in the Twenty-First Century.* Translated by Arthur Goldhammer. Cambridge, Mass.: Harvard University Press, 2014.

Porat, Ariel. "Private Production of Public Goods: Liability of Unrequested Benefits." *Michigan Law Review* 108 (2009): 189–227.

Post, Robert. "The Social Foundations of Privacy: Community and Self in the Common Law Tort." *California Law Review* 77 (1989): 957–1010.

Radin, Margaret Jane. *Reinterpreting Property.* Chicago: University of Chicago Press, 1993.

Ranganathan, Aruna. "The Artisan and His Audience: Identification with Work and Price Setting in a Handicraft Cluster in Southern India." *Administrative Science Quarterly* 63 (2017): 637–67.

Rawls, John. *Justice as Fairness: A Restatement.* Cambridge, Mass.: Harvard University Press, 2001.

———. *A Theory of Justice.* Cambridge, Mass.: Harvard University Press, 1971.

Reimers, Imke. "Copyright and Generic Entry in Book Publishing." *American Economics Journal* 11 (2019): 257–84.

Richards, Neil. *Intellectual Privacy: Rethinking Civil Liberties in the Digital Era.* New York: Oxford University Press, 2015.

Richards, Neil, and Dan Solove. "Privacy's Other Path: Recovering the Law of Confidentiality." *Georgetown Law Journal* 96 (2007): 123–82.

Ritchen, Fred. *After Photography.* New York: Norton Press, 2009.

Rhode, Deborah L. "#MeToo: Why Now? What Next?" *Duke Law Journal* 69 (2019): 377–428.

Roh, David. "Two Copyright Case Studies from a Literary Perspective." *Law and Literature* 22 (2010): 110–41.

Rose, Carol. "Introduction: Property and Language, or, the Ghost of the Fifth Panel." *Yale Journal of Law and the Humanities* 18 (2006): 1–29.

———. *Property and Persuasion: Essays on the History, Theory, and Rhetoric of Ownership.* Boulder, Colo.: Westview Press, 1994.

———. "Property as Storytelling: Perspectives from Game Theory, Narrative Theory, Feminist Theory." *Yale Journal of Law and the Humanities* 2 (1990): 37–57.

Rose, Mark. "The Author in Court: Pope v. Curll (1741)." *Cultural Critique* 21 (1992): 197–217.

———. *Authors in Court: Scenes from the Theater of Copyright.* Cambridge, Mass.: Harvard University Press, 2016.

Rosen, Jeffrey. "The Web Means the End of Forgetting." *New York Times,* July 25, 2010.

Rosenblatt, Elizabeth. "Intellectual Property's Negative Space: Beyond the Utilitarian." *Florida State University Law Review* 40 (2013): 441–86.

Rotenberg, Mark, Jeramie Scott, and Julia Horwitz, eds. *Privacy in the Modern Age: The Search for Solutions.* New York: The New Press, 2015.

Rothman, Jennifer. *The Right of Publicity: Privacy Reimagined for a Public World.* Cambridge, Mass.: Harvard University Press, 2018.

Sag, Matthew. "Internet Safe Harbors and the Transformation of Copyright Law." *Notre Dame Law Review* 93 (2017): 499–564.

Samuelson, Pamela. "Enriching Discourse on Public Domains." *Duke Law Journal* 55 (2006): 783–834.

———. "Freedom to Tinker." *Theoretical Inquiries in Law* 17 (2016): 563–600.

———. "Justifications for Copyright Limitation and Exceptions." In *Copyright Laws in the Age of Limitations and Exceptions,* ed. Ruth Okediji, 12–59. Cambridge: Cambridge University Press, 2017.

———. "Possible Futures of Fair Use." *Washington Law Review* 90 (2015): 815–68.

———. "Protecting Privacy through Copyright Law." In *Privacy in the Modern Age: The Search for Solutions,* ed. Mark Rotenberg, Jeramie Scott, and Julia Horwitz, 191–99. New York: The New Press, 2015.

———. "The Quest for a Sound Conception of Copyright's Derivative Work Right." *Georgetown Law Review* 101 (2013): 1506–64.

Scanlon, T. H. *Why Does Equality Matter?* New York: Oxford University Press, 2018.

Sen, Amartya. "Equality of What?" The Tanner Lecture on Human Values, Harvard University, 1979.

———. *Inequality Reexamined.* Cambridge, Mass.: Harvard University Press, 1995.

Shaver, Lea. "Copyright and Inequality." *Washington University Law Review* 92 (2014): 117–68.

Sheff, Jeremy. "Jefferson's Taper." *Southern Methodist University Law Review* 73 (2020): 299–350.

Shin, Patrick. "The Substantive Principle of Equal Treatment." *Legal Theory* 15 (2009): 149–72.

Siegel, Reva. "How Conflict Entrenched the Right to Privacy." *Yale Law Journal Forum* 124 (2015): 316–23.

Silverman, Kaja. *The Miracle of Analogy, or The History of Photography, Part 1.* Stanford, Calif.: Stanford University Press, 2015.

Singer, Joseph William. *Entitlement: The Paradoxes of Property.* New Haven, Conn.: Yale University Press, 2000.

Smith, Cathay. "Political Fair Use." *William and Mary Law Review* 62, no. 6 (2021): 2003–74.

Snow, Ned. "A Copyright Conundrum: Protecting Email Privacy." *Kansas Law Review* 55 (2007): 501–72.

Spaulding, Christina. "Anti-Pornography Laws as a Claim for Equal Respect: Feminism, Liberalism, and Community." *Berkeley Women's Law Journal* 4 (1988): 128–65.

Spoo, Robert. "Three Myths for Aging Copyrights: Tithonus, Dorian Gray, Ulysses." *Cardozo Arts and Entertainment Law Journal* 31 (2012): 77–110.

———. *Without Copyrights: Piracy, Publishing, and the Public Domain.* New York: Oxford University Press, 2013.

Standing, Guy. "The Precariat: From Denizens to Citizens?" *Polity* 44 (2012): 588–608.

———.*The Precariat: The New Dangerous Class.* London: Bloomsbury Press, 2011.

Stern, James. "ABC v. Aereo and the Humble Judge." *New York University Journal of Law and Liberty* 9 (2015): 81–91.

Stern, Simon. "From Author's Right to Property Right." *University Toronto Law Journal* 62 (2012): 29–91.

Subotnik, Eva E. "Artistic Control After Death." *Washington Law Review* 92 (2017): 253–313.

———. "The Author Was Not an Author: The Copyright Interests of Photograph Subjects from Wilde to Garcia." *Columbia Journal of Law and the Arts* 39 (2016): 449–63.

———. "Copyright and the Living Dead? Succession Law and the Postmortem Term." *Harvard Journal of Law and Technology* 29 (2015): 77–125.

Sunder, Madhavi. *From Goods to a Good Life: Intellectual Property and Global Justice.* New Haven, Conn.: Yale University Press, 2012.

———. "Novartis v. Myriad: The Indian and the US Supreme Courts on Patents and Public Health." *European Intellectual Property Review* 35 (2013): 711–14.

———. "Trade Secret and Human Freedom." In *Intellectual Property and the Common Law*, ed. Shyamkrishna Balganesh, 334–52. Cambridge: Cambridge University Press, 2013.

Sunder. Madhavi, and Anupam Chander. "The Romance of the Public Domain." *California Law Review* 92 (2004): 1331–73.

Syed, Talha, and William W. Fisher. "Global Justice in Healthcare: Developing Drugs for the Developing World." *University of California Davis Law Review* 40 (2006): 581–678.

Sylvain, Olivier. "Network Equality." *Hastings Law Journal* 67 (2016): 443–97.

Tehranian, John. *Infringement Nation: Copyright 2.0 and You.* New York: Oxford University Press, 2011.

———. "The New Censorship." *Iowa Law Review* 101 (2015): 245–95.

Toffler, Alvin. *The Third Wave.* New York: William Morrow, 1980.

Trachtenberg, Alan, ed. *Classic Essays on Photography.* Stony Creek, Conn.: Leete's Island Books, Inc., 1980.

Tribe, Lawrence. "Equal Dignity: Speaking Its Name." *Harvard Law Review* 129 (2015): 16–32.

Tushnet, Rebecca. "Fair Use's Unfinished Business." *Chicago-Kent Journal of Intellectual Property* 15 (2016): 399–411.

———. "How Many Wrongs Make a Copyright." *University of Minnesota Law Review* 98 (2014): 2346–74.

———. "Intellectual Property as a Public Interest Mechanism." In *The Oxford Handbook of Intellectual Property Law,* ed. Rochelle Dreyfuss and Justine Pila, 95–116. New York: Oxford University Press, 2018.

Tutt, Andrew. "Textualism and the Equity of the Copyright Act: Reflections Inspired by American Broadcasting Companies, Inc. v. Aereo, Inc." *New York University Law Review Online* 89 (2014): 1–9.

Van Houweling, Molly Shaffer. "Distributive Values in Copyright." *Texas Law Review* 83 (2005): 1535–79.

Vats, Anjali. *The Color of Creatorship: Intellectual Property, Race, and the Making of Americans.* Stanford, Calif.: Stanford University Press, 2020.

Waldman, Ari Ezra. "A Breach of Trust: Fighting Nonconsensual Pornography." *Iowa Law Review* 102 (2017): 709–33.

———. "Trust: A Model for Disclosure in Patent Law." *Indiana Law Journal* 92 (2017): 557–98.

Warren, Samuel D., and Louis D. Brandeis. "The Right to Privacy." *Harvard Law Review* 4 (1890): 193–220.

Westen, Peter. "The Empty Idea of Equality." *Harvard Law Review* 95 (1982): 537–96.

———. *Speaking of Equality.* Princeton, N.J.: Princeton University Press, 1990.

Yoshino, Kenji. "The New Equal Protection." *Harvard Law Review* 124 (2011): 747–803.

Yu, Peter. "The Anatomy of the Human Rights Framework for Intellectual Property." *Southern Methodist University Law Review* 69 (2016): 37–96.

Zuboff, Shoshana. *The Age of Surveillance Capitalism: The Fight for a Human Future at the New frontier of Power.* New York: Hachette Books, 2019.

Zuckerman, Ethan. "Mistrust, Efficacy, and the New Civics: Understanding the Deep Roots of the Crisis of Faith in Journalism." Knight Commission Workshop on Trust, Media and American Democracy, Aspen Institute, 2017.

Index

CPSIA information can be obtained
at www.ICGtesting.com
Printed in the USA
JSHW042253160422
25020JS00002B/4

9 781503 631915